A
Christian Defense
Of Polygamy
Through The Centuries

A Dialogue Of Polygamy, by Bernardino Ochino: *De Doctrina Christiana*, by John Milton: *Thelyphthora*, by Martin Madan: and *The History and Philosophy of Marriage*, by James Campbell are public domain and copyright free.

ISBN (Hardcover) - 979-8-9913155-0-0
ISBN (Paperback) - 979-8-9913155-1-7
ISBN (eBook) - 979-8-9913155-2-4

Published and Printed by Imgramspark

Author's Website – BiblicalFamily.Church

Other books by J.D. Langton
currently available on Amazon

Marriage, Sex, & Polygamy:
Its About To Get Biblical Up In Here

Polygamy: 6 Short Stories About Christian Families Who Obeyed The
Bible And Wound Up With Multiple Wives

Visit
BiblicalFamily.Church
To Learn More and Contact J.D. Langton

CONTENTS

INTRODUCTION

Households that include more than one wife have existed since the beginning of mankind, and until the rise of the Greco-Roman empire and the subsequent Catholic Church, nobody, not even Christians, questioned the legitimacy or normalcy of having more than one wife in a family. Despite the overwhelming presence of what we call "polygamy" in the Bible and God's direct endorsement of it, European Christians have argued the validity of this family structure for centuries. However, there have been well-known Christians throughout the centuries who have defended the Biblical nature of having more than one wife in a family.

This book is a compilation of the four most impactful and Biblical works on the subject throughout the last 5 centuries of Christian history. My hope is that it will serve as a helpful historical resource for those wishing to explore polygamy from a Biblical standpoint. (By publishing these works, I do not mean to imply that I agree with every point made in them.)

The works are presented in chronological order. The only change that has been made is replacing "F" with "S," where applicable, in the works with older English. No other alterations to the main content or footnotes have been made. The authors' mini-biographies are taken from *Marriage, Sex, & Polygamy: It's About To Get Biblical Up In Here*, by J.D. Langton.

May God bless you, strengthen your family, and give you grace to understand His Word as you read and study these works.

— J.D. Langton

Book I

A Dialogue Of Polygamy

Bernardino Ochino

1563

BERNARDINO OCHINO

- The Italian Reformer

Bernardino Ochino is best remembered for being one of the first reformers to preach to the people in their native tongue. He was a devout Catholic priest, and after being tasked to refute the writings of the reformers, he was converted to Christianity. When the Roman inquisition summoned him, he fled to John Calvin at Geneva, where he got married and became a pastor. Under King Edward VI, he played a prominent role in the Protestant Reformation. He also antagonized subsequent Catholic government by speaking out boldly against Catholic heresies.

In 1563, Ochino published a little book titled, "A Dialogue Of Polygamy And Divorce." In the first part, a fictional conversation occurs between two men about the permissibility of one of them taking an additional wife. While no doctrinal assertions are explicitly made, the character defending polygamy is clearly the winner of the fictional argument. It is a rather brilliant and funny piece of literature, but the leaders of Zurich didn't feel that way. They exiled Ochino for writing in support of polygamy, banishing him and his children (his wife had recently died) into the expanse of winter without mercy. The harsh elements quickly killed the Ochino family.

A

DIALOGUE

OF

POLYGAMY,

Written Originally in *Italian:*
Rendred into *English*
by a Person of Quality; and Dedicated
to the Author of that well-known
Treatise call'd,
Advice to a Son.

LONDON,
Printed for *Iohn Garfeild,* at the *Rolling-Press*
for *Pictures,* neer the *Royal Exchange*
in *Cornhill,* over against
Popes-head Alley, 1657.

A DIALOGUE OF POLYGAMY.

Between *Telypoligamus* AND *Ochinus.*

Tel.

I Desire your advice; which because I conceive you are both able and willing to afford me: therefore it is I address my self unto you.

Och.

I am indeed willing, provided it be within the reach of my understanding and ability.

Tel.

In the first place, I beg of you, That you will faithfully promise to keep my Counsel.

Och.

I am content, if I may do it, without dishonouring God.

Tel.

I have a Wife not suitable to my minde, so that I cannot love her, and as far as I can perceive, she is both barren, and unhealthful; and I finde my self so disposed, that I cannot want the Company of a Woman: also I desire to have Children, both for Posterities sake, and that I may instruct them in the fear of God. I could indeed keep a Concubine or two, but my Conscience will not suffer me: also I could falsly charge my Wife with Adultery, and so put her away; but in so doing, I should both offend God, and blemish mine own, and my Wives reputation, which I will not do. I could also poyson her, which is a thing I abhorre. But a thought is come into my minde, to take another Wife, so as to keep her that I have already, notwithstanding; and I conceive God has put this into my minde, and that I am thereunto called by him: my desire therefore is, that you will tell me whether, according to the word of God, I may lawfully do it.

Och.

In doubtful cases 'tis fit to take advice, but the case is clear, that a man ought not to have more Wives then one, because the condition of Mariage is such, that it cannot be between more then two.

Tel.

How can you make that appear?

Och.

God at the beginning made out of *Adam,* only one Woman, and gave her to him; signifying, that he ought to have but one and that Matrimony ought to be only of two persons. If he would have had a Man to have more Wives, he would doubtless have made him more, especially at the beginning of the World, when propagation was more necessary, then ever afterwards.

Tel.

I conceive, this Argument is of small validity. God gave to our first Father *Adam* one Wife, therefore it is unlawful for any man to have more.

Och.

If it had been the will of God that he should have more, he would have given him more, especially in that state of perfection, wherein he was pleased to put him.

Tel.

A bare act of God, without any precept added thereunto, does not obliege us to imitate the same; for if so, then we are bound to weare Coats of Skin, because God so cloathed our first Parents, and it were unlawful to wear Cloth or Silk. For your Argument would alwayes be of force. God cloathed them with Skins, and he could have cloathed them with Cloth or

Silk, if it had been his pleasure, that men should be so cloathed. If an Act of God alone do bind us as much as a precept, so that Gods giving *Adam* one Wife only, were as much in effect, as if he had said to him, I will and command, that every man have one only Wife; it would follow, that not only it should be unlawful for a man to have more Wives then one, but that every man that did not take a Wife, it being in his power so to do, should sin, which is contrary to the Doctrine of St. *Paul.*

O*ch.*

You must understand, that *Paul* is not contrary to God. For in that, God gave only one Wife to *Adam*, it was all one, as if he had said, I would not have a man to have more Wives then one, and it is my pleasure, that he have *one,* unless I shall call him to a single life, and give him the gift of Chastity, and that is the intent of *Paul.*

Tel.

And I for my part must say, that when God gave *Adam* one Wife, it was as if he had said, It is my pleasure, that a man shall have one Wife; if either he want the gift of continency, or I shall call him to a married condition. It is also my pleasure, that he shall have no more; unless he stand in need of more, or I shall call him to more: which is at this time my condition, who stand in need of, and am called to marrie another.

O*ch.*

That a single life is pleasing to God, the word of God shewes; but we are not thereby taught, that he is pleased, Men should have more then one Wife.

Tel.

Nay verily, both Gods word, and the Saints example, do reach the same, as we shall shew by and by. But go to; suppose, it had been Gods pleasure, that every man should have so many Wives, as it was possible for him rightly to govern, and instruct together with their Children: how many Wives must he have given *Adam,* thereby to signifie his pleasure in this point?

Och.

You suppose that which cannot be, seeing the having more Wives than one, is repugnant to true Matrimony.

Tel.

You have not yet made it clear to me, that to have more Wives then one is repugnant to Mariage, otherwise then by saying, that God gave *one* to *Adam,* Let us now suppose he had given him more; doubtless, from that first Institution you could not prove, that a man ought not to have more; nay, it would follow of necessity, that a man might have more. How many Wives therefore in such a case, had it been necessary for God to give *Adam,* to signifie his pleasure in this point?

Och.

Two would have been enough.

Tel.

Now then, if that Action of his had bin a precept, as you say, it would have bin unlawful for men to have had more or less then two Wives: which nevertheless, would not have been answerable to his will, seeing his intent was, that they should have as many as they could govern. We must therefore confess, that by a bare act of God: no command being added, we are not obliged to the imitation thereof. Otherwise it would be sin for a Minister to celebrate the Lords Supper, unless the Communicants were just so many in number, as the Apostles of Christ were, when he instituted the same.

Och.

Although it does not necessarily follow, that because God gave one Wife to *Adam,* therefore it is unlawful for a man to have more; yet is it doubtless, a very probable Argument, to perswade, & urges strongly, though it be not altogether compulsive.

Tel.

Nay verily, it urges not at all: since it may be said, that God gave one Wife to *Adam,* not to shew that his will was, that every man should have but one Wife; but that the rest of mankind being born as well of one Mother, as one Father, might love one another so much the more: also that *Eve* being made of the Rib of *Adam*, might be a figure of the holy Church, the onely Spouse of Christ.

Och.

Go to, let us come unto the words of the Text. Do you not think that *Adam* was moved by divine instinct, when he said; *For this cause shall a man leave his Father, and Mother, and cleave to his Wife?*

Tel.

Without doubt.

Och.

Do you not see how, in saying, he shall cleave to his Wife, (not, Wives) he teaches us, that a man is to have but one?

Tel.

Very good, when God commands a man to love his Neighbour, does he oblige him to love one or more?

Och.

All that are his Neighbours.

Tel.

That's false; for he sayes, Thou shalt love thy Neighbour, not thy Neighbours; and therefore whoever loves one of his Neighbours, has fulfilled that Command.

Och.

Christ, when he said, *Thou shalt love thy Neighbour*, spoke it in this sense, as if he should have said, Thou shalt love every one that is thy Neighbour.

Tel.

So likewise *Adam,* when he said: *he shall cleave unto his Wife,* did intimate, that he should cleave unto every one that shall be his Wife; And therefore not be proved by those words, that it is unlawful for a man to have more Wives then one.

Och.

But what will you say to those following words of his: *and of them twain shall be made one flesh?* for he does not say, of three or four. From these words it is doubtless manifest, that God would not have Marriage to be made between more then two.

Tel.

Adam says not, that of them two shall be made one flesh; but, *they shall be made one Flesh.*

Och.

But that was his meaning, as plainly appeares from the words of Christ, who citing the said speech, sayes, that God by *Adam* declared, *And they two shall be one Flesh,* adding moreover, this following clause: *They are no longer two, but one Flesh.*

Tel.

It is as if he had said, The Husband shall love every one of his Wives, as if she were the same flesh, and the same body with him; and so likewise, shall every Wife love her Husband.

Och.

But God said, they two shall be one: therefore there cannot be three or foure.

Tel.

You were in the right, if he had said, They two (only) shall be one. And therefore, as this Argument is of no force; Christ said, *If two of you on Earth shall agree about a thing, they shall obtain what they aske:* therefore if three or foure shall agree they shall not obtain the same: so is this no good inference; God said, *They two shall be one Flesh:* therefore if there be three, it is no true Marriage.

Och.

It is impossible for more then two, to become one flesh.

Tel.

In the primitive Church, there were not only two believers, but they were in great numbers, having nevertheless one soul, and one mind; and you believe, if a man had divers Wives, he could not become one flesh with them. If a man, while he cleaves unto an Harlot, becomes as *Paul* sayes, one body with her, although he have a Wife, should he not much more become one flesh with her, if he should make her his Wife?

Och.

Say what you will; To have more then one Wife, is a thing filthy, dishonest, and quite contrary, and destructive to the holy State of Matrimony.

Tel.

And yet you know, that *Abraham* had more Wives then one; as also *David,* and many other men under the old Testament; who, in case it had been unlawful for them, to have more then one Wife, they should have sinned in marrying divers Women; and the Children which they had by all their Wives, excepting the first; should have been Bastards, because not begotten in lawful Matrimony.

Och.

I will sooner grant all that you have said, then I will allow, or grant it lawful for one man to have more then one Wife. Those Ancients were holy men; yet did they sometimes sin. They were sinners, as being born of *Adam,* as appeares in the example of *David;* and they should have deceived themselves, if they had denied themselves to be sinners.

Tel.

That they sometimes sinned, I shall easily grant; but I will never yield, that they continued in their sins, till their day of death: which nevertheless they did, in case it was unlawful for them to have divers Wives. Whence it would follow, that they were all damned, as those who die while they keep a Concubine. As for us, we cannot hold them for Saints, seeing we know not for certain, that they ever repented. When *David* had committed those same Acts of Adultery and Murther, because he was one of Gods Elect, God sent his Prophet to him, to reprove him: as also when he numbred the People, contrary to the Command of God. Credible therefore it is, that if to have divers Wives, had been contrary to the Law of God, God would have used the like proceedings towards him, that he might not be damned. But though you read the whole Bible over, you shall never finde, that God has forbad the having of divers Wives. And yet, if it had bin a thing unlawful, *Moses* would never have dissembled the matter. Moreover, the Scriptures tell us, that *David* was a man after Gods own heart, and that he was obedient to all the Lords Commandements, all his life long, save in the matter of *Vriah*. So that had it been a sin to have divers Wives, seeing that also had been sufficiently known, the Authour would have accepted it, or he must doubtless, make himself a lyar; by saying, that *David* committed only that sin of *Homicide,* under which his Adultery is comprehended. Again, how could that be true, which God said to *David,* when blaming him for his unthankfulness he told him, that he had given him many Wives? which questionless, must have bin all Whores, except the first, and so it had not bin God, but the Devil that gave them unto him. Moreover, you shall finde, that God made a Law, that if any man had two Wives, the one beloved, the other hated; and had by them divers Children, the eldest of which, was the son of the hated Wife, it should not be allowed the Father, to make the Sonne of his beloved Wife his Heire. Now it might fall out, that the beloved Wife might be his first Wife, and so it should come to passe, that though the Husband had Children by the latter, sooner then by the first, yet they should be Bastards, if your opinion be true, and born of an Whore, and therefore ought not to be Heires. It is therefore clear by the word of God, that all the Children are legitimate, though sprung from divers wives by one and the same Husband; and that therefore not only the first, but the following marriages are lawful, seeing God did both approve and blesse them, in those holy men the first Fathers of the world.

O*ch.*

The first thing, which you say follows from my opinion, that all which died having many wives should be damned. I answer: If they are dead not having divorced all save their first wife; or without repenting of their sin, they are all damned. But as many of them as are saved did repent and put away all but their first and lawful wife.

Tel.

But, it is not apparent, that ever any did that; and yet if your opinion were true, mention ought to have been made thereof in the holy Scriptures, that we might know and understand, That to keep divers wives, is an abominable thing.

Och.

It was already known, that men ought not to have more wives then one, because God had commanded that the Husband and the wife, should of two become one-flesh.

Tel.

It is not likely that it was unlawful to have divers wives, and that the unlawfulness thereof was known, and *Abraham,* and *Jacob,* and *David,* and other worthy persons like them, should nevertheless marry more wives then one.

Och.

That's a good one! As if many holy men in ancient times did not sin, though they knew what they did, was unlawful.

Tel.

But they did not continue to their lives end in those sins, as those that married more wives then one, did.

Och.

I told you before that if they were of the number of Gods Elect, they did at last repent.

Tel.

But we ought no longer to reckon the Patriarchs for examples sake to be Saints, seeing we are assured that they sinned in having many wives; but we are not assured of their repentance.

O*ch*.

True, unlesse the word of God assures us that they were Saints: as we know (for example sake) *Abraham, Isaac,* and *Jacob* to be Saints, because Christ said, that *many should come from the East, and from the West, and sit down with* Abraham, Isaac *and* Jacob, *in the Kingdom of Heaven.* Now, I conceive, that as *Moses* because of the hardness of their hearts, suffered the Jews to put away their wives without just cause, so for the same cause he suffered them to have sundry wives, that is to say, he did not forbid or hinder it, nor punish the same by any Law enacted in his Commonwealth. But it follows not therefore, that they did not sin in Gods sight, and that they did not deserve punishment unlesse they repented.

T*el*.

That thing is permitted, which is neither punished, nor hindred, nor forbidden. Truly, I will not say *Moses* sinned, if to avoid a greater evil, and to comport with the hardness of the Jewes hearts, he permitted them to have divers wives; that is to say, he did not punish or hinder them. But if he permitted them so as not to forbid them, I cannot but say, he sinned. For *Moses* ought to have expresly forbidden, that any man should have more then one wife: which because he has not done, we must needs confesse that it is not a thing unlawful

O*ch*.

The having of many wives, was then (as it is now) so apparently filthy, dishonest, and vitious, that it was needless for *Moses* to forbid the same.

T*el*.

And was it not apparent, that Adultery was a thing filthy, dishonest, vicious? yea, much more then the having of many wives, and yet he expresly forbad adultery. But in case it had been unlawful to have many wives, he ought to have forbidden that, so much the more expresly, by how much the unlawlawfulnesse thereof, was lesse manifest then the unlawfulnesse of Adultery was. Is it not a clear case, that Homicide is unlawful, and yet he forbids that. In a word, What are the ten Commandements, but an Expression of the Law of Nature?

Och.

It may be said, that God might remit the transgressions against the second Table, because he is above, not only all Creatures, but his own Law: and peradventure he might remit the same to all mankind born before the death of Christ; and consequently be willing, that they might have more wives then one, without sin. And so it comes to pass, that those under the Old Testament that had many wives, did not sin; and under that consideration, God might give many wives to *David.* Though it may also be said, that he gave them to him, that is, permitted him to have them, in as much as he neither hindred, nor punisht him.

Tel.

That it is unlawful to keep more wives then one, if your opinion be true, is clear from the word of God, who said, *that two should be made one flesh;* but that God did so far remit of his Laws, that men should not sin in having more, does not appear in the word of God; that opinion therefore of yours, has no foundation.

Och.

If you consider well, you shall finde that *Lamech* a very wicked man, was the first that had two Wives. Other holy men that preceeded him, knowing the will of God, had onely one a piece.

Tel.

As if that *Abraham, Isaac,* and *Jacob,* were not more holy then those very men you speak of. But, in the first place, I cannot tell how you came to know that *Lamech* was the first man that had two wives, although he be the first man whom the Scripture mentions to have had two. But as this is a vain Argument, The Scripture no where mentions, that *Cain* had more then one Son; therefore, doubtlesse he had no more: so, as vain is this which follows: It is no where in Scripture recorded, that those men that lived before *Lamech,* had more wives then one: therefore none of them had above one wife. Moreover, where it is said, that *Lamech* had two wives, it is not charged upon him as a sin, but seems rather to be set down as a thing pleasing to God, that a man should have more wives then one, seeing by them he gave *Lamech* such ingenious Sons, as proved the inventors of Arts, both delightful and profitable. Neither can I see how you came informed, that *Lamech* was so wicked a man, as you talk of.

Och.

God plagued him, by suffering him to fall into the sins of murther and desperation, only because he had married two wives.

Tel.

But I cannot see, either that he was a murtherer or fell into despair; neither does the Scripture teach any such thing, if it be rightly interpreted: Or if the Scripture had intimated any such thing, (which I do not grant) yet does it not thereby appear, that God suffered him so to slip, because he had married two wives.

Och.

But we may conjecture, that his having two wives displeased God, seeing his murther is presently after mentioned.

Tel.

In the first place, I have already told you, that by the words of that Text, if they be rightly understood, there is no signification made, that either he was a man-slayer, or in desperation; and if such a thing were intimated, it does not therefore follow, that his plurality of wives was the cause thereof, or that God was offended with him therefore; inasmuch as presently upon the mention of his two wives, he commends their Sons, as if he would give us to understand, that he approves of plurality of wives. Add hereunto, that nothing ought to be affirmed or avouched in the Church of God, as necessary to salvation, if it cannot otherwise be known, save by conjectures only.

Och.

Seeing I cannot convince you out of the old Testament, I will try what I can do from the New.

Tel.

You are in an errour if you think the Old Testament is not sufficient to teach us all things necessary to salvation. If therefore that be the cause you betake your self to the New, you are deceived, seeing as *Paul* writes, *All Scripture of Divine inspiration is profitable for reprehension, correction and instruction, in righteousness, that the man of, God may be made perfect, furnished for every good work.* Now clear it is, that *Paul* in that place speaks of those Scriptures, in which *Timothy* was exercised from a child. And because the new Testament was not then written, you must be forced to confesse, that *Paul* in that place speaks of the Old. The old Testament therefore is profitable, not only to assert the truth of such things as are necessary to salvation, but also to confute falsities: and consequently to render a man perfect. For which cause, Christ speaking thereof said, *Search the Scriptures for in them is found life.*

Och.

Perhaps somethings are forbidden to us in the New Testament, which were not forbidden to them in the Old.

Tel.

In moral matters, verily what ever is unlawful and to us forbidden, was in like manner evermore forbidden to them; and whatever was allowed and commanded to them, the same is in like manner allowed and commanded to us. God was equally Author of the old Testament as well as of the New; nor was he ever contrary, or unlike himself.

Och.

That was allowed to those under the old Testament, because of their imperfection, which is not allowed to us, in whom carnal desires ought to be much more mortified.

Tel.

You take that for granted which you have not proved, *viz.* That it is unlawful to have more wives then one. Moreover, you are deceived, if you think, that it is a bad thing to have one wife, but worse to have two; For as the Act matrimonial, in him that has one wife, is a thing not in it self evil, nor repugnant to those actions, that are necessary to salvation: no more is it to have two wives, provided a man have a call from God to mary them, and be moved, not by the impulse of the flesh, but of the Spirit, that he may have children, and bring them up in the fear of God; his wife likewise doing the same. Whence it follows, that he may be as perfect that has two wives, as he that has but one or none. Nor had *Abraham,* because he had divers wives lesse Faith, Hope, or Charity, then Priests, Monks, or Friars that have none. Conjugal Chastity, is as well the gift of God, as that of a single State, For this cause *Paul* said, Every one is endued with his own gift from God, some one way, some another.

O*ch.*

In that place, the Apostle exhorted the *Corinthians* to a single Life, and that for no other cause, but that a married estate has many incumbrances attending the same: in as much as married people, being intangled with worldly affairs, are not so free to pray, and preach up and down, and do good to others, as single people are. Now, if so be the having of one wife, do bring so many impediments, any one may soon conjecture, what the having of divers wives will do. And therefore to have more wives then one is unlawful.

Tel.

You are in an error if you think, that the mind of *Paul* in those words was, that marriage was a stop to mens journey to Heaven, so that married people could not be saved; For then that which God said, would not be true, *viz.* That it was not good for a man to be alone; but it would rather be an excellent thing to be alone; and to marry a wife, the worst thing in the world, because in so doing a man should sin. Moreover, I and, that not only a married man may be saved, as well as a Bachelour, but be as perfect as he, inasmuch as he may attain as great perfection in Faith, Hope, and Charity as the other. And if he cannot personally performe some externall works which the single man can, as hindred by his married estate, yet he may in mind perform the same, and that is it which God regards.

O*ch.*

Though Matrimony do not hinder a man from going to God; yet the having of more wives then one, does.

Tel.

How prove you that?

Och.

From *Paul,* who speaking of Bishops, sayes, he would have them to be the husbands of one wife, meaning that they should have no more. It is therefore unlawful to have more wives then one.

Tel.

Nay rather when he tells them, by name, that they should have one, lest having more, they should be too much distracted with worldly businesse, 'tis easie to see that he allows other men to have more.

Och.

Some do thus interpret the mind of *Paul,* A Bishop is to have but one wife, that is (say they) one Church for his spiritual Spouse.

Tel.

Many reasons shew that to be a false opinion. First, because Christ only is the Spouse of Souls and Bridegroome of his Church. And if we that are ministers be his friends, we ought with *John Baptist,* as the friends of Christ, the only true Spouse of Souls, to send them to him their Bridegroom: and not to draw them to our selves. The Churches therefore of Christ are not the Bishops Spouses. And if they were, as the Husband is superiour to his Wife, so should they be to their respective Churches, against which *Paul* writes to the *Corinthians,* where he sayes, *We are not Lords over your faith, or over you, by reason of your Faith.* The Church therefore is not *Pauls* Wife. I confess indeed, that one Church is enough for one Pastor, and he does no small matter, if he can govern that well. In the ancient times of Christianity, one Church sometimes had divers Pastors, as appears from the Epistle to the *Philippians,* in which *Paul* salutes the Bishops, which were at *Philippi:* whereas now a dayes one Bishop has many Churches. Moreover, when *Paul* sayes. A Bishop ought to have one Wife, he speaks of the manners of him that was fit to be a Bishop. But if he be yet to be chosen, he is no Bishop; and therefore has no Church as yet, that might be called his wife. Hereby also it is manifest, that by Wife, he did not mean Church, because presently almost after those words, he makes mention of his Children, commanding that he govern his Family well, and have his Children subject to him, with all Reverence. For if a man cannot govern his own Family, how can he oversee the Church of God? In that place therefore he speaks of a Wife, and not of a Church.

Och.

Some say, that *Paul* in that place, forbids such men to be chosen Bishops, who have had divers Wives, though not at one and the same time.

Tel.

But I do not conceive, that *Paul* counted it sin after the death of a mans first wife, to take a second; for as much as he himself sayes, that after the death of the Husband, the wife is free, and may without blame marry another. So far is it from being unlawful for a man, after the death of his wife, to marry another.

Och.

They say, 'tis a shameful thing, when a mans first wife is dead, to marry another.

Tel.

If you weigh the matter rightly, and follow not the Opinion of the blind vulgar people, you shall finde that the matrimonial Act, is as free from turpitude, as the actions of eating and drinking; nor would God have commanded Matrimony, if it had bin evil, which nevertheless he did, when he said, Increase and propagate.

Och.

I condemn not matrimony; but the Iterations or Repetition thereof.

Tel.

The second Matrimony, is as true and valid as the first; and therefore you cannot condemn the Iteration of Matrimony, but you must withall, condemn Matrimony it self. Take an Example. A young man marries a Wife, she dies a few dayes after, he is somewhat incontinent, or is again called to a married condition: who knowes not, that he according to the Precept of *Paul,* seeing he cannot contain, ought to take another Wife.

Och.

Unless second Mariages were filthy, and unlawful, *Paul* would never, speaking afterwards of Widows, have commanded such to be chosen, as had only one Husband.

Tel.

Think you that *Paul* was superstitious?

Och.

I do not think he was.

Tel.

If a young Widow, somewhat incontinent, had asked *Pauls* advice, what think you *Pauls* answer would have bin?

Och.

That she should marry again, according to his own Doctrine.

Tel.

It is not therefore unlawful to marry again. Why then should *Paul* reject such Widows, as had had more Husbands then one? for it was possible that some Widow having had divers Husbands, might be more holy and honest, then they which had had but one. Also it might fall out, that she which had had divers Husbands, might live but one year with them: whereas the rest that had never had more then one, might have lived with him, thirty or forty years. In such a case truly, I cannot see why they should be more worthy to be chosen then she. I do therefore believe, that the mind of *Paul* in that place was this, that such Widows were not to be chosen that had had many Husbands, that is to say, who being divorced, had married again: their former Husbands who divorced them being yet alive. For either they were divorced upon a just ground, and then it was not fit they should be chosen; or upon an unjust ground, and so the Matrimony remained good, having never bin violated and then the divorced woman had sinned, if she married to another. By which meanes it came to passe, that all women divorced were infamous, not only such as married to other men; but such likewise as abstained from Mariage, especially amongst the Gentiles, who were not wont to divorce them; save for some fault or vitious quality. *Paul* therefore did never condemn those Women, who their former Husband being dead married another, nor did he forbid them to be Bishops, who their former Wife being dead, married another, which notwithstanding, the superstitious Papists observe, because they understood not the meaning of *Paul.* Though a man have kept divers Whores, they make him a Bishop; but if his first Wife being dead, he marry another, they will not: whence it comes to passe, that Matrimony amongst them is of worse report, then Fornication, Adultery, Incest, Sacriledge, Sodomie, and all imaginable abominations. This is therefore the mind of *Paul* (and this will make the third opinion) as has bin said of Widows, that he who has had divers Wives, because he divorced one, ought not to be made a Bishop. For if he divorc't her unjustly, he ought not to be a Bishop in that regard; if justly, yet the Infamy of his wife, redounding upon himself; for that cause *Paul* would not have him be a Bishop. Howbeit, I like not this Opinion; for he does not say, he must have bin, but that he must be the Husband of one wife: for he sayes, he must be unblamed, *viz.* as the Husband of one Wife: as he expressed it a little afterwards, touching Deacons, and writing to *Titus* about Bishops.

O*ch.*

Because a Bishop, in regard of the publick Office he beareth; as also the Deacons, have to do with all persons, not only with Men, but also with Women; to avoid suspicion, *Paul* would that they should be married; and this perhaps might be the meaning of those words. Also, it may be, that *Paul* foreseeing the Superstition of the Papists, who would forbid the Mariage of Bishops, that they might be without excuse, he said, they ought to be blameless, and to have a wise but that they should have no more then one, he did not say. Or he shewes, that a Bishop ought to have a wife, that is, he ought to be content with her, and not to have any thing to do with other Women, which is, as if he had said, that he ought to be honest.

Tel.

The mind of *Paul* is this, that it is lawful for the generality of Christians, to have many Wives; but for Bishops to have only every man one, not because it had bin a sin for them to have more; but because the duty of Bishops being to labour for the salvation of others, he feared lest multiplicity of Wives should be a pul-back, and hinder them from performing their Office, as they ought to do. For this cause he would have them to have but one: nor is it therefore unlawful for other men to have more. Yea verily, while he forbids Bishops and Deacons to have more then one, he closely allowes it to other men. Nor is it likely *Paul* would have forbidden Bishops to have more Wives then one, had it not bin the Custom of those times for them to have more. It was therefore in the new Testament forbidden to Bishops to have many Wives, as it was in the old Testament forbidden to Kings; not because it was in it self unlawful, but lest Kings, whose Office was of greatest consequence, being distracted by their Wives, should be corrupted, as it happened to *Solomon;* for if *Adam,* when he had but one, was notwithstanding perverted by her, 'tis easie to conjecture what might happen to Kings, if they should have many. Yet do I believe nevertheless, that as in the same place he forbad Kings to have many Horses, that is too great a multitude, least he should put his trust in them, rather then in God; for otherwise they were allowed to have many Horses; even so, they were forbid to have many Wives, seeing *David* a most holy man, had many; but that they should not have an immoderate multitude, especially such as were Heathens, and Worshippers of false Gods. To return therefore to our business, 'tis not credible, that *Paul* feared, lest *Timothy* should choose for Bishops, such as were *Gentile's* or *Jewes,* not baptized. There were therefore in the Church of Christ, and among the Christians, such as had more wives then one. And because from among them a Bishop was to be chosen: he would not have him choose one that had divers wives. But if to keep more wives then one, had bin contrary to the Law of God, as you say it is, and the first Wife only were right and true, the rest Harlots: 'tis not credible, that the Christians would have baptized any one that had plurality of wives, unless he had put away all saving his first. And if that had bin the practise, it had bin in vain for *Paul* to command, that he that was to be chosen Bishop, should be the Husband of one Wife, seeing Christians out of the number of whom the Bishop was chosen, had but each of them one a peece. But this I much marvail at, that many who have sometimes written and do believe, that to have more Wives then one, is repugnant to the divine Law, both moral and natural, and yet in expounding *Paul,* they say, that he writing to *Timothy,* warns him to take heed, that he choose not a Bishop that had plurality of wives; whence it follows, that seeing Election was not to be made of any out of the Church of God, that there were in Gods Church such as had more wives then one; and consequently, counted it not unlawfull to have more. Otherwise, if they had counted it unlawful, as they did not Baptize, or admit unto the Lords Supper any man that kept a Concubine, unless he would forsake her: in like manner they would not have Baptized, nor admitted to the Supper, nor suffer'd amongst them such as had many wives, unless they would divorce all save the first.

Och.

But what do you say to *Paul* who wills and commands, That every man should have his own wife? for in saying his own wife he excludes wives.

Tel.

Some say, his meaning is, Let every man have his own wife; that is, his own, not another mans: and nor, only one. As if some Father making shew of his Daughter, should say, This is my own Daughter; not denying that he has more Daughters, that are likewise his own.

Och.

In the same place the same *Paul* commands, That the Wife have her own proper Husband, that is to say, such a Wife as is proper to him alone, and not in common with other wives. Whence it follows, That as a woman ought to be proper to her husband, and not to belong to other husbands: so the man ought to be appropriated to his first wife, and not common to others: provided, you will (as you ought) expound the words of *Paul,* so as he may not contradict himself.

Tel.

Paul does not there dispute, whether an husband may have plurulity of wives, or no; but his intent is to shew, that such men as have not the gift of continence, should take them wives; and that women in the like case should marry

Och.

Is it possible that you should not see, that plurality of wives, is repugnant to the matrimonial contract, in which the man grants his wife, and the woman her husband, an honest use of their respective Bodies for ever? For which cause also *Paul* sayes, That neither the man nor the woman have power over their own Bodies, but each of one anothers. And in case a man have given the honest use of his Body to his wife, he can no longer give it to another, because he has already given it to the first.

Tel.

Yes, by the permission of the first he may, as *Abraham* did, when by the permission of *Sarah*, he married *Hagar*, and consequently by permission of the first and second, he may marry a third, which is true of other men as well as *Abraham:* especially the wives being instructed that it is no sin for their husbands, with their consent to marry other wives.

Och.

Do you believe, that *David* when he married *Bathsheba*, did it with consent of his other wives, and that others who married divers wives, did so likewise.

Tel.

Suppose they did not, yet were not their marriages the less true and lawful. For it was then a thing commonly known, and confirmed by example, That it was lawful for a man to have many wives. Therefore when a man by marriage, gave the use of his Body to his wife, he did not so totally give the same, as to bereave himself of all power to give it to other wives also: which the wives knew well enough by the publick custome then in force; and thereunto the wives did silently give consent, seeing their husbands married them with this condition being understood. Their marriages therefore were good and lawful.

Och.

An husband cannot marry a second wife without detriment of his first. It is not therefore credible, that wives did in their hearts consent, that their husbands should marry others.

Tel.

It is possible my wife may prove barren; in which case, it is her duty to consent that I should take another; yea and of her own consent to exhort me thereunto, as *Sarah* did of old. And if she would not approve thereof, this will of hers were unjust, and so it were lawful for her husband to marry another, contrary to her unjust mind. Also when a woman is with Child, and sometime after she is brought to bed, seeing she is then unfit for procreation, as also when she is old and sick, her husband may without injury to her, have to do with another wife; yea, though a mans wife were sound, and fit for generation, yet she ought to take it in good part, if enjoying the company of her husband at some certain times, as it is with other living Creatures, she leave it free for him to enjoy the carnal acquaitance of his other wives.

Och.

Do you think it lawful for one wise to have many husbands?

Tel.

No.

Och.

And yet there are sick Men, as well as sick women. Also a woman is able to have to do with more men, then a man can with women. Whence it seems more just, for one woman to have divers husbands, or at least lesse injust, then for a man to have many wives.

Tel.

Nay rather, since Matrimony is chiefly ordained for procreation sake, and a man having many wives, may in a short time have many more children, then a woman which has plurality of husbands: it is more equitable, that a man have many wives, then that a woman have many husbands. But the chief causes why women may not have many husbands, and yet men may have many wives, are these. First of all, because, if women should have many husbands, there would follow great disturbance and confusion in the world. For seeing no husband could certainly know that his children are his own, he might alwaies suspect, that they were some other husbands rather then his; and consequently he would not bring them up, nor instruct them, nor take such care for them, as now he does, knowing they are his own, though born of divers wives. Perhaps also being unassured that they are his own, he would not make them his Heirs. Another cause, why it is lawful for men to have many wives, but not for women to have many husbands, is this; The husband is his wives Head, and has authority and command over her, as being her Superiour; for which cause he may have divers wives, provided he can well rule and instruct them all. Nor is it a monstrous, but a comely thing for to have many members in one Body, though there he but one Head; but if the Body should have many Heads, it would be a monster: So for one husband to have many wives, is not monstrous; but for one wife to have many husbands, is monstrous. And therefore, as there would be dissention and discord, of in one Body there were many Heads, & they should be of contrary minds, as might well happen: so would there be discords, perturbations, and great inconveniences, if should have plurality of husbands, seeing it might happen, that they should will things contrary, and command their wives to do them.

Och.

If we regard discords and inconveniences, we shall finde they have been sometimes exceeding great, because one man has had two wives: as we see in the example of *Sarah & Hagar, Leah* and *Rachel, Hannah* and *Peninnah,* and others, amongst whom were continual dissensions: which I conceive, God did therefore suffer, to shew that he was not pleased, that one man should have more then one wife.

Tel.

Although among the first-born, and other brethren, many times grievous discords have arose, as appears in *Cain* and *Abel; Esau,* and *Jacob;* and many others: it is not therefore displeasing to God, that Fathers should have many Sons. As also between Mothers in Law, and Daughters in Law, though there is many times little quiet, yet is not Matrimony therefore displeasing to *God.* In like manner, although among divers wives of the same Husband, there has seldom bin good agreement, yet cannot either Marriage in general, or marriage of sundry wives be condemned; but only those wives, who were not so well disposed as they ought to have bin.

O*ch*.

Christians ought in this life to be contemners of pleasures, and to have more of the Spirit, then those men had, which lived under the old Testament. And therefore, though They had many wives, one a peece ought verily to content us.

T*el*.

I have already declared, and told you, to cohabit with plurality of Wives, is no unlawful thing, and that it may consist with the greatest degree of faith and perfection. And therefore I cannot tell how you can be assured, that some Christians are not called by God, to cohabit with divers wives, as well as some Jewes of old were called by Him thereunto.

O*ch*.

Say what you will, to have more wives then one, is a thing filthy and dishonest.

T*el*.

There are two things which bring you into that error. The first is custome; for if it were the Custom for men to have more then one, it would not seem to you blameworthy. Another is a feigned kind of holiness, which makes the having more wives then one, seem to you unlawful, though it be no whit repugnant to the holy Scriptures. Yea, and those that have more wives then one, are wont to be more grievously punished, then they should be, if they kept a thousand Concubines.

O*ch*.

'Tis hard for one man to content one woman, and you would have it lawful for him to have more.

T*el*.

An Husband is not obliged to satisfie all the carnal desires of his wife, but such only as are moderated with reason.

Och.

Under the old Testament when there were few men in the world, it was peradventure, expedient for men to have more wives; but now the world is full of people, it is not expedient.

Tel.

In the first place you know not, whether men if they had more wives, would have many more Children then they have: or if they should beget more Children (as is very likely) how know you that the fruits of the Earth will not suffice to afford them all that shall be necessary for their livelihood, and all other occasions. For the same God that gave increase of men, would likewise supply plenty of to nourish and maintain them. But suppose you were assured they should perish with famine, yet the souls of men are of so great price, that we should no wayes hinder their existence, especially if we be called thereto by God, as those holy men of old were, who had plurality of wives.

Och.

In these dayes a Christian ought not to have plurality of wives, if for no other cause, at least to avoid the offence which might thence arise, seeing all Christians do account the having of more wives then one, to be a most filthy and Diabolical thing.

Tel.

Even as, although men should account Matrimony an unlawful thing, yet ought you not to be moved with their offence taken thereat, but to marry, if need were: so ought you to marry more then one, if need be, or you be called thereunto by divine impulse.

Och.

A single man might indeed in such a case marry, to avoid fornication, although men should be therewith offended; especially, being called by God thereunto. But he that has one already needs not marry another, nor will God thereunto call him.

Tel.

Nay verily; if his wife be sick, or other impediments shall happen, so that he cannot enjoy her, and be incontinent, he must of necessity, to avoid fornication, marry another. Add hereunto, that God does not call men to marry, only for the avoidance of fornication; but chiefly for propagation, as of old he called *Abraham,* and other holy men.

Och.

Shall I make it clear and manifest to you, that the having more wives then one, is a thing forbidden? Christ says, if any man put away his wife, save for adultery, and shall marry another, he commits adultery. But if a man might have more wives then one, he should not commit adultery, as Christ sayes, whether he put away his former wife, or no.

Tel.

No man can expound those words of Christ, better then Christ himself, who in another place explaining the said words, sayes, Whosoever shall put away his wife, save for adultery, causes her to commit adultery, that is to say, he gives occasion to his wife, so unjustly put away, to commit Adultery. For the wife being by that meanes deprived of her true Husband, cannot marry any other, her former Husband living; but she shall commit adultery. Christ does not therefore say, If any man put away his wife, not for adultery, and marries another, he commits adultery; but that he gives occasion to his repudiated wife to commit adultery.

Och.

Both *Matthew, Mark,* and *Luke* record, that Christ said, If any man put away his wife, and marry another, he commits adultery, that is to say, by marrying that other. But if his intent was to shew, that by unjustly putting her away, he gave her occasion to commit adultery; it had been sufficient to have said, If any one put away his wife; not adding, *and marry another.* Christ therefore by those words of his in the fifth of *Matthew,* did not intend to explain that passage, which is recorded in the 19. Chapter of the said Evangelist: only he said, If any put away his wife, not for adultery, he makes her to commit adultery. But in the 19. of *Matthew,* he sayes another thing, *viz.* that if he marry another in the same kind, he commits Adultery, because the first was his wife, and he ought not to have more then one. Add hereunto, that the words of Christ in his Sermon upon the Mount, were uttered before those were, by which he answered the Pharises, when they asked him, Whether a man for every cause might put away his wife. Those former words therefore cannot be an Exposition of those were spoke afterwards.

Tel.

Whether the latter words were an Exposition of the former or no; it satisfies me; that his meaning is one and the same in both places, *viz.* that if any man put away his wife without just cause, he occasions her to commit Adultery. And as for those words, which in the 19. Chapter, are added over and above: Christ added them to shew, that a wife unjustly divorced, if she marry another man, commits adultery, though at the same time her former Husband marry another wife, seeing the first Matrimony is not void; but remains in full force. His meaning therefore is this; If he put her away unjustly, though he marry another, yet he gives her that is put away, occasion to commit adultery.

Och.

This interpretation of yours, is so forced and strained, that it is in danger of breaking. Moreover, we may see in Creatures irrational, that the Males have their Females, with whom alone they couple, as we see in Birds; and much fitter it is for men, especially Christians, to have the like.

Tel.

That is true only in such like Creatures, whose propagation is not very needful, to the maintenance of the life of man. But if you observe, you shall find, that one Cock has many Hens, one Bull many Cowes; and so in other Creatures which are profitable to mankind. If therefore God has ordained for the Commodity of Man-kind, that one Cock should have many Hens, much more has he ordained, that one man should have many wives, for the propagation of men, whom he so highly prizes, and so dearly loves.

Och.

If none of those live-Creatures you speak of were guelt, and they should all converse together, you should finde every male with his proper female; and men ought to do the same much more. But now, many of the males being guelt and separated, if one male couple, with divers females; it followes not therefore, that it should be lawful for one man to have many Wives. God put into the Ark of *Noah*, just so many males as females, to shew that every male ought to have only his own single female.

Tel.

If there were in the world as many Men as Women, I confess it were expedient, that every man should have his own single Wife. But seeing the number of Women is greater, I conceive it fit, that one man have many Wives; for it is not in vain, that *God* makes more Women. If there were in the World, for example sake, only three hundred Women, and as many men, and every man should have one Woman, they could not so soon propagate their kind: as if of six hundred, four hundred were Women, and two hundred men, every one of which should have divers Women. For this cause therefore, *God* ordained, that the number of Women, should be greater then the number of Men. The life of one Man equalls that of two Women.

Och.

In the first place, I do not believe that you know there are more Women in the World then men. Perhaps it seemes so to you, because commonly we rejoyce at the birth of Boyes, and grieve at the birth of Girles. But though there be more Women born into the World, yet they live not long for the most part, by reason of the more tender constitution of their bodies. Add hereunto, that many more men perish then women, by Warres, Shipwrack, and the Sword of justice: that reason therefore does not prove *Polygamy* or plurality of Wives. Moreover, the love of carnal society, is a most violent passion: and if dishonest love cannot endure a Rival, much lesse can that which is honest?

Tel.

Holy love rather extends to all, even our enemies.

Och.

Jacob was an holy man, and he loved barren *Rachel,* more then fruitful *Leah.* So also *Helkanah* loved *Hannah* that was barren, more then *Peninnah* that was fruitful. *Solomon* also said, that his beloved was one. It is therefore an hard thing, to share out a mans love, amongst many Wives, which notwithstanding, must be done in *Polygamy*. When a man has but one Wife, mutual love is better preserved, then if he had more; and if any falling out happen, reconciliation is more easily made. Where there are many Wives, there are divers understandings, divers Constitutions, Distractions and Discords.

Tel.

If there were a call from God, there would be his blessing. *Polygamy* is no enemy to charity. And therefore if any man should have plurality of Wives, and love were wanting between them, that were not the fault of *Polygamy*, but of the said Wives.

Och.

If the filthy love of an Harlot, is oftentimes the cause, that a man is content with her alone, much more ought the holy love of Wedlock, work the same effect.

Tel.

We see that filthy love is more effectual in some persons, then holy love is in others: as also in like manner, superstition produces more good works in some, then true Religion in others: all which comes to passe, by the instinct of Sathan.

Och.

That plurality of Wives, is a thing contrary to natural Reason, hereby appears, in that all Nations have always abstained therefrom, as from a thing unlawful.

Tel.

You know that the light of nature, that is to say, the Law which is imprinted in the hearts of men, is the gift of God, and that it is just, and that the Law of *Moses* is not contrary thereunto, but an explanation thereof. For if the Law of *Moses* were contrary thereunto, God would be contrary to himself, seeing both proceed from God, or rather, both are one and the same Law. And therefore if plurality of Wives, had bin contrary to the judgement of right Reason: neither would *Moses* verily have dissembled the same; neither would those most holy Patriarchs have used the same, nor would God have born with it. God by *Moses* commanding the *Jewes*, that when they came into the borders of the Gentiles, they should not imitate their vices, would have named *Polygamy,* among other vices, if it had bin unlawful; and he would have forbidden the same by *Moses,* which nevertheless, he did not do. We no where read, that ever God punished any man for having plurality of Wives, nor that he ever did by his Prophets, threaten such as had many Wives. If you would have the manners of the Gentiles, to be your rule and law, you shall finde amongst them much wickedness. And whereas you said, that all Nations abhorred *Polygamy,* that is false, as appeares by the *Jewes.* Also *Chremes* had two Wives, if we will believe *Terence:* also *Bocc••,* as *Salust* relates; in a word, *Socrates* himself, who notwithstanding, was the wisest of men, and had much of the light of nature.

Och.

Even wise men sometimes do amiss.

Tel.

Never any man condemned, or reprehended *Socrates,* for having two Wives, although for other things he hath been condemned. What needs many words? *Polygamy* was used as a good thing, and very profitable to Man-kind, by furthering propagation; not only among the *Jewes,* but also among the *Persians,* and the *Turks* likewise. Only in *Europe* it has been hateful; in which *Europe,* vice has abounded, if not more, yet not a whit lesse, then in all other parts of the world. Nay, & in the days of old, *Polygamy* was commended, even in *Europe.* Only they would not have in one house many Mistresses to rule the Family, which was a thing convenient to avoid confusion.

Och.

I will never confess, that it is a good thing, to have many wives.

Tel.

That is, because you coneive it is an unlawful conjunction, and you are over-powered with an old custome among the vulgar; which in tract of time, has wone the favour of the common people, and the Magistrates: by which it comes to passe, that the common opinion prevails more with you then the truth it self.

O*ch.*

But what do you say to the Imperial Laws, which are against you?

Tel.

In what place?

O*ch.*

First of all, the Emperors Diocletianus *and* Maximinus, *do forbid* Polygamy, *in these words:* That no man within the jurisdiction of the Roman Empire can have two wives: seeing also in the Edict of the *Praetor,* such men are branded with infamy: which thing a just judge, will not suffer to go unpunished. *Al|so, in the same* Code: That man doubtless that has two wives at once, is accompanyed with infamy.

Tel.

The Authors of the first Law, as you say, were *Diocletianus* and *Maximinus;* the other is taken out of a certain Rescript of *Valerianus* and *Galienus.*

O*ch.*

It is sufficient, that being Emperors, they had power to make Laws. It is to be observed, that in their daies, the condition of Matrimony, in the Heathenish Empire was such, that any man might put away his wife for light and frivolous causes, and keep Concubines without any shame. Howbeit, they had neither the name, nor authority of wives. The Emperors therefore thus decreed, not because they thought Polygamy was unlawful, seeing they allowed many lawful Concubines; but they judged it fit, that only the first should have the title and authority of a wife, especially seeing they might Divorce her, if she pleased them not. But we see that Concubines were forbidden by the Emperor *Constantine.*

Tel.

If you well weigh his words, you will find that his intent was, that it should be unlawful for him that had a wife to have Concubines; not that it was wholly unlawful, but he might not have them with him, that is, in his own House, where his wife dwelt, *viz,* to avoid brawlings, discords and countentions. But out of his house, he might have as many as he would, Moreover, the Roman-Emperor *Valentianus,* having the same Authority and power, did not only permit such as had wives to keep Concubines, but many wives also at the same time, in the same house, all dignifyed by the same name and of equal authority: and *Valentianus* himself, at the same time had divers wives; and therefore by the Law of *Valentianus,* which was afterwards made, the former Law of *Constantine* was abrogated.

O*ch*.

But *Justinian* in his *Code,* makes no mention of that Law of *Valentianus.*

Tel.

Yet that Law of his was, doubtless, published, as appears by the Histories. Add hereunto, that besides *Valentianus,* it is apparent, that *Constantius* also the Son of *Constantine* the great, had many wives. *Clotarius* also King of *France,* and *Heribertus* and *Hypericus* his Sons, had plurality of wives. I add *Pip•n* and *Charles,* the Great, of whom *Urspergensis* witnesseth, that they had more wives then one; Yea, and *Lotarius,* and the son of *Lotarius:* as also *Arnolphus* the seventh Emperor of *Germany,* and *Frederick Barbarossa,* and *Philippus Deodatus* King of *France,* and many more. Nor will I deny, that it is a wicked thing to do as some do, who having wives, leave them, travel into strange Countries, and marry others. But I speak of such as take care of both their wives, and are thereunto called by God.

O*ch*.

You suppose that which never was in the world, *viz.* That any man should be called by God to have two wives.

Tel.

Even as *Abraham, Jacob,* and many others were called by God thereunto, so may we. Nor do I see, why they had more need of this Remedy then we, nor why it was rather their duty to beget and bring up a numerous progenie, then ours.

Och.

Constantine will not have men to keep plurality of wives, nor will the Emperor that now reigns.

Tel.

Tell me what is just and fit, and not what men will. The Law of nature is unchangeable. And if in the daies of *Abraham,* it was agreeable to reason, to have plurality of wives, as a thing honest and just; otherwise, we may assure our selves *Abraham* would not have married above one; and therefore we must confesse, That it is at this day a thing fit and just, and so it was in the daies of *Constantine,* For though he were an Emperour, yet could he not make that to be unjust which was just in it self; Doubtless that ancient Church of Christ, had the knowledge of divine matters; and yet neither that Church, nor the Emperors of those times, did condemn or punish *Polygamy.* But men had rather seem to be good, then be so indeed, since they are so great haters of plurality of Wives, but not of Adultery. Finally, to condemn *Polygamy,* is for a man to prefer himself before God, who never condemned the same, and to strive to be more perfect then he. I spare to say, that I may not allow of the Lawes of the Emperors, in cases of Matrimony; seeing they refer the business to the Ecclesiastick Lawes.

Och.

If you will be tryed by them, I am Victor.

Tel.

Bring one *Canon* that makes for you.

Och.

In the times of the Fathers, *Polygamy* was accounted so filthy, and so notoriously and manifestly abominable, that they did not think fit to condemn it by words.

Tel.

But I, for my part, am verily perswaded, that those Fathers of the ancient Church, were contented with the Canon of *Paul,* who would have the Ministers of the Church, to be contented with one Wife; not because, it was in it self unlawful to have more, but that they might the better execute their Office: but he allowed others to live, according as they found themselves inwardly moved by God.

Och.

And yet plurality of wives was forbidden in the third and seventh *Neocaesariensian* Councel.

Tel.

I say, it was never forbidden, neither in them, nor in any other.

Och.

Sure I am, they ordained a penalty for *Polygamists,* which they would never have done, unless they had counted it unlawful to have more Wives then one. Moreover, they forbad all Priests to be present at the mariage of him, that would have more wives then one.

Tel.

True, but they did not forbid *Polygamy* it self.

Och.

They forbid it sufficiently, when they ordained punishments for it.

Tel.

Though you read all the Councels over, you shall never finde *Polygamy* forbidden. Nor can that be said to be the reason, because they conceived, it was forbidden in the holy Scriptures. For, neither is it forbidden, as we have showne already: and in the 17. Canon of the Apostles, it is decreed, that a man having two Wives, should be removed from the Episcopal and Priestly Function, and from all other Ecclesiasticall Offices. But if the Authours of those Canons, had seen that *Polygamy* was repugnant to the Scriptures, to charity, and the common good of mankind; they would have excommunicated such as had two Wives, nor would they only have kept them from the Communion; but they would have also punished them grievously. But those Apostolical persons, as *Paul* had done before them, did only forbid the Ministers of the Church to have more Wives then one, not as if it were a thing repugnant to common honesty; but because it would draw them away, and divert them from spiritual exercises. But because afterward, men began by little and little, to turn aside from the right way, so that many now fell to account Marriage unlawful; they were not ashamed to write, That a mans first Wife being dead, it was Adultery and not Marriage, to take another: touching which matter, you may see what *Gratian* writes. So also *Hierome,* and *Tertullian* interpret that saying of *Paul* and the Apostles, as if his intent had been, that he which had two Wives, though one after another, might not be a Minister in the Church of God: as also he that married a Widow, or a divorced Wife, which is observed at this day, by those most holy men (Sir Reverence) the Papists, who notwithstanding, create men of extraordinary and noted filthiness for their Bishops. But mark what I shall say: the life of a Courtier and a Souldier, is not sinful in it self, but many may be called by God to embrace the same; and yet in the twelfth Canon of the *Nicene* Council it was decreed, that those men should be severely punished, who having left the Warres, should become Souldiers again; notwithstanding in those times, Warre was seldom made, saying against Idolaters & Infidels. In like manner, though they decreed penalties for such as had 2 Wives; yet is not *Bigamy* therefore sinful, nor does it follow, but that many may by divine instinct, be called thereunto. There are many such Canons; especially, concerning Matrimony, which want amendment; nor are we tyed by any Canons, but such as have their foundation in the word of God. The Fathers have many times erred, as being men, and sometimes swarving from the rule of Gods word. Moreover, we ought to believe, that *Paul* taught the *Ephesians* (for examples sake) and the rest of the Churches, all things necessary to salvation, as himself testifies; and yet he taught them not, that any were to be tyed to one Wife, excepting Ministers of the Church.

Och.

He might therefore peradventure do that, to the intent, that others by their example, might by little and little, be brought to practise the same.

Tel.

In the first place, that which you say, is not founded upon any word of God; without which, it seems to me an impious thing to bind mens Consciences. Moreover, every thing that is convenient for Bishops, ought not to be propounded, as an example for all to follow.

Och.

Yet is it much, to say that the Church has erred, for the space now of a thousand two hundred years, in punishing *Bigamy*.

Tel.

That error is not to be attributed to the Church of God, but to men, who in the Church, have as much erred in forbidding Priests to marry; yea, and I would have you to take notice, that the *Neocaesariensian* Councel decreed not, that the second Wife should be divorced, nor that the second was no true Marriage.

Och.

The Councel declared that sufficiently, by decreeing penalties for such as had two Wives.

Tel.

Austin judges that man to sin, who, having made a vow of chastity, marries a wife; and yet he accounts it true marriage, and that it ought not to be made void. This Argument therefore, is of no force; the Councel enacted penalties for such as had two wives; and therefore the second was no true Marriage. Moreover, though above a thousand years are passed, since penalties were enacted against such as had two wives: yet is it not above four hundred years, since that decree was first received by the *Italians, Spaniards,* and *Germans.* For it is but an humane constitution; and the Bishops would have exclaimed against *Valentianus,* for his plurality of wives; but that he had the holy Scriptures on his side. And notwithstanding, they reprehended such as had more then one wife, as *Austin* and *Boniface* did, as persons that seemed over indulgent to the flesh; they did not therefore excommunicate them, or reckon them for such as could not be saved. *Ambrose* was a very sharp Reprover of sin; yet do we not any where read, that he reproved *Valentinianus,* for having two wives. Yea, and the said *Ambrose,* reprehending *Justina* his second wife; for being an *Arian,* must have reproved her also for being no true wife, but a Concubine, which notwithstanding he did not do. It is likewise recorded that *Leo* the fifth, when he heard that a certain Bishop in *Africa* had two wives, he only decreed, that by reason of the words of *Paul,* he should be degraded from that honour; but not that he should put away his second wife, or be otherwise punished for having two. *Gregory* likewise, Bishop of *Rome,* writing to *Boniface,* who was sent into *Germany,* to teach Christianity, an hundred and twenty years after the Nativity of Christ, beseeches him to take care, that such as had many wives, and all were dead save one, might content themselves with her alone, and marry no more. So that he exhorts men to shun plurality of Wives, just as he should exhort them to embrace a single life; which can be understood of none, but such as are called by God, to such a kind of life. The true Ecclesiastical Canons, which oblige us to their observance, are such as have their foundation in Gods word. But go to; read that Epistle which *Gregory* the third of that name, Bishop of *Rome,* wrote to the foresaid *Bonifacius,* there you shall find him write, to this effect. If any Man have a Wife, which by reason of some bodily infirmity, cannot afford her Husband due benevolence, he shall do well to abstain from her. But if he cannot contain (for that is a gift of God not given to all) it is better, that he should marry another Wife, then burn; provided, he allow his first Wife all necessary maintenance. Than which, what could be expressed more clearly?

Och.

All that you can say, though you talk till Doomsday, will never make me think it fit, and lawful for a Man to have more then one Wife.

Tel.

Suppose there are more Women then Men, what shall the poor Women do in this case?

Och.

They must do, just as the men should do, in case there were many more Men then Women, *viz.* pray to God to give them the gift of continence.

Tel.

In case a man is by God called to a married condition, and hath not the gift of continence, to live a single life, it would be in vain for him to pray to God, that he might have the gift to live without a Wife; for in my Opinion, he would never obtain his request, seeing God calls him to marry.

O*ch*.

The whole World has believed, that plurality of Wives is unlawful, nor can any man have more then one Wife, without giving the greatest offence imaginable, which all men ought to shun. Moreover, it is the will of God, that we obey our Magistrates; and they are so far from consenting to *Polygamy,* that they will put him to death, that shall have more then one wife.

T*el*.

But not, if he have many Concubines, or Whores. If any man being moved by divine instinct, to marry divers Wives, and it should be no sin so to do; if he married them, it were a scandal taken (as the Schools speak) and not given. Also he might, to avoid scandal, marry his second Wife privately.

O*ch*.

But such things are hardly practicable; and if he should be often seen in Company of his second Wife, men would take offence, as supposing her to be his Concubine. I shall therefore continually exhort all men to avoid *Polygamy;* and truly I exhort you to do the same. The Papists themselves do vow to live single, and shall we that are regenerate, spiritual, and Evangelical men, marry more wives then one?

T*el*.

Just; And how honest, that single life of theirs is, all the World takes notice. The Law it self condemns barren Matrimony; so far is it from not condemning voluntary and barren single life. Now I speak expresly, of such as have not the gift of continency, nor are called to a single life. The *Romans* did punish such as lived single, and rewarded those, who by abundance of Children, did augment the Commonwealth; and *Lycurgus* also, and *Ulpianus* decreed the same. Now what more blessed a thing can there be, then the preservation of humane kinde? which would wholly perish, were it not for Marriage. A man cannot transmit to posterity, a more honourable memorial of his name, then by leaving behind him Children, virtuously educated. And what greater folly can be imagined, then under a shew of holiness, to shun holy Matrimony, as a thing profane, which notwithstanding, has bin ordained by God, is dictated by nature, perswaded by reason, confirmed by Christ, praised by Authours, sacred and profane, commended by the Lawes, approved by the consent of all Nations; and whereunto we are invited by the Examples of good, and holy men? What more barbarous and inhumane, then to loath Matrimony, the desire whereof is implanted in us by nature? What more unthankful to the common nature of the World and Mankind, then not to beget Children, as our Ancestors and Parents have begotten us? For my part I make account, that such men are murtherers of as many as they might have begotten, in case they had embraced Matrimony; unless peradventure, they are carried by a Divine Impulse to live single. Questionless, it is a kind of Man-slaughter, not only by Medicaments, to cause abortion and barrenness; but also, without very just cause, to shun Marriage.

Och.

I do not condemn Matrimony, namely, the having of one Wife; but the having of two, or more.

Tel.

But what advice will you give me?

Och.

That you marry no more Wives, but pray to God for the gift of continence.

Tel.

What if he will not give it me?

Och.

He will, if you pray in Faith.

Tel.

What if he neither give me the gift, nor faith to ask it?

O*ch*.

If you shall then do that, to which God shall encline you, so that you be sure you are led by divine Instigation, you shall not sin. For it can be no Errour, to obey God. Other advice I cannot give you. And therefore I bid you farwel, and promise you, that I will seek God in your behalf.

Tel.

And that is it which I beseech you to do, that I may not offend God; but that I may give him all honour and glory, through Jesus Christ our Lord, *Amen.*

Book II

A Puritan Defense Of Polygamy

(Excerpt from De Doctrina Christiana)

John Milton

Appx. 1670

JOHN MILTON

- A Puritan Defense Of Polygamy

John Milton was a typical Puritan who believed in the sufficiency of Scripture and opposed religious institutions like the Church of England and the English monarchy. He married a woman who temporarily left him (presumably over political differences), but the couple reunited and had several children afterward. He married again after she died and a third time after his second wife died. Milton is best known for his 1667 publication, *Paradise Lost*. Some of you reading this have probably heard of it. It is considered by many to be the greatest epic poem ever written in English. It is a ten-volume piece that tells the story of Adam and Eve being tempted and removed from the Garden of Eden. His other major work is a massive systematic theology; *De Doctrina Christiana*. In it, when he comes to the subject of polygamy, Milton explicitly writes in defense of the practice. He uses Biblical examples to demonstrate that polygamy is not only marriage, but a form of marriage that God endorses as much as monogamy. It is a short, but capable, defense. Fans of Puritanism tend to treat this writing like Lutherans treat *On The Jews And Their Lies*; like it never happened. But try all we want, we cannot erase Milton's defense from Puritan history.

John Milton

On Polygamy

A simple English translation from the Latin

From De Doctrina Christiana

Originally in Latin

Published 1825

from original manuscripts

dated between 1620-1674

A Puritan Defense Of Polygamy

It is the peculiar province of God to make marriage prosperous and happy. Prov. xix. 14. *a prudent wife is from Jehovah,* xviii. 22. *whoso findeth a wife, findeth a good thing, and obtaineth favour of Jehovah.*

With regard to marriage, it is clear that it was instituted, if not commanded, at the creation, and that it consisted in the mutual love, society, help, and comfort of the husband and wife, though with a reservation of superior rights to the husband. Gen. ii. 18. it is not good that man should be alone; I will make him an help meet for him. 1 Cor. xi. 7-9. for a man....is the image of the glory of God, but the woman is the glory of the man: for the man is not of the woman, but the woman of the man; neither was the man created for the woman, but the woman for the man. The power of the husband was even increased after the fall. Gen. iii. 16. thy desire shall be to thy husband, and he shall rule over thee. Therefore the word [Strongs 0113 adown] in the Hebrew signifies both husband and lord. Thus Sarah is represented as calling her husband Abraham lord, 1 Pet. iii. 6. 1 Tim. ii. 12-14. I suffer not a woman to teach, nor to usurp authority over the man, but to be in silence: for Adam was first formed, then Eve; and Adam was not deceived, but the woman being deceived, was in the transgression.

Marriage, therefore, is a most intimate connection of man with woman, ordained by God, for the purpose either of the procreation of children, or of the relief and solace of life. Hence it is said, Gen. ii. 24. therefore shall a man leave his father and his mother, and shall cleave unto his wife, and they shall be one flesh. This is neither a law nor a commandment, but an effect or natural consequence of that most intimate union which would have existed between them in the perfect state of man; nor is the passage intended to serve any other purpose, than to account for the origin of families.

In the definition which I have given, I have not said, in compliance with the common opinion, of one man with one woman, lest I should by implication charge the holy patriarchs and pillars of our faith, Abraham, and the others who had more than one wife at the same time, with habitual fornication and adultery; and lest I should be forced to exclude from the sanctuary of God as spurious, the holy offspring which sprang from them, yea, the whole of the sons of Israel, for whom the sanctuary itself was made. For it is said, Deut. xxiii.2. a bastard shall not enter into the congregation of Jehovah, even to his tenth generation. Either therefore polygamy is a true marriage, or all children born in that state are spurious; which would include the whole race of Jacob, the twelve holy tribes chosen by God. But as such an assertion would be absurd in the extreme, not to say impious, and as it is the height of injustice, as well as an example of most dangerous tendency in religion, to account as sin what is not such in reality; it appears to me, that, so far from the question respecting the lawfulness of polygamy being a trivial, it is of the highest importance that it should be decided.

Those who deny its lawfulness, attempt to prove their position from Gen. ii. 24. a man shall cleave unto his wife, and they shall be one flesh, compared with Matt. xix. 5. they twain shall be one flesh. A man shall cleave, they say, to his wife, not to his wives, and they twain, and no more, shall be one flesh. This is particularly ingenious; and I therefore subjoin the passage in Exod. xx. 17. thou shalt not covet they neighbour's house, nor his man-servant, nor his maid-servant, nor his ox, nor his ass: whence it would follow that no one had more than a single house, a single man-servant, a single maid-servant, a single ox or ass. It would be ridiculous to argue, that it is not said houses, but house, not man-servants, but man-servant, not even neighbours, but neighbour; as if it were not the general custom, in laying down commandments of this kind, to use the singular number, not in a numerical sense, but as designating the species of the thing intended. With regard to the phrase, they twain, and not more, shall be one flesh, it is to be observed, first, that the context refers to the husband and that wife only whom he was seeking to divorce, without intending any allusion to the number of his wives, whether one or more. Secondly, marriage is in the nature of a relation; and to one relation there can be no more than two parties. In the same sense therefore as if a man has many sons, his paternal relation towards them all is manifold, but towards each individually is single and complete in itself; by parity of reasoning, if a man has many wives, the relation which he bears to each will not be less perfect in itself, nor will the husband be less one flesh with each of them, than if he had only one wife. Thus it might properly be said of Abraham, with regard to Sarah and Hagar respectively, these twain were one flesh. And with good reason; for whoever consorts with harlots, however many in number, is still said to be one flesh with each; 1 Cor. vi. 16. what, know ye not, that he which is joined to an harlot is one body? for two, saith he, shall be one flesh. The expression may therefore be applied as properly to the husband who has many wives, as to him who has only one. Hence it follows that the commandment in question (though in fact it is no commandment at all, as has been shown) contains nothing against polygamy, either in the way of direct prohibition or implied censure; unless we are to suppose that the law of God, as delivered by Moses, was at variance with his prior declarations; or that, though the passage in question had been frequently inspected by a multitude of priests, and levites, and prophets, men of all ranks, of holiest lives and most acceptable to God, the fury of their passions was such as to hurry them by a blind impulse into habitual fornication; for to this supposition are we reduced, if there be anything in the present precept which renders polygamy incompatible with lawful marriage.

Another text from which the unlawfulness of polygamy is maintained, is Lev. xviii. 18. neither shalt thou take a wife to her sister, to vex her, to uncover her nakedness, beside the other in her life time. Here Junius translates the passage mulierem ad sororem suam, in order that from this forced and inadmissible interpretation he may elicit an argument against polygamy. In drawing up a law, as in composing a definition, it is necessary that the most exact and appropriate words should be used, and that they should be interpreted not in their metaphoirical, but in their proper signification. He says, indeed, that the same words are found in the same sense in other passages. This is true; but it is only where the context precludes the possibility of any ambiguity, as in Gen. xxvi. 31. juraverunt vir fratri suo, that is, alteri, they sware one to another. No one would infer from this passage that Isaac was the brother of Abimelech; nor would any one, on the other hand, entertain a doubt that the passage in Leviticus was intended as a prohibition against taking a wife to her sister; particularly as the preceeding verses of this chapter treat of the degrees of affinity to which intermarriage is forbidden.

Moreover, this would be to uncover her nakedness, the evil against which the law in question was intended to guard; whereas the caution would be unnecessary in the case of taking another wife not related or allied to the former; for no nakedness would be thereby uncovered. Lastly, why is the clause in her life time added? For there could be no doubt of its being lawful after her death to marry another who was neither related nor allied to her, though it might be questionnable whether it were lawful to marry a wife's sister. It is objected, that marriage with a wife's sister is forbidden by analogy in the sixteenth verse, and that therefore a second prohibition was unnecessary. I answer, first, that there is in reality no analogy between the two passages; for that by marrying a brother's wife, the brother's nakedness is uncovered; whereas by marrying a wife's sister, it is not a sister's nakedness, but only that of a kinswoman by marriage, which is uncovered. Besides, if nothing were to be prohibited which had been before prohibited by analogy, why is marriage with a mother forbidden, when marriage with a father had already been declared unlawful? or why marriage with a mother's sister, when marriage with a father's sister had been prohibited? If this reasoning be allowed, it follows that more than half the laws relating to incest are unnecessary. Lastly, wheras the prevention of enmity is alleged as the principal motive for the law before us, it is obvious, that if the intention had been to condemn polygamy, reasons of a much stronger kind might have been urged from the nature of the original institution, as was done in the ordinance of the Sabbath.

A third passage which is advanced, Deut. xvii. 17. is so far from condemning polygamy, either in a king, or in any one else, that it expressly allows it; and only imposes the same restraints upon this condition which are laid upon the multiplication of horses, or the accumulation of treasure; as will appear from the seventeenth and eighteenth verses.

Except the three passages which are thus irrelevantly adduced, not a trace appears of their interdiction of polygamy throughout the whole law; nor even in any of the prophets, who were at once the rigid interpreters of the law, and the habitual reprovers of the vices of the people. The only shadow of an exception occurs in a passage of Malachi, the last of the prophets, which some consider as decisive against polygamy. It would be indeed a late and postliminous enactment, if that were for the first time prohibited after the Babylonish captivity which ought to have been prohibited many ages before. For if it had been really a sin, how could it have escaped the reprehension of so many prophets who preceeded him? we may safely conclude that if polygamy be not forbidden in the law, neither is it forbidden here; for Malachi was not the author of a new law. Let us however see the words themselves as translated by Junius, ii. 15. Nonne unum effecit? quamvis reliqui spiritus ipsi essent: quid qutem unum? It would be rash and unreasonable indeed, if, on the authority of so obscure a passage, and one which has been tortured and twisted by different interpreters into such a variety of meanings, we were to form a conclusion on so important a subject, and to impose it upon others as an article of faith. But whatever be the signification of the words nonne unum effecit, what do they prove? are we, for the sake of drawing an inference against polygamy, to understand the phrase thus - did not he make one woman? But the gender, and even the case, are at variance with this interpretation; for nearly all the other commentators render the words as follows: annon unus fecit? et residuum spiritus ipsi? et quid ille unus? We ought not therefore to draw any conclusion from a passage like the present in behalf of a doctrine which is either not mentioned elsewhere, or only in doubtful terms; but rather conclude that the prophet's design was to reprove a practice which the whole of Scripture concurs in reproving, and which forms the principal subject of the very chapter in question, v. 11-16. namely, marriage with the daughter of a strange god; a corruption very prevalent among the Jews of that time, as we learn from Ezra and Nehemiah.

With regard to the words of Christ, Matt. v. 32. and xix. 5. the passage from Gen. ii. 24. is repeated not for the purpose of condemning polygamy, but of reproving the unrestrained liberty of divorce, which is a very different thing; nor can the words be made to apply to any other subject without evident violence to their meaning. For the argument which is deduced from Matt. v. 32. that if a man who married another after putting away his first wife, committeth adultery, much more must he commit adultery who retains the first and marries another, ought itself to be repudiated as an illegitimate conclusion. For in the first place, it is the divine precepts themselves that are obligatory, not the consequences deduced from them by human reasoning; for what appears a reasonable inference to one individual, may not be equally obvious to another of similar discernment. Secondly, he who puts away his wife and marries another, is not said to commit adultery because he marries another, but because in consequence of his marriage with another he does not retain his former wife, to whom also he owed the performance of conjugal duties; whence it is expressly said, Mark x. 11. he committeth adultery against her. That he is in a condition to perform his conjugal duties to the one, after having taken another to her, is shown by God himself, Exod. xxi. 10. if he take him another wife, her food, her raiment, and her duty of marriage shall he not diminish. It cannot be supposed that the divine forethought intended to provide for adultery.

Nor is it allowable to argue, from 1 Cor. vii. 2. let every man have his own wife, that therefore none should have more than one; for the meaning of the precept is, that every man should have his own wife to himself, not that he should have but one wife. That bishops and elders should have no more than one wife is explicitly enjoined 1 Tim. iii. 2. and Tit. i. 6. he must be the husband of one wife, in order probably that they may discharge with greater diligence the ecclesiastical duties which they have undertaken. The command itself, however, is a sufficient proof that polygamy was not forbidden to the rest, and that it was common in the church at that time.

Lastly, in answer to what is urged from 1 Cor. vii. 4. likewise also the husband hath not power of his own body, but the wife, it is easy to reply, as was done above, that the word wife in this passage is used with reference to the species, and not to the number. Nor can the power of the wife over the body of her husband be different now from what it was under the law, where it is called [Strongs 05772 ownah], Exod. xxi.10. and signifies her stated times, which St. Paul expresses in the present chapter by the phrase, her due benevolence. With regard to what is due, the Hebrew word is sufficiently explicit.

On the other hand, the following passages clearly admit the lawfulness of polygamy. Exod. xxi. 10. if he take him another wife, her food, her raiment, and her duty of marriage shall he not diminish. Deut. xvii. 17. neither shall he multiply wives to himself, that his heart not turn away. Would the law have been so loosely worded, if it had not been allowable to take more wives than one at the same time? Who would venture to subjoin as an inference from this language, therefore let him have one only? In such case, since it is said in the preceding verse, he shall not multiply horses to himself, it would be necessary to subjoin there also, therefore he shall have one horse only. Nor do we want any proof to assure us, that the first institution of marriage was intended to bind the prince equally with the people; if therefore it permits only one wife, it permits no more even to the prince. But the reason given for the law is this, that his heart turn not away; a danger which would arise if he were to marry many, and especially strange women, as Solomon afterwards did. Now if the present law had been intended merely as a confirmation and vindication of the primary institution of marriage, nothing could have been more appropriate that to have restricted the institution itself in this place, and not to have advanced that reason alone which has been mentioned.

Let us hear the words of God himself, the author of the law, and the best interpreter of his own will. 2 Sam. xii. 8. I gave thee thy master's wives into thy bosom....and if that had been too little, I would moreover have given unto thee such and such things. Here there can be no subterfuge; God gave him wives, he gave them to the man whom he loved, as one among a number of great benefits; he would have given him more, if these had not been enough. Besides, the very argument which God uses towards David, is of more force when applied to the gift of wives, than to any other, - thou oughtest at least to have abstained from the wife of another person, not so much because I had given thee thy master's house, or thy master's kingdom, as because I had given thee the wives of the king. Beza indeed objects, that David herein committed incest, namely, with the wives of his father-in-law. But he had forgotten what is indicated by Esther ii. 12, 13. that the kings of Israel had two houses for the women, one appointed for the virgins, the other for the concubines, and that it was the former and not the latter which were given to David. This appears also from 1 Kings i. 4. the king knew her not. Cantic. vi. 8. there are fourscore concubines, and virgins without number. At the same time, it might be said with perfect propriety that God had given him his master's wives, even supposing that he had only given him as many in number and of the same description, though not the very same; even as he gave him, not indeed the identical house and retinue of his master, but one equally magnificent and royal.

It is not wonderful, therefore, that what the authority of the law, and the voice of God himself has sanctioned, should be alluded to by the holy prophets in their inspired hymns as a thing lawful and honourable. Psal. xlv. 9. (which is entitled A song of loves) king's daughters were among thy honourable women. v. 14. the virgins her companions that follow her shall be brought unto thee. Nay, the words of this very song are quoted by the apostle to the Hebrews, i. 8. unto the Son he saith, Thy throne, O God, &c. as the words wherein God the Father himself addresses the Son, and in which his divinity is asserted more clearly than in any other passage. Would it have been proper for God the Father to speak by the mouth of harlots, and to manifest his holy Son to mankind as God in the amatory songs of adultresses? Thus also in Cantic. vi. 8-10. the queens and concubines are evidently mentioned with honour, and are all without distinction considered worthy of celebrating the praises of the bride: there are threescore queens, and fourscore concubines, and virgins without number ....the daughters saw her and blessed her; yea, the queens and the concubines, and they praised her. Nor must we omit 2 Chron. xxiv. 2,3. Joash did that which was right in the sight of the Lord all the days of Jehoida the priest: and Jehoida took for him two wives. For the two clauses are not placed in contrast, or disjoined from each other, but it is said in one and the same connection that under the guidance of Jehoida he did that which was right, and that by the authority of the same individual he married two wives. This is contrary to the usual practice in the eulogies of the kings, where, if to the general character anything blameable be subjoined, it is expressly excepted; 1 Kings xv. 5. save only in the matter of Uriah the Hittite. v. 11, 14. and Asa did that which was right.....but the high places were not removed: nevertheless Asa's heart was perfect. Since therefore the right conduct of Joash is mentioned in unqualified terms, in conjunction with his double marriage, it is evident that the latter was not considered matter of censure; for the sacred historian would not have neglected so suitable an opportunity of making the customary exception, if there had been anything which deserved disapprobation. Moreover, God himself, in an allegorial fiction, Ezek. xxiii. 4. represents himself as having espoused two wives, Aholah and Aholibah; a mode of speaking which he would by no means have employed, especially at such length, even in a parable, nor indeed have taken on himself such a character at all, if the practice which it implied had been intrinsically dishonourable or shameful.

On what grounds, however, can a practice be considered dishonourable or shameful, which is prohibited to no one even under the gospel? for that dispensation annuls none of the merely civil regulations which existed previous to its introduction. It is only enjoined that elders and deacons should be chosen from such as were husbands of one wife, 1 Tim. iii. 2. and Tit. i. 6. This implies, not that to be the husband of more than one wife would be a sin, for in that case the restriction would have been equally imposed on all; but that, in proportion as they were less entangled in domestic affairs, they would be more at leisure for the business of the church. Since therefore polygamy is interdicted in this passage to the ministers of the church alone, and that not on account of any sinfulness in the practice, and since none of the other members are precluded from it either here or elsewhere, it follows that it was permitted, as abovesaid, to all the remaining members of the church, and that it was adopted by many without offence.

Lastly, I argue as follows from Heb. xiii. 4. Polygamy is either marriage, or fornication, or adultery; the apostle recognises no fourth state. Reverence for so many patriarchs who were polygamists will, I trust, deter any one from considering it as fornication or adultery; for whoremongers and adulterers God will judge; wheras the patriarchs were the objects of his especial favour, as he himself witnesses. If then polygamy be marriage properly so called, it is also lawful and honourable, according to the same apostle: marriage is honourable in all, and the bed undefiled.

It appears to me sufficiently established by the above arguments that polygamy is allowed by the law of God; lest however any doubt should remain, I will subjoin abundant examples of men whose holiness renders them fit patterns for imitation, and who are among the lights of our faith. Foremost I place Abraham, the father of all the faithful, and of the holy seed, Gen. xvi. 1, &c. Jacob, chap. xxx. and if I mistake not, Moses, Numb. xii. 1. for he had married (a Cushite, Marginal Translation, or) an Ethiopian woman. It is not likely that the wife of Moses, who had been so often spoken of before by her proper name of Zipporah, should now be called by the new title of a Cushite; or that the anger of Aaron and Miriam should at this time be suddenly kindled, because Moses forty years before had married Zipporah; nor would they have acted thus scornfully towards one whom the whole house of Israel had gone out to meet on her arrival with the father Jethro. If then he married the Cushite during the lifetime of Zipporah, his conduct in this particular received the express approbation of God himself, who moreover punished with severity the unnatural opposition of Aaron and his sister. Next I place Gideon, that signal example of faith and piety, Judg. viii. 30, 31. and Elkanah, a rigid Levite, the father of Samuel; who was so far from believing himself less acceptable to God on account of his double marriage, that he took with him his two wives every year to the sacrifices and annual worship, into the immediate presence of God; nor was he therefore reproved, but went home blessed with Samuel, a child of excellent promise, 1 Sam. ii. 10. Passing over several other examples, though illustrious, such as Caleb, 1 Chron. ii. 46, 48. vii, 1, 4. the sons of Issachar, in number six and thirty thousand men, for they had many wives and sons, contrary to the modern European practice, where in many places the land is suffered to remain uncultivated for want of population; and also Manasseh, the son of Joseph, 1 Chron. vii. 14. I come to the prophet David, whom God loved beyond all men, and who took two wives, besides Michal; and this not in a time of pride and prosperity, but when he was almost bowed down by adversity, and when, as we learn from many of the psalms, he was entirely occupied in the study of the word of God, and in the right regulation of his conduct. 1 Sam. xxv. 42, 43. and afterwards, 2 Sam. v. 12,13. David perceived that Jehovah had established him king over Israel, and that he had exalted his kingdom for his people Israel's sake, and David took him more concubines and wives out of Jerusalem. Such were the motives, such the honourable and holy thoughts whereby he was influenced, namely, by the consideration of God's kindness towards him for his people's sake. His heavenly and prophetic understanding saw not in that primitive institution what we in our blindness fancy we discern so clearly; nor did he hesitate to proclaim in the supreme council of the nation the pure and honourable motives to which, as he trusted, his children born in polygamy owed their existence. 1 Chron. xxviii. 5 of all my sons, for Jehovah has given me many sons, he hath chosen, &c. I say nothing of Solomon, notwithstanding his wisdom, because he seems to have exceeded due bounds; although it is not objected to him that he had taken many wives, but that he had married strange women; 1 Kings xi. 1. Nehem. xiii. 26. his son Rehoboam desired many wives, not in the time of his iniquity, but during the three years in which he is said to have walked in the way of David, 2 Chron. xi. 17, 21, 23. Of Joash mention has already been made; who was induced to take two wives, not by licentious passion, or the wanton desires incident to uncontrolled power, but by the sanction and advice of a most wise and holy man, Jehoida the priest. Who can believe, either that so many men of the highest character should have sinned through ignorance for so many ages; or that their hearts should have been so hardened; or that God should have tolerated such conduct in his people? Let therefore the rule received among theologians have the same weight here as in other cases: "The practice of the saints is the best interpretation of the commandments."

Book III

Thelypthora, or A Treatise On Female Ruin...

Martin Madan

1780

(Chapter V Omitted for lack of relevancy)

MARTIN MADAN

- The Evangelist Who Cared For Women

A convert of John Wesley's, Martin Madan was a well-known Methodist evangelist of the mid-late 1700s. He is best known for his chaplaincy at the Lock Hospital for women in London, his implementation of hymn-singing into the Christian worship service (Thank you, brother!), and his powerful defense of George Whitefield and the Methodists against a vicious attack by Samuel Foote in 1760; but his initial claim to fame was his co-authorship of the Christmas song, "Hark! The Herald Angels Sing." Madan was a capable defender of the faith and gifted evangelist who led many people to Christ through his preaching in England. The Lock Hospital, where he served for over thirty years, was the first of its kind and continues to operate through similar facilities to this day. The hospital focused on caring for former prostitutes and other women who needed medical aid. Madan demonstrated a consistent concern for the welfare of women in general, as proven by his long years of service at the specialty hospital.

Over the course of his time there, he began to speculate how these women could be re-integrated into Christian families. For almost thirty years, he tried, and failed, to find a sufficient mode of providing these women with good husbands and homes. After much labor, he came to the conclusion that polygamy was the answer. Upon observing the uneven amount of women and men in England, logic left him with no alternative to allowing men to care for multiple wives. After studying the Scripture and gleaning from history, he also concluded that polygamy would be beneficial for Western society as a whole, as it would keep more women off the streets and deter men from fornication. While his reasoning was far more expansive than what I'm capturing here, these were some of the general principles that initially inspired his thinking.

In 1780, Martin Madan published *Thelyphthora; or, A Treatise On Female Ruin, In Its Causes, Effects, Consequences, Prevention, And Remedy; Considered On The Basis Of Divine Law.* (Book titles were really long back then.) It ended up being a three-volume release. Volumes II and III dealt more with divorce and legality, but Volume I dealt exclusively with polygamy. *Marriage, Sex, & Polygamy* aside, *Thelyphthora* is the largest Biblical work on polygamy in history. A couple of other substantial works were published, but they were far more social and political than Biblical, and neither of them received English translations. Madan's *Thelyphthora* was remarkably thorough when considering the unique nature of the topic. Only one future work would appear that could honestly be compared to it (which is the final work in this volume).

Thelyphthora was a shield and a rescue plan. Madan's primary goal was to continue caring for women in need, just as he had been doing for almost thirty years. The treatise was simply his method of transferring women out of his care and into the care of godly families. Its subtitle begins with, "A Treatise On Female Ruin," for, in modern phrasing, he wanted to stop females' lives from being ruined. Any notion that the book sought to oppress women or "put them in their place" is misplaced, at best. Rather, the book was actually a poignant condemnation of the Western systems of monogamy that have left women single, lonely, and destitute, just as its Greco-Roman predecessors had done; yet it didn't stop there. Madan surgically exposed many relevant Scriptures to make His case a Biblical one. If appraised honestly, he left little doubt that the common arguments for monogamy-onlyism were rooted in tradition, not Scripture. It truly was the first work of its kind and it didn't go unnoticed.

As expected, his work on polygamy caused quite the stir. No longer was the idea confined to a fanatical group of Anabaptists or one random Puritan in a sea of other Puritans. Martin Madan was an Evangelical Methodist and preached the gospel on the heels of one of the greatest Christian revivals the world has ever seen. Due to his prominence as a minister and hymn-writer, his shocking treatise wouldn't circulate quietly. Debates surrounding his proposals became the talk of the country, eventually crossing the sea to America. From casual conversations over tea to adaptations in entertainment, *Thelypthora's* polygamy-centric message made waves across England in more ways than one. Historian Sarah Pearsall reports;

This publication provoked a wave of reviews and countertreatises, newspaper notices, poems, plays, and prints. By the end of the year, the topic formed a staple of London debating societies. As one critic observed: "Witness the infinite letters, epigrams, and lampoons, in almost every news-paper, on this subject; witness the public disputations in places of amusement. ... Witness also the ridiculous and contemptible figure exhibited ... in ... many of our print-shops." Even beyond the metropolis, Madan's doctrines were purported to be the subject of intense discussion. According to a Cheshire preacher, *Thelyphthora* was, despite its weightiness, "much read, and more talked of," indeed "the general topic of conversation, in almost every company where I go."[1]

She also noted that the work was more talked about than read, as debating such a controversial topic was more appealing to most people than reading a large, theological work. Many of Madan's critics obviously never read his book either, as all of their criticisms attacked systems of thought that Madan himself refuted, and all of their doctrinal objections were ones that Madan had clearly addressed in the book. Madan also didn't see himself as opposing the steady stream of Christian progress. Rather, he saw himself as continuing the Protestant Reformation, helping the true Church to fully escape the clutches of Rome. He once said, "As Rome was not built in a day, so neither could it be demolished in a day. The Protestant Reformers did much towards its demolition, but they could not do all."

---

1   Sarah M. S. Pearsall – Polygamy: An early American History, Yale University Press: New Haven and London (2019) p. 190-191

LOCK HOSPITAL, HYDE PARK CORNER.

THELYPHTHORA,

OR,

A TREATISE ON FEMALE RUIN,

IN ITS

CAUSES, EFFECTS, CONSEQUENCES,

PREVENTION, AND REMEDY;

considered on the basis of the

DIVINE LAW:

Under the following HEADS, viz.

Marriage,	Adultery,
Whoredom,	Polygamy,
Fornication,	Divorce;

With many other INCIDENTAL MATTERS;

Particularly Including

An Examination of the Principles and Tendency of

Stat. 26 Geo. II c, 33.

Commonly Called

The MARRIAGE ACT.

In Two Volumes.   Vol. I.

The Second Edition, Enlarged.

What in me is dark

Illumine, what is low raise and support;

That, to the height of this great argument,

I may assert Eternal Providence,

And justify the way of God to men.

Milton.

LONDON:

Printed for J. DODSLEY, in Pall-Mall.

M.DCC.LXXXI

Preparing for the Press - and speedily will be published,

THELYPHTHORA,

VOL III.

I. Shewing by what *means*, and by what *degrees*, the *laws* of Jehovah concerning *marriage*, were *opposed* and *abrogated*, and a new system invented and established by Christian Churchmen. Extracted from the most authentic *records*, from the earliest times of the Christian Church after the Apostles, to the *decrees* of the Council of Trent, anno 1563, *inclusive*.

II. Observations on the foregoing uninterrupted series of incontestable evidence, and the whole applied to the subjects of this treatise.

III. The true origin and necessity of marriage-ceremony.

With *many* other incidental matters.

TO THE
PRESIDENTS,
VICE-PRESIDENTS,
AND OTHER
GOVERNORS

Of those well-intended Charities, and beneficent Institutions

The *Asylum—Misericordia—Magdalene* and *Lock—Hospital.*

THE Author of the following Treatise cannot fix on a more proper patronage for a work of this kind, than that of those noble and honourable persons, whose compassion on the miseries of the female sex, has led them to institute public charities for its preservation and relief.

As our laws are at present framed, women are exposed to *seduction, prostitution,* and *ruin,* almost without controul;—they seem to be looked upon as lawful prey to the lust, treachery, cruelty, and mean artifices of licentious and profligate men, who can seduce and then abandon them at their will.

That a want of good government among us in these respects, is one source of all those evils, which your disinterested and humane endeavours are intended to prevent or remedy, is surely apparent on the slightest consideration.

A system of laws which leaves the horrid crime of *adultery* not only out of the lift of its *capital punishments,* but even exempts it, as a *public* offence, from any animadversion whatsoever in our courts of criminal judicature, must be attended with all those mischiefs that arise from the encouragement which impunity affords to vice.

The fame may also be observed, with respect to the defenseless state, in which the *weaker sex* in general is left against the *stronger*; so that any man may seduce, and abandon at his pleasure, the unhappy and deluded objects of his brutal appetite.

To exhibit a system far different from this—to set forth the *divine law* as the contrivance of *infinite wisdom*, for the security, peace, preservation, and protection of the *female sex*, is the purpose of the following pages. Were this to be made the basis of our *municipal laws*, it would prove an adequate remedy for all those mischiefs, which, in comparatively few instances, can now only find a partial palliation, from benevolence like yours, but which must, in general, be still the portion of those, whom GOD's law was formed to protect.

Many of you, my LORDS and GENTLEMEN, are members of the LEGISLATURE; and if, from what shall be said on the matters treated in this book, they should become the subjects of your serious consideration in your *legislative* capacity, the author will gain one desirable end of his labours.

This surely must be allowed—that, in point of fact, the alarming increase of *female prostitution* and *ruin*, calls loudly for some remedy: the *self-evidence* of this, is the very foundation of those benevolent designs, which distinguish the several public charities to which you so generously contribute.

Let Government adopt the system of heavenly wisdom, which adorns the pages of the SACRED VOLUME, and it will find remedy in its own hands— what that system is, it has been the author's most serious endeavour to enquire, and to recommend it to all, but more especially to the consideration of those, whose care, expence, and vigilance, for the good of their fellow-creatures, has occasioned them the trouble of this address from

Their most humble servant,

And ardent well-wisher to their good designs,

THE AUTHOR.

PREFACE

TO THE

FIRST EDITION.

THE subjects of the following treatise, being of the utmost importance have been considered with the most serious attention, and are laid before the reader on the highest authority, that is to say, on the authority of the *holy scriptures*.

Nothing less than this ought, or can, determine on the points herein treated, because they concern, not only the *present*, but *future* welfare of mankind: these, as taken in connection together, must depend, first, on *knowing*, and then on *doing* the will of God. What His *will* is, can only be known from the several revelations, or discoveries, which it hath graciously pleased Him to make of it, *by men, who spake not of themselves, but as they were moved by the Holy Ghost.* 2 Pet. i. 21.

To imagine that, without such revelation, mortals can understand, or know the mind and will of GOD, is an absurdity, even greater than to suppose we can know the thoughts of each other, without any declaration of them either by words or actions. But to admit the necessity of a divine revelation, *to* receive the scriptures as *that* revelation, and not to make them the only infallible *rule* and guide, in all matters which relate to the mind and will of GOD therein revealed, is, so far, to lay aside the revelation of God, to make it *void and of none effect*, and to place ourselves in no better situation, than if no such discovery of the mind and will of God had ever been vouchsafed us.

Thus we rob God of His honour, by slighting His *word*, and thus are people led to set up the determinations of human wisdom against it, and expose themselves to *be carried about with every wind of doctrine*, which the folly and superstition of *weak* men, and the wickedness and craft of *designing* men, may happen to invent.

By such means it has been, that so many errors of various kinds have found their way, in all ages, into the *church*, and have maintained their empire over the minds of men. Long *usage* has made them venerable—the prescriptive power of *custom* has given them establishment—and *both* there have prevailed on *human legislatures*, to afford them the awful obligation of their most solemn sanctions[2].

It cannot want many arguments to prove, that sundry *practices*, as well as *opinions*, which are found among the heathen nations, are abhorrent from all our conceptions of propriety, decency, and even humanity itself. All these have but one source - *They do err, not knowing the scriptures.*

Where *revelation* is received, yet if it be not adhered to as the *only* rule of *faith* and *manners*, and this unreservedly, the opinions and practices of men will be as wide from the mind and will of God, as those of the *Heathen* are. I might here instance in the opinions and practices of the *Pharisees* of old, as well as of many nations called *Christian*, in more modern days, and who are members of that *society* of professing *Christians* which insolently and exclusively styles itself "THE HOLY APOSTOLICAL CATHOLIC CHURCH" amongst whom the most devout are worshipping a *wooden* god, which they call a *crucifix*[3], and a

---

2   I cannot forbear mentioning here that valuable, learned, and excellent work of *John Leland, D. D.* on the *Advantage and Necessity of the Christian Revelation* - wherein that author hath, with a strength of judgment, and depth of learning and erudition peculiar to himself, so proved his point, as to deserve the thanks of all who know how to set a just value on the scriptures, as well as of those who would wish to do it. This valuable author says, "It is the mighty advantage of a *written revelation*, that by an impartial consulting it, the deviations from it may be detected, and things may again be reduced "to the original standard." Vol. i. p. 453.

3   This invention of the crucifix, or image of Christ on the cross, is but old heathenism new vamped. *Maximus Tyrius*, a Platonic philosopher, who was master to *M. Antoninus*, says - "The divine nature stands not in need of images or statues; but the nature and condition of man being very weak, and as far distant from the Divinity as heaven is from earth, framed these signs for itself, and attributed to them the names and titles of the gods" - and he thinks that the legislators acted wisely in contriving images for the people. See *Leland*, vol. i. p. 338. The wise men and *philosophers* pleaded for images as necessary helps to human infirmity. Ib. 424.

breaden god, which they call the *host*; and, besides these, they worship *saints* and *angels*, and many *such like things they do*. The foundation of all which is still one and the same - *They do err, not knowing the scriptures*; for though the *Papists* have the scriptures, yet they do not adopt them as the only rule of faith and *worship*. *Their fear towards* God *is taught them by the doctrines and commandments of men*[4], If. xxix. 13. which take place of the mind and will of God, as revealed in His holy word.

Happy would it be, could *we*, reformed *Protestants*, clear ourselves of this charge in all respects!

To prove that we cannot, in some points of the utmost consequence, is the purpose of the following pages; which, while the *reader* peruses, I could wish him to weigh in the *balance of the sanctuary*, to lay his *Bible* before him, and to call every argument, observation, and doctrine, to the strictest and most severe account, before that unerring tribunal. If he shall find any thing that is *wrong*, or detect any thing that is *false*, let him freely set it down to the *Author's* account. But whatever he shall find agreeable to, or clearly proved *by*, the *word* of GOD, let him not listen to the lying testimony of *prejudice* or *vulgar error* against it, but treasure it up in his mind, for the direction of his own *judgment and conscience*, in all situations and conditions of life.

---

4   Two of the articles in the famous creed of Pope Pius IV. are as follows:

XIII. I most firmly admit and embrace *apostolical* and *ecclesiastical* traditions, and all other observations and constitutions of the *one catholic and apostolic church*.

XIV. I do admit the holy scriptures in the same sense on that *holy Mother Church doth*, whose business it is to judge of the true sense and interpretation of them, and I will interpret them according to the unanimous *consent of the fathers*.

The *Popish canon law* frequently affirms—that *the church is above the scriptures*.

Omnis quæ nunc apud nos eft scripturæ authoritas ab ecclesiæ authoritate necessario dependet.— "All the authority which we attribute to the scriptures, necessarily depends on the authority of the church." *Pighius de Hierar. Eccl.* Lib. i. c. 2. *Eccius,* in his *Enchiridion de Authoritate Ecclefiæ,* maintains - *Ecclesiam esse scripturis antiquiorem, & scripturam non esse authenticam, nisi ecclesiæ authoritate.*—"The church is more antient than the scriptures, and the scriptures are not authentic, save by the authority of the church."

Hermannus goes farther, and affirms—*Scripturas tantum valere quantum valent Æsopi fabluæ, nisi accederet ecclesiæa testimonium.*—"The scriptures are no more to be valued than *Asop's Fables,* unless it were for the testimony of the church." See *Hist. of Popery,* vol. i. p. 214.

If the *judgment* be mis-led or mis-informed, the more conscientious a man is, the farther will he be led into error, and the more firmly will he be attached to it; therefore it is well for us to listen to the counsel of the *wise man*—Prov. iv. 7. "WISDOM is the principal thing, therefore get WISDOM; and with all thy getting get UNDERSTANDING."

As to differences, or even *errors*, (if *mistakes* about indifferent matters can be so called) where mere outward *forms* are concerned, and those of human invention, the *Author* desires *to think*, and *to let think*, and wheresoever the scriptures are *silent*, to be so too. He does not esteem it worth his while to expend a single drop of ink in such controversies. He does not suppose, that, had he lived in the second *century*, when the *Roman* and *Asiatic* Christians quarrelled about the keeping of *Easter*, and ran to such indecent lengths of animosity and discord, as make the very *heathen* blush, he would have ventured a single scratch of his finger, to have had it decided whether it was to be held "on the fourteenth day after the first moon in the new year," or "on the same stated day in every year," or "on the first *Sunday* after the first full moon." All this rout was made to very little purpose: and had the *Author* been weak enough into the dispute, had he sided with the *Asiatics*, and been excommunicated by Pope *Victor* for his pains, it would not, according to his present notions, have given him a moment's uneasiness.

But where the peace and well-being (I had almost said the very *being*) of society are concerned, where disorders, of the most malignant kind, have infected the general mass, to the destruction of millions down to this moment, and threaten the destruction of millions yet unborn, and those chiefly from among the most defenseless part of the human species; when the lust, treachery, cruelty, and villainy of men, are let loose to ravage, as they can, on the weakness and credulity of helpless women; and when all this is apparently the effect of abolishing those parts of the *divine* law, which were evidently made to prevent it, and the introduction of a *system of human* invention is the means of its daily increase; too much cannot be said to point out the cause of the *disease*, and to lead to the *remedy*. The *former* is from the substitution of the *wisdom* of man, in the place of the *wisdom* of God; the *latter* can only be discovered and rendered effectual, by restoring the *wisdom* of God to its due place in our esteem, and by making it, as it is found revealed to us in the scriptures, the *basis* of our *municipal laws*—the *line* of our conduct—the *rule* of our *obedience*.

Perhaps some may think, that there are *points* handled and discussed in this *book*, which had better been left under the clouds of obscurity which have long overwhelmed them, and hidden them from vulgar observation, lest disputes should be raised, and abuses committed by the perversions of the evil and licentious. It is written concerning the scriptures themselves, that, to some they are the *savour of life unto life*[5], and unto others the *savour of death unto death.* 2 Cor. ii. 16. And again—that the *unlearned and unstable wrested the epistles of Paul, as also the other scriptures, to their own destruction.* 2 Pet. iii. 16. As therefore there is nothing in this *book*, which is not to be found in those scriptures, as to the *points* above hinted at, the Author ventures it forth, confiding in Him who hath said—*As the rain cometh down, and the snow from heaven, and returneth not thither, but watereth the earth, and maketh it bring forth and bud, that it may give feed to the sower, and bread to the eater; so shall My word be, that goeth forth out of My mouth: it shall not return unto Me void, but it shall accomplish that which I please, and it shall prosper in the thing whereunto I sent it.* Is. Iv. 10, 11.

He cannot be of the mind of *Synesius* the *Platonist*, who was raised to be a *Bishop* in the *Christian* church but continued to be a determined *Platonist*; and had so far imbibed the spirit and doctrine of that school as to declare his sentiments thus: "As darkness is most proper and commodious for those who have weak eyes, so I hold that[6] lyes and *fictions* are useful to the people, and that *truth* would be hurtful to those who are not able to bear its light and splendor." And he adds—"If the laws of the church would dispense with it, that he would *philosophize* at home, and talk abroad in the common strain, preaching up received *fables*." See note z, Leland, vol. ii. p. 344.

---

5   Haurit lethiferum bufo de flore venenum, Quo mel nectareum fedula promit apes.
At the same flow'r the *toad* and *bee* may meet, *That* suck the *poison*—*this* exhaust the *sweet*.

6   *Maximus Tyrius* faith - "a lye is often profitable and advantageous to men, and truth hurtful." So *Plato*, and others of the *philosophers* - the *Stoics* especially, who held that "a wise man might make use of a lye for many conveniences and managements in life." See *Leland*, vol. ii. p. 220. Many of the early *Fathers* and *Christians* adopted the same principle, which has been called by the softer term of *pious fraud*, and would *lye* by wholesale—but this *only for the good of the church*—however, this has never been got rid of, as *Popery* can fully attest. See *Mosheim*, vol. i. p. 209.

The antient philosophers had an *exoteric* doctrine—εξωτερικού—which they openly taught to the people; and an *esoteric* doctrine—ἐσωτερικού—which they taught privately to their select disciples, whom they let into the secrets of their scheme. It was a maxim among them that "it was lawful to deceive the people for the public good." Ib. 342—3. So the sect of *Foe* in China, have an *exterior* and *interior* doctrine with regard to a *future state*—they publicly preach it to the people, but their *interior* doctrine rejects it. See Ib. 344, note z.

Such is human prudence and wisdom!—But the *divine wisdom* saith— *He that hath My word, let him speak My word faithfully*. Jer. xxiii. 28. *There is nothing covered that shall not be revealed; and hid, that shall not be known. What I tell you in darkness, that speak ye in the light; and what ye hear in the ear, that preach (κηρύξατε, proclaim, publish) upon the housetops*. Matt. x. 26, 27. Comp. Mark iv. 21, 22. *Truth* is like him *that doeth the truth—it cometh to the light, that its deeds may be manifest, that they are wrought in God. Error, like every one that doth evil, hateth the light, neither cometh to the light, lest its deeds should be reproved*. John iii. 20, 21.

God never revealed anything but that it should be known. When men want to conceal any part of divine revelation from the knowledge of others, it is too frequently with a purpose of preventing the detection of some errors in *human systems*, which, from some sinister view or other, they dread the discovery of. Thus the Church of *Rome*, jealous of the light of Scripture, knowing that the whole dominion of *popes* and *priests* over the understandings and consciences of the laity is founded in ignorance, keep, as far as they can, the scriptures out of their hands.

Others there are, who, from well-meant, but mistaken zeal, for principles which they have been taught to *venerate*, dread that these should be attacked; as thinking the cause of *religion itself* is involved with the *supposed truth* of what they are accustomed to believe. There can be no doubt that when our *reformers* first attacked the Pope's *supremacy*, the worship of the *Virgin Mary*, the *celibacy of priests*, and other pious lies and forgeries of the *church* of *Rome*, many *devout* and *zealous* people thought that *religion itself* was, like the *ark* of old, 1 Sam. iv. 10, 11. about to be delivered into the hands of the *Philistines*; and cried out, like *Micah*, when the *Danites* took away his *Levite* and his *Teraphim—Ye have taken away my gods which I made, and the priest—and what have I more?* See *Judges* xviii. 24[7].

If there be anything in the *Bible* which ought to be *concealed*, it would be no very hard matter to prove that it ought never to have been *revealed*. But as it often happens with private individuals, they are afraid of looking too narrowly into the Scripture, for fear of meeting with something to shake their preconceived opinions and prejudices; so is it with all public and *national systems*. As these have been fashioned by *human* contrivance, they are not, for very obvious reasons, over-fond of too narrow a scrutiny on the single footing of *divine revelation*; lest, as they are formed like the *feet of the image* in *Nebuchadnezzar's* dream, which were *part of iron, and part of clay*; so these being composed of the *heterogeneous* mixture of *divine wisdom* and *human contrivance*, a too curious investigator should, like the stone *there* mentioned—*fall upon them, and break them to pieces*.

The Author of the following sheets professes himself a *Free-thinker*; not in the usual sense of that word, as what he has written must abundantly testify, but as an assertor of that right, which every reasonable creature is invested with, to *search*, think, and *judge* for himself. He, therefore, has endeavored to lay some points, which he cannot but esteem of the utmost consequence, before the world, that others may exercise their privilege as the Author hath done *his*.

As for the *abuse* which any subject herein treated may be liable to—What is not *abused*? What in nature, providence, or revelation, has not been *abused* and perverted to some vile purpose or other? The very Gospel of Peace hath been *abused* to sanctify fraud, violence, oppression, and persecution—to justify massacres, tortures, murders, even to men's *roasting alive* their fellow-creatures, and *thinking they did God service!* Insomuch that, were we to judge of the great Head of our *holy religion*, by the *abuse* which has been made of His authority, we should invert what He says in *Luke* ix. 56, and imagine, that He came *not to* save men's lives, *but to* destroy *them*. Even the *grace of our* God has been, and *is* by many, *turned into lasciviousness*. (See Jude iv.) But what does all this prove? Nothing but the ignorance, perverseness, cruelty, and wickedness of human nature; and that *corruptio optimi sit pessima*: but it does not prove that the God of heaven, who

---

7   In 1547, Gardiner, Bishop of Winchester, said, "that he thought the removing of images, was on design to subvert *religion* and the *state* of the *world*."—*Burnet*, Preface to Hist. Ref. vol. ii. p. 11.

foresaw and foreknew such *abuses*, should not have revealed His *mind* and *will* to mortals; nor that *any* part of that revelation should be concealed, suppressed, or hidden from the eyes of men, for fear of its being *abuse*d. For this may be taken as a certain rule, that no *abuse* of the scriptures ever yet happened from a real understanding and knowledge of their contents, but from ignorance, either in ourselves, or imposed on us by the design and artifice of others.

The grand question to be tried is, "whether a system, filled with *obligation* and *responsibility*, of men to women, and of women to men, even unto *death* itself, and this established by infinite wisdom, is not better calculated to prevent the ruin of the female *sex*, with all its horrid consequences, both to the public and individuals, than a system of *human contrivance*, where neither *obligation* nor *responsibility are* to be found, either of men to women, or of women to men, in instances of the most important concern to *both*, but more especially to the *weaker sex?*"

The whole of the evidence on both sides is faithfully collected, and laid open, without any reserve or disguise, in this book—let every reader look upon himself as impanelled on the *jury*— let him impartially hearken to the *cause*—and give a true *verdict* according to the *evidence*.

PREFACE

TO THE

SECOND EDITION.

Notwithstanding the disadvantages under which this work has laboured, a *second edition* has long been called for, and now makes its appearance, in as expeditious a manner as the necessary delay of printing would permit.

The *author* would therefore fain hope that the book has made its way by dint of that intrinsic *truth* which it contains—the *importance* of the subjects treated—the important *ends* proposed—and that conformity to the *oracles* of God, which it professedly makes the *basis* of its contents.

A work which militates against the received *notions*, long *customs*, and inveterate *prejudices* of mankind, can expect but little quarter from the world in general, and, of course, but little of that sort of *candor*, which is shown to performances of *authors* who write on the *popular* side of a question.—This was fully experienced at the *Reformation*—when *Luther*, and others, published against the ridiculous fopperies and gross villainies of Popery, they had *volumes* written against them, in which they were represented in every odious light imaginable.—They were "*heretics—anti-Christs—factors for the devil*" - and, in short, all that was *bad*;—But the abuse of their adversaries had one good effect—it proved how much at a loss these were for fair argument grounded on scripture-evidence, and how little able they were to meet their *opponents* with the *weapons* of a *spiritual warfare*. (see 2 Cor. x. 4). Seldom does *abuse* serve any better purpose in *controversy* than to create a very strong presumption that those who *give* it have nothing better on their side and, therefore, are in the *wrong*, and that those who receive it are, therefore, in the *right*.

With regard to the article of *abuse* of an *author*, if it be of the *personal* kind, let him set it down as so much gained; if it lights upon his *book*, let the book answer for *itself*, and if it cannot do *this*, let him set down the abuse which it meets with, as what it *deserves*.

Another expedient, which some critics have used to depreciate a work, is, to separate some given *subject* from the *rest*, destroy its connection with the main argument, and then, by selecting, in like manner, detached sentences or paragraphs, make these appear to their readers in a light not only different from the author's intention, but diametrically opposite to his whole meaning.

Owing to this, it has been said that the subject of *polygamy* has been selected, and the *indiscriminate practice* of it said to be recommended by the author of *Thelyphthora*. To guard against this, in the plain and express manner which he has done (vol. ii. p. 174-177, 288, and n. and 335, n.), he is sorry to find was to little purpose: these passages were overlooked, whether intentionally or not, is to be left to those who best know. However, let the whole that the author has written on the subject be taken fairly and candidly together, and it will appear that nothing more is said than is warranted by *scripture, nature, and reason*, and to prove that the *indiscriminate* prohibition of it in all cases, however circumstanced—which is nowhere warranted by the law of God—is one source of *public prostitution*—which, *Montesquieu* truly says, "may be looked upon as the greatest of misfortunes in a popular state."

I know no book, the *Bible* itself not excepted, which may not be abused by partial quotation;—and by that which is one consequence of it, *misrepresentation.*—We may prove *atheism* on *David*, as having said, Ps. xiv. 1. *There is no God*;—a recommendation of *drunkenness* from Ps. civ. 15, where he says, *Wine maketh glad the heart of man*;—or we may suppose that the prophet *Isaiah*, and the apostle Paul meant to encourage the licentiousness of a Sçavoir vivre club—by saying—*Let us eat and drink, for tomorrow we die.* If. xxii. 13. 1 Cor. xv. 32.

Something like the *disingenuousness* which would attend such proofs as these, has attended the misrepresentation of the author's treating *polygamy.*— He has maintained its forming a part of the *divine plan*, which was so evidently calculated for the preservation of the *female* sex from desertion and *prostitution*— but by a part only of what is said on the subject being taken, and placed in another point of view, he is accused of recommending *polygamy* as an *indiscriminate practice*, to the subversion of the peace and domestic happiness of every family in the *kingdom*—an idea as foreign from his purpose, as it was from the *Apostle's* (1 Tim. v. 23.) to make *Timothy* a *wine-bibber* (οινοποτης) - See Prov. xxiii. 20. Matt. xi. 19.—when he exhorted him to—*drink no longer water, but to use a little wine for his stomach's sake*, and his often *infirmities*. Thus *polygamy* is mentioned in no other light, throughout this treatise, but as[8] *expedient* in some cases,[9] *necessary* in others, to prevent mischiefs of an infinitely more deplorable kind, both to individuals in particular, and to the public in general, than can possibly arise from every man's being obliged to keep, maintain, and provide for, as the scripture has commanded, the women he *seduces*—but in order to this, its *lawfulness* must be proved, for if it be disallowed of God—there is an end of all questions upon the subject, and we must sit down contented under the present ruinous state of things, which is every day increasing the licentiousness of our men, the destruction of our *women*, and the[10] *depopulation* of the land. As for partial and unfair representation, it has been a usual way of injuring arguments which do not easily admit of plain and fair answers.

Thus the *Papists* served *Erasmus*, upon his publishing his "*Translation* and *Paraphrase* on the New Testament." A great clamor was raised against him by the *faculty* of *divinity* at *Paris*, as before at *Basel*; and "*Natalis Bedda*, a doctor of

---

8   see vol. ii. p. 178.

9   See Exod. xxii. 16. Deut. xxii. 28, 29.

10   We were lately told, in one of the public prints, how truly I cannot say, that—"a noble Lord stated in the House of Commons, with his usual accuracy, that the decrease of people in this country, within these last 90 years, has been ONE MILLION EIGHT HUNDRED THOUSAND." Surely this must be an exaggeration—but yet it might be worthwhile to examine the *increase* or *decrease* of the people.

divinity, who was at that time *Syndic* of the *faculty*, collected several propositions which, as to the full import and general sense of them, were lame and imperfect, being separated from what went before and from what followed after, and thereby might be taken in an ill sense; whereas, if they were read with what went before, and what followed after, it would be found they were sound and orthodox." And thus, at length, a decree was passed against him, and "those *doctors* who were on the side of *Erasmus*, were obliged to hold their peace, left by "speaking their thoughts freely, they should become odious, and their lives be made uneasy." See Du Pin, Cent. 16. p. 267—8. *Eng. Transl.*

What *Erasmus* wrote on the treatment which he met with from many quarters, on account of his publication, deserves our notice, as containing a proper admonition to those who *condemn*, because they read with *prejudice*; and to those who are *profligate* enough to *condemn*, without reading *at all*.

"Sic oportet ad librum legendum accedere lectorem, ut solet ad convivium conviva civilis. Convivator annititur omnibus satisfacere: & tamen siquid apponitur, quod hujus aut illius palato non respondeat, urbanè vel dissimulant, vel probant etiam, ne quid contristent convivatorem. Quis enim eum convivam serat, qui tantùm hoc animo veniat ad mensam, ut carpens quæ apponuntur, ne vescatur ipse, nec alios vesci finat?"

"Et tamen his quoque reperias inciviliores, qui palam, qui fine fine damnent ac lacerent opus, *quod nunquam legerint*. Atque hoc sane faciunt quidam, qui se *Christianæ pietatis doctores* profitentur, & *religionis antistites*; cum fit plus quam *sycophanticum*, damnare quod nefcias."

As I have too much reason to think that some of the *unlearned*, as well as the learned, stand much in need of being acquainted with the above, I will give it in English.

"A reader should come to the perusal of a book, as a courteous guest comes to a feast. The giver of the feast does his endeavor to satisfy all; yet, if anything is brought to the table which may not be agreeable to the palate of this or that person, they politely dissemble their dislike of who has invited them. For who could *approve*, rather than *grieve* him, to bear with that guest who comes to the table only with a disposition to find fault, and neither to partake himself nor suffer others to partake of the entertainment?"

"Yet you may find others more *uncivil* than these, who openly, and without end, will condemn and tear a work to pieces, which they have never read. And *some* do this, who profess themselves *teachers of Christian piety* and *eminent*[11] *professors* of religion. Whereas, to condemn that of which you are ignorant, is beyond the baseness of the[12] *basest informer*." I could easily make some *strictures* on the above passage, but I forbear saying any more, than *Erasmus* has said for me.

I would recommend it, however, to all who have, or shall criticize on this *work*, to be very certain they *understand* it; for I have a shrewd suspicion, that this has not been the case with *all* its *readers*; perhaps I might name some highly-respected characters, that have been *foremost* in very *unbecoming language* relative to *certain subjects* of it. If *those subjects* are *not* treated, in direct consonance with the law of God, as revealed by *Moses*, they have my free liberty to say what they please; but otherwise, let them take care, lest their *wit, raillery,* and *pious sarcasms,* do not ultimately tend to vilify and ridicule the God *that made them*—let them beware, lest that question, once put on a very serious occasion, be not put to them, in *an hour* when they will find more difficulty than they seem at present aware of, to answer it—*Whom hast thou reproached and blasphemed? And against whom hast thou exalted thy voice, and lifted up thine eyes on high? Even against the Holy One of Israel.* 2 Kings xix. 22. Let them remember, that He will not only *convince the ungodly, of the hard speeches, which they have spoken against Him,* (Jude xv.) but, sooner or later, will *deal* with persons of a more *decent character,* and whose sayings have borne the *semblance of religious zeal, after their folly,* in that they *have not spoken of Him the thing that is right.* See Job xlii. 8.

As to the *Ladies,* who, I am told, are *extremely displeased,* I hope I have

---

11   *Antistes* properly denotes a *chief priest, prelate,* or *bishop*: "but is also used for any man *eminent* among others. Ainsworth."

Erasmus probably used it in the *former sense.* The *author* uses it in the *latter,* for a *reason* which *some* of his *readers* have *more* cause, than he wishes they had, to see the propriety of.

12   *Sycophanticum,* rendered literally, would afford no information to the *unlearned* reader; the term is therefore *paraphrased,* in such a manner, as to give an idea of the *sort* of people which the *Greeks* called *Sycophants,* and, of course, what *Erasmus* means by *Sycophanticum.* For the derivation and meaning of *Sycophants* among the *Athenians,* see *Chambers' Diet.*

too much good manners, to presume to enter into any controversy with *them*; only I would recommend to them also, a very serious attention to what is said in the preceding *paragraph*—and to take great care, that their *objections* do not fall on Him, who knew the situation He had placed them in, when He made His *laws* for the protection of their *frail sisters* from ruin and destruction.—They will, however, permit me to assure them, that if the *author* had found anything in the *divine economy*, which tended to support the *pride* of one part of the *sex*, at the expense of the *ruin and prostitution* of the *other*, he would most faithfully have declared it; and if his fair *readers* should *search the scriptures* with the intent of finding such a thing, he would very earnestly caution them, on *whom* they lay the *blame* of the disappointment that will most certainly attend their inquiries.

The additions which have been made in this *edition*, are such, as tend to elucidate the passages where they occur, and to show the respect and attention, which the *author* most gratefully pays, to any pertinent and candid observations, which have fallen in his way.

I now conclude this *Preface*, with the contents of a paper which I received from a very respectable *Clergyman*, who was *candid* enough to let his *prejudices* submit to his *judgment*, and had *honesty* enough to *own* it.

The following *queries* contain so accurate an *epitome* of the work and are so much to the purpose, as to save the *author* the trouble of introducing them, with any further remarks whatsoever.

"As the subject of a late publication, entitled 'Thelyphthora; or, a Treatise on Female Ruin', &c. is much misunderstood, and misrepresented by many people, who have, some of them, never read it at all, and the rest but partially, and not without prejudice, and therefore oppose it; 'tis judged best to send its opposers the following *questions*, for them to answer: the doing of this, 'tis thought, will bring the matter to a point, enter upon particulars, and be a means to discover where, and with whom, *truth* is, and where, and with whom, *error* is."

1. Are the mischievous, shocking crimes of whoredom, fornication, and adultery, got to an enormous and increasing height in this land, and is the land defiled and deluged by them, or not? And is the frown, or curse of God upon the land, or is it not?

2. Is it needful, and is it our bounden duty, to cry aloud against these

God-provoking, and nation-ruining sins, and to seek a remedy against this monstrous evil, or is it not?

3. Is there anything destructively horrible in the lives, and anything shockingly dreadful in the deaths of abandoned women, alias, common prostitutes, or is there not?

4. What *number*, how many thousands are there of these miserable creatures in our land? And do they have any evil effect on the male sex, or not?

5. Do our laws, as they now stand, hinder this ruinous evil, or do they not? And can they, or *can* they *not*?

6. Do our laws encourage, or discourage, honorable marriage, or celibacy? encourage, or discourage population?

7. Do our laws, in any cases, put asunder those, whom God has joined together, and keep together those, whom He has ordered to be put asunder, or do they not?

8. Is there any *remedy* at all spoken of in God's word, against the great evil of lewdness; and if there be, what is that particular remedy?

9. Does God, in His word, order that whores, adulterers and adulteresses shall be *put to death*, or does He not? See Leviticus xx.10. Deut. xxii. 21, 22.

10. In particular instances of some persons injuring others, does GOD, in his word, enjoin any *recompense* that the injurers and offenders shall make to the injured, or does He not?

11. Are some of our laws, in this land, framed upon the Divine laws, in the above-mentioned particular, and do they inflict punishment on some transgressors and offenders, in any cases, according to the spirit of the Divine laws, or not?

12. Is there any *particular* recompense that God, in his word, orders an *unmarried* man to make to a virgin whom he has defiled, or is there not? and if there is, what is it? See Exodus xxii. 16, 17. Deut. xxii. 28, 29.

13. Is there any particular recompense that a *married* man is enjoined to make to the virgin whom he has defiled, or is there not? If there be,

what is it? Is the virgin, in the above case, to receive a recompense, and the virgin, in this, to receive none, and be abandoned? See the above scriptures.

14. Is our marriage ceremony, in the church, so the essence of marriage as to *constitute* marriage; and, therefore, none are married in God's sight, but those who are joined together, by a priest, with that ceremony?

15. Is the marriage of the people called *Quakers*, in this land, marriage *in* God's sight? and also according to our laws?

16. Were the marriages performed by justices of the peace, in the last century, for eighteen years together, marriages in God's sight, and according to our laws?

17. In what way, or by what form, were all those people of old joined together, whose marriages are recorded in scripture-history?

18. In what way, or by what form, were Christians married for upwards of a thousand years immediately after the birth of Christ?

19. Was our church marriage-ceremony the consequence of Pope Innocent the 3rd, putting marriage, as a sacrament, into the hands of Popish priests, or was it not?

20. What reasons can be assigned for God's permitting so many people, and, particularly, some of his distinguished saints of old, to live allowedly in the practice of *Polygamy*, and to die, without ever reproving them, calling them to repentance, (if it was a *sin*), and without their ever expressing any sorrow for it, and showing any evidences at all of their repentance? And if God's word be the rule of our conduct, and if the example of these saints be written for our learning, what are we to learn from them, respecting their polygamy?

21. If these saints of old lived and died in *sin*, by living and dying in the allowed practice of *polygamy*, what is the *name* of the sin? By what term is it to be distinguished? Was it adultery? or, whoredom? or, fornication? Was their commerce licit or illicit? What commandment did they sin against? Were they adulterers,

whoremongers, or fornicators? What does the scripture-history of the lives and deaths of these saints teach us to call this their practice?

22. Were Hannah, and Rachel, and (after Uriah's death) Bathsheba, whores or adulteresses; or, were they lawful and honored wives? How are they spoken of, and how were they treated, as the scripture-history informs us?

23. Were Joseph, Samuel, and Solomon bastards, or honorable legitimate sons? In what character were they spoken of and treated? Did God show favor to them, or dislike of them?

24. Were not Hannah, Rachel, and Bathsheba, whores or adulteresses; and Joseph, Samuel, and Solomon bastards, according to the *laws of our land?*

25. Are there any things unscriptural, as well as impolitic, in the late act of Parliament for the preventing clandestine marriages, and if there be, what are they, and why? And why did half the House of Lords, save one single voice, move for a *repeal* of this act?

26. In what way can a stop be put to these following ruinous, detestable, horrible, and national evils; namely, brothel-keeping, murdering of infants by seduced women; pregnant virgins committing suicide; medicine-taking to procure abortion; the venereal disease; seduction; prostitution; whoredom; adultery; and all the deplorable evils accompanying and following the mischievous sin of lewdness in this land? If GOD's law respecting the commerce of the sexes was observed, and if the laws of our land were to enforce that, might we not expect His blessing of such means used to accomplish so needed and desirable an end?

27. On the supposition that polygamy be a practice disallowed by God, is the *other* part of the scheme for preventing the horrible evils of lewdness in our land, scriptural and practical, or not?

28. Is the design and aim of the book to hinder lewdness, and its deplorable effects, or not?

After these questions are answered, not in a trifling, superficial, and merely specious and declamatory manner, but in a full, plain, fair, scriptural, and reasonable manner; and the answers are open and honest, free from paltry subterfuge, and all deceiving equivocation, and reservation, and all the answers are founded on truth and facts, we shall then notice what the *consequences* will be of such a right mode of answering these questions; and so find out whether the arguments in "Thelyphthora" be scriptural, reasonable, and defensible, or not; whether the scheme in that book has a good or a bad tendency; whether to be reprobated or received; and whether the friends and abettors of it are friends or foes to their country? the cause of God? the temporal, spiritual, and eternal welfare of their fellow-creatures?"

THELYPHTHORA.

INTRODUCTION.

To call into question the truth of long-received *opinions*, is a sort of employment which *few* choose to be engaged in; not only from the natural indolence and supineness of the human mind, but from the reception which such attempts are likely to meet with from the *generality*, who are always jealous of whatsoever may seem an attack on *principles* which have the sanction of *antient custom*; and from thence, even of laws themselves, for their support.

We need only look[13] back to the times of the *Reformation*, in order to see this abundantly verified. Our *Reformers* no sooner began the salutary work of enquiry after *truth*, and its infallible consequence, the detection of error, than the whole *Christian world*, so-called, was in arms against them. *Councils* were

---

13   If we carry our researches into the history of the Heathen world, we shall find that it was an established maxim adopted by *Plato*, and in which all the other *philosophers* without exception concurred, that "every nation should worship the gods according to the established laws and customs, to which also every private person in his own practice ought to conform." By this artifice of the *devil* (who is emphatically styled the "*god of this world*, that *blinds the minds of men*," 2 Cor. iv. 4.), not only the Heathen world but a great part of the *Christian* world has been enslaved in chains of error and delusion. On the footing of this maxim, it was, that when *Socrates*, who was the wisest of the *philosophers*, attempted to awaken his countrymen to a more rational and spiritual sense of *divine things* than they had been accustomed to, he was accused at *Athens* by *Anytus* and *Melitus,* that "he did not believe those to be gods which the city believed, and that he introduced other new gods—for this he was put to death. How many *Christians* have been put to death on a similar principle, let the annals of those declare who are now crying, *How long*, O LORD, *holy and true, dost thou not judge and avenge our blood on them that dwell on the earth!* Rev. vi. 9,

So *Cicero* binds it as a duty upon the people "to follow the religion of their ancestors. Cic. de Leg. Jib. ii. c. 8.—*ritus familia patrumque servante.*

87

summoned, *synods* held, and their sentences were, in substance, what that of the "*men, brethren,* and *fathers,*" of the *Jews* was against that supposed *innovator, Paul* of *Tarsus,* when they said, "*Away with such a fellow from the earth, for it is not fit that he should live.*" Acts xxii. 22.

When *Paul* and *Silas* were apprehended and carried before the magistrates at *Philippi,* the charge against them ran in the following terms:—*These men, being Jews, do exceedingly trouble our city and teach customs which are not lawful for us to observe, being Romans.* But why was it not *lawful* for the *Romans* to observe what Paul had been teaching? Because of the contrariety of the *Roman* laws and superstitions to God's word—for a like reason, the *Reformers* taught things which it was not *lawful* for the subjects of this kingdom to *observe,* because the system of the laws of church and state were opposite to the *Bible*—and, as far as they are so still, so far will a writer against them be deemed no better than a *troubler of the land,* and a teacher of *customs which it is not* LAWFUL *for us to observe.* He likewise stands fair for being called one of those, who would *turn the world upside down.* See Acts xvi. 20, 21; xvii. 6.

Had not Luther quarrelled with *Pope Leo X,* and brought himself into difficult and dangerous circumstances, it is not impossible but that the light of that great *reformer* might have remained hidden under the[14] *bushel of monkery.* However, it pleased God to order it otherwise, and, in His gracious providence, to overrule *Luther's* situation, for the investigation and promulgation of the *faith once delivered to the saints.* Jude 3. This extraordinary man was led to search, think, and judge for himself; and (drawing his *artillery* from the inexhaustible *arsenal* of the *holy scriptures*) first to[15] attack, and then to overthrow, *errors,* which had been received as the most sacred *truths* for ages, and which had been maintained by

---

14   Matth. v. 15.

15   I would observe, that *John Wickliffe,* an *Englishman,* educated at Oxford in the reign of Edward III, has the honor of being the first person in Europe who publicly called in question, and boldly refuted, those doctrines, which had passed for *certain* during so many ages. Guth. Gram. vol. i. 247. For this, he was sorely persecuted during his life; and after his death, his bones, which had been buried forty-one years, were dug up and burned. This by a solemn decree of the Council of *Constance.* See Fox's Martyrs, vol. i, p. 529. He was the first translator of the New Testament from the *Latin Vulgate* into *English.* He died about 1387. Jortin Rem., vol. v, pp. 479-80.

every support that the credulity and superstition of mankind, aided by laws and powers *ecclesiastical* and *civil*, could give them.

From whence I would infer that no *opinions* or doctrines whatsoever receive any *conclusive* proof of their truth from the suffrages of men, however wise, learned, or however supported by human *maxims*, customs, or *laws*. To take it for granted that truth must be where there are these supports is at once to give up our privilege of inquiring and judging for ourselves; and, if so, we might as well have been born without *reason* and *judgment* as with them. Upon such a principle as this, a *Mohammedan* has as good [16] a reason for the truth of the *Koran* as we have for the truth of the *Bible*; for the former has as much the *customs* and *laws* of *Turkey* for its support, as the *latter* has those of *England*. "*Idolatry* at *Pekin* (says a late writer), *Mohammedanism* at *Constantinople*, *Popery* at *Rome*, and *orthodoxy* at *Westminster*, will be all equally right. The earth will turn round in *England*, and stand still in *Italy*; and our holy religion will be true in *Europe*, but an arrant falsehood throughout all the continent of *Asia*." *Humanum est errare* is too true respecting *every* man and *all* men, as fallible creatures. *Churches* and *councils*, as well as other communities[17], are therefore liable to be mistaken, as is modestly

---

16   So had the ancient *Heathen* for the truth of their systems. Many of the *philosophers* actually resolve all *moral* obligations into merely *human laws and constitutions*; making them the *only* measure of right and wrong, good and evil: so that if the people had a mind to be instructed what they should do or forbear, they sent them to the laws of their several countries, and allowed them to do whatsoever was not forbidden by those laws. *Leland*, vol. ii. 81, 82. *Plato* is for people's "worshiping the gods appointed by the laws of the state, and in the manner there prescribed." Ib. p. 119. note p. So before him *Pythagoras*,

Ἀθαναίος μεν πρῶτα Θεος ΝΟΜΩ ΩΣ ΔΙΑΚΕΙΤΑΙ

Σεβα—

First the immortal gods, *as is by law ordain'd*,

Worship.

When *Erasmus* was about to publish his edition of the New Testament, he was sorely abused for presuming to amend the *text* by correcting some blunders in the commonly received readings. In his account of the arguments of his opponents, he says, among others, *Quidam hic nobis tradunt Lesbiam regulam, ut id habeatur pro recto, quod vulgo receptum est.* "Some here lay down for me the Lesbian rule, that, that should be esteemed *right* which is commonly received." At this rate, how unprofitably does a man pass his time in endeavoring to instruct himself, with the hope of instructing others?

17   By paying little deference to *general councils*, few inconveniences arise, compared with those

confessed by the Church of *England* in her 21st *article*, "Of General Councils."

"When they are gathered together (for as much as they are an assembly of men, where not all are governed by the Spirit and word of God), they may *err*, and sometimes *have erred* in things pertaining to God. Wherefore, things ordained by them as necessary to salvation have neither strength nor authority, unless it can be declared that they are taken from the Holy Scriptures."

The writer of the following pages would humbly hope that, having such venerable authority for calling into question the truth of certain matters which are most *assuredly believed amongst us*, he shall not be deemed impertinently contentious if, touching some points, he differs from the generality of his countrymen. They, contenting themselves with *notions* and opinions *received by tradition from their fathers*, have never thought of looking after the foundations on which they are grounded and have therefore mistaken the *fallible* authority of men like themselves for the divine and *infallible* authority of truth *itself*.

That our *brothels* are filled with *harlots*, our streets with *prostitutes*, and our land with *impurity* is too dreadfully true. *Magdalens*, *Asylums*, and all the kind and benevolent interventions of public charities, however we Magdalens may suppose them, with respect to some few individuals, to answer their benevolent designs, are inadequate to the cure of so crying an evil. A tree is not to be destroyed by plucking off a few leaves, or by cutting away here and there a branch; nor can so general an evil, as we have spoken of, be reformed by so partial, so precarious a remedy, as, from the nature of things, it is in the power of the best disposed, as matters are now constituted amongst us, to administer.

The *ax must be laid to the root*—this is divine wisdom. The truth is that the evil mentioned above, as all others, arises from the neglect and contempt of the divine law, and the substitution of human[18] laws in its stead. The wisdom

---

which inevitably follow a blind and tame submission, in points of faith, to human decisions, and to *public wisdom*, as some of our controversial doctors have loved to call it, which may be *public folly*. "*Public wisdom* is a mere *Proteus*; and, not to consider it in *Pagan* or *Mahometan* countries, amongst the *Jews* it once was the *wisdom* of *Ahab* and Jezebel, and afterwards of *Annas* and *Caiaphas*. It sets out with a great shew of religion, it begins with the *Gospel according to St. Matthew*, and it often ends in the *Gospel according to Mr. Hobbes*." Jortin Rem, vol. ii. p. 193-4.

18   This *practice* exactly harmonizes with the *principles* of Lord *Bolingbroke*, who concludes a very

and goodness of God, which He has shown in the provision graciously made for the protection and defense of the *weaker* sex, from the villainy, treachery, and cruelty of the *stronger*, are disregarded. God's laws are laid aside for that system of baseness and barbarity, which permits men, with impunity, first to *seduce*, and then to betray, to infamy, want, misery, disease, and even death itself in many instances, thousands and tens of thousands of unhappy women, who (were the laws of Heaven regarded, as they ought to be, and made the foundation of our *municipal* laws) instead of becoming nuisances, and reduced to the state of *Devils*[19] incarnate, might have been the comforts of their families, the delight of their friends, the ornaments of civil society.

As to what shall be advanced on these, and on the other subjects of the following discourse, the *author* is not wild enough to imagine that what he has to say will meet with any better reception than *that book* does from whence he takes his authority; or that any person who does not regard the *Bible* so far as to pay an implicit regard to its sacred dictates will be in the least persuaded by what will be offered: much less that there will be any alteration in our *national* system of laws, until, *as* a nation, we practically adopt, as we certainly profess to believe, and as it is evidently *true*, that God is to make laws for man, and not man for God; or, in other words, that the *world* is to conform to the *Bible*, and not the *Bible* to the *world*.

It is now long since Christ charged the *Jewish rabbis* with *making void the*

---

horrid sentiment on the *commerce* of men and women, with these words: "*Increase and multiply* is the law of nature. The manner in which this shall be executed, with the greatest advantage to society, is the *law* of man." Here this matter is left wholly to political considerations and human laws, without any *divine law* to restrain or regulate it.

19   This expression will not be thought too strong when the appendages and concomitant vices of *prostitution* are considered, such as *profane cursing* and *swearing—blasphemy—obscene* talking, *drunkenness—lying—thieving—*and even the *unnatural crime* mentioned in Rom. i. 26. This is so *frequent* that it has even become *common*. When such are the gradual consequences of eradicating every principle of *modesty* and *virtue* from the *female* mind, how ought that *law* to be reverenced which was ordained by Heaven for their protection! *Montesquieu, L'Esprit des Lois*, vol. i, Liv. 16, c. 12, observes, that "there are so many evils attending the loss of virtue in a woman, the whole soul is so degraded by it, and so many other faults follow upon it, that in a popular state, *public incontinence* may be regarded as the greatest of misfortunes."

law of God through their traditions and teaching for doctrines the commandments of men, hereby proving themselves the children and followers of those of whom he complains (Isaiah xxix. 13). *This people draw near me with their mouth and with their lips do honor me, but have removed their heart far from me, and their fear towards me is taught by the precept of men.* Human nature is[20] just the same *now* as it was *then*, and the same leaven has run through *human systems*, more or less, to this hour.

Our laws concerning *marriage*, especially since the famous *marriage-act*, are full of this, and hence in part arises the mischief complained of. By substituting a human *ceremony of man's invention,* in the place of the *only* ordinance of marriage which God ever instituted or revealed, we have reduced the most solemn of all ties to a sort of *civil institution*, the most sacred of all obligations to a mere *civil contract*; and where the latter can be avoided, the *former* is *as totally* vacated as if it had never been.

By God's express command from *Mount Sinai*, where the laws concerning *moral* good and evil were eternally and unalterably fixed, no man could *take* a *virgin* and then *abandon* her. *He shall surely endow her to be his wife.* Exod. xxii. 16. And again, Deut. xxii. 29. *She shall be his wife*; BECAUSE HE HAS HUMBLED HER, *he may not put her away all his days.*

Will any say—"these laws are[21] antiquated?" I answer, "they are as unchangeable as the God that made them." His *law* is His *will*, and therefore can no more *change* than Himself. *The strength of* Israel *is not a man that He should repent* נחם *change his mind, opinion,* or *purpose.* 1 Sam. xv. 29. *I am* Jehovah, *I change not*, is the character which he records of himself, Mal. iii. 16; and to show

---

20   August 1, 1543, the *Parisian* divines assembling the people by the sound of a trumpet, published twenty-five heads of *Christian doctrine*, proposing the bare conclusions and determinations without adding reasons, persuasions, or grounds, but only prescribing, as it were by authority, *what they would have believed.* These were printed and sent throughout all France, confirmed by the King's letters, under most grievous punishments against whosoever spoke or taught otherwise." Brent. Hist. Coun, Trent. 105.

21   We read in the memoirs of the great *Scriblerus* that one of the *philosophical works* of that *profound* genius was entitled, "A complete digest of *the laws of Nature*, with a review of those that are *obsolete* or *repealed*, and of those that are ready to be *renewed* and put in *force*."

that he hath stamped the same *unchangeableness* upon his *laws*, he says, Deut. iv. 2. *Ye shall not* ADD *unto the word which I command you, neither shall ye* DIMINISH *ought from it, that ye may keep the commandments of the* LORD *your* GOD. And again, Deut. xii. 32. *What thing soever I command you, observe to do it, thou shalt not* ADD *thereto, nor DIMINISH from it.*

Now, I do take it for granted that He, who, speaking to the people of *Israel*, calls Himself THE LORD YOUR GOD, is also The Lord Our God. *Is He the God of the Jews only ? Is he not also of the Gentiles? Yes—of the Gentiles also.* Rom. iii. 29. For which very evident reason, I do conclude that both *Jews* and *Gentiles* are equally subject to those laws which the Lord Their God once revealed and established for the *moral* government of the world: and therefore (as we may learn from the testimony of the *Apostle* of the Gentiles under the New Testament, *Gal.* iii. 10, as well as from *Moses* under the Old Testament, Deut. xxvii. 26) *Cursed is every one, that continueth not in* ALL *things which are written in the* Book Of The Law, *to do them.*

These laws therefore stand on the same footing with what we usually call the *Ten Commandments*—and are no more subject to *decay* or *alteration* than *they* are. I say they stand on the same footing because they were equally delivered by God to *Moses,* on the same divine *veracity,* the same awful, and indisputable *authority,* and are guarded by the same tremendous *sanction.*

That the merely *ceremonial* laws are *waxed old* and *vanished away,* Heb. viii. 13, is certain because they were only established for the *time then present,* Heb. ix. 9, to point out and prefigure *things to come.* They had their end and accomplishment in CHRIST and, of course, their utter abolition. This, far from arguing any *change* of mind or will in GOD, is one of the highest and most illustrious proofs of the uniformity and consistency with which He has laid down, carried on, and perfected the same one design from the beginning.

But the *moral* laws which respect the well-being of society, the prevention of disorder, confusion, and all other appendages of *moral evil*, must endure, as long as the objects to which they relate endure on the face of the earth. When *St. Paul*, Gal. iii. 10, and Rom. x. 5, cites the sanctions of the *moral* law from the Old Testament, he shows very clearly that it still remains as an invariable rule of conduct, from which all the people of God, whether *Jews* or *Gentiles*, are equally forbidden to depart.

Can any person therefore, in his sober senses, imagine that it was *unlawful* in the sight of God (because expressly by a *positive* law forbidden) *three thousand* years ago, to take a virgin and then abandon her, but that now it is *lawful*? or, because there is no law of this land against it, it is therefore less offensive in the eyes of God, than at the instant He forbade it? Or that God's law is only binding on the consciences of men, where it has the sanction of human[22] institutions to enforce it? If it be *time* which wears out the malignity of such an evil, or the obligation of the divine law against it, we may as well imagine that other crimes stand in the same predicament, and the most atrocious violations of the security and happiness of mankind will have a *prescriptive* innocence to plead in their excuse.

That all such reasonings are not only without foundation, but directly opposite to the *divine truth*, we learn from that *truth itself*, which has assured us that "*it is easier for heaven and earth to pass, than one tittle of the law to fail.*" And that we may be assured He stamped the most permanent authority on that law, and particularly on the part of the law of which we have now been speaking, He adds, in the very next words—"*Whosoever putteth away his wife, and marrieth another, committeth adultery; and whosoever marrieth her that is put away from her husband, committeth adultery.*" This is no *new* law enacted by our blessed *Saviour* on the subject, but an application and explanation of that very law which he had, immediately before, said,— "could never fail," and which was given to *Moses* at mount *Sinai*. See *Luke* xvi. 17, 18.

When our Lord, in His Sermon on the Mount, as recorded by *St. Matthew*, is about to explain the *moral* law and vindicate it from the false glosses which the *Scribes* and *Pharisees* had put upon it, He prefaces His explanation with these remarkable words— "*Verily I say unto you, 'till heaven and earth pass, one jot or one tittle* (one, even the most seemingly inconsiderable part of a single letter) *shall in no wise pass from the law, till all be fulfilled.*" ἕως ἂν πάντα γένηται. *Until all things be done.* Which, with the learned *Dr. Hammond* on Matth. v. 18, I would

---

22 We may say of human laws, ceremonies, and institutions, which interfere with the obligation of God's ordinances or commandments, as *Henry* II, King of *France* said of the *papal* dispensations, that—"they are not able to secure the conscience, and are nothing but a shadow cast before the eyes of men, which cannot hide the truth from God."

thus paraphrase: "Till the world be destroyed, and all things come to an end, no one least particle shall depart from the law, or be taken away, or lose its force and obligation." "*Whosever, therefore*, saith Christ, ver. 19, *shall break one of these least commandments, and shall teach men so, he shall be called the least in the kingdom of heaven; but whosoever shall do, and teach them, the same shall be called great in the kingdom of heaven.*" After such a testimony as this to the[23] *immutability* of the divine law, it would hardly be decent in me to attempt an addition to its force, by any further arguments.

I will therefore now proceed to examine the subjects proposed, which I shall do singly on the authority of God's word; and this, not by detaching one text here and there from the rest of the sacred scriptures; but by examining carefully the *whole* throughout, *comparing spiritual things with spiritual,* 1 Cor. ii. 13, and thus allowing the word of God to be, what God doubtless intended it should be, the *best comment* upon *itself.*

Nor shall I venture to rest any one point on the authority of even the best[24] *translations*, but constantly have recourse to the *original scriptures*, being desirous to follow that sensible maxim, that "nothing should be received in proof, but on the best testimony which the nature of the thing will admit of." If, in matters of *civil* property, "a copy will not be admitted in evidence where the original can be come at," how much doth it behove us, in matters of *eternal concern*, to have the best evidence for our determinations? *Satius est petere fontes quam sectari rivulos.*

I have endeavoured to clear my imagination of all *worldly* systems and *human inventions* whatsoever, whether *Popish* or *Protestant*, and to allow no authority more modern than the sacred scripture, *less* weighty than inspiration

---

23   The Psalmist faith, Pf. cxix. $9.

בַּשָּׁמָיִם   נצב   דברך   יהוה   לעולם in the heavens is settled Thy word O Jehovah! For ever I must therefore declare it, not only as my *opinion*, but as a fixed article of my *faith*, that a single *atom* of the *moral law* can never be changed— *nor will God alter the thing that has gone out of his lips.* Ps. lxxxix. 34.

24   Whosoever reads the strictures on, or rather *against*, the sacred scriptures, of that ignorant and malicious reviler of them, *M. de Voltaire*, may see how he has been led into his mistakes by some of the *Latin* and *French* translations.

itself, to amount to a proof of what is *true* or *false*. As for the writings of primitive[25] *fathers*, Christians, &c. the whole rabble of *schoolmen*, together with the decrees of *councils*, *churches*, *synods*, etc., a man who wishes to know the *truth* should no more receive a matter of *doctrine* on their authority than he should a matter of *fact* on the testimony of a *Popish* legend. Nay, I will go farther and say that the[26] dying words and unshaken constancy of *saints*, *martyrs*, and *confessors* ought to prove no more than that "they themselves believed what they said," unless the *holy scriptures* bear testimony to their opinions.

However clear the *Spring* is, when it divides itself, flowing from the fountainhead into different channels, it will naturally present to the *eye* the *colour*, and to the *palate* the *taste*, of the different soils through which it may happen to take its course. I have therefore found little encouragement to rest anything on the authority of *commentators*; who, being prejudiced by education, influenced by

---

25 These were but *fallible men*, like ourselves, at best; and if we consider the strange opinions which are to be found in their writings, we must acknowledge them to be very faulty. Though they have been so mutilated, changed, interpolated, and corrupted by the various *sects* who have wanted their testimony to speak for them, it is difficult to know what is *genuine* and what is not. I remember having met with the following dismal, though short, account of the writings of the *fathers*,—"Scatent erroribus tum veterûm tum recentiorum *hæreticorum*." They abound with the errors, as well of the old, as of the more modern heretics." Burnet observes, that "there was a great mixture of *sophisticated stuff*, that went under the *antient names*, and was joined to their *true works*, which critics have since discovered to be *spurious*." Hist. Ref. p. 30, 2nd edit., vol. i. The *apostle*, Titus 1:14, warns us against *Jewish fables*; we should be equally careful of *giving heed* to those which seem to bear a *Christian stamp*.

We might as well recommend a *young man* to the study of so many volumes of *newspapers* to make him an accurate *historiographer*, as to the study of the fathers to make him a *sound divine*. How far they may make him a *rotten* one may be seen in the *Life of Dr. Clarke by W. Whiston*, p. 143, 151, 155.

26 Much has been built on the constancy with which the *martyrs* suffered—but when we find people dying with equal constancy for opposite opinions, nothing is conclusively proved on either side, but that each believed his own tenets.—See Burnet's Hist. Ref. vol. ii. p. 112. 9th edit. the case of *Joan* of *Kent*, and of *George Van Pare*, a *Dutchman*.

It is a dangerous thing to build our faith on *equivocal* testimony, instead of the ONE INFALLIBLE EVIDENCE of God's WRITTEN WORD—which can neither *lye* nor *deceive*; and *against* which there can lie no appeal, to any *other writings* in the world, nor to any *other testimony* of any kind whatsoever.

custom, and misled by others who have gone before them—instead of *thinking as the Bible speaks,* too frequently make the *Bible speak* as *they think.* The conclusion of the matter therefore ought to be—*To the LAW and to the* TESTIMONY! Is viii. 20.

CHAPTER I.

Of MARRIAGE *as a Divine Institution.*

WHEN the great and all-wise Creator had formed man upon the earth, *male* and *female*, He *blessed them, and said unto them, Be fruitful and multiply, and replenish the earth.* Gen. 1:28. This command was to be fulfilled in a way of God's own appointment; that is to say, by *the union of the man* and *woman* in *personal knowledge of each other.* This is the only[27] *marriage-ordinance* which we find revealed in the sacred scriptures. Wherever this *union* should come to pass, though *two* distinct and independent persons before, they now were to become as *one. They shall be one[28] flesh*, Gen. ii. 24. and so indissolubly *one*, as to be inseparable. *What God hath joined together, let not man put asunder.* Matt. xix. 6.

That this oneness arose from this *act* of *union*, and from the command consequent upon it, that *they should be one flesh*, is evident from the *Apostle's* reasoning, 1 Cor. vi. 15, 16. *Know ye not that your bodies are the members of* CHRIST? *Shall I then take the members of* CHRIST, *and make them the members of an[29] harlot? God forbid! What, know ye not that he that is* JOINED *to a harlot is*

---

27 By this expression, I would be understood to mean *that* by *which* the parties become *one flesh* in God's sight, *so as not to be put asunder.* See Matt. xix. 5, 6.

28 לבשר אחר—*as one flesh*—εἰς σάρκα μίαν, Gr. Teft. The Hebrew ל prefixed, hath often this sense. See Josh. vii. 5. Lam. i. 17. So the *Greek* preposition εἰς, which answers to it. Compare 2 Sam. vii. 14. with Heb. i. 5. where the לבב and לאב of the Old Testament are rendered by εις πατέρα and εις υἱόν in the New Testament; and clearly evince the names of *Father* and *Son* to be *economical* names of *office* in the covenant of redemption, not descriptive of an inferiority and subordination in the persons of the GODHEAD. Compare Luke i. 35..

Also הוה with ל, and a noun following, denotes some change of condition, state, or quality, and signifies—to *become.* Gen. ii. 7. 24. Xvii. 4. Exod. iv.4. & al. freq.

29 πόρνη, from πέρνημι, or πέραω, *to sell. A whore*, a woman who prostitutes her body for *gain.* So the Latin *meretrix* is from *mereor, to earn, get money*: and our *English* word *whore*, from the German

ONE BODY? *for two*, saith he, *shall be* ONE FLESH.

This question of the Apostle's—*Know ye not that he that is joined to an harlot is one body?* and what follows, being taken together, have a plain reference to what *Adam* said, Gen. ii. 24, and seems very fully to determine not only the strictness of the *marriage-union* but also what constitutes it in the sight of God. In all this, there is not the least hint, or most distant allusion, to any *outward* rite or ceremony administered by any person whatsoever; but the whole is made to rest simply and only in the *personal*[30] union of the *man* and *woman*. It is this *alone*

---

buren (Dutch *buren*) to hire. Thus *Ovid*. lib. i. eleg. 10.

> Stat *meretrix* certo cuivis *mercabilis* ære,
> Et miferas juffo *corpore quarit opes*.

See Parkhurst's Gr. Lex

30 It may be presumed that in what *Adam* said, Gen. ii. 23, he had an immediate reference to her formation out of a *part of himself*; but that there was also an allusion to the personal *union* of the *male and female* in what he says, ver. 24, is clearly proved by the *Apostle's* argument, 1 Cor. vi. 16. Otherwise, his citing this passage of Gen. ii. 24 would have been nothing to the purpose to show that *this* makes them *one flesh*. The Hebrew באשתו דבק is rendered by the LXX, ΠΡΟΣΚΟΛΛΗΘΗΣΕΤΑΙ, προς την γυναικα αυτά, in Matt. xix. 5. ΠΡΟΣΚΟΛΛΗΘΗΣΕΤΑΙ τη γυναικι αυτε.. Let the *reader* compare all this with the *Apostle's* ΚΟΛΛΩΜΕΝΟΣ τω πόρνη, and it will be very easy to see that the same *idea* runs through the whole; which is, that those who are *thus joined*, are *one body*, and pronounced by God—*one flesh*. This will appear still more evidently if we consider our Lord's expression, as represented by the *Evangelist*, Matt. xix. 6, where he uses the word ΣΥΝΕΖΕΥΞΕΝ, hath *joined*, or *yoked together*, as the *effect* of the *cause* expressed by προσκολληθήσεται. All this will appear still more evidently if, with the accurate *Ar. Mont.*, we translate באשתו ודבק, *& adhærebit IN UXORE SUA*.

A very candid critic on *Thelyphthora*, asks "how the above idea (of κολλώμενος) is reconcilable with the context in which the same word is applied to the Lord,—'Ο κολλώμενος τω κυρίω, *He that is* JOINED *to the Lord*," &c. It is a pleasure for me to give a candid question as candid an answer.

The idea contended for, where κολλώμενος is made use of as denoting the union of a *man* with a *harlot*, cannot be the same as that where it denotes the union of the believer *in one spirit with the Lord*: the *one* is evidently a *carnal* idea, the other as evidently *spiritual*; yet the *marriage union* is emblematic of the *spiritual* union between CHRIST and the believer, as to the strictness and indissolubility of the union itself, and many other particulars, which the reader may find. Eph. v. 22-33. where (v. 31.) the *Apostle* quotes Gen. ii. 24. and expressly assimilates it to the union of CHRIST *with the church*, v. 32. Thus are *earthly* things made use of to teach us *heavenly* truths; and indeed in this dark and imperfect state of *mortality*, this is the *only* way by which we can become acquainted with them; they are therefore made use of for this gracious purpose, throughout the whole *Bible*.

The *Apostle* is showing, in this passage of 1 Cor. vi, the horrid inconsistency of *believers* who, in

which, according to the *Apostle*, makes them *one flesh*.

If the licentious and temporary union with an *harlot* makes a man become *one body* and *one flesh* with her, we may suppose that the sin of *fornication* receives no small share of its malignity from the abuse thereby committed of the *ordinance* of *marriage* as established by God: entering into it without any intention of abiding by it, but merely to gratify a transient lust, and that with a woman who departs from one to another as gain or evil desire may lead her. Nevertheless, the *Apostle*, on the authority of Gen. ii. 24, says *he that is* JOINED *to an harlot* is *one body* and *one flesh* with her, by being engaged in *that ordinance*, of which these things are declared in the passage referred to, to be the inevitable consequences.

From what has been said, it appears that *marriage*, as instituted by God, simply consists (as to the essence of it) in the *union* of the *man* and *woman* as *one body*; for which plain and evident reason, no outward forms or ceremonies of man's invention, can add to or diminish from the effects of *this union* in the sight of God. What ends these things may serve, as to civil purposes, I shall not dispute: but I cannot suppose that the[31] *matrimonial*-service in our church, or any other,

---

a *spiritual* sense, are *joined to the Lord* (compare John xv. 5) and become *one spirit* with Him (so that their very bodies are *temples of the Holy Ghost*, ver. 19), taking those *bodies* from the *sanctified* use (see 1 Thess. iv. 4, 5) to which they ought to be dedicated and *joining* them in carnal commerce with an *harlot*, by which they become *one body* and, of course, *one flesh* with her.—This is not glorifying God in *their bodies and in their spirit* , &c. ver. 20 but a profanation and defilement of *both*.

31   Our marriage-ceremony, or form of *solemnization* of *matrimony*, was settled by *Archbishop Cranmer* and twelve others in the reign of Edward VI, i.e., about 232 years ago, or 1548 years after the canon of scripture was closed, and is certainly the method by which the *civil contract* is established among us, provided it be administered agreeably to a subsequent act of *parliament* (26 G. II. c. 33); but how far must the mind be gone in superstition and prejudice to suppose that a human ceremony can control or alter the fixed and determinate *laws* of *Heaven*, or have the least influence on what *does* or *does not* make the parties *one flesh* in God's sight! Grotius, de Jur. lib. ii. c. 5. § 8. states - "Conjugium naturaliter esse existimamus talem cohabitationem maris cum femina, quae feminam constituat quasi sub oculis et custodia maris. Nam tale consortium in mutis animantibus quibusdam videre est. In homine vero, qua animans est utens ratione, ad hoc accessit fides, qua se femina mari obstringit. Nec aliud, ut conjugium subsistat, natura videtur requirere. We account marriage to be naturally such a cohabitation of the *male* with the *female*, as may place the female, as it were, under the eye and custody of the *male*; for such a fellowship [or intercourse] is to be seen among certain brute animals. But as to man, as he is an animal having the use of reason, to this (natural conjunction) has acceded a solemn contract, by which the female binds herself to the

can make the parties more *one flesh* in the sight of GOD, supposing them to have been *united*, than the *burial*-service can make the corpse over which it is read more dead than it was before.

Supposing they have not been *united*, they are not *one flesh* in the sight of GOD, by any virtue in the words of the service, any more than a piece of *wafer* becomes *flesh and blood* by a Popish priest's consecration. It is not *man*, but GOD, who makes the *twain one flesh*; neither is it *man's ordinance*, but God's *institution*, which brings that to pass. If this be not so, why, notwithstanding the words of the service, does incapacity, inability, or impotency in either party render all that has been done *null* and *void*? See Burn, Eccl. Law, vol. ii. p. 39.

By observing the *outward* ordinance, the intention of the parties is publicly recognized, and they are pronounced *man* and *wife* in the sight of the world; but they are not so in God's sight, unless by anticipation, as it were, with respect to the mutual promises made to each other, which the sacred scriptures call *betrothing* or *espousing*; but the contract is then, and only then, *complete* in the sight of God, when the only ordinance that He has appointed has passed between them; and therefore, it is very properly styled—*the consummation*.

As to the person celebrating the marriage—the place where—the manner how; it is very certain that these things are wholly of human invention, and therefore not only various in different parts of the world, but also in the same country. We have amongst us *Jews, Papists, Quakers*; all these observe an outward form or ceremony different from each other. As for the Church of *England*, we have differed from ourselves; for the same ceremony which would have constituted a *legal* marriage before the 26th of the late King George II will not do it now, unless certain circumstances, introduced and insisted upon by act of Parliament,

---

male. Nor does nature seem to require anything else for the subsistence of marriage.

Gronovius notes on part of the above passage, as follows, viz.

Custodia maris.] Videtur addendum, procreationis, & mutui auxilii caufa.

The custody of the male.] It seems there should be added–for the sake of procreation, and of mutual help. Acceffit fides.] Tacite significat fidem quam dat maritus uxori non esse a natura, fed ab instituto.

Acceded a solemn contract.] Here is tacitly signified, that the faith which the *husband* pledges to the *wife*, is not from nature, but by (positive) institution.

be observed.

But the *all-wise Legislator of the universe* hath not left His divine institutions on so vague, so precarious, so uncertain a footing. *But see, said* He to *Moses, that thou make all things according to the pattern shown thee in the mount.* Heb. viii. 5. We find every particular, down to the very pins in the tabernacle, every *rite* and *ceremony*, even to the minutest circumstance, exactly delineated and revealed. But we find no *marriage service*, or *religious ceremony of an*[32] *outward* kind, so much as mentioned. The business of *marriage*, by which I understand the parties *actually* becoming *one flesh* in God's sight, was left as at first ordained, to the one simple *act* of union. A conclusive proof of this is that nothing else is of *divine* institution; consequently, that nothing else is essential to constitute a marriage in the sight of God but that *this* is.

Should the *Reader* retain the least doubt about the truth of what has been said, or be under any difficulty in understanding what is meant by those words— *They shall be one flesh*, we may refer to a very clear explanation of the matter, not only by reviewing St. *Paul's* words, 1 Cor. vi. 15, 16, but also by considering more minutely what is meant by those passages mentioned before, from the law of *Moses*; but as the *texts* are not cited at length, I will here set them down as they stand in the places referred to.

Exod. xxii. 16, 17.

If a man entice a maid who is not betrothed, and lies with her, he shall surely endow her to be his wife. If her father utterly refuses to give her to him, he shall pay money according to the dowry of virgins.

By this passage, as from many others in the sacred scriptures, it appears that fathers, during the minority of their daughters, as in every other instance (see Numb. xxx. 3,4,5) so in the business of contracting marriage, had a negative impact in their own power: therefore, *if a woman being in her father's house in her youth,* i.e., being under age, as we term it, *betrothed* or *espoused* to a man, the

---

32 As for the manner of celebrating marriage, *Moses* has left no direction about it. We do not find it accompanied by any religious ceremony, such as going to the Tabernacle or Temple, offering sacrifices, or even if it was performed by or before a *priest*. See Ant. Univ. Hift. vol. iii. p. 145.

former by[33] *verba de futuro*, the *latter* by *verba de præsenti*, as the *civilians* speak; both which were held so sacred, that *defiling* either a *betrothed* or *espoused* woman was considered a species of *adultery*, and punished with death:—yet, if the father withheld his consent, neither the *betrothing* nor *espousals*, nor any contract arising from them, could lawfully be carried into execution. But in the passage before us, matters were gone too far to be recalled. The man had not only *enticed the maid*, but had actually *lain with* her; and therefore, God commands that he *shall surely endow* לו לאשה *sibi in uxorem*. Mont. *for his wife*. For now the primary institution took place, *they shall be one flesh*; and what God *had joined together* (by pronouncing them *one flesh*) man could not *put asunder*. Therefore, the 17th verse does not say, "If the *father utterly refuse to give her unto him*, such marriage shall be *null* and *void*; but—*if*—*or*— [34] *though the father utterly refuse to give her unto him, he shall pay money according to the dowry of virgins*. Which is but explanatory of what goes before, he *shall* SURELY *endow her to be his wife*, by paying מהר *the dower* into the hands of the father *after becoming one flesh* with her, as he ought to have done, and was usually done, *before-hand*. מהר is supposed to be a *dowry* or portion which the husband paid into the hands of the bride or her father as a kind of purchase of her person. This is, to this day, the practice of several[35] eastern nations; and this was not to be withheld because the husband

---

33 Spousals *de futuro* are, according to our ecclesiastical law, a mutual promise, or covenant of marriage, to be had afterwards; as when the man saith to the woman, "I will take thee to my wife"; and she then answereth, "I will take thee to my husband." Espousals *de præsenti* are a mutual promise or contract of present matrimony; as when the man doth say to the woman—"I do take thee to my wife,"— and she then answereth—"I do take thee to my husband." 2 Burn 16.

34 So אם is often rendered, as in *Judg.* xiii. 16. Ps. xxvii. Isa. x. 22. Jer. xv. 1. Lam. iii. 32. & al. freq.; and so I think it ought to be understood here (although I may differ from the *Talmudists*) in order to make this verse consistent with the preceding, where it is said:—ימהרנה, מהר *endowing* he shall *endow her*, &c. as well as to avoid the very great difficulty of supposing that such an action as *enticing the maid, lying with her*, and *then leaving her* on the father's refusal, was of no higher consequence than paying a *small* sum of money; כסף-ן *silver* paid, amounted to very little, and rather seems to be payable as an acknowledgment of the contract, than anything else. See Nold. Heb. Part. אם, No. 13. translated by *quamvis—although:*—where the reader will find many authorities.

35 See Parkhurft's Heb. Lex. fub voc. מהר
   Tacitus L. de Mor. Germ. mentions such a custom among the *Germans*. Dotem non uxor

had married the woman either *without* or *against* the father's consent. In short, the man was not to take advantage of his own wrong. But,[36] אם *whether* the father refused or *not*, the dowry must be paid according to the law, and thus the contract be publicly ratified.

Having seen what was to be done where a man *enticed* a *maid* and took actual possession of her, *against* the father's *consent*; let us next see what was to be done when a man took a maid without even the father's *knowledge*; not by a seduction or enticement, but on a sudden and unexpected interview, by meeting her without any previous intent.

Deut. xxii. 28, 29.

If a man find a damsel that is a virgin, which is not betrothed, and lay hold[37]

---

marito, sed uxori maritus offert, interfunt parentes et propinqui, ac munera probant: In hæc munera uxor accipitur, hoc maximum vinculum, hæc arcana sacra, hoc conjugales Deos arbitrantur. "The wife doth not bring a dower to the husband, but the husband to the wife; the parents and relations are present, and approve the gifts. On these gifts the wife is accepted; this is the chief bond: these are sacred mysteries, with which they "think the Gods are married." This was called among the *Romans-coëmptio nuptialis*, and was reciprocal, as well on the woman's side as on the man's. To this Virg. Georg. I. 1. 31. seems to allude:

Teque sibi generum *Tethys* emat omnibus undis.

36 This is also one sense of the Hebrew particle אם *an—utrùm—whether* or *not—*of which *Noldius* gives many examples. See Nold. p. 65. No. 2. edit. 1734. It is to be remarked that *Noldius* has not mentioned Exod. xxii. 17. as an example of any of the senses here given, viz. either as *fi-quamvis—*or *utrùm*.

37 The word ותפשה seems here to be rightly rendered by *lay hold on he—Prendra* Fr.—*take her*. The *Jewish* doctors construe this into that sort of *violence* and *constraint* which we call *rape*. But this is spoken of at verse 25, where the word חזק is used; which is a much stronger expression than תפש *to take*, or *lay hold on*; and so our translators have (ver. 25.) observed, in their translating והחזיק by—*force her*. That this is the true idea of the word may be seen by comparing 2 Sam. xiii. 11, 14, when *Amnon* commits a *rape* on *Tamar*. The word חמש does not necessarily signify violence, which חזק does. *Omnis significatio est vehementia, fortitudo. Calasio*, sub voc. This place in Deut. xxii. 28 is rather to be understood of "defiling a maid, that being occasionally *laid hold on*, did presently yield, not being solicited beforehand, and drawn to it by degrees. But Exod. xxii. 16 speaks of such as did *entice a maid*, with promise of marriage, and then defiled her." *Clark*. The two passages taken together shew that in neither case shall the man *abandon* the *virgin* he hath *taken*. We must conclude there is a reason for using different words at ver. 25, and ver. 28, in the *Hebrew* text, though the LXX.

on her and lie with her, and they be found; the man that lay with her shall give unto the damsel's father fifty shekels of silver, and she shall be his wife; BECAUSE HE HATH HUMBLED HER, *he may not put her away all his days.*

The word *shekels* is not in the original but inserted by our translators; in the passage of Exod. xxii. 17, there is the same word כסף *silver,* or *silver-money;* there it is said in general, *according to the dowry of virgins.* Here it is said חמשים כסף *Quinqua ginta argentinos, fifty pieces of silver-money.* By comparing the two passages, we may therefore look upon this as the assessment of the usual *dowry of virgins* paid to the father. It was to be paid in *this* case as well as the *former,* for in *both,* the father's consent was precluded; but in no case was he to be defrauded of the מהר or dowry. This was as much to be paid when his daughter was taken *against* his consent, as when *with* it, and so when taken *without* his knowledge and consent, as in this latter case. But whatever account the money was to be paid, it alters not the point in question, for, saith God, *She shall be his wife,* or *woman*—Fr. *Elle lui sera pour femme*—Because HE HATH HUMBLED HER, *he may not put her away all his days.* This is clearly explanatory of the *original* institution—*they shall be one flesh,* and what *God hath joined together* (by pronouncing them *one flesh) let not man* (either the parties themselves, or any human power whatsoever) *put asunder.*

I should rather chuse to let the scripture answer for itself, than appeal to human authority for its explanation. I will only here just observe that I am by no means singular in my views of these things. Our *ecclesiastical* courts have proceeded on this principle, have called this *personal intercourse,* previous to any *outward* ceremony, a *marriage de facto,* and have compelled the parties to a public recognition of it *in facie ecclesiæ,* in the *face of the church.* See *Blackstone's* Comment. vol. i. 435, 439:—and in *Burn's* Ecc. Law, Tit. *Marriage,* there is this remarkable passage, "Nor was he or they to be dismissed or absolved, if those spousals *de futuro,* by reason of *carnal knowledge,* or some other *act* equivalent,

---

translate them both by βιασάμενΘ—probably חמש is a more general word than חזק, and signifies *laying hold on,* or *apprehending,* whether by *violence* or otherwise. Among the *Athenians,* if a man had *ravished* a young woman (so she were free-born), he was fined 1000 *drachmæ,* and, besides that, was obliged to *marry* her, unless it could be made to appear she had taken something of him in consideration. *Rous's* Archæol. Atticæ, 190.

did *become matrimony.*" By this it does appear that, in the judgment of our *canon law*, if a man had promised a woman to marry her at a *future time*, and in the meantime *lay with her*, or used the *freedoms of a husband* with her, such promise did, by such acts, become *matrimony.*

So sacred have our *canonists* esteemed this *act,* that where one of the parties has forsaken the other, and married another than the person to whom they have been *thus* joined, the *ecclesiastical courts* have pronounced a sentence of divorce with regard to the *second* marriage, *causa precontractûs,* by reason of *precontract.* With what authority will appear by-and-by.

In Bacon's Abr. vol. iii. p. 574, we find the following case:—A. contracts himself with B. and after marries C. B. sues A. on this contract in the spiritual court. There sentence is given that A. *shall marry* and *cohabit* with B., which he does accordingly. They are *baron* and *feme,* without any[38] divorce between A. and C; for the *marriage* of A. and C. was a mere *nullity*[39].

That I am not singular in my opinion respecting the one divine ordinance of *marriage,* will also appear from the very remarkable statute of Henry III; which, as it is very short, I will transcribe.

"To the king's writ of bastardy, whether one born *before* matrimony may inherit in like manner as he that is born *after* matrimony: all the *bishops* answered, that they would not nor could not answer to it, because it was against the common order of the church. And *all* the *bishops* instanted the *lords,* that they would consent, that all such as were born[40] *before* matrimony, as to the succession of

---

38   In the time of H. VIII, an act was passed that marriages solemnized and consummated should stand good, notwithstanding any *precontract* that had not been consummated. But this was done only to gratify the *King,* and therefore in the next reign (2 Ed. VI.) this act was repealed.

39   The law since 26 Geo. II. c. 33. is quite the reverse, the *precontract* between A. and B. would be a *nullity,* and the *marriage* between A. and C. *valid.* Such are the liberties which mortals have presumed to take with the *ordinance of Heaven.* But this cannot alter either the *thing itself,* or God's views of it.

40   "*Constantine,* to discourage *concubinage,* and to encourage *matrimony* in persons who lived together in that way, ordered that if a man married his *concubine,* the children which he had by her *before marriage* should become legitimate. But the *church* meddled not with these distinctions of the civil laws, but regarding only the law of nature, approved *every conjunction* of one man with a

inheritance, should be legitimate, as well as they that are born *within* matrimony, for so much as the *church* accepteth SUCH TO BE LEGITIMATE. And all the *earls* and *barons* answered with one voice that they would not change the laws of the realm, which hitherto have been used and approved."

Here was a strong push made, that the ordinance of GOD should be in some measure recognized, as to its scriptural import and validity, in our municipal laws; but human wisdom forbade it!

In ancient *Rome*, there were three kinds of marriage, distinguished from each other by the names of *consarreation, coëmption,* and *use.*—the last of these came very near to the simplicity of the divine institution. It was, when the accidental living together of a man and woman had been productive of children, and they found it necessary or convenient to continue together; when, if they agreed on the matter between themselves, it became a valid marriage, and the children were considered as legitimate.

By the first law of the 12th table, relative to *marriages,* it is declared that "when a woman shall have cohabited with a man for a whole year, without having been three nights absent from him, she shall be deemed *his wife.*" By which it appears that the *Romans* considered living together, or *conjugal* cohabitation, as the very essence of matrimony. *Broughton* Hist. Lib. tit. *Marriage.* This may

---

woman, if it was with one woman and perpetual; and the more so because the holy scriptures employ the name of *wife* or of *concubine* indifferently."

"The first council of *Toledo,* A.D. 400, hath this canon: He who with a *believing wife* hath a *concubine,* is excommunicated; but if his *concubine* is in the stead of a *wife,* and he adheres to her alone, whether she be called *wife* or *concubine,* he is not to be rejected from communion." See Jortin Rem. vol. ii. p. 294, 295; who adds—"This canon shews that there were *concubines* approved by the church."

I would here add, that *Austin, De fide & oper.* c. 19. says—"If a *concubine* should profess to know no other man, although she should be dismissed from him to whom she is subjected, it may well be doubted whether she ought not to be admitted to receive baptism." So that it appears very plainly, there was a time when the conjunction of the man and woman did not depend, for its validity and lawfulness, upon human ceremonies and inventions.

In how many matters, as well as in many of the above circumstances, hath the *church* (as it is called) changed its notions of things! I have often thought that if *Methuselah* had begun his long life with the era of the *Christian church,* and had lived his 969 years in the *Christian world,* his life must have been a very miserable one, unless, like the *vicar of Bray,* of famous *versatile* memory, he could have changed with the times and held at least as many different opinions as he was years old.

be reckoned one instance, in which, to the disgrace of *us Christians, the Gentiles, which had not the law, did, by nature, the things contained in the law*. Rom. ii. 14.

According to the laws of *Scotland*, cohabitation with a woman for some time, and openly acknowledging her as a wife, confirms the marriage, and renders it valid in law. Mem. of *Cranstoun*, p. 30. So where a man and woman have lived together 'till they have children, if the man marries the woman, even upon his death-bed, all the antenuptial children become legitimated, and inherit the honours and estate of their father.

The case is famous in *Holland*; with this difference only, that all the children to be legitimated must appear with the father and mother in the church at the ceremony of their marriage. See the *History of Women*, by *W. Alexander*, M. D vol. ii. p. 252, 267.

Our system in *England* is very injurious and cruel, as it destroys one grand inducement to matrimony, where a man and woman have lived together and had children, by stamping bastardy on the issue without remedy. Whence so inhuman a plan should be derived into the common law of the realm, cannot well be devised; but it must be supposed to have commenced in some of the darkest ages of ignorance and barbarism; for at the latter end of the twelfth century, *Pope Alexander* III. made a constitution, that "children born before the solemnization of matrimony, where matrimony followed, should, to all intents and purposes, be as legitimate as those born after matrimony." By which it should seem that the institution of *Constantine* had been totally laid aside; also, that the *church* thought very differently of marriage, from what it did in the fourth century. See before, p. 31, note.

Upon the whole, it may be concluded, that such laws as are above mentioned would never have been thought of, unless the proposers and framers of such schemes of *post-legitimation* had been convinced that the *conjugal cohabitation* of the man and woman was a lawful marriage in God's account, consequently the issue legitimate in His sight: therefore they were willing to reconcile matters as well as they could between *human invention* and *divine institution*.

Having, I trust, established this truth, that where a man and a virgin are united by the *communication of their persons* to each other, they become *one flesh* in the sight of God, so made by his express command, insomuch that the man *may not put her away all his days*; it follows, that they are *indissolubly* united, beyond the power of *disunion* by any human authority whatsoever.

It is the contempt of this law, this primary law of nature, or rather of the God of nature, established from *the beginning*, and afterwards enforced and explained by the positive laws above-mentioned, which lies at the root of the evils complained of. For, if *a man* כי איש, which is the scripture's way of saying *any man, every man,* without distinction (for God makes none in the texts we have been considering, nor in any other) was deemed the *husband* of the *virgin he lay with,* and was obliged to make a public recognition of it, as enjoined by God so to do, without any liberty to *put her away all his days;* if the law of the land was as positive as this, as the law delivered from God to *Moses* above-cited, we should see a wonderful change in the manners of the people, as well as a stop put to the daily ruin of innocent girls. Would the *great* and *opulent* debauch their tenant's or laborer's daughters, or their own servant-maids, if they knew that this put it into the power of such poor creatures to claim their *seducers* as their *husbands*? Certainly not, at least not in one instance out of ten thousand where it now happens. Must we not suppose that the great and merciful Creator enacted His laws for the protection of the[41] *weaker* sex against the *stronger*, as well as for the prevention of *confusion and every evil work,* which must ensue from men and women coming together and parting ὡς ἄλογα ζῶα φυσικά (as the *Apostle* says) *like natural brute beasts which are without reason?* As, therefore, a contempt of the laws of Heaven, is evidently the cause of the evil, it is as evident that nothing but restoring their due *respect and efficacy* can ever cure it.

How great an impediment to matrimony does this also prove, among the profligate and licentious part of mankind? (which, as the world goes, I do not

---

41   The *Atheist* and *Hobbist* deny any principle of *right* or *natural justice* before the invention of *civil compact*, which, they say, gave being to it; and accordingly have had the effrontery to declare that a *state of nature was a state of war.* See Pope's Works, quarto, 1769, vol. i. p. 534-5, note.

This seems to coincide with the *vulgar* notion of throwing the *marriage-union* on a human *outward* ceremony or *civil compact*, without which the sexes *are in a state of war*, and each makes what depredations they can on the other: little adverting to the wise and holy provision which the CREATOR ordained against this long before *civil compact*, arising from *marriage-ceremony*, was invented, or existed.

suppose to constitute a very small part of it)—for if men can gratify their passions, and indulge their love of variety, without the least danger of much further trouble than it costs them to seduce a poor unwary girl, they will hardly bind themselves to the painful economy of a family-life, or confine themselves to the attention and concern which a family must require.

In every point of view, the contempt of God's law is very shocking; but be it remembered that, though we have no municipal law to enforce its obligation, it ought to be binding and obligatory on *every man's conscience in the sight* of the divine *law-giver*.

There is no *statute* which punishes the defilement of our neighbor's wife, though it is a *capital* offense by God's law, and punished with the *death* of *both* parties; yet surely none will say that it is the less criminal before God: or, because the seventh *commandment* has no human municipal law to enforce its rigour, that therefore the consciences of individuals are under *less* obligation to observe it, or have more liberty to transgress it, than if it had.

But it sometimes happens that a man, having *enticed a maid*, &c. lives with her for a season, and then turns her off for another, not perhaps without making *some* provision for the *first*, and the conscience of the man is salved by this piece of *generosity*, as it is called. But the law of God is directly against such a proceeding—He *shall* SURELY *endow her to be his wife, saith the Most High:* and the reason given for this can never alter nor cease, because the *act* from which it arises can never be recalled. The law of GOD therefore as much remains in force against *such* a *putting away* as against *theft or murder.*

It is not unusual for women *so put away*, to marry other men; nay, sometimes they are portioned by the *seducer* for this very purpose. This fashionable way of getting rid of women, includes in it *many* crimes. First, it is a breach of that positive law—*He shall surely endow her to be his wife*—and again—*She shall be his wife; because he has humbled her, he may not put her away all his days.* Secondly, it is therefore a species of unlawful, forbidden *divorce.* It is, thirdly, *adultery* in the woman *so* put away to marry another. And fourthly, *He that marries her that is put away commits adultery.*

We never allow anything to be *adultery* except the *outward ceremony* has passed; but GOD's positive commands are not subject to the control of *human invention.* It would be a solecism in philosophy, to talk of setting the *sun* to the *dial*, and not the *dial* to the *sun*; it is as great a one in divinity, to argue that the law of God is to be accommodated to the law of man, and not the law of man to the law of God.

Let us suppose for a moment that, as it is said to have been the case amongst the *Spartans, theft* was not to be looked upon in a scandalous point of view, but[42] rather allowable and commendable, if done so dexterously, as that the persons were not detected in the fact; Would this shake the authority of the *eighth commandment,* or be pleadable before God as a justification of the *thief? Consider the work of* God, *that which is crooked cannot be made strait, and who can make that strait which he hath made crooked?* Eccl. i. 15. vii. 13.

From what has been said, I think it may be fairly concluded:

1. That *marriage* is a divine institution, and, as such, to be abided by as revealed to us by its holy and blessed author.

2. That those who look upon it merely as a *civil contract*, and therefore subject to the alteration and control of men, have different views of it from those given us in the scriptures.

3. That a woman's *person* cannot be separated from her self; wherever she bestows the *one*, the *other* is bestowed also.

4. That when she delivers her *person*, and consequently her *self*, into the profession of a man, she is (if not betrothed to another) by *that* act, inseparably united to him, so indissolubly joined, that she cannot leave him, *nor may he put her away all his days.*

5. That if these truths were received, as they are indeed the truths of God, millions of women (especially of the lower sort) would be saved from ruin; for, being protected, received, and provided for as God's law enjoins, as the *wives* of those men who first enticed them, they could not be turned out upon the wide world, with the

---

42 *Aulus Gellius,* lib. xi. c. 18. tells us, out of an antient lawyer, that the old *Egyptians* held all manner of thefts to be lawful, and did not punish them. *Diodorus Siculus* mentions this law among them, that they who live by robbery were to enter their names, and bring what they stole to the *priest,* who muleted the man that was robbed, a fourth part, and gave it to the thief. See *Patrick* on Gen. xlvi. 34.

loss of reputation, friends, and consequently all power of helping themselves, but by ways too dreadful to think of!

Before I conclude this point, I must desire not to be misunderstood, as if I meant to undervalue or despise *human ordinances*; they have excellent use, and, in this mixed state of things, are necessary to maintain that order and decency, which are so necessary for the regulation of the outward actions of men. I would rather infer their use and necessity, than doubt of either. When I say that the *marriage-service of the church,* doth not constitute a marriage in the sight of God, I say true; because by finding no such *service* in the *Bible,* and that marriages were had and solemnized without it, I therefore conclude *that* cannot be it which constitutes a marriage in the sight of God; for, if so, we must suppose that people before the invention of such service were not *married at all,* but lived in *sin*; which is absurd and impossible. That *some* service, or ceremony, is expedient, for many good and laudable purposes, must be allowed—as, for the public recognition of the mutual engagement of the parties to each other—to ratify their union as to inheritances, and many other laudable ends of *civil* society; and as none can live together as *man* and *wife*, without offence, unless they[43] *submit to the ordinance of man*, it ought, where it possibly can, *to be submitted to for the Lord's sake.* 1 Pet. ii. 13.

But it is a great *abuse* of such things to put them in the place of the institution of GOD; so that *this* is of no force or validity in GOD's sight without the other. Hence it is, that men thinking they are not *married,* unless by a *priest* in a *church,* take advantage of their own villainy, and thus *seduce* women and *put them away* at their pleasure; whereas GOD's law binds them, in the *first instance,* and declares the bond *indissoluble.* So that, as to the purposes of the divine

---

43 This golden rule of 1 Pet. ii. 13 appears, by the context, to relate to that obedience which we owe to the *civil* powers. But then the laws of *civil* government must not be inconsistent *with,* or repugnant *to,* the law of God, for if they are, we must not *submit* to them, but rather *suffer* than *obey.* When *Nebuchadnezzar* set up his *golden image,* the three children of *Israel* would not obey the king's *decree* to worship it; they chose rather to endure the *fiery furnace.* Dan. iii. 17, 18. So Daniel vi. 10. And as it is with *civil,* so is it with *ecclesiastical* ordinances of men; these must be consonant with God's word; otherwise, we must act as the *apostles* did, *Acts* iv. 19. Men may make laws for the public recognition of a *marriage* in the *sight of the world*; but to ordain what *marriage* shall consist of in the *sight of* God, is out of their jurisdiction, and depends solely on the appointment of God's *own* law.

institution, if a thousand *priests* were to read a thousand *services* over the parties, these cannot add to, nor diminish from their union before GOD, which, as in His sight, is created by the Almighty *siat—they shall be one flesh.* This surely must be as evident, from the whole tenor of the scripture, as that the pouring water on a person, or dipping him in water, in the name of the *Blessed Trinity,* is the complete divine ordinance of *baptism,* though no *act* is done, or *word* said, besides.

There are no where in the *Hebrew* of the Old Testament, or *Greek* of the New Testament, any specific names for *married persons,* such as the *English* words *husband* and *wife*—but אשה and איש *man* and *woman*—So Ἀνὴρ and γυνή, which also signify persons of the *male* or *female* sex in general; but when coupled with pronouns possessive, as אשת *her man*—אשתו, *his woman.* Ὁ ανηρ σου, *thy man*—ἡ γυνη ἑαυτȣ, *his women,* they then denote the *marriage-relation:* but *how* that relation is entered into, so as to become indissoluble on both sides, hath already been shewn; to which we may add some observations on the word בעל which we translate *husband, married.* See Gen. xx. 3. בעלת בעל *maritatus marito.* Mont.; literally, according to our idiom, *married to a husband.* Isa. lxii. 4. ר וארצך תבעל *terra tua erit maritata.* Mont.; *and thy land shall be married.* Now בעל signifies *to have,* or *take possession,* or *authority over,* as a participial noun—Ὁ ἔχων—he *who* hath.

Hence it signifies *to marry,* to *take possession of a woman,* to *have her,* as we say. See Deut. xxiv. 1; xxi. 13. In *Niph,* to *be married,* taken *possession of as a wife.* Isa. lxii. 4; liv. 1. See *Parkhurst's* Heb. Lex.בעל. So *Calasio.* "Significat dominium, magistratum, dominatus est, habuit, possedit ut dominus, mauritius fuit, rem habuit cum muliere." It signifies dominion, the place or office of a[44] master or governor." "As a verb, he governed, had, *possessed,* as a[45] lord or master, he was married, or *had to do with a woman.*" By all which, taken together, it appears that this *last* circumstance is *that* which *brings* her into the possession and reduces her under the *dominion* of the man, according to that of Gen. iii. 16. latter part.

---

44 Our English word *husband* hath this *idea,* according to *Johnson*—"*Husband, master,* Danish; from *bouse* and *bonda, Runic,* a master." See Dict.

45 The *husband* is called, Exod. xxi. 3.בעל אשה *mulieris dominus,* Mont. *Lord of a woman, Maritus.* Marg.

See Deut. xxii. 29, where it is expressed by עָנָה. *Compressit eam.* Mont.; He *hath humbled her.* English translation. Surely this affords an additional and conclusive proof that a man's *taking possession of a woman* in the sense above-mentioned, is in the language of scripture *marrying her,* or making her אשתו *his woman.*

This appears also from Deut. xxiv. I, where the word בעל, according to *Pagninus,* is used in this sense—

כי יקח איש אשה ובעלה

eá cum coierit & fæminam vir ceperit si.

Pagninus. Mont. Marg.

Here the *taking* the *woman,* and *lying with her,* most clearly appears to make her the *man's wife,* as the rest of the verse and the three following demonstrably shew.

Bishop Patrick, on this place, observes, that "the *Hebrew* Doctors make a difference between these two: understanding by *taking a wife,* espousing her to be his wife, and by *marrying her,* his completing the contract by *lying with her.*" The former signified by יקח the latter by בעלה.

There is another word which denotes a *wife,* viz. שגל—from the root שגל—which in Kal signifies to *lie carnally with a woman.* See Deut. xxviii. 30, also Ps. xlv. 9, and Neh. ii. 6. In both which latter places, we have translated it *Queen;* but this term does not signify in any other sense, but as the King's *wife.* Ar. Mont. renders it as *conjunx—a yoke-fellow* or *wife;* συγκοιτος—*Aquila.* See that learned and useful work. *Parkhurst's* Heb. & Eng. Lex. fub voc. שגל.

I should now proceed to consider marriage, or *matrimony* as it is called, in another point of view, namely under *civil* confederations, and, as such, an object of *human laws:* but before this can be done in a proper manner, some incidental points must be fully understood and discussed. Therefore the subject *matrimony,* as a *civil* contract controllable by *human* legislature, must be deferred for a season.

CHAPTER II.

Of WHOREDOM *and* FORNICATION.

WHEN GOD, the CREATOR and LORD of all, was pleased to ordain and establish the means by which His creatures were *to increase and multiply and replenish the earth*, in which primary command His *reasonable* creatures were equally interested with the brute part of the creation, and in some respects, if we consider *this* world as connected with *another*, infinitely more, and therefore the command was particularly addressed to them, Gen. i. 28—it could not be but that the *act*, whereby mankind was to be propagated, must be totally *innocent* in itself: otherwise it could not have been consistent with the state[46] of *innocence*

---

46 We are told, Gen. i. 31, that God *saw every thing that He had made, and behold, it was* טוב מאד *very good*. We cannot, consistently with this account of things, doubt that every endowment of human nature, whether of body or mind, came under this description; consequently, that those *desires* which were necessary to lead man to the propagation and continuance of his species, were without any evil whatsoever. We cannot sufficiently abhor the folly and blasphemy of *Jerome* and some others, who say that *"Adam's* desire to *know his wife* was the first sin which made GOD repent that He had made man, and was the occasion of turning him out of *Paradise."* Coitus præmium mors—says *Jerome* contr. *Jovinian.*

No inconsiderable difficulty awaited this scheme, which arose from the question—"How then was the world to be peopled, if not by natural generation?" But this was easily solved, by imagining that "the *earth* would have been supplied with *men*, as the *heavens* are with *angels*, by the immediate creative power of GOD, without the interference of any *generation* whatsoever." See *Du Pin's* Eccl. Hist. Eng. Trans. Cent. 5, p. 31, where *St. Chrysostom* delivers himself to this effect.

When such monstrous opinions can have been maintained by those who, in their day, were looked upon as *fathers of the church*, let it warn thee, Reader, against searching for truth anywhere but in the blessed word of GOD; dread as much to leave it for an instant, as a blind man would dread to walk amidst pits and precipices without a guide, or a mariner to sail among rocks and shoals without a pilot. Remember what the Psalmist says, Ps. cxix. 105. *Thy word is a lamp unto my feet, and a light unto my path.*

in which man was when *marriage* was first ordained. But that this *act*, innocent in itself as any other function of the body, might be kept within due bounds of *order* and *decency*, and all confusion and disorder avoided; GOD enacted certain[47] *positive* laws for this very purpose, to confine within such bounds as seemed good to Himself to limit, that *natural*, but *violent* passion, which, for the great purpose of propagating the *human species*, was made an *inseparable* adjunct to the *human frame*.

Those who imagine that this appetite is in itself *sinful*, either in the *desire* or *act*, *charge* God *foolishly*, as if He could ordain the *increase* and *multiplication* of mankind by an *act* sinful in itself: an absurdity little short of *blasphemy! Sin*, we are told, on the most infallible authority, *is the transgression of the law*, 1 John iii. 4;—and *where no law is, there is no transgression* Rom. iv. 15:—when therefore, this act is done agreeably to God's will, it is like all *other* acts done, *good* and *not evil*. In order to make it *evil*, it must be done against some precept of God's law, otherwise, it is as innocent as satisfying our *hunger* with *eating* or our *thirst* with *drinking*. These may become *sinful* by their *abuse or excess*; so may the *other*; but in *itself*, and in its *lawful* use, it is as perfectly *innocent* as the two *former*.

We have observed before that when a man and woman become *personally* united to each other, they are *one flesh* and are forbidden to *put each other away*. This is the[48] ordinance of marriage and the *only* one revealed in the scriptures; therefore, we may call it the *only* one that God ever ordained.

But when men *corrupted their ways upon the earth*, Gen. vi. 12, this ordinance of *marriage*, sanctified by God's *blessing*, Gen. i. 28, and ratified by His own *express command*, Gen. ii. 24, was, as every other *divine* institution,

---

47 *Conjunctio maris cum fæmina, per quam propagatur genus humanum, dignissima res est legum curá.* Grot. de Verit. lib. ii. §13. "The conjunction of the *male* with the *female*, by which the human race is propagated, is a matter most worthy of the care of laws."

48 Unless we agree on defining the terms made use of, no argument can be properly understood, or satisfactorily concluded. I would therefore repeat, what I have already said—that, "as in God's sight, by *marriage ordinance* I mean, *that*, by *which* the parties become *one flesh*—and by *marriage*, the *actually becoming so*." This *was*, *is*, and ever *must be* one and the same, in all *ages*, *times*, and *places*, however mankind may differ about the adventitious circumstances of *human ceremony*—whether *Jewish, Papist, Protestant, Mahometan*, or *Heathen*.

corrupted, perverted, and abused; and men, to satisfy their desires at as cheap a rate as possible, without the incumbrance of a wife and family, or confining themselves to the sober duties of maintaining, taking care of, or providing for their households, chose to have intercourse and commerce with women, like *brute beasts*, for the sake of mere appetite, and then to leave the women for the service of the next comer. Something of this sort may not improbably be the meaning of Gen. vi. 2, where it is said that *they took them* נשׁים *women of all which they chose.* For though this word, in certain connexions, denotes what we call *wives* (as Deut. xxi. 15) yet it signifies primarily the *female sex,* or *women in general.* Such traffic was offensive to God, an abuse of His *ordinance* (see 1 Cor. vi. 15, 16) and tending to destroy the *marriage-obligation,* not only by rendering the bond which was created by it ineffectual but by inducing mankind to despise it, and set it at naught. All *genealogies* must be confounded, inheritances obscured, and relationship itself destroyed; for who could ascertain these things, so necessary to the existence of all civil society, in the commerce with *harlots? Confusion,* and every *evil work,* must ensue; and therefore the all-wise *Governor of the universe* forbade *whoredom* and *fornication* on pain of death *temporal* and *eternal.* See 1 Tim. i. 8, 9, 10.

The *Hebrew* word זנה is particularly appropriated to this offence in the Old Testament, as πορνεία is in the New Testament; and we shall never find it mentioned but with divine *abhorrence.* We have no law to enforce the punishment which God annexed to it, or to treat an *harlot* or *whore as a capital* offender; but it is nevertheless offensive to God, and will now, as ever, meet with marks of His displeasure. *Know ye not,* saith *Paul,* 1 Cor. vi. 9, *that the unrighteous shall not inherit the kingdom of* God? *Be not deceived, neither fornicators, nor idolaters, nor adulterers,—&c.—shall inherit the kingdom of* God.

So odious is *whoredom* in God's sight, that it is not only said to defile the parties who are guilty of it, but the very *land itself* was said to be *defiled* thereby, Jer. iii. 9. Though this *text* may perhaps primarily relate to *idolatry,* which is *spiritual whoredom,* yet it serves to show the malignant nature of *whoredom;* otherwise this would not be made use of, as *adultery* is in the same verse, in a figurative sense, to denote the other.

GOD expressly commanded that there should *not be a whore among the daughters of Israel, Lev.* xix. 29. *Deut.* xxiii. 17; and ordained, that a woman *playing*

119

the whore, if the daughter of a common person, should *be stoned to death, Deut.* xxii. 21. but if the daughter of a *priest,* she was to *be burned with fire,* Lev. xxi. 9. I mention these things as proofs of the sinfulness of an act, innocent in *itself,* when committed against a divine positive law. No human power or custom can alleviate its guilt, or make it less offensive to GOD than His word has made it; the person's conscience that thinks otherwise is sadly deceived.

Though what has been already said may serve as a definition of this offense, yet, to save the *Reader* the trouble of looking back, as well as to be still more explicit upon the subject, I would define זנה, or *whoredom,* to be "a woman's *giving* her person to a man, without any intent of *marriage,* but either for the mere gratification of *lust,* or for *gain* or *hire,* and departing from that man to others for the *same*[49] purposes." This is what the *Hebrew* scriptures call זונה, an *harlot* or *whore.* See Gen. xxxviii. 15, 16. The radical idea of the Hebrew זנה seems to be, to *encompass, encircle, infold, enclose;* and denotes *unlawful embraces* between the *sexes.* Hence we render it, *to commit whoredom.* See Parkhurst's Heb. and Eng. Lex. sub voc.

As *whoredom* is generally used in our translation, as denoted by the word זנה, and seems rather appropriate to signify the *woman's* share in the offense; so the term[50] *fornication,* which is expressed by the same word in the original, seems to be the name given to the offense which the *man* commits in such *illicit* commerce. Though this observation may not hold in all cases, yet it is the best reason which

---

49   After reading the above, it is hard to conceive with what eyes people have read this book, and yet charge the *author* with giving no definition of *whoredom.*

50   Our English word *fornication,* seems to be derived from the Latin *fornix;* which literally signifies *an arch or vault in houses*—and by a *metonymy*—a *brothel-house,* because these were in *vaults* underground. Ainsworth. Hor. Epist. 14. 1. 21, 22. says to his *steward—Fornix* tibi, & uneta popina;

Incutiunt urbis defiderium, video.

"For well I know, a tavern's greasy steam,

"And a vile *stew,* with joy your heart inflame."

FRANCIS.

Hence the haunters of those places were called *fornicators.* See *Johnfon's* Dict. Hor. Sat. lib. i. Sat. 2. 1. 30, 31.

occurs to me for our using *different* words, to denote an offence of the *same* kind.

I readily confess, that the revival of GOD'S antient laws against *whoredom*, amongst us, would be very dreadful, and indeed *unjust*, unless the whole consistent scheme which GOD has laid down was *all* to be revived together. The women, under GOD'S law, could *force* their seducers to take them as their wives; or rather were deemed so *actually* married, as not *to be put away*. A woman had but to summon her *seducer* before the *judges*, to prove the fact against him, and their sentence, which must have been according to the law, must have been obeyed on *pain of death*. Deut. xvii. 12. Unless this were (as it ought to be) the case among us, it would be oppressive, unjust, and cruel to the last degree to punish women with death, for being, by the treachery and villainy of men, forced into a way of life (however abhorrent in itself, or culpable) which is the natural, and in most instances, the inevitable consequence of their being deserted by those who ought to have protected them, but against whom they have no remedy or means to make them act the just and honorable part.

Under this head of *forbidden* lewdness, I would mention the practice of taking an *harlot to keep* for a time, and then, when pleasure or convenience prompts, dismissing her. This is usually called *keeping a mistress*; but as there is no intention of *marriage,* and this is only done for the *mere* gratification of *lust,* it is not only a very evil example to others, and a defiance of the laws and good order of society, but doubtless comes under the *condemnation,* as it must be ranked under the description of *fornication* and *whoredom.*

This was not the situation of the פילגשים or[51] *concubines* amongst the *Jews*; these seem to have been looked upon as *wives*, though, in some respects, of an

---

51   *Dr. Johnson*, in his Dictionary, makes a *concubine signify*— "a woman kept in fornication, a whore, a strumpet:" but no such meaning of the word שגליפ is to be found in the scriptures. It is greatly owing to such interpretations of words which are used in our *translation*, that we are led to have very false conceptions, not only of words, but of whole passages, in the sacred volume.

So the word *adultery*—instead of keeping to the unvaried use of the Hebrew נאף, we make it signify everything which our ideas have annexed to the *English* term *adultery*. At this rate, the truth of scripture can never be fixed, but must alter with the languages into which it may happen to be translated, or with the ideas which changes of times, or opinions, may affix to certain words in those languages.

inferior rank. They were so far considered as *wives*, that the man who took them had such a propriety in them, as to make it a very great offence, if not *adultery* itself, to violate them; as appears in the case of *Jacob*'s concubine *Bilhah*. *Reuben*, the eldest son of *Jacob*, had lain with her; and *Jacob*, Gen. xlix. 4. *calls* it *"going up to his bed and defiling it."* For this crime *Reuben* was disinherited, and put from the right of the *first-born*. Compare Gen. xlix. 3, 4. with 1 Chron. v. I.

Though the children of the *concubine* did not inherit as the children of the *wife* in most cases, yet in one very remarkable one we find they did, and that by the disposal of God Himself. *Leah* and *Rachel*, are called the *wives of Jacob*; *Bilhah* and *Zilpah* were his *concubines* (as may appear from *Gen. xxxv. 22.*); yet the children of *these* inherited the land of *Canaan* equally with the children of the *former*.

I confess myself not master enough of the subject, to define exactly the difference between אשה a *wife*, and פילגש a *concubine*, in all respects; neither have I been fortunate enough to meet with so precise a definition in any author, as to warrant a determination of the question. What I have found upon the subject, I submit to the Reader, in the notes below[52], and in the *appendix* to this chapter,

---

52   The authors of the *Univ. Hist.* (vol. iii. p. 141.) call the נשים *wives of the first rank*, and the פילגשים *wives of* the *second rank*; "which last, say they, though most versions render by the word *concubines, harlots,* and *prostitutes,* yet in none of those places of scripture where the word is used, which are about thirty-six in number, is any such sinister sense implied." However, they state a two-fold difference between *these* and the *wives of the first rank*. "First—that the *latter* were taken with the usual ceremonies, and the *former* with out. Secondly, with respect to their authority, and the honour paid to them and their children."

This is very clear, that the sacred *tongue*, made use of by the *Holy Ghost* in the scriptures, makes distinctions, which amount to demonstration of there being no foundation for confounding the פילגשים with *whores* or *harlots*. The words אשה and פילגש are sometimes used for the same person. See Gen. xxv. 1. 6. (xxxv. 4 with xxxv. 22.); but פילגש and זונה are never thus used.

Calasio defines פלגש as—*Ancilla unita & addicta viro absque scriptura,* i.e. *contractu dotali & sponsalibus.* "An handmaid united and devoted to a man, or husband, without writing—*i.e.* without any contract for dower or espousals.

Busbequius expressly affirms, "that a *wife* is distinguished from a *concubine,* in *Turkey,* merely by a *dowry,* which seems also to have been the distinction among the *Jews*." See *Outlines of a new Commentary on Solomon's Song* (a most ingenious and excellent work) p. 21. written by an author to whom the world is highly indebted, for *"Observations on divers passages of scripture,"* in two *volumes*—a work, which, by laying before us the *manners* and *customs* in the *East*, elucidates the

which he will see at the end of this *volume*.

This is certain, no mark of disapprobation is set upon *concubinage* in the scriptures, though they speak so severely against *whoredom*; which, to me, is an evident and conclusive proof, that there is some specific difference between them. Indeed we find the owner of the *concubine* called her *husband*; *she his wife*. So the text, *Judges* xix. 1. A certain *Levite* took to him אשה פילגש *uxorem pellicem*. Mont.; *a wife concubine*: and in verse 3. he is called אשה *vir ejus*. Mont. *her husband*, as we translate it. So the Fr. of D. Martin, *son mari*; and this translation seems to be very proper, because, the damsel's father is called, ver. 4. his (the Levite's) חותן *father-in-law*; and ver. 5. the Levite is called חותנו *his* (the damsel's father's) *son-in-law*; each of these relations by marriage being expressed by the word חָתַן. Surely this affords a conclusive proof, that the *concubines*, in those days, were in some sense *wives*; but, in what sense, it may be very difficult to determine exactly. The root חָתַן signifies to *contract affinity by marriage*. Gen. xxxiv. 9. Josh. xxiii. 12. In this last passage, the *LXX* render it by ἐπιγαμίας ποιεῖν, to *make marriages*. So that though we cannot state the precise difference between the *wife* and the *concubine* in every particular, yet there was too great a similarity between them, not to be both widely different from what we call a *kept mistress*, in whom the man claims not a jot more property, than in an horse hired for a day's journey, nor is more care or concern usually taken about them, when once the fancy or humour of the *keeper* leads him to resolve upon dismission.

The remedy of this mischief depends on that of the others which have been mentioned; all must stand or fall together.

---

scriptures of the Old Testament beyond any other comment that has yet appeared. It may be truly said of *Mr. Harmer*, that he has the happy art of making "dark things plain," in a way, which, at the same time that it *instructs*, highly *entertains* the reader.

CHAPTER III.

Of ADULTERY.

I COME now to consider an offence against the positive precepts of God, which is of the most malignant kind, that of *commerce between the sexes*, where the woman is the *wife*, consequently the inviolable and unalienable property of *another man*.

This is truly and properly *adultery*, and described in the *seventh* commandment by a word, which, throughout the whole *Hebrew* scriptures, is confined to that single idea. Hence it is, that it is used, in a figurative sense, to denote the turning from God to the worship of *idols*. God calls himself the *husband* of His church; the church is represented under the figure of a *spouse* or *wife*; therefore, apostatizing from *Jehovah* to *idols*, is called, in a spiritual sense, *adultery*, II. liv. 5.[53] *Thy Maker is thine husband.* Jer. iii. 14.

Turn, O backsliding children, for I am married to you. Then God complains, ver. 20. *Surely as a wife treacherously departs from her husband, so have ye dealt treacherously with me, O house of Israel, saith the Lord of hosts.*

It is the misfortune of ours, as of all arbitrary languages, to want[54] precision;

---

53 The words in the original are רישׁע ילעב in the plural number, *thy husbands, thy makers*; then follows, *Jehovah Sabaoth is his name.* Surely here, as in Eccl. xii. 1. and in many other passages, the careful reader must see a *plurality* of persons in *Jehovah* openly revealed. To imagine, as many do, that this fundamental of *true religion* was reserved to the days of the *New Testament*, is one of those consequences of ignorance with respect to the Hebrew scriptures, under which we *Christians* content ourselves.

54 One great reason of which is, the aptness of such languages to acquire new meanings by length of time. This is remarkably the case with ours; for instance, the word *knave* formerly meant a *boy*—a *male child*—then a *servant boy*, and by degrees, *any servant man*. In some old English translations, I am told, that Παυλος δουλος Ιησου Χριστος, is rendered, Paul a *knave* of Jesus Christ. These meanings are obsolete, and now it signifies a *petty rascal, a scoundrel, a dishonest fellow.* See *Phillips's* Dict. and

125

so that when we speak of *adultery*, we include in it every idea that is usually affixed to the word by *custom*, whether right or wrong. There is a[55] precision in the *Hebrew* language peculiar to itself; every word is derived from some fixed *root* or is itself that *root*, which has a fixed and determinate meaning. Though the word branches into so many different and seemingly contradictory senses, the original

---

Johnson. So the word *lust*, which now generally, if not always, carries with it an idea of something filthy and unlawful, was used by the translators of the *Bible* to signify *lawful desire*, (Deut. xii. 15. xiv. 26.) as well as that which is evil. In *Phillips's Eng. Dict.* 6th edit. 1706, the word *lust* is thus defined—"unlawful passion or *desire*—wantonness—leachery"—so that its signification of *desire, in a good sense*, is totally excluded. But this cannot affect the import of the Hebrew חָמַד, or the Greek ἐπιθυμία. Dr. *Johnson* (Dict. sub voc.) defines it by, 1. *Carnal desire*—2. *Violent* and *irregular desire*. See Ps. xxxviii. 12. Prayer Book Translation. Other instances of such mutation might be given. But this cannot be the case with the *Hebrew* language; if it could, it must cease to be the word of God, and become the word, the uncertain word, of man.

In short, it would amount to a creation of *new laws*, which still must vary with the new use of words, and thus, from time to time, create *new offences*, in proportion to words acquiring new meanings. But the *mind* of God hath been graciously delivered to us in a language as unchangeable and fixed as *itself*. Therefore, what the *words* meant when recorded by the *sacred penmen*, they mean to this hour, and will mean for ever—for which very conclusive reason, it is impossible that any word of the Old Testament can acquire a new meaning under the New Testament. Wherefore the word נָאַף *adultery*, can never admit of any other meaning or construction, than it received in the books of *Moses* and the *prophets*—what that was, will appear in the sequel.

How arbitrary languages have always been subject to change, by their being governed by fashion and custom, we may learn from *Horace*:

—Mortalia facta peribunt,
Nedum sermonum stet honos, & gratia vivax.
Multa renascentur, quæ jam cecidere: cadentque
Quæ nunc sunt in honore vocabula si volet usus,
Quem penes arbitrium est, & jus & norma loquendi.

All *things* shall perish, and shall words presume
To hold their honours and immortal bloom?
Many shall rise, that now forgotten lie,
Others, in present credit, soon shall die,
If custom will, whose arbitrary sway,
Words, and the forms of language, must obey.

Francis.

---

55   The *Hebrew* language is worthy its *omniscient author*, equally free from *deficiency* or *hyperbole*: not so the *modern* languages; they have indeed *letters* to form *sounds*, but the words they compose are *arbitrary*, *uncertain*, and frequently *false*. *Hutch*. Abr., p. 41.

idea contained in the *root* will always circulate, as the same sap from the root of a tree will always flow through the stem to the several branches, be they are ever too many. From the want of such precision in our language, we are apt to fix meanings to the words of Scripture, which, when considered in the original, they will not bear: and in few areas are we more mistaken than in the meaning (the scriptural meaning) of the word *adultery*.

The words of the seventh commandment are—לא תנאף—which we very properly translate—*Thou shalt not commit adultery*. But what is the true meaning of the word נאף *adultery*? The only certain way to know this is to consider its uniform signification throughout the whole *Hebrew Bible*; and whoever does this will find that it is never used but to denote the defilement of a[56] *betrothed or*

---

56   The learned authors of the *Ant. Univ. Hist.* vol. iii. p. 137. rightly observe, that "adultery was punishable with death in both parties, whether they were both married, or only the woman." But, they add—"We cannot affirm the punishment of a married man to have been the same, who *committed adultery* with an *unmarried woman*." This solecism of "a married man's *committing adultery* with an *unmarried woman*," arises from the popular and improper ideas which are annexed to the English word *adultery*, and from not attending to the single and only idea annexed to the Hebrew נאף throughout the *Bible*. Consistently with this, *Antonius Matthæus*, the civilian, affirms, that "adultery cannot be committed between a *married man* and an *unmarried woman*." This is certainly true; because no trace of such an use of the word is to be found throughout the *Bible*.

And indeed, fixing a determinate meaning to the word נאף *adultery*, was of the utmost importance, for every man who committed *adultery* was guilty of a capital crime and liable to be punished with *death*.—This was, therefore, too serious a matter to be left in a state of uncertainty, respecting what did or did not constitute the offense.

What *Wetstein* says on Mark x. 12 is worth attending to on this point.—*Potiora fuisse jura mariti quam uxoris inde manifestum est, quia uxor jure & consuetudine Judeorum erat in manu ac potestate viri. Porro uxor cum juvene rem habens, adulterii erat rea et morte punienda: non item vir rem habens cum innupta; quod etiam apud veteres Christianos obtinuit.*

Basil. Can. 21. αν ἀνὴρ γυναικὶ συνοικῶν, ἐπεὶα μὴ ἀρεσθεὶς τῷ γάμῳ, εἰς πορνείαν ἐμπέσῃ, πόρνον κρινόμενος τοι δίον· οὐ μέλλοι ἔχομεν κανόνα τῆς μοιχείας αὐτὸν ὑπαγάγειν ἁπλῶς, ἐὰν εἰς ἐλεύθεραν γαμῆ· ἡ ἁμαρτία γενήται οὐ μέγιστη πορνεύσας καὶ ἀποκλείσει ἀφεῖται τῆς πρὸς τὴν γυναῖκα αὐτοῦ συνοικήσεως, ὡς ἡ μὲν γυνὴ ἐπαινοῖται ἀπὸ πορνείας τὸν ἄνδρα αὐτῇ παραδεξαῖς, ὁ δὲ ἀνὴρ μιανθήσεται τῶν οἴκων αὐτῇ ἀποπεμφθείς. Καὶ τοιγαρ οὖν ὁ λόγος οὐ ῥάδιος, ἡ δὲ συν θεῖα κατκράπικε.

"From hence it is manifest, that the laws which related to the husband were more eligible than those which related to the wife, because, by the law and custom of the *Jews*, the wife was in the *hand*, and under the power of the husband. Moreover, a wife having to do with a young man was guilty of *adultery*, and to be punished with death. But it was not so with the husband who had an affair with an unmarried woman, which also obtained among the antient *Christians*."—*Basil, Can. 21. "If a married woman;* except in the *figurative* sense above mentioned, with respect to *idolatry,* where the *same* idea is exactly preserved.

In *Lev.* xx. 10. we have an accurate and clear explanation of the significant word נאף as well as of the commandment where it is found. *If a man commit adultery with his neighbour's wife, the adulterer and adulteress shall surely be put to death.* What is here called *committing adultery with his neighbour's wife,* is called, Ezek. xviii. 11. *defiling his neighbour's wife;* and Prov. vi. 29. *going in to his neighbour's wife.* If we turn to Deut. xxii. and consider the exposition of the *seventh* commandment which Moses was directed, by the *Holy Spirit,* to deliver to the rising generation, before their entrance into *Canaan,* from ver. 13. to ver. 29. inclusive, we shall find this idea uniformly preserved[57] throughout. See also Lev.

---

man cohabiting with a wife, afterwards, not pleased with marriage, should fall into *fornication,* we judge such an one a *fornicator.*—We have not any *canon* (or rule) to bring him under an accusation of *adultery,* if the sin should be with a woman free from marriage—nor indeed shall he that (thus) committeth *fornication,* be shut out from cohabitation with his wife: so that the wife shall receive the man returning from *fornication* to herself, but the man shall send away from his house a defiled wife. The reason of these things is not easy to conceive, but thus hath the custom prevailed."

57   It is to be observed, that *Basil* lived in the fourth century. If the above rule was of so long standing, as to be called συνήθεια, a *custom,* it proves demonstrably, that the very early *Christians* did not consider *adultery* as relating to any thing but to the *defilement* of a *married woman,* and of course, that the interpreting the New Testament so as to rank *polygamy* with *adultery,* is a much more *modern* invention than is usually supposed.

"נָאַף." Mœchatus est, adulteravit, adulterium commisit. *Prov. vi. 32.* per *metaphoram*—Idola coluit. *Jer.* iii. *9.* Dissert a זָנָה quod generaliter *scortari* significat, ut liquet ex Oseœ iv. 14. at hoc verbum non nisi in *nuptam* competit. Mercer in Pagn.

"R. Solomon Jarchi notat dici tantum de nuptâ."

Leigh's Crit. Sacr.

נאף "To commit *adultery* with matrons. See Litt. Dict. Mœchor. to *adulterate,* to *commit adultery* [with a married woman] Prov. vi. 29, 32-34. Metaphorically, to *worship idols,* Jer. iii. 9. It differs from זנה , which signifies *whoring* in general, as is plain from *Hosea* iv. 14. But this word *only* belongs to incontinency with a *married woman.*

"R. Solomon Jarchi observes, it is only used where a *married woman* is concerned."

Aben Ezra thinks, that it signifies all *illicit commerce,* even whoredom—"But I see, saith *Grotius,* on Exod. xx. 14. that this word is taken by the *Hebrews* in the sense of *adultery* only, and so it is translated in this and the other places where it is used, by the Greeks, Latins, and other interpreters." See Leigh, ib. and margin.

The *LXX* always render it by μοιχεύειν and μοιχᾶσθαι. However, not to rely on the faithfulness

xviii. 20.

So strict is this law with regard to this offence, that it even reaches to the defilement of a *betrothed* woman, who, in God's sight, is reckoned as the man's *wife* to whom she is betrothed. *If a man be found lying with a woman married to an husband, then they shall both of them die, both the man that lay with the woman, and the woman; so shalt thou put away evil from Israel.* Deut. xxii. 22. By these latter words we are taught, that the sin of adultery, like that of *murder,* was not to be looked upon merely as a personal offence, which was of no further consequence than to the parties committing it, but, if not punished as God commanded, brought guilt upon the very land itself, which could only be *put away* by the punishment of the offenders. Then follows ver. 22. *If a damsel that is a virgin be betrothed unto an husband, and a man find her in the city and lie with her, then shall ye bring them both unto the gate of that city, and ye shall stone them with stones that they die: the damsel, because she cried not, being in the city ; and the man, because he hath HUMBLED HIS NEIGHBOUR'S WIFE.*

Such is the law of THE MOST HIGH against *adultery,* or the *defilement of a man's wife.* Yet it is not the object of our *municipal* law as any *public* offence whatsoever. The injured husband may bring a civil action for private damages; but neither the *adulterer,* nor the *adulteress,* can be indicted or punished,[58] as a *public offender,* by any one *statute* throughout our whole code of laws. How far

---

of *translators,* the accuracy of *lexicographers,* or the wisdom of *commentators,* either critical or explanatory, we must have recourse to the *word itself* in the original; and if we find, that in all its connections throughout the *Hebrew* scriptures, it never is used but in *one single sense,* we are not warranted to put any *other* upon it.

58   "In the year 1650, when the ruling powers found it for their interest to put on the semblance of a very extraordinary strictness and purity of morals; not only *incest* and wilful *adultery* were made capital crimes, but also the repeated act of keeping a brothel, or committing fornication, were (upon a second conviction) made felony without benefit of clergy. But at the restoration, when men, from an abhorrence of the hypocrisy of the late times, fell into a contrary extreme of licentiousness, it was not thought proper to renew a law of such unfashionable rigour. And these offences have been ever since left to the feeble coercion of the *spiritual court,* according to the rules of the canon law; a law which has treated the offence of incontinence, nay even *adultery itself,* with a great degree of tenderness and lenity; owing perhaps to the celibacy of its first compilers. *The temporal courts* therefore take no cognizance of the crime of *adultery,* otherwise than as a private injury." *Blackstone,* vol. iv. p. 64. *Id.* vol. i. 433.

this is seen to be for the comfort of society, and the honour of a *Christian* nation, let others determine; I can only say, that, if the law of God (which by the way is as clear and positive a law as can be conceived) took place, we should hardly hear of such daily offences against it, as now disgrace, dishonour, and defile the land. Such however is the *consistency* of our *statute laws*, such their *conformity* to the law of *God*, that they make a man a *felon*, and, but for the *benefit of clergy*, liable to suffer *death*, if he have *two* wives of *his own*; but he may seduce and debauch as *many wives* of *other people*, as may fall in his way, and he is free from punishment, except, as I said before, by way of *civil action* for the wrong done to the husband.

It is said, indeed, that[59] "our law considers marriage in no other light but as a *civil contract*, and leaves the holiness of the marriage-state to the *ecclesiastical courts*;" but surely in a *Christian* land, "the holiness of the marriage-state" ought to be an object of the *municipal* laws, as of infinitely greater consequence to the *public*, and to the peace and welfare of society, than many other offences, which are properly deemed objects of their utmost severity. For what are the consequences of *adultery*, even in a temporal view? *All* its evils cannot be reckoned—but only to mention a *few*—It must introduce a total confusion as to the offspring, a defeating of rightful heirs, an utter obscurity as to family descents and pedigrees; for where *adultery* is, no man can know his own children, or even ostensible brothers and sisters ascertain their relation to each other: for which, as well as for many other wise causes, doubtless it was (as well as to preserve the sanctity of the marriage-institution) made *capital* by the *DIVINE LAWGIVER*. This we may humbly presume to be the case; for this offence is introductory of that kind of disorder, which must, in the very nature of it, tend to destroy every bond of *civil* and religious society, and make the world, in a moral sense, a mere *chaos*.

Why then is *adultery*, notwithstanding it is condemned by the positive law of God, so frequently, so shamelessly, so openly practiced? It is because the law of God being disregarded in the conscience, and not enforced by the laws of

---

59   Bishop *Burnet*, in his history of the Reformation, speaking of the state of the church before that period, said—"The unmarried state both of *seculars* and *regulars* gave infinite scandal to the world; for it appeared that restraining them from having *wives of their own,* made them conclude that they had a *right to all other men's*: and the inferior *clergy* were no better, &c." See Crit. History of England, p. 141. Blackstone Comm.

the land in all its terror, its importance is not adverted to. For though outward laws may not reach the heart, they frequently, by restraining the outward actions of men, may lead them to view such offenses in a different light than when there is no punishment attending them.

Such is the depravity of mankind, that we find the saying of the *Preacher* generally true: *Because sentence against an evil work is not executed speedily, therefore the heart of the sons of men is fully set in them to do evil.* Eccl. viii. 11. *Impunity begets security*; and this must produce and multiply *transgression*.

As to those reliques of the *Pope's* tyranny in this country, commonly called the *ecclesiastical courts*[60], their power is but very *feeble*; for which I and every free Protestant ought to be thankful. This sort of *imperium in imperio*, which excludes trials by *juries* in criminal matters, and substitutes paper depositions in the place of *vivâ voce* evidence, is too abhorrent from every principle of our free constitution to be endured; and I am astonished, that at the Reformation, their very being was not annihilated, as that of the *star-chamber* was afterwards, 16 Car. I. These[61] courts, however, have cognizance of the crime of *adultery*, for which they can set the offender on a *joint stool* in a *white sheet*, under title *Penance*; unless,

---

60   An instance of the oppression of these courts, and the tyranny they exercise where they can, may appear from the following case:—*Ann Jenkinson* was presented at the *primary* visitation of the *Archbishop of York*, 1777, for *fornication*, she being with child by C. D. a *single man*. The case was, that the man had *promised her marriage*, not only privately to herself, but also before the *Justice*, when she swore C. D. to be the father of the child. He soon after married another woman. The *spiritual* court proceeded against the *poor girl*, thus abandoned by the man, and without ever citing her, sent an *excommunication* down, which was *red and returned* accordingly. Another was *cited* on such an account, but could not take out *her penance*, because she could not pay a certain *sum of money* which was demanded: so that it is possible she may also have been *excommunicated*.

The late Mr. *Shenstone*, in his works, vol. ii. p. 258. 4th edit. gives several definitions of the word *church*. Among others is the following, viz.— "A body of people who too frequently harrass and infest the *laity* according to law, and who conceal their *real names* under that of a *spiritual court*."

No man, says Bishop *Burnet*, was more sensible of the abuses of the court called the *spiritual court*, than Archbishop *Usher* was. No man knew the beginning and progress of them better, nor was more touched with the ill effects of them. Life of Bishop *Bedell*, p. 85.

61   In antient times, the *King's* courts, and especially the *Leets*, had power to enquire of and punish *fornication* and *adultery*; but by 13 Ed. I. Stat. 4. called the statute of *circumspecté agatis*, these matters were turned over to the *ecclesiastical* courts. See 1 *Burn*, 662, 663. Also 2 *Burn*, 144, 145.

under title[62] *Commutation*, he or she can buy off their sin and shame with a *sum of money*. See 1 Burn. Ecc. Law, 663, quarto. Whatever be the cause, most certain it is, that the crime of *adultery* daily increases amongst us, insomuch, that one would think many of the *British ladies*, once famed for their modesty, chasity, and sobriety, either never red their *Bibles* at all, or else only that edition of it which was printed by the company of *Stationers*, in the reign of *Charles* the *First* (and for which *Archbishop Laud* fined them severely in the *star-chamber*) wherein they printed the *seventh commandment* without the word *not*, so that it stood, *Thou shalt commit adultery*.

But if in reading the *Hebrew Bible* we restrain the word נאף *adultery* in the *seventh* commandment, to the *married woman* only, and to the *man who defiles her*, do we not leave the man, who, having *one wife*, takes *another*[63], out of its reach?

---

62   All this wicked traffic of *penance* and *commutation* was originally derived from the doctrine of *indulgences*; concerning which, *Tetzel* and his associates, when describing the benefit of *indulgences*, and the necessity of purchasing them, a little before the *Reformation*, thus express themselves:—"The efficacy of indulgences is so great, that the most heinous sins, even if one should *violate* the *mother of* God, would be remitted and expiated by them, and the person freed both from *punishment* and *guilt*. For *twelve-pence* you may redeem the soul of your father out of *purgatory*."

Tetzel was sent into *Germany*, in the time of *Leo* the *Tenth*, with a large cargo of *indulgences*, which he disposed of for the raising a sum of money for the *Pope*. *Tetzel* affirmed, that he could not only pardon *sins past*, but also *sins to come*; whereupon a *German* gentleman bought *such* a pardon of him, and afterwards robbed *Tetzel* of the money. *Tetzel* threatening him, the other said, he had *bought his pardon*, declaring *that* was the sin which he determined to commit. To which *Tetzel* could not reply.

63   The wise, holy, uniform, and connected scheme of God's *moral* government, with respect to the *commerce of the sexes*, has *two* principal ends in view. The *one*, to prevent all *confusion of issue*—the *other*, to secure the *female sex* from that which must lead to it. Therefore a woman's going from *one man to another* is in all cases made a *capital offence*, and punishable with *death*. On the other hand, no man could *take* a woman, and then wantonly *forsake* her. This, being apparently the source of *adultery* and *prostitution*, is positively forbidden. The law which forbids this, though conceived in *general* terms, without any limitation or exception, must, in some cases, fail of the provision it has made for the above purposes, without the allowance of *polygamy*; as, where the man *taking* the woman was *married before*. It is therefore necessary for us to enter deeply into this question; which I shall endeavour in the next *chapter*, not on the precarious footing of *popular prejudice* and *vulgar opinion*, concluding that we are wiser than the inhabitants of more extensive parts of the globe; but on the firm basis of *divine revelation*, concluding that God is *wiser* than *man*.

I answer—It is not for us to judge in this matter, but by the rule of *God's* word; if *that* brings such a case within the reach of the *seventh commandment*, or of any one interpretation of it which is to be found in the *book of that law*, then such a man is *condemned*: if otherwise, he is free—*For where there is no law, there is no transgression.* Rom. iv. 15. *And sin is not imputed* (ελλογεῖται, reckoned, charged, brought to account) *where there is no law.* Rom. v. 13.

By the *book of the law*, I mean the *Pentateuch*, or *five* books of *Moses*, delivered by *God* himself to that eminent *servant* and *prophet* of the Most High, and by him committed to writing, and delivered to the people. To the *book of this law* the great *apostle of the Gentiles* evidently refers, Gal. iii. 10. where he says, *Cursed is every one, that continueth not in all things which are written in the book of the law, to do them.* Our *Lord's* forerunner, *John the Baptist*, declared *the law was given by Moses, John* i. 17. There is therefore *no* law but that which was given by *God* to *Moses*, nor was any *new law* enacted after the canon of the *Pentateuch* was closed by the death of *Moses*. The distinction and difference of *moral good* and *evil* were then unalterably fixed, and the nature of *both* invariably to remain the same. *What God doeth, it shall be forever; nothing can be added to it, nor anything taken from it: and God doeth it that men should fear before Him.* Eccl. iii. 14.

As I am fully persuaded, on the most mature deliberation, that taking from *God's* law in *some* points, and adding to it in *others*, are the chief causes of the evil complained of, with regard to the ruin of *one* sex, by the lust, cruelty, treachery, and perfidy of the *other*; I shall examine the subject before us the more freely: not supposing that *polygamy*, being made *felony* by that sanguinary statute 1 Jac. I. c. 11. is therefore *sinful* in the sight of *God*, any more than that *adultery* is *innocent* before Him, or one jot the more so, because our statute-book has ordained no punishment for it whatsoever. Nor does its being looked upon with detestation and abhorrence in this part of the world, any more prove the *unlawfulness* of *polygamy* in the sight of *God*, than the approbation and practice of it in other more extensive parts[64] of the globe, can prove its *lawfulness*. All must stand or fall

---

64   The *pride* and *self-importance* so natural to fallen man are the true reasons why people of all climes and countries are apt to imagine themselves in the *right* and all others who differ from them in the *wrong*. The *Turk* despises the *Christian* because he is not a *polygamist*; the *Christian*, in his turn, abhors the *Turk* because he is—What shall decide between them? *Custom, usage, prejudice of*

by God's own revelation of His *own* will, in His *own* law. To suppose that His law can be different in different parts of the world, which he hath made, and upholds *with the word of His power*; or that His one uniform jurisdiction doth not equally and invariably extend over all His reasonable creatures; is to think of Him as the poor idolatrous, ignorant *Syrians* did—*The* Lord *is* God *of the hills, but he is not the* God *of the vallies*. 1 Kings xx. 28.

Near akin to this, is the supposition that *God* can change his mind, and be of one mind in the *Old Testament*, and of another in the *New Testament*; if so, He may now have changed His mind again, and neither of these books contain a single syllable which can be depended upon; so that after all the pains we can take to acquaint ourselves with the *divine* mind and will, we may be as utter strangers to them as the savages in *America* are.—But when we search the indelible records of truth, we find that the attribute of *unchangeableness* shines, with a distinguished lustre; *I am Jehovah*, saith He, *I change not*. Mal. iii. 6. God is *one*—His will is *one*—therefore *this*, no more than *Himself*, can know any alteration, diminution, or change. What was *law*[65] at the *beginning* will be *law* to the *end*; and therefore what that *law* is, as touching the point in question, I will now proceed, with the

---

education, national belief, municipal laws—have as much to plead on one side as on the other. These may say—

Non nostrum inter vos tantas componere lites.

The only decisive appeal which can be made, must be to the *Hebrew* scriptures, unless we are to suppose that the *Great Moral Governor* of the *universe* had no *mind* or *will* concerning the matter, or that he left his church and people in the dark for four thousand years together, touching an affair of such infinite consequence. As for imagining that he left the adjustment of *marriage* to the days of the New Testament (which is a popular notion amongst us) having suffered the *Jews* to live in ignorance and error concerning it for so many preceding ages—this is as false in point of fact, as if it were said, that they lived without any *revelation* at all. As surely as the writings of *Moses* contain the law of God, so surely was the law of *marriage* adjusted and settled in the minutest particular. Among other reasons why this must necessarily have been the case, is that very conclusive one, which arises from the dependence of the lawfulness of the *issue* on the lawfulness of the *marriage*, and of course the preservation of true *genealogy* throughout the whole *Jewish* dispensation; a matter in which our dearest and eternal interest is concerned.

65   This is true even of the *ceremonial law*, as to its *meaning* and *substance*. It cannot be less true of the *moral* law, which is founded in the relation that mankind bears to God and each other, and therefore must be as *immutable* as that *relation* is.

confidence which the love of truth inspires, and with a proper disregard for the fallacious and unscriptural reasonings of men, in the freest manner to consider.

CHAPTER IV.

Of POLYGAMY.

I PROMISED the *Reader*, that the proofs for what I advance should be drawn from the *word of* God; and, for my own sake, as well as that of the *truth*, I find myself more especially bound to keep this promise, with respect to the subject before us: for if I were to go to *human* authorities, I should wander into such an endless labyrinth of difference and contradiction, as to lose sight of everything but fruitless[66] disputation.

That the mischiefs which must inevitably attend *polygamy* on the *woman's* side, do not accrue from it on the part of the *man*, is very clear: and on this principle, we may account for the total difference which is put between them in the *divine law*—the one punished with *death*, the other not so much as mentioned in a *criminal* light. So far from being prohibited or condemned by the *law*, we find it *allowed, owned*, and even *blessed* of God: and in no one instance, amongst the many recorded in scripture, so much as *disapproved*.

By *polygamy*, I would be understood to mean[67], what the word literally

---

66   Fruitless indeed! For the great *Puffendorf*, B. vi. c. i. §17. says— "Whether or not this practice be repugnant to the *law of nature*, is a point not fully settled among the learned." He then gives the arguments on both sides, "leaving the decisive judgment to be passed by the reader." So that upon the footing of *human wisdom—adduc sub judice lis est*. The author therefore only considers it on the footing of the *divine law*, conceiving it impossible to determine its *lawfulness* or *unlawfulness* in God's sight by any thing else. According to this law will all men be judged at the last day: therefore, to appeal to any other, in matters of conscience, is absurd to the last degree. There is no other principle or means of discovering the mind and will of God touching this, or any other religious truth, no other rule or measure of judging and determining any thing about it or concerning it, but only the *writing* from whence it is taken, it being wholly of divine revelation, and that revelation being only expressed in that writing. See Dr. Owen on the Scriptures, p. 18.

67   *Polygamy*, strictly speaking, is of two sorts; either when one woman promiscuously admits of more husbands than one, or when one man is at the same time joined in marriage to more than

imports, the *having* and *cohabiting with more than one wife at a time*. Whether taken together, as seems to be the case of king *Jehoash*, 2 *Chron.* xxiv. 3. or first *one* and then *another*, as *Jacob*, Gen. xxix. 28. or *David*, 1 Sam. xxv. 43; it was *this* which was *allowed* of *God*, consequently practised by His people. The *putting away* or divorcing *one* woman, in order to take *another*, was as much forbidden in the Old Testament as in the *New*. *God* says, Deut. xxii. 29. *She shall be his wife; he may not put her away all his days.* So before, ver. 19; and again, Exod. xxi. 10. *If he take him another wife, her food (i.e. of the first wife) her raiment, and her duty of marriage, he shall not[68] diminish.* Putting away or *divorcing* a *first* wife in order to take a *second*, is a palpable breach of these laws, and therefore treated by the great and infallible *interpreter* of them as a heinous offence against *God*, it being a breach of that obligation, laid upon the man, to consider his wife as *one flesh* with himself, and, as such, to cleave to her for life, as *bone of his bone, flesh of his flesh*, Gen. ii. 23; which our *Lord* cites, and reasons upon, to prove the abomination of such a proceeding, as absolutely contrary to the original institution of the *marriage-bond*.

This, however, was the common practice of the profligate *Jews* of that day, who abused the liberty of *divorce* permitted by *Moses* in certain cases, to the most licentious purposes, so as to make *marriage* little better than a pretence for gratifying their lusts, divorcing *one*, in order to take *another*, and thus profaning the holy ordinance of God, by giving it no higher place in their esteem, than as a means of indulging their depraved appetites. A monstrous practice! against which *Christ's* discourse, *Matth.* xix. 4, &c. is levelled, not against *polygamy*, as considered simply in itself. If we interpret this passage as such an explanation of *God's* law *from the beginning*, as will serve to prove all *polygamists are[69]* adulterers,

---

one woman—The former of these is too abhorrent from *nature, reason,* and *scripture*, to admit of a single argument in its favour, or even to deserve a moment's consideration. The author therefore, by the word *polygamy*, only means the *latter*, throughout this treatise.

68 לא יגרע —not *withhold— withdraw— keep back— ἀποσερήσει, LXX*; much less shall he *put her away.*

69 *Adultery* is marked as a mortal sin, Gen. xx. 3. in the history of *Abimelech* king of *Gerar,* and *polygamy* therein stands as utterly distinguished from it—this in the judgment of *Jehovah himself.*

we must condemn a large generation of *God's* dearest servants and children; and instead of believing that *all these died in faith, Heb.* xi. 13. we must say, that many of them died in a state of *unbelief* and *disobedience*; and instead of looking for *Abraham, Jacob, David,* &c. in the kingdom of *heaven*, we must look for them in the kingdom of *Satan*; for his they were, and him they served, if *polygamy* be an offence against the law *from the beginning*, under which these people lived and died, without the least repentance, or any signs of it, as *adulterers, fornicators, and whoremongers*. That is the infallible[70] consequence of the common interpretation of this passage; for *Christ* does not ground the authority of what *He* declares on any *new law* which he was introducing, but on an explanation of God's *law* from the *beginning*, revealed first to *Adam*, afterwards recorded by *Moses*, that it might be transmitted to all succeeding generations, as the one rule of faith and practice, for all those to whom *God's* word should come, to the end of the world. *Neither with you only*, saith *Moses* to the people (then present at the re-publication of God's law, Deut. xxix. 14, 15.) *do I make this covenant and this oath, but with him that standeth here with us this day, before the* Lord *our* God, *and also with him that is not (or those who are not) here with us this day*, i.e. with all succeeding generations, till time shall be no more.

Therefore Christ, so far from altering, changing, or destroying the law delivered from *God by Moses*, enters a *caveat* against such a supposition (Matt. v. 17.) *Think not that I am come to destroy the law or the prophets; I am not come to destroy, but to fulfil: for verily I say unto you, 'till heaven and earth pass, one jot or one tittle shall in no wise pass from the law, 'till all be fulfilled*—ἕως ἂν πάντα γένηται—*until all things be done. Hammond.* And again (Luke xvi. 17.) *It is easier for heaven and earth to pass, than one tittle of the law to fail.* This not only stamps *unchangeableness* upon the *law*, but upon its *import, sense,* and *meaning*, as *one*

Comp. Gen. xxvi. 9, 10, 11. See post.

70   *For sin is the transgression of the law.* 1 John iii. 4. *All unrighteousness* (i.e. *all unconformity to the law) is sin.* 1 John v. 17. *The soul that sinneth, it shall die.* Ezek. xviii. 4. *The wages of sin is death.* Rom. vi. 23. *Whoremongers and adulterers God will judge.* Heb. xiii. 4. The weak arguments which have been made use of to excuse the *sin of polygamy*, as some call it, in the *patriarchs*, and the Old-Testament *saints*, will be fully considered and exposed in this chapter.

and the *same* throughout all ages and generations, as an invariable rule of life for the members of *God's visible church* upon earth, even to the least *jot* or *tittle*.

Notwithstanding, as this passage of Matt. xix. is the chief ground on which that absurd position is built, that "*Polygamy*, though allowed under the law, is forbidden under the *gospel*;" or, "though permitted under the Old Testament, is[71] forbidden under the *New*" (as if there could be a law in the New Testament contradictory to that in the Old Testament) it may be worth our while to consider the matter more minutely.

The question put by the *Pharisees*, Matt. xix. 3. is not, "whether it be lawful to marry two wives at a time, or to take one to another?" but—"*Is it lawful for a man* to put away *his wife for every cause?*" The question concerns *divorce*, and *divorce only.* When we consider *who* it was that is to give the *answer*, we may be certain of its entire pertinence to the *question*. It follows (ver. 4. &c.) *He answered and said unto them, Have ye not read, that He which made them at the beginning, made them male and female, and said, For this cause shall a man leave father and mother, and cleave unto his wife, and they twain (i.e. the man and his wife) shall be one flesh? Wherefore they are no more twain, but one flesh. What therefore God hath joined together, let not man put asunder.*

---

71   The notion that *marriage* under the *New Testament*, is different from what it was under the *Old Testament*, which, as will appear in the *third volume* of this work, is true genuine *Popery*, reminds one of *Moliere's Médecin malgré lui*, where Sganarelle sets forth his profound *medical* and *anatomical* knowledge; as an instance of the *last*, he places the liver on the *right* side, and the *heart* on the *left.*—Geronte says—*On ne peut pas mieux raisonner sans doute. Il n'y a qu'une seule chose qui m'a choqué. C'est l'endroit du foye & du cœur. Il me semble que vous les placez autrement qu'ils ne sont. Que le cœur est du côté gauche, & le foye du côté droit.*

Sganarelle. *Oui cela étoit* autrefois ainsi: *mais nous* avons change' *tout cela, & nous faisons maintenant* la médecine d'une methode toute nouvelle.

Geronte. *C'est ce que je ne sçavois pas, & je vous demande pardon de mon ignorance.*

Sganarelle. *Il n'y a point de mal, & vous n'êtes pas obligé d'être si habile que nous.*

Geronte. "One cannot, doubtless, discourse better on the subject.—There is but one thing that has displeased me—I mean the situation of the *liver* and the *heart.*—It seems to me, that you place them otherwise than they are—that the *heart* is on the *left* side, and the *liver* on the right."

Sganarelle. "Yes, it was formerly so; but we have changed all that, and now-a-days we practise *physic* after a *method entirely new.*"

Geronte. "That I did not know, and I ask your pardon for my ignorance."

Sganarelle. "There's no harm done.—You are not obliged to be as skilful as we are."

With so close, so apposite, so conclusive an answer, grounded on the *old* marriage-institution, not on any *new* dispensation; they ought to have been satisfied that *divorce* was *unlawful*. But they urge him farther, and (ver. 7.) *said unto him—Why did Moses then command to give a writing of divorcement, and put her away? He saith unto them, Moses, because of the hardness of your hearts, SUFFERED you to put away your wives, but from the beginning it was not so* (i.e., that *men* should *put away* their *wives*). *And I say unto you, that whosoever shall put away his wife, except it be for fornication, and shall marry another, committeth adultery; and he who marrieth her who is put away, committeth adultery.*

This last is the verse which has made the difficulty; for if this were meant to condemn *polygamy*, it amounts, so far, to a *contradiction*, or rather *repeal*, of the *old law*, which permitted it; and then more than a *jot or tittle has passed from the law*. If it means that it was *always sinful*, and against the law of GOD, it condemns, as was before observed, all that ever practiced it, and falls heavily on some of the greatest saints that are recorded in scripture as patterns of *faith*, *holiness*, and *obedience*.

This difficulty, like many others in the Scriptures, can only be solved by attending to the character of the speaker, the peculiar circumstances of the persons spoken to, and the particular occasion on which the words were spoken; for want of this, we are apt to interpret the Scriptures more by *sound* than *sense*, and thus make them speak what they never *meant*[72].

The *Jews* at the time of their dispute with Christ on the subject of *divorce*, were fonder of *tradition* than of the Scriptures, and of the teachings of their

---

72   You then whose judgment the right course would steer,
     Know well each antient's proper character;
     His fable, subject, scope of every page;
     Religion, country, genius of his age:
     Without all these at once before your eyes,
     Cavil you may, but never *criticize*.
Eff. onCrit.

If such requisites are necessary for judging properly of the *shallow* productions of mortals, how much more are those above mentioned necessary, that we may judge aright of the *deep things* of God.

rabbis, than of the law of God; insomuch that Christ charges them (*Matt.* xv. 9) with *teaching for doctrines the commandments of men*: and (*Mark* vii. 9, 13.) with *rejecting* and *making the word of God of none effect, through their tradition.* There were several famous *rabbis,* whom they highly reverenced, but particularly *Shammah, Hillel,* and *Akiba.*

The[73] school of *Shammah* taught that man could not be lawfully divorced from his wife "unless he had found her guilty of some action which was really infamous, and contrary to the rules of virtue." But the school of *Hillel*[74], who was *Shammah*'s disciple, taught, on the contrary, that "the least reasons were sufficient to authorize a man to put *away his wife.* For example—if she did not dress his victuals well, or if *he found any other woman he liked better.*" *Akiba* was still more indulgent than *Hillel,* for he affirmed that "it was sufficient cause for a man to *put away his wife,* if she were not agreeable to her husband."

Josephus and *Philo* show very sufficiently that, in their time, the *Jews* believed *divorce* to be lawful for every trivial cause. That the *Pharisees* had learned to explain the toleration of *Moses* in a like extensive manner, may be gathered from the question which they put to our SAVIOR. The above observations may therefore serve as a key to the scripture under consideration. The *Pharisees* (who asked, whether it *was lawful for a man to put away his wife for every cause?*) seem to have been deeply tinctured with that position of *Hillel* and to have adopted that particular cause of *divorce* mentioned by him, that of *seeing a woman they liked better, so putting away one* whom they liked *less* in order to take *another* whom they liked *more.* Against this, CHRIST may be understood to level his answer—

---

73   See *Cruden,* under *divorce.*

74   Shammah and Hillell are supposed to have lived about an hundred years before the destruction of the second temple. Some say they were contemporaries with Herod the Great. See Ant. Univ. Hist. vol. x. p. 429, 469.

Of Akiba it is said—Circa ea tempora vixit—"he lived about those times." Athan. Vinc.

Dr. Owen on the Scripture, p. 227, makes him *armor-bearer* to the Pseudo-Messias *Barchochab,* in the days of *Adrian*; when, in the pursuit of a design to restore their *temple* and *worship,* the *Jews* fell into a rebellion against the *Romans* all the world over. This was about the year 135. From these different accounts, it seems probable that there was more than one person of the name of *Akiba,* or, as some call him, *Aquiba.*

Whosoever putteth away his wife, except for the cause of fornication, and marrieth another, committeth adultery, &c. not as condemning *polygamy* in itself, against which there *was no law*, but under the particular circumstance of unlawful *divorce* to effect it, against which the law of God was from the *beginning*. Such a thing was not contained in Moses's *permission*, nor mentioned therein, but was contrary to the very *institution of marriage*; and, as our Lord shows clearly, verses 4, 5, 6, it was virtually forbidden by the very words of it. It is as unlawful for a *man* to put away or *divorce* his wife for *another woman*, as for a *woman* to put away or *divorce* her husband for *another man*: the *marriage-bond* being *equally* binding in the matter of *putting away*. We may also observe, that though the *saints* of God, of whom we read so much in the Old Testament[75], practiced *polygamy*, yet they did not put away *one wife* in order to make room for *another*. This was as directly forbidden to them by the law of GOD, delivered by *Moses*, as by CHRIST, on the authority of that law, to these *Pharisees*.

Here I would observe that our translators of the *Bible* seem to have paid too much attention to the *Scribes* and *Pharisees* in rendering the passage referred to for the justification of their doctrines about *divorce*. The *Pharisees* say, *Moses* commanded *to give a writing of divorcement, and put her away*. Thus, the *rabbis* construed *Deut.* xxiv. 1, &c. in the *imperative* mood; and we, by doing the same in our translation of that passage, have justified their misinterpretation, and even justify the *divorced woman*'s going to be *another man's wife. She may go* and *be another man's wife*; so we translate, verse 2. No marvel, if this be the case, that

---

75 "The example of the *Heathens* and *Mahometans* may indeed be of no great force in the argument for *polygamy*, because it appears that those people are guilty of many violations of the law of nature; but the *polygamy* of the *fathers* under the *old covenant* is a reason which ingenuous men must confess to be unanswerable." See *Puffendorf*, lib. vi. c. 1. § 18.

Some have thought that the examples of *Abraham, Jacob*, and the other Old-Testament saints are too far removed into antiquity to serve as proofs for the lawfulness of *polygamy*.—But did ever anyone object to the history of *Cain* as an example of the criminality of murder or of God's thoughts on that subject? Or does the *Apostle*, in the Epistle to the *Hebrews*, scruple to recapitulate, by *name* those heroes of antiquity, who did such mighty works by the power of faith, as examples to us? In short, does he not assure us, Rom. xv. 4. *That whatsoever things were written afore-time were written for our learning?* But what can we *learn* from either the *precepts* or *examples* of *old time* if we are to suppose that God has changed His mind upon the subjects which they hold forth to us?

Christ is supposed to *condemn* something which was before *allowed*; whereas the whole passage is suppository or *hypothetical*, and only introductory to that positive law, ver. 4. The whole should be rendered thus if we would avoid the absurdity of supposing *Moses* to *command* what God positively forbade, and to consign a *married woman* into the arms of an *adulterer* in the very face of the *seventh* commandment, by saying, "She *may go and be another man's wife*," ver. 2. This would be establishing[76] adultery by a solemn law.

The Hebrew text should be rendered—*When* (or if) *a man hath taken a wife, or woman, and married her, and it come to pass that she find no favor in his eyes, because he hath found some uncleanness in her, and (IF) he write her a bill of divorcement, and give it in her hand, and send her out of his house, and she shall have departed out of his house, and* (IF) *she go and be another man's wife, and IF the latter husband hate her,* (here we explain the ₁ by an IF, why not before?) *and write her a bill of divorcement*, &c. or *if the latter husband die, which took her to be his wife, her former husband, which sent her away, may not take her again to be his wife after that she is* DEFILED, *for that is abomination before the* LORD, *and thou shalt not cause the land to sin, which the* LORD *thy* GOD *giveth thee for an inheritance.*

Thus the Greek[77] interpreters express the sense of these four verses, and the *Vulgar Latin*, yea, and the *Chaldee* paraphrase may be so understood. So

---

76   The learned *Dr. Whitby*, in order to get rid of this consequence, is for supposing, that these divorces dissolved the *bond of marriage*; but this is directly contrary to what CHRIST asserts, for his whole argument shews, that nothing can do this, but *adultery* in the wife. The *Doctor* was certainly led into this mistake, by our wrong translation of the passage, in *Deut.* xxiv. 1-4.

77   To the testimonies here mentioned, for this interpretation of the *Hebrew* text, we may add that of the learned *Buxtorf*, who observes that in the words of *Moses*, Deut. xxiv. 1-4 (see Jer. iii. 1), this one prohibition only is contained—"*That a man shall not receive again to his bed a wife whom he hath once put away*"—but that the custom itself of *putting away wives* is, in that place, neither approved by *Moses* nor plainly condemned, but left, as it were, indifferent. And the observation of our *Saviour* that this *permission* was given by *Moses, because of the hardness of their hearts,* sufficiently makes it appear, that the *Mosaical* indulgence doth not amount to an approbation, but signifies only a bare toleration, or connivance, exempting from *civil* punishment. See Puffend. b. vi. c. 1. § 23. So *Clark* on Matth. xix. 8. intimates that "*Moses* permitted divorce to prevent a greater civil mischief. He did so far allow of it, as to exempt them that did it from any *civil* punishment, but still it was a transgression of the *moral* law, and so a sin against God."

Tremellius renders the words, and *Vatablus* explains them, *Scripsitque ei libellum repudii et dederit Ei in manu, ejeceritque,* &c. If *he shall have written her a bill of divorce,* &c. "This is not an absolute sentence," saith *Vatablus*, "but ought to be joined to the words following, which show that if such things happened, that if a man divorced his wife, and if another took her, the former husband might not take her again, she having been *defiled*." This proves the same thing contended for by our Lord in His discourse with the *Pharisees*, that those *permissive divorces*, which, says He, *Moses permitted*, ἐπέτρεψεν—not, as the *Pharisees* would have it, ἐνετείλατο, *commanded*—made *no* difference as to the *marriage-bond* in the *sight* of God. The man who *put away his wife* for no other cause than marrying *another*, which was the practice of these people, committed a great sin, not only by not *cleaving to his wife*, as God had commanded, but by *putting her away* for *another woman*, and thus *causing her to commit adultery* with another man. See Matt. 5:32. And in this sense, as *accessory* to his divorced wife's crime, might himself be said to *commit adultery*. But more of this hereafter.

If those *divorces* could have operated, as a *dissolution* of the *first* marriage, she would not have been DEFILED by marrying another man; but this not being the case, she was DEFILED[78] in the sight of GOD, when put away by *unlawful divorce*, as when she went to another man without *any divorce*. Very striking are the words of Jer. iii. 1. *They say, If a man put away his wife, and she go from him, and become another man's, shall she return to her again? Shall not that land be greatly polluted?*—But where is anything like this said of *polygamy*? That *polygamy* was practiced throughout all ages of the *Jewish* economy cannot be denied. It is equally evident that it was the deliberate, open, avowed, and wilful practice of the most *holy* and *excellent of the earth*, of *Abraham*, the *father* of the *faithful*, the *friend of* GOD, Isa. xli. 8., as well as of the most illustrious of his children; and this without the least *reproof* or *rebuke* from GOD or the most distant hint or expression of his displeasure, either by *Moses* or any other of the prophets. No trace of *sorrow, remorse,* or *repentance* touching this matter is to be found in any one instance, and therefore *commentators* are at a loss to maintain the *sinfulness* of

---

78 The word (Deut. xxiv. 4.) which we translate *defiled*, is אמט. The same word is used, Ezek. xviii. 6, 11, 15. for *violating another's wife*.

polygamy, but at the expense of *scripture, reason, and common sense.*

Some say: "It was a *sin*, but God[79] allowed it because of the *hardness of their hearts.*" That *Moses suffered* (ἐπέτρεψεν, *permitted, tolerated*) *divorce*, so far as not to exact the outward punishment of it in certain cases, is evident from the *supposed* circumstances in *Deut.* xxiv. 1, &c. But this was in order to avoid worse mischief among the wicked and profligate part of the community, such as maltreating, beating, or even killing their *hated* wives. This is what we may suppose, at least in part, to be meant by our Lord when He says—*Moses, because of the hardness of your hearts, suffered you to put away your wives.* This is said of *divorce*, not of[80] *polygamy*, as plainly appears by the words of the text. And herein *Moses* seems to have acted more as a *politician* than as a *lawgiver*—by *permission*, not by *commandment*, like that of *Paul*, 1 *Cor.* vii. 6. It is not said—GOD *suffered it*—but *Moses suffered you to put away your wives*: but, Christ adds, *from the beginning it was not* so—i.e. that men should *put away their wives.* Here is not the least hint about polygamy.

Can we suppose, however, that God suffered *Abraham, Jacob, David,* and others of His saints, to break His law, and this for the *hardness of their hearts?*—If they had *hearts of stone*, who ever had a *heart of flesh*? Ezek. xi. 19. Do not reason and common sense start back at *such* a supposition?

Others have absurdly said, "that God, being the sovereign, has a right to *dispense* with his own laws, and having[81] done this, *polygamy* was no sin."

---

79   The idea of JEHOVAH'S allowance of *sin*, and that for ages together, is placing Him, in point of holiness, purity, and justice, below the notion which the heathen had of their gods—*Homer* says—

Οὐ γὰρ χείλια ἔργα θεοὶ μάκαρες φιλέεσι. Odyf. Ξ. Ver. 85.
Yet for the gods their impious acts detest,
And honor justice, and the righteous breast

80   The learned authors of the *Universal History*, vol. iii. p. 137, observe that *Moses*, among other things, "was forced to indulge them (the *Jews*) in *polygamy*." But what could this have to do with *Abraham, Jacob*, and those who lived before *Moses*? It is evident that *polygamy* was practiced by the holiest of the saints, ages before *Moses* existed; therefore, ascribing the practice of it to an *indulgence* of *Moses* is as great a mistake as ascribing the origin of *circumcision* to the *law of Moses*. Comp. Gen. xvii. 10—14. with John vii. 22.

81   The elaborate *Noldius*, after long arguments upon the subject, pro and con, of his own and

We find particular occasional instances of God's dispensing with the rigor of His laws on certain emergencies and for particular purposes, as in David's eating the *shew-bread, which it was not lawful for any but the priests to eat.* Also, in some other instances which might be mentioned. But where do we find a *total* suspension of one of the commandments of the *moral* law for ages together? If it was as great a sin for a man to have *two* wives as for a woman to have *two* husbands, why suspend it on the part of the *man* and not on the part of the *woman*? Why invariably ordain punishment on one side and not on the other, if each was equally sinful against the law itself? *Doth* God *pervert judgment? Or doth the Almighty pervert justice?* Job viii. 3. God is *no respecter of persons.* Acts x. 34. He *accepteth* (*i.e.* with undue and partial favor) *no man's person.* Gal. ii. 6. *As many as have sinned in the law shall be judged by the law.* Rom. ii. 12. Nor is it conceivable that the righteous Judge of all should Himself depart from the rule laid down for His *vice-gerents,* the *judges of the earth (Deut. i. 17.) Ye shall not respect persons in judgment.* No other account then can consistently be given of the matter than what may be gathered from the uniform and unvaried use of the word נאף—*adultery*—in the *seventh* commandment, as relating to the *wife*; that is to say, as forbidding *polygamy* on *her* side, but not to the *husband* as forbidding *polygamy* on his.

Others would make the wise, holy, great, and good men, who were

---

other people's, which may all be seen Heb. Part. Annotat. 225. concludes—*Sanctos veteres polygamos non peccasse coram Deo, quia habuerunt dispensationem specialem & extraordinariam.*—"The *old saints,* who were *polygamists,* did not sin before GOD, because they had a *special and extraordinary dispensation.*" But, 1. Where is such a *dispensation* recorded? 2. The very supposition of such a thing is as absurd as it is profane; more becoming the character of a *Pope of Rome* than of the HOLY GOD. 3. The idea of a *special and extraordinary dispensation* to some, and the leaving others under the *guilt* of sin, seems to be borrowed from the speech of one of the doctors (*Soto*) at the famous Council of *Trent,* who said, "The antient *fathers* had *many wives* by dispensation, and the others, who were not dispensed with, did live in perpetual sin."—*Hist.* of *Council* of *Trent,* Eng. Transl. by *N. Brent,* p. 671. This directly militates against the *universality* of the law, Deut. xxi. 15, which is conceived in as general terms as possible, and most clearly supposes that *any man* might have *two wives.* The *Levirate,* or *law,* Deut. xxv. 5, 6, which *Noldius* calls a *dispensation* for marrying the brother's wife, contrary to Lev. xviii. 16, is very improperly called so, it being a *positive commandment,* established for a *particular purpose,* and both the law itself, and the reason of it are there set down. This is not the case with *polygamy,* for there is no law which prohibits it, nor any to establish a *partial* allowance of it.

polygamists, wholly *ignorant* of the law, as to the true meaning thereof, and say—"*The times of ignorance* God *winked at*"—wresting this text (*Acts* xvii. 30) which speaks of the blind *Gentiles*, who were without the *written law of* God, and making it relate to the *Jews*, to whom *were committed the oracles* of God *Rom.* iii. 1, 2. But, waving this, was Abraham, that *prophet* Gen. xx. 7. whom God, from the familiar intercourse He had with him, calls His[82] friend (Isa. xli. 8.)—was *Jacob*, who spoke with God *face to face* (Gen. xxxii. 30.) *ignorant*? Could Moses, the sacred penman and expounder of the law, be *ignorant*? So *ignorant*, as not to know its true meaning? Could David be *ignorant*? If so, to what little purpose was his *study in it all the day long*? Ps. cxix. 97. Are we to suppose *Solomon* ignorant, to whom God said, Lo, *I have given thee a wise and understanding heart, so that there was none like thee before thee, neither after thee shall any arise like unto thee?* 1 Kings iii. 12. See 1 Kings iv. 29, &c. Compare Matt. xii. 42. Luke xi. 31. Such a solution of the matter will more easily prove the *ignorance* of such commentators than their assertions prove *ignorance* in the holiest and wisest men that ever lived under the light of the Old Testament, where alone God's law is to be found, and on the authority of which the whole New Testament can only[83] stand. The *kings* of *Israel* were expressly commanded to write a copy of the law with *their own hand*; it was to be *with them*, and they were to *read in it daily*. Deut. xvii. 18, 19. The *Priests* and *Levites* could not be *ignorant*; for their *lips were to keep knowledge*, and the people were to *seek the law at their mouth. Mal.* ii. 7. As for the *people*, they not only heard the law constantly but were commanded to write it upon the very *doorposts of their houses*. Deut. vi. 9. Whatever else, therefore, their *polygamy* proceeded

---

82   God saith, *Gen.* xviii. 19. *Shall I hide from Abraham that thing which I do?—for I know him, that he will command his children and his household after him, and they shall keep the way of the* LORD, *to do justice and judgment. How Abraham* could teach others to *keep the way of the* LORD, and yet be ignorant of it himself, cannot easily be conceived. *If the blind lead the blind, both shall fall into the ditch.* Matt. xv. 14.

83   *Ignatius*, Epist. ad Philadelph. c. 8, introduces a *Jew* saying, "Ἐὰν μὴ ἐν τοῖς ἀρχαίιος εὕρω ἐν τῷ Εὐαγγελίῳ πιςεύω—nisi invenero in antiquis (vaticiniis) Evangelio non credo: which I heartily assent to, thus paraphrased—"What I do not find in *Moses and the prophets*, I'll not believe in the *gospel*." But there is no danger of this, no hazard of being put to such a trial; for certainly the New Testament states *none other things than Moses and the prophets did say should come to pass.* Acts xxvi. 22. See Rom. xv. 4. Luke xxiv. 44, 45.

from, it could not be derived from *ignorance*. They could not be *ignorant* of the *seventh* commandment; and supposing that many of them, like their descendants in later times, lost sight of its *spiritual intent*, yet the meaning of its *outward letter* they could hardly be at a loss for, especially as they must observe its uniform and unvaried use throughout the whole of their scriptures. If, therefore, *polygamists* sinned against the *seventh* commandment, they did it with their eyes open; and whoever can believe that such men as we have mentioned could do this without any scruple beforehand, or sorrow afterwards, or the least sign of repentance, must believe more than, for their sakes, and the sake of thousands of God's saints (who though not mentioned as *polygamists*, doubtless were so) I could wish even to surmise, or than is in the least consistent with the account which we have of them in the holy scriptures.

I shall only observe further on this head, of attributing the practice of *polygamy* by the Old Testament saints to *ignorance*, that we must charge *ignorance* on God's high priest *Jehoiada*, who stands recorded in 2 Kings xii. and 2 Chron. xxiv. as one of the wisest, best, and greatest characters that ever lived, as well as one of the most exemplary promoters of God's honor, and a chief instrument of the reformation of religion in *Judah*, in the reign of king[84] *Jehoash*. If so, our charge of *ignorance* will not stop here, but even reach the *Spirit* of God *Himself*. For He says that *Joash did right in the sight of the* Lord *all the days of Jehoiada the priest* (2 Chron. xxiv. 2, or, as it is 2 Kings xii. 2), *all his days, wherein Jehoiada the priest instructed him*; And yet we are told, ver. 3. that *Jehoiada took for him* two wives, *and he begat sons and daughters.* On whom shall the commentator fix *ignorance*? On *Jehoiada* the high priest, for teaching his pupil King *Jehoash* to be a *polygamist* by taking *two wives* for him? Or on *Jehoash*, who received them and *cohabited with them*? Or on the *Holy Ghost*, who bears testimony to the *rectitude* of king *Jehoash*'s conduct *all his days wherein Jehoiada the priest instructed him?*

The learned Bishop Patrick, on 2 Chron. xxiv. 3. says that "*Jehoiada* did not take these *two wives* for the king, but for himself." Supposing it to be so, the proof of the lawfulness of *polygamy* in *Jehoiada*'s opinion is equally strong. But this sense of the *Bishop*'s will hardly arise from the position and construction

---

84 Called Joash also, 2 *Chron*. xxiv.

of the *Hebrew* text: for it does not stand in the order of our translation—*And Jehoiada took for him two wives*—so as to make *him* the relative to *Jehoiada*; but

uxores duas Jehoiada ei tulit Et. Mont. נשים שתים לו יהוירע

[85]וישא Wives two Jehoiada him to brought And So that the לו—*to him*—stands as the relative to the chief subject of the preceding verse, which is evidently King *Jehoash*, whose history the sacred penman is here recording, as a part of which this action of *Jehoiada*'s is here related.

The Bishop is conscious of a difficulty in his interpretation, arising from a constant tradition of the *Jews*, that the *high-priest* was to have but *one wife* at a time, which was founded on Lev. xxi. 13, 14. This he endeavors to get rid of by saying—"It is not certain that *Jehoiada* was *high-priest*, for he is everywhere called *Jehoiada* the *priest*, and but once only (ver. 6) the *chief*."—this is no argument at all against his being *high-priest*, for *Abiathar*, who was *high-priest*, is nowhere called so in the Old Testament, but always *the priest*; so his father *Abimelech*, as the *Bishop* himself observes on 1 Sam. xxi. 1; so *Eli the priest*, 1 Sam. ii. 11; *Zadoc the priest*, 1 Kings iv. 2; 1 Chron. xxix. 22; and even *Aaron* himself, Ps. xcix. 6. The title of ראש—the *chief*, or *head*, which is given to *Jehoiada*, ver. 6, signifies certainly more than "the chief of one of the courses of priests."—His having apparently the conduct and management of everything[86] relating to the temple, his anointing *king Jehoash* (comp. 1 Kings i. 45.) and many other circumstances related of him, bespeak him plainly to be no less than high-priest; and therefore the word ראש— *chief*, or *head*—denotes this here, as it does that Seraiah was a[87] high-priest, 2 Kings xxv. 18. For all which reasons it seems clear that *Jehoiada* (who had before married *Jehoshabeath*, the sister of king *Ahaziah*, 2 Chron. xxii. 11.) took not these *two wives* for himself, but for King *Joash*.

---

85   The verb נשא certainly signifies to take a wife for *one's self*—but it also signifies to *take* or *bring* a wife *for another*. See Ezra ix. 2, 12. Neh. xiii. 25; in which passages the word אשא is used in both these senses.

86   As well as the entire management and command over all the Priests and Levites, See 2 Chron. xxiii. 4-8.

87   That *Seraiah* was defended in a right line from *Eleazar* the son of *Aaron*, appears 1 Chron. vi. 4-14. and of course succeeded to the *high-priesthood*. As such he is registered. Ibid.

These things are too plain not to force conviction on the minds of many; therefore it is that they have said with the learned author of the *"Historical Library"*—*"Polygamy*, though not expressly *allowed*, is however *tacitly implied* in the law of Moses." This goes farther than those I have mentioned, but yet does not come up to the matter. For if it is forbidden by the *seventh* commandment, or by any other law, it is as contradictory to scripture to say that it was *tacitly implied* as that it was *expressly allowed*. This last is the truth; it was *expressly allowed*, and that by God *Himself*: a direct proof that it was not forbidden by the *seventh* commandment, or by any other law, unless we can suppose the all-wise God to be so inconsistent with Himself, as to *forbid*, and yet *allow*, the same thing under the same circumstances.

Some have found out that *"polygamy* was allowed for the more expeditious peopling of the world."—Supposing it is a means of increasing[88] population (which by the way will admit of great doubt), yet where was the use of this amongst the *Jews*, when, before their entrance into *Canaan*, they were as the *stars in heaven for multitude?* Deut. 1:10; and yet *polygamy* did not cease after

---

88   This common notion, or rather *vulgar error*, is adopted by *St. Augustine*, De Civ. Dei, lib. xvi. c. 38. where, speaking of the antient *polygamy*, he says it was lawful—*Quoniam multiplicanda posteritatis causa plures uxores lex nulla prohibebat.* "Because, for the sake of *multiplying posterity*, no law forbade many wives."—Thus thought many of the *fathers*, and the *Romish* Church in general, until the doctrine of *dispensations* was introduced; then they said it was a *sin*; but God gave a *dispensation* to some to practice it—thus artfully making the *Holy* God a dispenser with *sin*, and setting an example for the *Pope's* first *making sins*, and then *dispensing* with them. But let us suppose ten men and ten women—can it be imagined that if these ten women are each severally married to one man, they are not likely to have as many children as if they were all married to one of the men? *Porter*, in his Observations on the *Turks*, says, p. 292, that the number of children in *Turkish* families is not what the idea of *polygamy* suggests; that they have not, in general, so many children as are found in common families of *Christians* and *Jews*—he even uses this as an argument against *polygamy*. On the other hand, many have contended for the permission of *polygamy* as "a speedier means of peopling the world; it appearing that in *polygamous* countries, people abound more than in others that are *monogamous*." But I take the real state of the case, upon the whole, to be this; wherever there are the most *married* women, there the increase of the people will be the greatest. *Polygamy*, therefore, as tending to increase the number of *married* women, must certainly tend to *population*. But then we are to suppose, that women who are married under *polygamous* contracts, would not otherwise be married at all; for in no other view can *polygamy* be said to increase *population*; in this it certainly must.

their entrance into the *promised* land.

As for all *popular* arguments against polygamy, which the wisdom of this world has invented and believed as so many certain conclusions on the side of truth, they equally apply against the wisdom and holiness of God in *allowing* it, as against those who *maintain* it: Therefore, as *He will be justified in His sayings and clear when He is judged,* Rom. iii. 4. the best answer which can be given for the present is that included in the awful question of the *Apostle,* Rom. ix. 20, "*Nay but, O man, who art thou that repliest against* God?" Though this immediately relates to another point, yet it is applicable to all the vain reasonings of men against the dispensations of *Providence,* either in the *natural* or *moral* world. Such reasonings, when thoroughly canvassed and set in their true light, will appear to be neither more nor less than the pleadings of human *pride* on behalf of human *ignorance.* Our prejudices and our opinions reciprocally affect each other, and, upon examination, they will usually be found as much alike as the *image* and the *mold* it is cast in.

> "Go wiser thou, and in thy seale of sense,
> Weigh thy opinion against *Providence*—
> Call imperfection what thou fanciest such,
> Say, *here* He gives too little—*there* too much—
> "Snatch from His hand the balance and the rod,
> Rejudge His justice, be the God of God.
> "In pride, in reasoning pride, our error lies,
> All quit their sphere, and rush into the skies;
> And who but wishes to invert the laws
> Of *order*, sins against the ETERNAL CAUSE.
> All this dread *order* break—for whom?—for thee?
> Vile worm! Oh madness! pride! impiety!
> Go teach ETERNAL WISDOM how to rule,
> Then drop into *thyself*—and be a *fool.*
> From pride, from pride, our very reas'ning springs—
> Account for *moral*, as for *nat'ral* things:
> Why charge we *Heaven* in *those*, in *these* acquit?—
> In *both*, to *reason right*, is to *submit.*"

Essay on Man.

In fewer, but still more forcible and humbling words, Paul expresses himself to the *self-wise* among the *Corinthians*—and in *them* to *us*—1 Cor. iii. 18, 19.—*Let no man deceive himself*—*If any man among you seems to be wise in this world*—εν τω αιωνι τχτω—like the philosophers, *politicians*, and *rabbis* of the *age* (GUYSE) *let him become a* fool *that he may be wise*—*for the wisdom of this world* is foolishness with God.

Though it be beside my design, in this treatise, to consider the subjects thereof on any other footing than as they appear in the scriptures; yet I will so far depart from my purpose, as to take notice of a *popular* argument *against polygamy*, which, in the minds of some learned and considerate men, has been of such importance as to outweigh all that could be said *for* it. It is this—"The *males* and *females* brought into the world are nearly on a balance, only allowing a little excess on the side of the *males*; whence it follows that nature intends only one wife for the same person; if they have more, some others must[89] go without any." This

---

89   So must it be, even upon the principle of *monogamy*; for if, according to these calculators, there are more *males* than *females*, it is not possible that *every* man can have a *wife*; some *must go without*. However, a departure either way from the original proportion of *one male* and *one female* destroys all arguments which can be drawn from thence against *polygamy*; for the precedent which this might otherwise have been, being departed from by the *Creator* Himself, it of course ceases with respect to His creatures. Major *Grant* observes that a little excess on the side of the *males*—"is to make up for the extraordinary expense thereof in war and at *sea*"—to which others have added, as a consideration also, "the laborious and dangerous employments in which men are engaged and women are not." As for *war*—it is written—*Whence come wars and fightings among you? Come they not hence, even of your lusts* (ἡδονῶν, the desires after sensual gratifications) *which war in your members? Ye lust and have not, ye kill and desire to have, and cannot obtain,* &c. James iv. 1, 2. So *Plato* in his Phædo, § 10, Edit. Cantab. 1673, p. 88. και γαρ πολεμος και στασεις και μάχας δεν αλλο παρέχει η το σωμα και οι τοῖς ἐπιθυ μιαι. *"For nothing but the body and its lusts* (or evil desires) *produce wars, seditions, battles."* Can it be reasonably supposed that the *Almighty*, whose gracious command is—*Thou shalt love thy neighbor as thyself*—is directed, in the proportion of *males* and *females*, by the most horrid and fatal proofs which men are daily giving of their enmity to Him and each other? And that more men than women are born into the world on this account? These *wars*, together with the extension of commerce and the calls of numberless artificial wants which luxury has introduced, certainly expose the lives of men to the dangers of the *sea*. *But who has required this at their hands?*—Let a *heathen* give the answer:

Nequicquam DEUS abscidit
Prudens oceano diffociabili
Terras, si tamen impiæ

argument, plausible as it may seem, wants one essential to *solidity*, which is truth. For saying which, I will, by way of justification, transcribe a few paragraphs from Dr. FORSTER'S "*Observations during a Voyage round the World*"—published 1778. This ingenious author, who seems to be a most strenuous *monogamist*, after speaking of "*Monogamy* established in the isles of the *South Sea*," very candidly says—"But here I find myself obliged to confess, that I am not as yet persuaded of the great and universal argument for *monogamy*, viz. the *equal proportion of women to men*; as, in my opinion, it is not clearly proved that this just proportion holds place in all countries and climates. On the contrary, I am of opinion, that

---

Non tangenda rates transiliunt vada.
Audax omnia perpeti
Gens humana ruit per vetitum nesas.

Hor

Divided by th' unhabitable main,
If ships profane, with fearless pride,
Bound o'er th' inviolable tide.
No laws, or human or divine,
Can the presumptuous race of man confine.

Francis.

God *hath made man upright, but they have sought out many inventions*, saith *Solomon*, Eccl. vii. 29. To imagine that the providential dispensations of the ALL-WISE GOD are to be accommodated to *these*, or regulated by them, is surely too absurd to bear an argument.

As for "laborious employments, many of which are attended with danger, and which usually fall to the share of the males," let as many of these be selected as can be deemed *necessary*, and then, against them, let us set—the many diseases to which *females* are peculiarly liable, and to which *men* are *not*—let us add to these the peril of childbirth, and then, this last supposed *reason* for more males being born than *females*, will be as groundless as the two former.

I should imagine that no opinions whatsoever, however false and absurd, are without having *reasons* given for them. Nor is it to be doubted that a *Ptolemaist* would give as many reasons for the *sun's* going *round the earth*, as a *Copernican* would for the *earth's* going *around the sun*.

The following question is said to have been once laid before a certain very learned body:—Take a tub of water weighing one ton—into which put a *salmon* of thirty pounds weight; Why will not the tub be heavier than before the fish was put into it? The fact being taken for granted, produced many *wise* reasons for it; but none were thought *so wise* and adequate as—*Corpora non gravant in loco suo*—therefore, the *fish* being in its *place* or proper element lost its power of adding any thing to the weight of the tub of water. At last, it was proposed to weigh the tub, both with and without the fish; when, to the confusion of all their reasonings, the matter ended as the reader may conceive.

the constitution of food and climate, and the prevailing custom of marrying many wives, have, by length of time, produced a considerable disparity between the numbers of men and women; so that now, to one man, several women are born. This observation is really confirmed by fact; for *all* the voyagers unanimously agree, that among all the *African* nations *polygamy* is customary; nor has any one observed that there are men among these nations *without wives*, for every one is matched to *one* or *more* females." Here he refers to Bosman's "Description of the coast of *Guinea*," "who likewise," says the Doctor "expressly declares, that the number of women *much* exceeds that of the men."—"When a *polygamous* nation lives in the neighborhood of *monogamous* nations, there is always a probability that the women necessary for so many men who have *more* than one wife are obtained by stealth, force, or by commerce from the neighboring nations; but in *Africa*, all the nations are *polygamous*; every man is *married* and has *more* than *one* wife. They procure these wives from the neighboring tribes where the same custom prevails. It is therefore, in my opinion, a clear and settled point that the women born among these nations must be more numerous than the males.

Though the colonists at the *Cape of Good Hope* are *monogamous*[90], I observed, in the various families of the town and country, the number of females to prevail.—It has been observed[91] in Sweden, more females than males have been born during the latter part of this century—it is reported in the kingdom of *Bantam*, even *ten* women are born to *one* man;" and refers to Lord *Kames's* Hist.

---

90   *Kempfer*, on numbering the people of *Meaco*, in the kingdom of *Japan*, found the females to *exceed* the males in the following proportion:

Females, 223,573

Males,   182,072

41,501 more *females* than *males*.

Spirit of Laws, vol. i. p. 373

91   How far this observation may hold good in this kingdom I know not—but, being lately on an occasional visit to the *vicar* of a country village, I had the curiosity to look into the parish register of births; I took ten years in the latter part of the last century, *viz.* from 1670 to 1679, inclusive, and there appeared to have been born in that space 19 more *males* than *females*.

In the space between 1770 to 1779, inclusive, the number of *females* born exceeded that of the *males* by 27.

of Man, vol. I. p. 176." *Montesquieu*, Spirit of Laws—Eng. Trans. 4th edition, octavo—vol. i, p. 374. mentions this—"I confess," says he, "if what history tells us be true, that at *Bantam* there are *ten* women to *one* man, this must be a case peculiarly favorable to *polygamy*."

From all this it appears to me, that, unless we can find that GOD delivered to *Moses* as many different laws to govern the actions of His reasonable creatures, as there are different parts of the globe inhabited by them, so as that there is one law for the inhabitants of *Asia* and *Africa*, and another for those of *Europe*, this sort of arguments, drawn from the outward appearances of things in different parts of the world, proves nothing on either side of the question, but the exceeding ignorance of mankind as touching the acts and dispensations of that INFINITELY WISE BEING, whose *judgments are unsearchable, and His ways past finding out!* Rom. xi. 33.

The best and fairest, and indeed the only way to get at the truth, on this as on every other occasion where religion is concerned, is to lay aside *prejudice*, from whatever source it may be derived, and to let the *Bible* speak for itself. Then we shall see that *polygamy*, notwithstanding the *seventh* commandment, was allowed by God *Himself*, who, however others might mistake it, must infallibly know His own *mind*, be perfectly acquainted with His own will, and thoroughly understand His own *law*. If He did not intend to allow *polygamy*, but to prevent or condemn it, either by the *seventh* commandment, or by some other law, how is it possible that He should make laws for its *regulation*, any more than He should make laws for the *regulation* of *adultery, theft,* or *murder*? How is it conceivable that He should give the least countenance to it, or so express His approbation of it, as even to *work miracles* in support of it? For making a woman *fruitful* who was naturally *barren*, must have been the effect of[92] supernatural power.—He *blessed*, and in a distinguished manner *owned* the issue—and declared it legitimate to all intents and purposes. If this is not *allowance*, what is? As to the *first*, namely, his making laws for the *regulation* of *polygamy*, let us consider what is written, *Exod.* xxi. 10. If he (*i.e.* the husband) *takes him another wife* (not—in so doing he sins against the *seventh* commandment, recorded in the preceding chapter—but) *her food, her*

---

92   Ps. cxiii. 9. *He maketh the* barren woman *to keep house, and to be a joyful mother of children.*

raiment (i.e. of the first wife), *and her duty of marriage, he shall not diminish*—לא
יגרע—he shall not *subtract* or *withhold*, εκ αποϛερήσει,. Compare 1 Cor. vii. 5. Here
God positively forbids *neglect*, much more the *divorc*ing or *putting away of the first
wife*, but charges no *sin* on taking the *second*.

Secondly. When *Jacob* married *Rachel* she was *barren*, and so continued
for many years; but GOD did not leave this as a punishment upon her for marrying
a man who had *another wife*. It is said, Gen. xxx. 22, that GOD *remembered
Rachel, and* GOD *hearkened unto her and opened her—and her womb—and she
conceived and bare a son—and said,* GOD *hath taken away my reproach.* Surely
this passage of scripture ought to afford a complete answer to those who bring
the words of the marriage-bond, as cited by CHRIST, Matth. xix. *They twain
shall be one flesh,* to prove *polygamy* sinful; and should lead us to construe them,
as by this instance, and many others, the LAWGIVER Himself appears to have
done; that is to say, where a woman, not *betrothed to another man,* unites herself
in *personal knowledge* with the man of her choice, let that man's *situation* be what
it may—*they twain shall be one flesh.* How otherwise do we find such a woman as
Rachel, united to *Jacob,* who had a wife then living, praying to GOD for a blessing
on her intercourse with *Jacob,* and GOD *hearkening unto her, opening her womb,*
removing her barrenness, and thus, by miracle, *taking away her reproach?* We also
find the offspring legitimate, and inheritors of the land of *Canaan;* a plain proof
that *Joseph* and *Benjamin* were no *bastards,* or born out of lawful marriage. See
a like palpable instance of God's miraculous blessing on *polygamy* in the case of
Hannah, 1 *Sam.* i. and ii.—These instances serve also to prove, that, in God's
account, the *second* marriage is just as valid as the *first,* and as obligatory, and that
our making it *less so,* is contradictory to the divine wisdom.

Thirdly. God blessed and owned the issue. How eminently this was the
case with regard to *Joseph,* see Gen. xlix. 22-26; to *Samuel,* see 1 Sam. iii. 19. It
was expressly commanded that a *bastard,* or son of a woman who was with child
by[93] *whoredom,* should not *enter into the congregation of the* LORD, *even to his
tenth generation.* Deut. xxiii. 2. But we find *Samuel,* the offspring of[94] *polygamy,*

---

93 ἐκ πόρνης. LXX.

94 See Appendix, No 1. vol. ii.

ministering to the LORD in the tabernacle at *Shiloh*, even in his *very childhood, clothed with a linen ephod before* ELI *the priest.* See this whole history, 1 Sam. i. and ii. Who then can doubt of *Samuel's* legitimacy, consequently of GOD's *allowance* of, and blessing on *polygamy?* If such second marriage was in God's account *null* and *void*, as a sin against the *original law* of marriage, the *seventh* commandment, or *any other* law of GOD, no mark of *legitimacy* could have been found on the issue; for a *null* and *void* marriage is tantamount to *no* marriage at all; and if no marriage, no legitimacy of the issue can possibly be. Instead of such a blessing as *Hannah* obtained, we should have found her and her husband *Elkanah* charged with *adultery*, dragged forth and *stoned to death*; for so was *adultery* to be punished. All this furnishes us with a conclusive proof that having *more* than *one wife* with whom a man cohabited was not *adultery* in the sight of God; or, in other words, that it never was reckoned by Him as any sin against the *seventh* commandment, the original *marriage-institution*, or any other *law whatsoever.*

Fourthly. But there is a passage (Deut. xxi. 15) which is express[95] to the point, and amounts to a demonstration of God's allowance of *polygamy*. *If there be to a man* נשים שתי—two wives— (compare Gen. iv. 19. 1 Sam. i. 2. xxx. 5.)—the one beloved and the one hated, and they have *borne him children, both the* beloved *and the* hated, *then it shall be, when he maketh his sons to inherit that which he hath, that he may not make the son of the* beloved *first-born before the son of the* hated, *which is indeed the first-born, by giving him a double portion of all that he hath; for he is the beginning of his strength, and the right of the first-born is his.*

On the footing of this law, the marriage of *both* women is equally *lawful*. God calls them both *wives* (for so the word נשים must be rendered in this place, as the context shews plainly), and He can't be *mistaken*, if He *calls them so*, they certainly *were so*. If the *second* wife bore the first son, that son was to inherit before a son born afterwards of the[96] *first* wife. Here the issue is expressly deemed *legitimate*, and inheritable to the *double portion of the first-born*; which could not be if the *second* marriage were not deemed as lawful and valid as the *first*.

---

95   "Herein is a law, tacitly implied at least, for a man to have two wives." Ant. Univ. Hist. vol. iii. p. 141.

96   This could not happen where there were *two wives* in *succession*.

The *wisdom of this world*, as at present constituted, would say—the man was an *adulterer*—the *second* wife an *adulteress*—our law would make the man a *felon*—our *ecclesiastical* courts would pronounce the *second* marriage *null* and *void*—the issue would be *bastardized*—and our *devout* people would lift up their hands and eyes, and deem the whole a monstrous piece of wickedness! Which view of the matter is most agreeable to the *mind* and *will* of God, must be left to the *judicious* reader to determine.

Dean *Delaney*, who cannot venture to deny absolutely that this text relates to *polygamy*—yet, in a note, endeavors to get rid of its evidence, by saying, that "this one expression—*her's that was hated*—see our translation—makes this law appear rather to be understood of the children of two *successive wives*."—But the Hebrew runs thus—והיה הבן הבכר לשניאה—*and the first-born son be to the hated* - so that the stress laid on the words of our translation, her's that was hated, is good for nothing. See Reflections on *Polygamy*, p. 56.

The learned *Dr. Rutherforth* has also taken no small pains to get rid of the conclusive evidence of this text in favor of the divine allowance of *polygamy*. That learned professor, in his lectures which he read at *Cambridge*, on *Grotius* de *Jure*, found this *text*, in the plain and obvious meaning of the *Hebrew*, by no means conformable to the position which he had laid down, that *polygamy* was contrary to the *law* of *nature*; he therefore is for *supposing* the two wives to have been in *succession*, and that the *first-born* was the son of the *first wife*. See *Institutes of Natural Law*, b.i. c. 15.

But it is very extraordinary, if this were the case, that it should not be so expressed. This is a point of too much consequence, to be established on words, which do not carry that meaning, and no other, on the face of them: so far from it, the only terms used in the description of the *women are*—"*The one beloved and the one hated*"—who can say which was which? Consequently, presume to determine, of *which wife* the *first-born* was, in point of time?

Dr. Rutherforth, as well as Dr. Delaney, in his treatment of all *scriptures* which pose his *law of nature* scheme, puts one in mind of *Kolben's* account of the *Rhinoceros*—"This creature, in order to get at his *prey*, marches towards it in a *right line*, tearing his way very furiously through all opposition of trees and bushes. When he is upon the march, he is heard at a great distance, forcing his way through thick bushes and snapping off trees."

As for *Grotius* and *Puffendorf,* they both allow that the *Jewish* law permitted *polygamy,* as they both declare; and both mention this text as one proof of it. See *Grot. de Jure,* lib. ii. c. 5. §9. Marg. *Pussend.* lib. vi. c. 1. § 16—The like may be said of the great *Mr. Selden, Bishop Patrick,* and every other learned *commentator,* who had not a very *interesting reason* for imitating *Peter Kolben's Rhinoceros* above-mentioned.

One particular occasion of this law seems to have been what had happened in the case of *Leah* and *Rachel, Jacob's* שתי נשים—*two wives*—the one beloved and the one hated. See Gen. xxix. 30, 31. *Reuben was the first-born of Leah—Joseph of Rachel. Jacob* disinherited the son of the *hated,* and gave the *right of the first-born* to the son of the *beloved.* But this was not a mere act of *caprice* and undue *preference* against the law of inheritance on account of *Jacob's* partiality to *Rachel;* but an act of *justice* on account of *Reuben's* crime, who had gone up to his *father's couch* and defiled his *concubine Bilhah.* He therefore disinherited him as a punishment, and the *birth-right* thus became *Joseph's,* who was the *first-born of Jacob* by *Rachel.* See I Chron. v. 1, 2.

As this might have been made a precedent among the *polygamous Jews,* and what had been an act of *justice* in *Jacob,* made use of to justify an indulgence of undue partiality for *one wife* before *another,* to the *dispersion* of the *first-born,* and to the overturning the sacred rights he was invested with, as a *type* or *figure* of *Him that was to come*—who, as the great *antitype,* is *styled,* "the *first-born of every creature.*" Col. i. 15.—therefore this law seems to have been made, and stands as an irrefragable proof of the lawfulness of *polygamy;* because it stands as a proof, not only of the *allowed* practice of it, but of the *legitimacy* of the *issue* in the sight of God; which is evinced to demonstration in the above case of *Joseph,* who could not have inherited the right of the *first-born,* on any other principle.

Simeon was the next son of *Leah* but could not take the *inheritance,* not being the *first-born* of his mother. But *Joseph was,* and therefore, as the only *legitimate heir,* took the birthright, on the disinheritance of Reuben, the first-born of Leah.

But farther. To say that *polygamy* is sinful (for if it ever *was* it certainly *is,* and if ever it *was not* it certainly *is not,* unless some positive law hath made an alteration, or unless good and evil change their nature by length of time, like the fashion of our clothes) is to make God the *author of sin*; for[97] not to forbid that which is evil, but even to countenance and promote it, and this uniformly for ages together, is being so far the *author* of it, and accessory to it in the highest degree.—And shall we dare to say, or even to think, that this is chargeable on Him *who is of purer eyes than to behold evil, and who cannot look on iniquity?* Hab. i. 13. God forbid!

When He is upbraiding David by the prophet *Nathan* for his ingratitude towards His *Almighty benefactor* (2 Sam. xii.), He does it in the following terms: ver. 8. I gave thee[98] *thy master's house* and thy Masters Wives Into Thy Bosom, and

---

97 *Puffendorf*, b. vi. c. 1. § 16. observes that the *Mosaical* law was so far from forbidding this custom that it seems in several places to suppose it, and refers to Deut. xxi. 15; xvii. 16, 17; and 2 Sam. xii. 8.

98 When *Esau* met *Jacob* with his wives and children, he *asked—who are those with thee? and Jacob* said—*The children which* God *hath graciously given thy servant (Gen. xxxiii. 5)*. Now, can we suppose that God's *gracious gifts* are peculiarly bestowed on acts of rebellion against His positive laws? Yet we must either suppose this, or that *Jacob's polygamy* was no transgression of the law. See Gen. xxx. 16, 17, 18, another remarkable instance of God's special blessing on *polygamy*.

The mention of Esau reminds me of a remarkable part of his history. He took *two wives, both Hittites,* idolatresses—*who were a grief of mind unto Isaac, and to Rebekah* (Gen. xxvi. 34, 35). But whence arose this grief of mind in *Esau's* parents? Not on account of his *polygamy*, but because he had married *heathen women*, as is clear from xxvii. 46. Therefore, *Jacob* is sent to *Padan Aram*, that he might not take a *wife* from the *daughters of Canaan*, but from his *mother's family*. And when *Esau saw that the daughters of Canaan pleased not Isaac his father, he went and took a wife of the daughters of Ishmael, unto the wives which he had*—but we hear of no lamentation of *Isaac and Rebekah*, over this *fresh act of polygamy*. As for *Jacob*, we read of his return out of Syria with no less than *four wives*—that when he came to *Mahanaim*, and heard of *Esau's* approach, he rose up that night, and took his two *wives*, and *his two women-servants* (called also his *wives*—See Gen. xxx. 4. 9.) and his *eleven sons, and passed over the brook Jabbok.* Gen. xxxii. 22. And *Jacob was left alone, and there wrestled a man with him*, &c. This *man* is called אלהים ver. 30. *God*; in Hos. xii. 4. מלאך *an angel*; and ver. 5. the *Lord God of Hosts*—which, all put together, shews us, that it was not a *mere man*, nor *created angel*, but מלאך יהוה the *angel* Jehovah—the *messenger of the covenant, Mal. iii. 1.* who appeared often in an human form under the Old Testament, in token of His *future incarnation* under the New Testament, even *the man, the God-man* Christ Jesus—He who is represented by commentators as ranking *polygamy* with *adultery*, Matt. xix. 9. But what was his conduct towards *Jacob?*—Doth He reprove Him for the *sin of polygamy*, in which he was living? No—He said, *Thy name shall no more be called Jacob, but Israel; for as a prince hast thou power with God and with men, and hast prevailed*—and he blessed *him there.* Comp. *Deut. xxvii. 26. and Gal. iii. 10.*

I gave thee the bounty of Israel and Judah, and if that had been too little, I would moreover have given thee such and such things.

Can we suppose God giving *more wives than one* into David's *bosom*, who already had *more than one*, if it was *sin* in David to *take* them? Can we imagine that God should thus transgress (as it were) His own commandment in *one* instance, and yet so severely reprove and chastise David for breaking it in another? Is it not rather plain, from the whole transaction, that David committed *mortal* sin in taking another *living* man's wife, but none in taking the widows of the *deceased* Saul? That, therefore, though the law of God condemned the *first*, yet it did not condemn the *second*?

This passage of 2 *Sam.* xii. 8 is so conclusive a proof of God's allowance of *polygamy* that writers on the other side of the question have not been able to get rid of it, but by a downright corruption of the text. Instead of the plain, obvious, and literal meaning of the word חיק—which signifies the "*breast* or *bosom*, from the *throat* to the *pit of the stomach*"—they have construed it into *power* and would tell us that "God gave Saul's *wives* into David's *power*, as a *sovereign*, not into his *bosom* as an *husband.*"

Take this expression in its strongest and 'most strict sense' (says the late reverend and learned[99] *Dean Delaney*, in a book called Reflections on *Polygamy*, printed at London, 1737, under the name of *Phileleutherus Dublinensis*): 'as where *Sarai* tells *Abram* that she had *given her maid into his bosom* (Gen. xvi. 5), what more can be meant by it, than that she gave her into his *power?*' We have but to look at the whole context of that passage, and this learned man's question receives a full and explicit answer, and his whole argument an absolute refutation. Gen. xvi. 1. &c. Now *Sarai*, Abram's *wife, bare him no children, and she had an handmaid, an* Egyptian, *whose name was* Hagar; *and* Sarai *said unto* Abram, *Behold now the* Lord *hath restrained me from bearing. I pray thee go*[100] *in unto*

---

99   This *Reverend* gentleman is so candid as to tell us,—"that he has ventured to differ from all the commentators he has ever met with, in the sense of *every text relating to this point,*"—i.e. of *David's polygamy.*—So that, by his own confession, he stands *alone,* in his interpretation of *every text* upon the subject. See Reflections on *Polygamy,* p. 3.

100   The sequel of this chapter seems to afford, to every candid mind, a very conclusive proof, that

my maid, *it may be that I may* obtain children by her. *And* Abram *hearkened unto the voice of* Sarai: *and* Sarai, Abram*'s wife, took* Hagar *her maid, the* Egyptian, *and gave her to* Abram *to be* his wife *(לאשה) and* he went in unto Hagar, *and she conceived; and when she saw that she had conceived, her mistress was despised in her eyes: and* Sarai *said unto* Abram, *My wrong be upon thee; I have* given my maid into thy bosom, *and when she saw that she had conceived, I was despised in her eyes; the* Lord *judge between me and thee.* This scripture is too plain to need any comment. I will therefore, after observing that חק no more signifies *power*, than it signifies an *horse*, only add, that if Saul's *wives* had not been given into David's *bosom*, in the plain and[101] usual sense of that expression, the circumstance itself could not have afforded that striking aggravation, so beautifully intimated in *Nathan's* parable, of the *rich man's sparing to take of his own flock, and his own herd, to dress for the wayfaring man that was come unto him, but taking the poor man's lamb, &c.*

The learned *Dean*, as well as some other commentators on this famous passage, go still farther, and tell us, David could not enjoy these widows of Saul as *wives*, because in so doing he would have committed *incest*, they being *mothers-in-law* to Michal, Saul's daughter, who was David's wife. But where is such an union forbidden? I have carefully examined the degrees of *affinity* and *consanguinity* wherein marriage is forbidden, and do find a man must not marry his *own mother-in-law*, (Lev. xviii. 8.) but as to his *wife's mother-in-law*, there is not a trace of such an impediment. As for Michal's *own mother*, she, if living, must be put out of the question. See Lev. xviii. 17.

These things being considered, the observations of such commentators evaporate into just what Nathan's parable and remonstrance must do, supposing

---

this proposal of *polygamy* to *Abram* by his wife *Sarai*, was not *sinful*, neither *Abram's* complying with it in the least displeasing to *God*; for on *Hagar's* departure from *Sarai*, on account of *hard usage*, ver. 6. the *angel of the Lord* recommends it to her to *return*, and promises to *multiply her seed exceedingly, that it should not be numbered for multitude*—tells her *she should bear a son*—בן—which promise was fulfilled, ver. 15. Now, for all this to happen, in support of, and as a blessing *upon*, a *polygamous* marriage, if such marriages were *sinful*, and of course abominable in the eyes of *God*, is, I freely own, past every notion which I have conceived of the *scripture-character* of the *holy* God of *Israel*. See Gen. xvii. 20.

101   Deut. xiii. 6. תשא קיח—uxorem sinus tui. Mont.— *The wife of thy bosom.*

such criticisms to be true; that is to say, into—nothing at all. David's ingratitude to God, and to his[102] worthy Uriah—were not to be marked by Nathan, because David had a number of women whom he could *not enjoy*; but because he might have *enjoyed* them whenever he pleased: therefore his taking Uriah's *wife* was the more inexcusable, and his rebellious ingratitude against God, who gave him so many women *into his bosom*, the more aggravated.

These truths have not failed universally in their influence, but have forced themselves into the consciences of some; who, not being able to resist their conviction, have confessed that "*Polygamy* was *allowed* of God to the *Jews*, but yet it is[103] *forbidden* to Christians"—which is just as true as if it was said, that "the people under the Old Testament were *men* and *women*, but Christians[104] are not; for to suppose that the *human species* is changed, is not more absurd than to suppose a change either of the *original* design of God in the institution of marriage, or of the sense and meaning of the *seventh* commandment, as forbidding or condemning that *now*, which was not forbidden or condemned, either by the one or the other, for so many ages *before*. As for the positive law of the *seventh* commandment, it is attended with such pains and penalties in the breach of it, that it is impossible but that some instance of God's disapprobation of *polygamy* must have been met with, had that been within the meaning of it; otherwise the absurdity must follow, of supposing a suspension of this law for 1500 years after it was ordained of God, delivered to *Moses*, and by him to the people at *Mount Sinai*—and all this for the indulgence of *mortal sin* in one sex, while it was punished with death in the other.

In the first place, I would observe in general, that *polygamy*, in its proper

---

102   2 Sam. xxiii. 39.

103   *Polygamy* is prohibited among *Christians*, but was allowed, by *Divine appointment*, among the *Jews*. Chambers, Tit. *Polygamy*.

104   Or to say with *some of the* antient fathers, who were *wiser* than the scriptures, that the *crescite & multiplicamini* of the Old Testament has nothing to do with *Christians* under the New Testament—Quia hodie, repleto mundo, non tam necessarium quam olim; and again—hodie non pertineret ad tempora ante *Christum*, sed nos qui alio vivimus ævo—mundum jam non desiderare illud *crescite et multiplicamini*. "The command—*Be fruitful and multiply*, &c. is not necessary, as once it was, because the world is filled with people.—That belonged to the times before Christ, not to us who live in another age—the world now wants not that—*Increase and multiply*."

sense, as practiced under the Old Testament by the people of God; that is, the taking *two wives together at once,* or *one to another,* and *cohabiting with both,* is not so much as[105] mentioned any where, that I can find, from the *first* chapter of *Saint Matthew* to the *last* of the *Revelation of Saint John,* inclusive: therefore it cannot be said to be[106] *condemned.* The famous passage in Matt. xix. which has been already considered, and will be more fully hereafter, certainly relates to[107] *divorce,* and, properly speaking, not to *polygamy;* for this, simply considered, does not come in question. The people there, so far from intending *polygamy,* meant nothing less, for they meant to have but *one wife at a time;* else why were they for *divorcing one,* in order to take[108] *another?* Their sin was this, not the *taking* and *cohabiting* with *more than one* at a time. They imagined themselves *totally free* from the *first,* before they married the *second.*

The New Testament was not to introduce a *new law* concerning this, nor anything else. Nothing is to be found there which was not in the Old Testament, only as to the *manner;* the *matter* is one and the same. Otherwise, how could *Paul* derive any strength to his argument, Gal. iii. 10, by citing the sanction of the *old* law, to prove the necessity of *salvation by grace?* If the law be in a single instance altered, or changed in one single point, how can it be said by an inspired *apostle* of Christ—*Cursed is every one that continueth not in* all things *which are written in the book of the law to do them?*—which, as it never had, so it never can have but one sense and meaning; and our Lord shews, that it not only condemned the *act,* but the very *thought* of *adultery.* Did it only begin to do this, when Christ said, *Whosoever looketh upon a woman to lust after her, hath already committed*

---

105   Unless incidentally, 1 Tim. iii. 2. 1 Tit. i. 6. where nothing is said, either good or bad, as to the matter itself in general.

106   Judge *Blackstone* says, very gravely—Comm. vol. i. p. 436.—"*Polygamy* is condemned by the law of the *New Testament.*"

107   So our *translators* undoubtedly thought; for in the summary of the contents printed at the head of the *chapter,* they only say—"Christ answereth the Pharisees concerning *divorcement.*" ver. 3—10. So Mark x. 2. *"Touching divorcement."*

108   Here the word ἀλλην, Matt. xix. 9. is supposed to signify *another* (i.e. *any* other *woman*) according to our translation. But that this may not be the sense of it, see after.

adultery with her in his heart[109]? Matt. v. 28. (but then this must mean such a woman[110] as *adultery* could be committed with, supposing the *thought* brought

---

109   *Per γυναῖκα autem intelligitur uxor alterius.* "By the word γυναῖκα—*woman*—the wife of another is understood. 2 Sam. xi. 2, 3, 4. Job xxxi. 1, 7. Prov. vi. 27. Ecclus ix. 7, 8, 9. xxvi. 9. Sus. viii. 9, 32." See Wetft. on Matt. v. 28.

110   The word γυνὴ—like the Hebrew אִשָּׁה—is certainly a general term, and signifies a *woman*, as distinguished from a man; and in this sense it is used *Matt.* xiv. 21. *Acts* v. 14. & al. freq.

But this cannot be the sense of it here; for if it be sinful to *look* with *desire* on any *woman* whatsoever, then it would be sinful for a man to *desire* his own wife, to whom he is actually married, or a virgin to whom he is contracted; and this would lead us into all the absurdities of the antient misogamists, who held *marriage itself* to be *sinful*.

In this place, therefore, it certainly means a *woman* considered as *related to a man*; and that, whether *betrothed* or *espoused* only (See Matt. i. 20, 24. Luke ii. 5.) or that hath cohabited with her husband, (Luke i. 5, 13, 18.) for with no other can *adultery* be committed; and it is very evident that *our Saviour's* discourse is on that subject; as forbidden and condemned by the *seventh commandment*, which He is explaining.

Γυνὴ in the New Testament, like אִשָּׁה also in the Old Testament, is the term made use of to denote a *married woman*—when *others* are designed, we meet with κοράσιον, a damsel, Fr. damoiselle—παρθένος, a *virgin*—χήρα, a widow—but I believe it would be difficult to find a single passage in the New Testament, where γυνὴ is used necessarily to denote an *unmarried woman.* μεμέρισται ἡ γυνὴ ἡ παρθένος, 1 Cor. vii. 34. Afterwards the παρθένος is called ἄγαμος—the γυνὴ, γαμήσασα.

For want of such distinction, some *commentators,* by letting their own imaginations loose, have filled those of many *readers* with matter of sore distress and bondage of *conscience*, as if the *desire* after any *female* whatsoever, came within what they call the *spiritual* import of the seventh commandment

I once knew a gentleman, who often assured me, that he never approached *his own wife*, without finding a secret uneasiness in his mind, lest he was doing wrong. He was a great admirer of what are called *spiritual expositors.* These are, too often, a species of *commentators,* who, neglecting the scriptural sense and meaning of the *original*, wander into every conceit which a warm, or perhaps a wild imagination may suggest, from the sound of words in a translation. Some instances of this have been given in this work, and as many more might be given, as would furnish ample materials for a work by itself.

N. B. Let every man be sure he understands the *original letter*—before he *presumes* to descend upon the spirit of it; or he will bewilder himself and his readers; and what is worse, be setting forth many things as the *word* of God, which are not so.

Such people there always were.—Among the *heathen*—*Democritus oculos sibi eruit, quòd mulieres fine concupiscentiâ aspicere non possit. Sed nihil aliud fecit, quam quod fatuitatem suam urbi manifestam fecit.* Tertull, in Apologet.—"*Democritus* plucked out his eyes, because he could not behold women without concupiscence. But he did nothing else than expose his folly to the city."— Among the *Jews*, we read of a sect of *Pharisees*, who were called *Talpæ* or *Moles*, because they walked about with their eyes shut or blindfolded, lest they should behold a woman; and, says my author—*sæpe in muros impingerint & sanguis profusus fuerit*—"They often got bloody noses by running against walls." See Christoph. Gerson, in Talmud. p. 24.

We are told of a *Jesuit, called Alphonsus Redicin, who*, though he served at the mass 44 years, and had given absolution to thousands, had never beheld the face of a woman in all that time. General Mar. 31 Oct. p. 577

Another was so *pious*, and so avoided the sight of all women, that he would not even see his *own mother*. Ib.—To what does this amount?—A delusion of the Devil—an arraignment of the wisdom and holiness of the Creator in our formation, by condemning as evil, those appetites which He hath implanted in our nature, for the purpose of incitement to marriage, and, of course, to the continuance of the human species. To avoid such errors, one safe rule may be laid down, viz. That no *desire* is, or can be *unlawful*, but where the object of it is *unlawful* for us to possess. Let us keep to this, and then we shall not be whittling away the strong, noble, manly sense of scripture, into the ridiculous whims and fancies of visionaries and enthusiasts.

Notwithstanding the length of this note, I cannot help taking notice of a text, which is supposed to be the ground of the *Talpean* austerity above-mentioned, and which is as likely to be abused to the purposes of *self-righteousness* as that of Matt. v. 28. It is that of xxxi. 1. *I made a covenant with mine eyes, why then should I think upon a maid? Job* is asserting his integrity with respect to many circumstances of his life and conversation, and among the rest, with regard to fleshly incontinence; and this chapter begins with—*I have made a covenant with mine eyes.*—ברית כרתי לעיני ומה אתבונן על בתולה—*Et quid confiderabo in virgine.* Mont. Our translation is near enough to the original to give us the sense of it; however, that *sense* must be interpreted according to the analogy of the *divine law*, and not according to the mere *sound* of the words; for *Job* (ver. 2, 3.) shews us, that he means to express a very grievous offence, such as excludes from *all portion of* God, and *inheritance in the kingdom of heaven* (Comp. 1 Cor. vi. 9.) and which bringeth *destruction on workers* of such *iniquity.* This is sufficient to make it impossible that *Job* can speak the truth, if nothing more is meant than is literally expressed. In the first place, *Job* had made no such *covenant, &c. as not to think on a maid*, for he had married one. Secondly, this can be no sin, simply considered in itself; for if so, men must plunge into sin, or there must be an end of the world; which but ill agrees with—increase and *multiply, &c.*

Some have therefore construed this to mean that *Job* was content with one wife and did not verge towards *concubinage* or *polygamy.*—Neither of these were forbidden or condemned by the *law*, but, as has been shown at large, practiced openly by the greatest *saint*, and allowed and blessed of God; therefore, cannot answer to ver. 2, 3.

For which reasons this text is very difficult to interpret agreeably to the analogy of faith, unless the word בְּתוּלָה—*maid, or virgin*—be taken here, for what it certainly imports elsewhere, בְּתוּלָה אֲרֻשָׂה—*virgo desponsata*—a *betrothed* or *espoused virgin*, who still was called בְּתוּלָה. See Joel i. 8. and perhaps Jer. ii. 32. Comp. Is. lxi. 10. latter part. See Deut. xxii. 23, 24, 25.

That *Job* should not suffer himself to *think* on (*i.e.* so as to *desire*) such a one, is of a piece with what he says, ver. 9, 10, 11, 12; for such a one was, in the eye of the law, *another man's wife*. Deut. xxii. 23, 24. So that *Job* is not to be understood as making *transgression where there is no law*, like the *Talpæ* and the *Jesuit* above-mentioned; but as professing his innocence with respect to *adultery*, in

forth into act). And does not the Old Testament say the same thing? What else is the meaning of the *tenth* commandment, which says, *Thou shalt not covet thy neighbour's wife?* or of Prov. xxiv. 9. *The thought of foolishness is sin?* The word זמה not which we translate *the thought,* signifies a *wicked imagination, prava aut mala cogitatio. Mont. — an evil thought. The law is spiritual,* says *Paul, I had not known lust* (i.e. to know it to be evil) *except the law had said, Thou shalt not covet.* Rom. vii. 7. Therefore, when our *Saviour* preached on the *Mount,* He did not make, ordain, or publish any *new law,* nor did he make the law more *spiritual* than when published at *Mount Sinai;* but He set it forth, and vindicated it from the false glosses of the *Scribes* and *Pharisees,* who, in their teaching, dwelt on the *outward* letter only, throwing a veil of obscurity over its *spiritual* sense and meaning. The *seventh* commandment was just as *spiritual* under the Old Testament as under the New. The very *thought* of *adultery* in David, was as sinful as it would have been in *Saint Paul.* How then can it be imagined, that the commandment against *adultery* meant not as much in the times of *Moses* and the *prophets,* as in the days of Christ and His *Apostles?* or, in other words, as much under the Old Testament as under the *New?* How can it be thought to condemn anything amongst *Christians,* which it did not equally condemn amongst the *Jews? Whatsoever things the law saith, it saith to them that are under the law* (whether Jews or Christians) *that every mouth may be stopped, and all the world become guilty before God.* Rom. iii. 19. If then the law ever condemned *polygamy* as *adultery, whoredom,* or *fornication,* it certainly does it now; but, as hath been shewn, it never did condemn it in any one instance, not only *from the beginning,* by any construction put on the *original marriage-institution,* but also for 1500 years together after the giving the law at Mount *Sinai;* therefore it never has condemned it since: for Christ gave no *new* meaning to this or any other of the commandments, but only vindicated and restored the *old.* What *was* murder is *now* murder—what *was* theft is *now* theft—what *was* adultery is *now* adultery—and what *was* none of these, *is* still none of these.

---

every sense of the word, as not suffering himself to *look on,* so as to *lust after,* a *virgin betrothed,* much less to commit *actual adultery,* by defiling his *neighbour's wife* ver. 9, 10, 11, 12.

    Solomon Jarchi construes the passage very liberally indeed, or rather *paraphrases* it thus, viz. *"I made a covenant,* &c. that I would have no knowledge of any man's wife." See *Chappelowe* on Job, vol. i. p. 425.

God's *law* is His *will*, and His *will* is His *law*; a change of *one* must infer a change in the *other*, and either of these a change in Himself: an idea which is wholly irreconcilable with the *scripture-character* of God, *with whom there is no variableness, neither any shadow of turning. James* i. 17.

Men may cobble, and vamp, and alter, and repeal laws, and indeed it must be so, as mischiefs, which escape all human prescience and foresight, must daily arise; but it cannot be so with Omniscience. *All things are present and open to Him. Heb.* iv. 13. He ordained the propagation of mankind—*He blessed them, and said unto them, Be fruitful, and multiply, and replenish the earth.* Gen. i. 28. He made the woman, and *brought her to the man*, and said—*A man shall cleave to his wife,* Gen. ii. 22, 24. (by which expression, according to *St. Paul's*[111] interpretation, 1 Cor. vi. 15, 16. is meant the act of[112] copulation or *marriage*) *and they shall be one flesh*—thus creating between them so indissoluble a bond, as never to be divided more. Though these words were spoken immediately by Adam, yet, doubtless, he spoke under the influence of the *divine Spirit,* as may appear from Christ's manner of applying the words, Matt. xix. 4, 5. and may therefore, as what Moses and the *prophets* spoke under the same holy influence, be styled— *"The word of* God." The circumscription and regulation of the whole was provided for by fixed, determined, and immutable laws, calculated for all times, places, and ages of the world, wherein He should be pleased to make them known. These laws, on the establishment of the church, on its deliverance out of EGYPT, were given to Moses, and enforced and explained by him, and the subsequent *prophets,* under the immediate command and teaching of God; and continue, like the *holy Lawgiver Himself, one* and the *same* forever. Who *may* marry together, and who may *not*— what is lawful marriage in God's account, and what is not so, was not left to the uncertain or presumptuous determinations of mankind, but immutably fixed by *written laws* of God. To these it is our bounden duty to conform, and to say to

---

111   See before, 19, 20, and note.

112   This is the literal import of ותשאב קבד—*agglutinatus erit in uxore sua.* Mont. (See before p. 20. note,) ill expressed by—*shall cleave to his wife.*—The verb Προσκολληθήσεται, LXX. Matt. xix. 5. and Eph. v. 31.—and the participle κολλημενος, 1 Cor. vi. 16.—are in the *passive voice.*—For the *Author's* idea of the word *marriage,* see before, p. 48. note.

all subsequent inventions of men, as well those which forbid marriage entirely, as those who would put *asunder those whom* God *hath joined together,* under pretence of greater purity and holiness, as the angel did to Peter, Acts x. 15. *What* God *hath cleansed, that call thou not common or unclean.*

I have mentioned the law being explained by the *prophets.* There were extraordinary messengers whom God raised up, and sent forth under a special commission; not only to *foretell things to come,* but to *preach* to the people, to hold forth the *law,* to point out their defections from it, and to call them to repentance under the severest terms of God's displeasure, unless they obeyed. Their commission, in these respects, we find recorded, Is. lviii. 1. *Cry aloud, spare not, lift up thy voice like a trumpet: shew my people their transgressions, and the house of Jacob their sins.* This commission was to be faithfully executed, at the peril of the *prophet's* own destruction, as appears from the solemn charge given to *Ezekiel,* chap. iii. 18. *When I say to the wicked, Thou shalt surely die, and thou givest him not warning, nor speakest to warn the wicked to save his life, the same wicked man shall die in his iniquity, but his blood will I require at thine hand.*

These *prophets* executed their commission very unfaithfully towards GOD and the people, as well as most dangerously for themselves, if *polygamy* was a sin against God's law; for it was the common practice of the[113] whole nation, from the *prince on the throne* to the *lowest of the people*; and yet neither Isaiah, Jeremiah, nor any one of the *prophets,* bore the least testimony against it. They reproved them sharply and plainly for *defiling their neighbours wives*; as *Jer.* V.8; xxix. 23.— in which fifth chapter, we not only find the *prophet* bearing testimony against *adultery,* but against *whoredom* and *fornication,* ver. 7. for that they assembled themselves by *troops in the harlots houses.* Not a word against *polygamy.* How is it possible, in any reason, to think that this, if a sin, should never be mentioned as such, by God—by[114] Moses—or any *one* of the *prophets*?

---

113   *Josephus* calls it εθνικός—which answers to what we mean by the word *national.*

114   Moses mentions all the sins of the *nations of Canaan,* as warnings to the *Israelites* not to be guilty of them; but their *polygamy* is nowhere mentioned or condemned, nor are the *Jews* warned against it. See *Levit.* xviii. 3. 24, &c.

Here I may particularly mention *Elijah* the *Tishbite,* who could with truth say of himself, 1 Kings xix. 10. קנא קנאתי—*zelando zelatus sum.* Mont. Which emphatical reduplication we translate by—*I have been* Very Jealous *for the* Lord Of Hosts. This holy man was fired with zeal for God's law and was a most faithful and undaunted reprover of sin, even to the very face of *King Ahab* (who at that time reigned in *Israel,* and was doubtless a *polygamist,* by his having *seventy sons)* yet not a word is said about his *polygamy;* which could hardly have been omitted, had it been a sin against either the *primary* law of marriage or the *seventh* commandment. The same zeal which led *Elijah* to tell *Ahab,* that *he and his father's house had troubled Israel* by *forsaking the commandments of the* Lord, *and following Baalim,* must surely have led him to reprove *Ahab's* polygamy, had that also been a *forsaking of the commandments of* Jehovah. The scripture, 1 Kings xvi. 31, strongly remarks, as an aggravation of *Ahab's* superlative wickedness, that he married an *idolatress,* contrary to Deut. vii. 3. Had his *polygamy* been contrary to *Exod.* xx. 14, this would hardly have escaped the reproofs of the prophet *Elijah,* who did not forget *Jezebel,* and the *prophets which ate at her table.* 1 Kings xviii. 19.

We may also observe that *Ezekiel,* ch. xxii. sets down very particularly the sins of *lewdness,* which the *Jews* were addicted to in his day, ver. 10, 11. but not a word of *polygamy* is there to be found.

Although it be true that none of the *prophets before the captivity* mention it as a *sin,* yet did not MALACHI, after the *return from the captivity,* speak of it, and in very severe terms *condemn* it? thus closing the canon of the Old Testament with a most awful reprehension of it? Mal. ii. 14, 15.

As this famous passage is taken for granted to be a condemnation of *polygamy* under the Old Testament, let us examine it, and we shall find that it does not even relate to the subject: if it did, it would be very strange that so material a point should escape *all* the *prophets* that went before him, *Moses* himself not excepted. This single circumstance should make one suspicious of the common interpretation given to this portion of scripture by the general run of *commentators,* who, mistaking the *sound* of the words for the *sense* of the text, have followed one another like sheep, who keep the same track, only because others have gone before them. The words, as they stand in our translation, are these— The Lord *hath been witness between thee and the wife of thy youth, against whom thou hast dealt treacherously: yet she is thy companion and the wife of thy covenant. And did not He make one? yet hath He the residue of the spirit. And wherefore one? That He might seek a godly seed. Therefore take heed to your spirit, and let none deal treacherously against the wife of his youth,* for the Lord God *of* ISRAEL *saith, that he hateth* PUTTING AWAY.

The *last* words are a key to the rest, and shew that the instance in which they *dealt treacherously with their wives,* was *putting them away*; and this, in order to take *heathen* women in their room. This is manifest from Ver. 11. JUDAH *hath dealt treacherously,* and an abomination is committed in ISRAEL and JERUSALEM; for JUDAH *hath prophaned the holiness of the* LORD *which he loved, and hath married the daughter of a strange god.*

EZRA[115], who lived about this time, hath recorded the fact at large and fully explains the matter; *chap.* ix. 1. *The people of* ISRAEL *and the priests have not separated themselves from the people of the lands, for they have taken of their daughters for themselves, and for their sons, and the holy seed have mingled themselves with the people of those lands.*

Ver. 10. *And now, O* LORD, *what shall we say after this? for we have forsaken thy commandments, which thou hast commanded by thy servants the prophets, saying, The land which ye go to possess is an unclean land,* &c.

Ver. 12. *Now therefore give not your daughters unto their sons, neither take their daughters to your sons,* &c.

Chap. x. 2. *We have trespassed against our* GOD, *and have taken strange wives of the people of the land. Now therefore let us make a covenant with our* GOD, *to put away all the wives, and such as are born of them,* ver. 3.

The *putting away* of these heathen women was a *duty,* and this by the positive law of GOD. For GOD having, as it were, forbidden the *banns* in express words (Deut. vii. 3.), their marriages were absolutely null and void *ab initio;* they could contract no valid marriage whatsoever with them, and therefore must *put them away.* This affords us a strong proof of the *lawfulness* of *polygamy,* where the woman was not excepted against, as by the law above mentioned, or by some other: for if this were otherwise, we should hear of *putting away* all but the *first*

---

115   See also *Nehemiah* xiii. 23-29.

in all cases. GOD would not have suffered any marriage that was contrary to the *seventh* commandment, any more than those which were contrary to *Deut.* vii. 3. When we compare EZRA and MALACHI together, we find by the *former*, that the *Jews* took *heathen women for their wives;* and by the *latter*, that they not only did this, but *put away* their *Israelitish* wives for *that very purpose*. This is plainly what ver. 14. calls *dealing treacherously* with their wives, their divorcing them for this *unhallowed* purpose. There the *prophet* uses the like arguments against them as he had before used, ver. 10. with regard to their *dealing treacherously with their brethren—Have we not all one father? hath not one GOD created us? why do we deal treacherously every man against his brother, by profaning the covenant of our fathers?* When they put away their *Jewish wives,* and married the *heathen* idolatrous women, they *profaned the covenant of their fathers;* that is, that command of GOD delivered to their fathers, not only in the *original* institution of marriage, which forbade *putting away*, but also that positive law, Deut. vii. 3, which forbade marriage with *heathens*. They *dealt treacherously with their brethren;* that is to say, with the *parents* and *relations* of their unjustly-*divorced wives*, who gave them their *daughters* or *sisters* in marriage, to *abide* with them, not to be *put away*. They *dealt treacherously also with their wives*, in *putting them away.*—Therefore, the *prophet* reproves them, and calls them to repentance by the following considerations, ver. 14, 15; which I will endeavour to lay before the *reader* in a paraphrase suitable to the literal and true meaning of the *original* Hebrew, and conformable to the *analogy* of divine revelation, as delivered to us by MOSES and the *prophets*. Then it will appear, that these distinguished servants of GOD were not guilty of concealing, disguising, or dissembling the truth; nor GOD Himself capable of suffering His *seventh* commandment, as well as the *original institution of marriage*, to be transgressed, not only with impunity, but *allowance*, uniformly through so many ages, or of leaving His church and people utterly ignorant of His mind and will touching so important a matter, for all that time.

ולא אחד עשה—*Et ne unus fecit?* Mont.—*And did not one make?* Here our *commentators*, misled by our *translators*, and these by the vulgar error of the *sinfulness* of *polygamy*, tell us, that "these words signify GOD's making but *one woman* at the beginning; He had the *residue of the spirit*, and therefore could have made *more women* for ADAM if He *had pleased*." One misfortune attending so ignorant a comment, is, that the word אחד cannot signify *one woman,* unless, among other changes, *women* were of the *masculine* gender under the Old Testament, though of the *feminine* under the New Testament; for אחד is certainly of the *masculine* gender—אחת is the feminine—See Judges ix. 53.—אשה אחת— *mulier una.* Mont. & al freq. This, besides an undue transposition of the words, is, I take it, a conclusive reason for saying they mistake the passage. It is not—*Did not he make One?*—but—*Did not One[116] make?* Like ver. 10. *Have we not all* One *Father? Did not* ONE GOD *create us?* Did not *One,* or THE ONE, make both you and your *Jewish wives?* Did He not form both of you (see Deut. xxxi. 6.) *naturally* of the same seed of *Abraham*—*spiritually* by the same holy dispensation and ordinances? At ver. 14, it is said—היא בריתך—*She is thy companion,* or associate— ואשת בריתך—and *a wife,* or woman, *of thy covenant*—i.e., a partaker with thee in the covenant made with *Abraham* and his seed after him. So the *prophet* Zech. ix. 11, where GOD says to the *daughter of Zion*—As for thee—בדם בריתך—*In* (or by) *the blood* THY COVENANT, *I have sent forth thy prisoners,* &c. where בריתך—*thy covenant*—compared with the context in this place of Malachi, clearly determines the meaning to be as above, and it stands here as opposed to the *daughter of a strange* GOD, ver. 11.—ושאר רוח לו—And *He hath* (or hath He not?*) the *remainder of the Spirit*—Hath He not the same *power* He ever had?—Is His hand shortened at all, so that He cannot complete your restoration if He pleases, or punish you still more severely, if you continue disobedient to His commandments? *Spirit* is here used for *power[117],* mighty, but especially *irresistible power;* as Ps. cxxxix. 7; Is. lix. 19; Is. lxiii. 14; Is. xxxiv. 16.—ומה האחד מבקש And what did THE ONE

---

116 If the attentive reader will compare the דחא—*one,* in this place, with דחא לא—*one* GOD, ver. 10. surely he must see, that the same *Almighty Person* is meant. *There* he is said to *create*—*here* to make. Comp. Gen. ii. 3. latter part.

117 So the *power* of the *Spirit* is often used for the *Spirit itself.* Comp. If. xxxii. 15. Luke xxiv. 49. Acts i. 8. See also *Judges* xiii. 25; xiv. 19; xvi. 17, 20. Rom. i. 4. with 1 Cor. vi. 14. & al. freq. In an old edition of the *Bible,* printed in the year 1615, there are short notes added in the margin; and in the note on the word *Spirit,* in this text, it is explained to mean *power and* virtue.

seek? זרע אלהים—a[118] *seed of* GOD—an[119] *holy seed* (see Ezra ix. 2, compare ver. 14) therefore *take heed to your spirit*—that is, your *temper—affections*—as רוח is very often applied (see Num. xiv. 24; 1 Sam. i. 15) *and none of you deal treacherously against the wife of thy youth,* (whom thou hast married when a virgin) by *putting her away,* and *taking* these *idolatresses; for I, the* Lord, *hate putting away.* The consideration of the relation they stood in to Jehovah—their *common Father—they* His professing *children,* was one argument against their separating—another was, that, as the Lord sought a *godly seed* in their offspring, by their being devoted to Him in their earliest infancy, then brought up in the *nurture and admonition of the* Lord, this design would be defeated by their taking *idolatrous* women who, instead of devoting the children to Jehovah, would be for bringing them up to the[120] *worship* of their *idols,* and an *ungodly seed* be the consequence. See *Deut.* vii. 3, 4. Lastly, God had forbidden *divorce* from the beginning (see Gen. ii. 24), for He *hateth putting away* at any rate; but how much more to see His own professing daughters *put away,* that His own professing sons might *marry the daughters of a strange God?* This was indeed *doing an abominable thing which* God *hated.* Jer. xliv. 4.

This I take to be a clear, consistent view of this famous passage, and agrees exactly with what Ezra says, chap. ix. &c. and chap. x. 2. &c., who did not *rend his mantle and garment, and pluck the hair off his head and beard, and sit down astonished,* because the people did what their fathers Abram, Jacob, David, etc., had done without the *least reproof,* and had been constantly, openly, avowedly praised by the holiest of their forefathers, without the least

---

118   Et quid Unus querit nifi femen Dat. *Vulg.*

119   This can have nothing to do with *polygamy,* because, if it had, we should have hardly found it *allowed* by GOD, and practised by His saints; or, in fact, have found some of the most distinguished and blessed men that ever lived as the offspring of *polygamous* marriages; witness holy *Joseph* and the prophet *Samuel.* Besides all this, we may observe that the *Jews,* who are in this place of *Ezra* emphatically styled *the holy seed,* were descended from the *twelve sons of Jacob,* half of which were born under *polygamy.*

120   We find that these idolatrous women laid a fair foundation for this by bringing up their children in the knowledge of the heathen tongues of their several countries, so that they could not understand the language of God's law. See Neh. xiii. 23, 24.

scruple[121] on their part, or condemnation on God's part—but because they had married *heathen* women, and, as appears by *Mal.* ii. 14, had *dealt treacherously* against the *Jewish lawful* wives, by *putting them away* in order to do it.

As to the notion expressed by *commentators*, in their apparently misconceived ideas of this text of Malachi—that because God created but *one man* and *one woman* at first, therefore He intended that "no man should have more than one wife at a time ever after," I do humbly conceive that if God had *meant* so, He would somewhere have *said* so, and not have left it to the wisdom of men to put their[122] interpretations on what He was pleased to do: For *who hath known the mind of the* Lord, *and who hath been His counselor?* Rom. xi. 34. Some may argue that because it was said—"*A man shall cleave to his wife, not wives,* therefore it is unlawful for a man to have *two or more wives in*[123] succession, and can only have

---

121   When *Joseph* was solicited by *Potiphar's* wife, he *answered with abhorrence*—"*How can I do this great wickedness, and sin against God?*" (Gen. xxxix. 9, latter part).—But when *Abraham's* wife *Sarah* proposed her *husband's taking Hagar to wife* (Gen. xvi. 2, 3), he does it without the least objection. So *Jacob* took *Rachel* after *Leah*, there being then no law against marrying a *wife's sister*. This, and the many other instances, clearly prove that the wisest and best of God's saints never dreamt of *polygamy's* having any relation to the sin of *adultery*.

122   As for putting our construction on any acts of God, so as to draw them into *precedents*, unless clearly instructed by Him so to do, it would in many cases be attended with great mischiefs—for instance: Suppose we were to argue for *brothers* and *sisters* intermarrying, because this must have been the case among the immediate children of *Adam and Eve?* The creation of only *one man* and *one woman,* would at least be as good an argument *for* incest, as *against* polygamy. But it can have no weight in either case, because God, by a positive law (Lev. xviii. 9), prohibited the *first*, and by as positive a law (Deut. xxi. 15-17) allowed the *second*. It pleased God, that the whole *human nature* should reside in one common *federal head*, who was to be the common *representative* of all his subsequent naturally-engendered offspring; and by *one woman* taken out of *himself,* to convey that nature which was in him to his own immediate children, and by them to his posterity, to the end of the world. Let anyone read *Rom. v.* with attention, and consider in what respects *Adam* was a *figure of Him that was to come* (ver. 14), and then it will be seen that no man who ever *was*, or *will be naturally* engendered of the offspring of *Adam,* can have been or be in the same circumstances and situation that *Adam* was. Wherefore, a precedent against *polygamy* is no more to be drawn from him than against natural generation from *Eve's* being made out of *one of his ribs,* or from his own being immediately formed out of the *dust of the earth.*

123   There was a time in the *Christian* church, when this was looked upon as only "a more specious and decorous kind of *adultery*," and reckoned *infamous.*

one so long as he lives, because *Adam[124]* had but *one.*" This sort of conceits is like supposing that God forbad the wearing cloth, or silk, or linen, because He *clothed* our first parents *with skins.* Gen. iii. 21; or supposing, like those mad *heretics* of the *second* century, who called themselves *Adamites*, that *Christians* are to meet together stark *naked* without any *shame*, because it is said (Gen. ii. 25.) *Adam* and *Eve were naked, and were not ashamed.* If we take upon ourselves to interpret this or any act of God merely by our imaginations, we take upon us what does not belong to us. We are told, Deut. xxix. 29. Secret things *belong unto the* Lord *our God, but those things which are* revealed, *to us and our children forever, that we may do all the words of His law.*

That God might have created *10,000 men, and as many women, is certain.*

The *Montanists* affirmed *second* marriages to be as *scandalous* and *sinful* as *fornication.* In the *three* first *ages* of the *church*, "*second marriages* were reputed *scandalous*; nay, they were *condemned by some persons.*" *Dupin*, Eccl. Hist. vol. i. 182. Engl. transl. But more of this hereafter.

124   *Milton* represents *Adam* as saying—

—O why did God,
Creator wise, that peopled highest heav'n
With spirits masculine, create at last
This novelty on earth, this fair defect
Of Nature, and not fill the world at once
With men as angels without feminine,
Or find some other way to generate Mankind?
Par. Lost, B. 10.

We may presume that God made the rest of the animal creation by *pairs*, the *male and female*— Comp. Gen. i. 20-25. with Gen. vi. 19. Gen. vii. 2, 3, 9, 14-16: therefore, to draw arguments against *polygamy* (which, by the way, the scriptures have nowhere done) from a similar creation of the human species, would, if pursued to the utmost, prove *too much*, and of course prove *nothing.* So when God was about to destroy the earth by the *deluge*, he commanded *Noah* to come into the *ark*—"*Thou and thy sons, and thy wife, and thy sons wives with thee,*" in all *eight persons* (see 1 Pet. iii. 20) "*and of every living thing of all flesh, TWO OF EVERY SORT—they shall be male and female—seven pair of the clean, and two pair of the unclean*, the MALE and HIS FEMALE."—ותשאו שיא—*Virum & uxorem ejus.* Mont. So that in the preservation of the *brutal*, as well as of the *human* species, we read of them in *pairs*—and these *pairs* are described by the same *Hebrew* words, which, in other parts of the scriptures, we render—*a man and his wife.*—For the *exact words* of these abridged *passages*, see the scriptures above referred to.

Why He did not, He hath no where told us, any more than why He created only one man and one woman. This and all things else are to be resolved into His *own good pleasure, and the counsel of his own will.* Eph. i. 11. Rev. iv. 11. Our attempting to account for any of His holy acts or dispensations, any farther than the revelation of His word expressly authorizes us, is to be wise *above what is written,* to involve ourselves in endless mazes of error, till—*professing ourselves wise, we become fools.* Rom. i. 22.

God's bringing *the woman to the man*—that solemn denunciation— *therefore shall a man leave father and mother, and cleave unto his wife, and they shall be one flesh*—form a conclusive argument against wanton and causeless *divorce*; and are expressly made use of by Christ for that purpose in His dispute with the *Pharisees,* Matt. xix. 4, 5; but it is nowhere, in the whole scripture, made use of as an argument against *polygamy.* There were, doubtless, opportunities enough in the *antediluvian,* as well as the *postdiluvian* world, to have given occasion for it, had any[125] such thing been intended.

The first instance of *polygamy* which is recorded, we find Gen. iv. 19. *And*

---

125   One weighty reason for the creation of only *one man* and *one woman* at first, may perhaps be gathered from Acts xvii. 26. where it is said—*He hath made of* one blood *all nations of men, for to dwell on all the face of the earth.* Had more men and women than *Adam* and *Eve* been created at first, this strict affinity of relationship *by blood* could not have existed; but this was wisely and graciously contrived, as a reason for, and cement of, brotherly love—as a means of hiding pride, and boasting of one above another, with respect to their original pedigree; so that none, on this account, should despise or set at *nought his brother.* This thought is well expressed in that well-known epitaph:

> Nobles and heralds, by your leave,
> Here lie the bones of *Matthew Prior,*
> The son of *Adam* and of *Eve,*—
> Let *Bourbon* or Nassau go higher!

Although, in this corrupt and mixed state of things, civil government is necessary, therefore outward distinctions of men are necessary; for without these no civil polity could exist; yet, *in that day,* when the *governors* and *governed* shall appear before the *Great Governor of all,* they will be constrained to say, with *Joseph*'s brethren, Gen. xlii. 11. *we are all one man's sons;*—and then will know, however little attention they may give to it now, that God is *no respecter of persons.* See Acts x. 34. If these humbling considerations were improved as they ought, they would furnish us with motives of humility, benevolence, brotherly-kindness, long-suffering, mercy, and charity to each other, beyond all the arguments of the wisest moralists of *Greece* and *Rome.* See Mal. ii. 10.

LAMECH took unto him two wives, the name of one was Adah, *the other* Zillah. Here our commentators think they have found out the *sin of polygamy*—"It was one of the degenerate race of Cain," saith one, "that first transgressed the law of marriage, that *two only* should be one flesh." These are the words of one of the wisest and best (Mr. *Henry*) among our *English* commentators and serve to show how far men will go to support a popular notion, or preconceived opinion, even to the[126] *corrupting of the Bible.* There are no such words as *"two only"* in the law of marriage referred to.—It stands, Gen. ii. 24. *they shall be one flesh*; and, as mentioned by Christ, Matt. xix. 5. οἱ δυο—*they twain shall be one flesh.* So Mark x. 8. Had the words *"two only"* been there, we should not have read so frequently afterwards of God's countenancing, or His saints practising *polygamy*, any more than of His countenancing, and *their* practising *adultery.* I must here take notice of the *Evangelist's* introduction of the words οἱ δυο—*they twain,* or *the twain*—which certainly was not done as an *addition* to the original words, or as an *interpolation,* in order to introduce some *new doctrine,* but merely as a sort of *paraphrase* to explain their import, sense, and meaning—that a *man* and *his wife,* though before marriage they were *two*—that is, separate, unconnected,

---

126   See *Henry* on Gen. iv. 19. When I saw the word *only* interpolated by Mr. *Henry,* I really thought it a *corruption* worthy the *church of Rome.* In this I find I was not mistaken, for the *council of Trent* thus dogmatizes—"*Adam* did pronounce the bond of matrimony to be perpetual, and that only *two persons may be joined* therein; a thing more plainly declared by Christ." See *Brent.* 784.—Now, here is an *interpolation* of the word *only,* and a downright *lye* to justify it—for where does Christ *more plainly declare,* that only *two persons* can be joined together in marriage?

Mr. *Henry* goes on to tell us, that "Hitherto *one man* had but *one wife* at a time."—(How did he know that? See *Le Clerc* on Gen. iv. 19. and Thelyph. vol. ii. p. 161. n.)—"But *Lamech* took two— *From the beginning it was not so*"—this he would prove from Mal. ii. 15. which is nothing to the purpose. See above p. 132-139. He then falls into the usual misapplication and perversion of Matt. xix. 8. where the words *"in the beginning it was not so"*—clearly and necessarily refer to the preceding sentence, which mentions nothing but *"putting away their wives."*

Mr. *Henry* concludes his annotation on Gen. iv. 19 with two practical inferences:—"1. That those who desert God's church and *commandments* (which said *commandments* are, on this occasion, the entire *forgery* and *invention* of the *commentator*) lay themselves open to all manner of temptation.—2. That when an ill custom is begun by *ill* men, sometimes *men of better characters* are, *through unwariness,* drawn in to follow them; *Jacob, David,* and many others, who were *otherwise good men,* were afterwards ensnared in *this sin,* which *Lamech* had begun." — N. B. This is called an *Exposition* of the scriptures of the Old Testament!

independent of each other, so that they might or might not come together, yet afterwards they are *no more two*, separate, unconnected, independent persons, but as *one flesh, εις σαρκα μιαν*—The words of *οι δυο—the twain*—are not to be taken in their *numerical*[127] sense, for if they be, what follows ver. 6.—*so that they are no more twain*—would not be true; for certainly a man and woman are as much *numerically* two *after* marriage, as they are *before* it, and therefore cannot be *numerically one*; but in the same sense in which they were spoken of as *two* before, they now become *one*, that is to say, in consideration of law.

The marriage destroys their unconnectedness, distinctiveness, and independence on each other, so that in all *legal* consideration they are *no more twain, but one flesh*. Therefore, the consequence is proved which our blessed Lord meant to prove—it could not be *lawful for a man ἀπολῦσαι— to divorce his wife for every cause,* or for *any* cause *except one,* which, of itself, divided their persons again, and amounted to a total dissolution of the marriage bond: for to make a man live with an *adulteress,* would be to make him father other people's children, defeat his own rightful heirs, and introduce that confusion into his family, which it was one grand object of the *seventh* commandment to prevent. For want of considering the words οι δυο—*they twain,* or *the twain*—in the *legal* sense above-mentioned, our commentators have jingled them in their fancies, till they have blundered into their *two only—two and no more*: thus interpolating and corrupting the words of the marriage institution, as it stands recorded. Gen. ii. 24. and what is worse still, making our *blessed Saviour* do the same, by representing Him as using the words in their *numerical* sense. This stamps untruth, nay, downright nonsense on what He says, ver. 6; for it is not true that a *man and his wife* are no more *(numerically) two;* and to say that persons who are *numerically two* are yet *numerically one* is downright nonsense. As the word *twain is* to be understood in a *legal* sense, so *they shall be one flesh,* cannot be understood in a *literal* sense, as if by a kind of matrimonial *transubstantiation* they became literally *one body (see 1 Cor. vi. 16);* but that they are so in a *legal sense* is very certain; and therefore, as a man cannot

---

127   Non *unitas essentialis,* sed *unio seu conjunctio mystica vel conjugalis* describitur.—"Nold. Part. Edit. Tymp. 750. Not an *essential unity,* but an *union* or *conjunction mystical* or *conjugal is described."* Matt. xix. 5. 6. Mark x. 8.

separate his *bones* from his *flesh,* nor his *flesh* from his *bones,* without destroying himself, so neither can a man *put away his wife* unjustly (who, in the estimation of God's law, *is bone of his bone and flesh of his flesh)* without offending against the holiness and destroying the positive obligation of the marriage-institution.

Those, who by the legerdemain of this same *numerical* interpretation of the word *twain,* added to the *sound* of the former clause of ver. 9. make Christ condemn *polygamy* as *adultery,* represent Him as using the word נאף — *adultery*— in an unauthorized unconformity to the *Hebrew* scripture (as our Lord doubtless spake in *Hebrew*); for no where is that word used, to denote a man who had one wife, *taking another to her, and cohabiting with both* (which I take to be the true and genuine notion of *polygamy);* nor is it used in any other sense, but to denote the *defilement of a married woman.* Our Saviour, who constantly appealed to the *Hebrew* scriptures for what he delivered to the people, can hardly be supposed to have advanced a doctrine so unsupported by *them*; and *that* before an audience of those very *Pharisees,* who we are told, Luke xi. 54. *were laying wait for him, seeking to catch something out of His mouth, that they might accuse Him.* Again—by making Christ declare *polygamy* to be *adultery,* they charge Him with asserting a falsehood, both in point of *law* and *fact,* by declaring all such *after-taken women* not to be the real *wives* of the men who took them; for if they were, *adultery* must be out of the question. Let us examine this on the footing of scripture. It is said, 1 Sam. xxv. 42, 43 Abigial *became* David's *wife,* and David also took Ahinoam of Jezreel, *and they were also both of them his wives.* So witnesseth the *Holy Ghost,* and this, though ver. 44. tells us, he had at that very time *another wife* living. By saying *they were also both of them his wives* (for that must be the meaning of נשים in this context) it is making each *one flesh* with him, so that he could not *divorce* either; and if either had gone to another man, she would have been an *adulteress,* and the man who took her would have been an *adulterer.* I say this, taking it for granted that the *Holy Ghost* would not have called them *his wives,* לו לנשים—*fibi in uxores.* Mont.—unless they *really were so.* See also 1 Sam. xxvii. 3.

Thus, on the authority of the *Hebrew* scripture, an *after-taken* woman is as much a man's *wife* who takes her, as the *first* is—therefore it is neither true in point of *law* or *fact,* that a man having *one wife,* and taking *another,* committeth *adultery*; for which reason it is[128] impossible Christ should ever say so, and those who make Him say so, wrest His words from their true meaning.—But as this portion of scripture will necessarily fall under farther consideration hereafter, I will now return to the history of Lamech.

Whether he did right or wrong does not appear, for it is only said—Lamech *took him two wives*. His being "of the degenerate race of Cain" made it not a jot the *worse,* or a tittle the *better*, any more than the same thing done by Jacob made it either the one or the other, because he was "of the blessed race of Seth." The invention of music, which was afterwards made such considerable use of in the *temple* of God—of *agriculture* and the *care of cattle*—of *working* in *brass* and *iron*, were all found out by Lamech's children; yet I cannot conceive that they are the less innocent in themselves, or less useful to mankind, than if they had been found out by Abraham, Isaac, and Jacob. We can only say of such observations on scripture, that they are *very silly*; but if the word of God is to be corrupted in order to serve as a foundation for them, they are very *wicked*. See Deut. iv. 2; xii. 32. I only mention Mr. *Henry,* but I might name others; *one* who goes so far in corrupting the text that he represents it as the command of God, "that *two, and no more*, should be *one flesh*, Gen. ii. 24." The words simply are והיו לבשר אחד—*Et erunt in carnem unam.* Καὶ ἔσονται οἱ δύο εἰς σάρκα μίαν. Matt. xix. 5. *They twain shall be one flesh.* The words ἔσονται οἱ δύο—*they two shall be, &c.*—relate to the *man* and his *wife,* mentioned in the same verse, and answer to the והיו Gen. ii. 24, which signifies *they shall be*—meaning the איש and ואשתו the *man* and his *wife,* Gen. ii. 24. So that though here is a small variation between *they shall be* and *they twain shall* be, yet it is merely *verbal* in point of quotation; the *sense* is just the same, whether, speaking of a man and woman, we say—*they,* or—*they twain*: but adding the word *only*, or *they two and no more*, is a very material alteration, so material as to alter the whole sense of the passage, and to make every *polygamist*

---

128   It is very certain that the whole law of *Moses,* even the *ceremonial* part of it, was at this time in all its force and obligation—therefore to represent Christ, who came to vindicate its honour, and enforce the respect due to it, as laying down a proposition in direct contrariety to the whole tenor of the *Jewish* law, is to represent Him as uttering a downright falsehood, and this in the face, as it were, of the whole *Jewish* nation, which He so constantly referred to the writings of *Moses,* for the truth of what He said.

that ever lived an offender against the original *institution of marriage*. Rather than fail in this, even the learned *Beza* himself will condescend to talk nonsense. On 1 Cor. vi. 16, where the *apostle* cites our Lord's words—*Two shall be one flesh*—"this οἱ δύο," says he, "is not mentioned by *Moses*, but is rightly added, as well in this place as in Matt. xix. 5 and Mark x. 8, because there is only mention made of a man and of *one wife*, but not of *wives*; nor is it true that a *polygamist* is *one* with each of his several wives when he is rather *divided into as many parts as he has wives*". Though this learned man represents a *polygamist* as *Judges* xix. 29 represents the *Levite's concubine*, whom *he divided, together with her bones, into twelve parts, and sent her into all the coasts of* Israel, yet the *polygamists* which we read of in scripture were as *entire* individuals, in a *moral* as well as a *natural* sense, as those who had but *one wife;* otherwise each woman could not have called the man[129] *her husband,* 1 Sam. i. 8, 22, 23, nor could each woman be called *his wife,* ver. 2. Now whatever parties, being united, in God's account are *man* and *wife,* they are also[130] *one flesh,* therefore it is *true,* "that a *polygamist* is *one* with each[131] of his several wives"— that is to say, in the *legal* sense above-mentioned; nor can all the reasonings of men prove them otherwise, 'till they can prove themselves wiser than He is who declares them to be so. And I do verily believe, that if a man had *seduced* any wife of a *polygamist,* and had been arraigned before the judges of *Israel* on that

---

129 It is, in our law, commonly said, that each *joint-tenant* is seised of the land, which he holdeth jointly, *per my & per tout—"by the half, or by part, and by the whole." "Et sic totum tenet, & nihil tenet*—scil.—*totum conjunctim, & nihil seperatim,"* says *Lord Coke.*—"And thus he holdeth the whole, and holdeth nothing—that is to say, the *whole jointly,* and *nothing separately.*" COKE LITT. 186. a. LITT. § 288.

130 This phrase, according to the *Hebrew,* denotes all relationship, whether of *affinity* by marriage, as Gen. ii. 24. or *consanguinity.* See Gen. xxix. 14. Judges ix. 2. 2 Sam. v. 1. 1 Chron. xi. 1. 2 Sam. xix. 12, 13. So that the conjuration of *Beza,* and other commentators, who have found out that a man can only be *one flesh* with *one woman,* may also find out that but *one* of his relations can be of *his bone* and of *his flesh,* or be called so with any propriety. In Lev. xviii. 6. *a man's near of kin* is in the Hebrew שאר בשרו—*remainder of his flesh.* Eng. Marg.—every near relation being, as it were, a *remnant,* or remainder of the same flesh and blood of which we ourselves consist.

131 Even as CHRIST, the *husband of the church* (comp Is. liv. 5. with 2 Cor. xi. 2.) is as really *one* with every *several* believer, as with the whole church collectively or as the *head* is *one* with *each* and *all* the members of the body. See post.

183

statute, Deut. xxii. 22. *he* must, as well as the *woman*, have been condemned to die, notwithstanding what *Beza* has said, or what all the reasoners in the world could have said on the subject of *polygamy*, in *arrest* of judgment.

But there is a text in the Old Testament, which is looked upon by some to be a direct forbiddance of *polygamy*; for it stands in the margin of our Bibles—*Thou shalt not take one wife to another*. If this be the right rendering of the *Hebrew*, then the saints of old time sinned against *light, knowledge,* and *law*[132] with a witness! But it is translated in the text—*Neither shalt thou take a wife to her sister, to vex her, in her life-time*. Lev. xviii. 18. First, I would observe, that the marginal reading—*"one wife to another"*—disunites entirely the 18th verse from the preceding context to which it belongs; this only treats of marriages which are unlawful with respect to *affinity* and *consanguinity*. The *brother's wife* had there been spoken of, ver. 16; here, most naturally, as a necessary part of the prohibition of *incest,* the *wife's sister*. Secondly, This rendering of the text is agreeable to the grammatical sense of the *Hebrew*, which the other is not. This is demonstrably shewn in *Tympius's* note on *Lev.* xviii. 18. in *Noldius*, Heb. Part. אשה p. 30. But as I find the meaning of this important passage better explained by the learned *Bishop Patrick on the place*, than I can express it in any words of my own, I will transcribe the *Bishop's* note as it stands:

"There are a great many eminent writers who, following our marginal translation (*one wife to another*), imagine that here *plurality of wives* is expressly forbidden by God, and they think there is an example to justify this translation,

---

132   Ipsos quoque Judæos hanc legem de *polygamia* haud accepisse, perpetua consuetudo plures sibi ex hac gente jungentium uxores ostendit. Non autem videntur tanto impetu per *vetitum nefas* ruisse, præcipuè legis divinæ cætera studiosissimi, si expresso hujusmodi mandato hac de re cautum fuisset. Tympius in Nold. p. 30, note r.

"That the *Jews* themselves did not understand this law as concerning *polygamy*, their constant practice of marrying a plurality of wives demonstrates; for it is not probable that they should have rushed with such violence into prohibited wickedness, especially those who were most observant of the divine law in all other respects, if cautioned against it by so express a commandment."

This is certainly very *improbable*, yet not so *improbable,* as that, if *polygamy* be against the original institution of marriage, and, as such, here forbidden by a *positive law*, God should nowhere appear to disapprove it, or enact any *judicial law* against it, on the side of the man, as on the side of the woman. See Lev. xx. 10, where the *wife* who is defiled, and the *man* who defiles her, are condemned to *capital punishment*.

Exod. xxvi. where *Moses* is commanded to take care that the *five curtains* of the tabernacle were coupled together, *one to its sister,* as the *Hebrew* phrase is, meaning *one to another*; which, if it were true, would solve several difficulties: but there are such reasons against it, as that I cannot think it to be the meaning. For as *more wives than one* were indulged *before* the law, so they were *after.* And *Moses* himself supposes as much, when he provides, a man should not prefer a child he had by a *beloved wife,* before one he had by her whom he *hated,* if he was the *eldest son*; which plainly intimates an allowance in his law of *more wives than one.*"

Here, by the good and learned *Bishop's* leave, I would observe that he expresses himself rather inaccurately; for by saying—"Moses himself supposes as much," and by calling the law he is mentioning, "*his* (Moses's) law"—it looks as if Moses was speaking by his *own* wisdom, and establishing some law merely on his *own* authority; whereas Moses, under the immediate inspiration of the *Holy Ghost (Numb.* xi. 17, 25. and 2 Pet. i. 21.) is the mouth of God Himself to the people; to whom He says, *Deut.* iv. 5: *Behold, I have taught you statutes and judgments, even as the* Lord *commanded me, that ye should do so in the land whither ye go to possess it.* The only instance in which Moses acted by his *own* authority, was in the matter of *divorces.* When our Saviour is mentioning this, *Matt.* xix, He does not say—God *suffered,* but—Moses, *because of the hardness of your hearts, suffered you to put away your wives; but from the beginning it was not so*; plainly intimating that such *divorce* was not of God's ordaining, but merely of Moses's *permission,* as an expedient to obviate the mischiefs of his enforcing the letter of the law in every instance, by compelling them to retain their wives; thus subjecting them to their ill treatment and brutality, even to the beating and perhaps killing them. So that, in this *toleration of divorce* for, or upon account of, the *hardness of their hearts,* Moses might say as PAUL, 1 Cor. vii. 12. *To such speak I,* Not *the* Lord—but as to other things, not I, but the Lord, ver. 10.—The *Bishop* proceeds—"And so we find expressly their *kings* might have, though not a *multitude, Deut.* xvii. 17; and their *best* king, who red God's law *day and night,* and could not but understand it, took *many wives* without any reproof: nay, God gave him more than he had before, by delivering his (late) master's *wives* to him, 2 Sam. xii. 8. And besides all this, Moses, speaking all along in this chapter of *consanguinity* and *affinity,* it is reasonable, as *Schindlerus* observes, to conclude he doth so here, not of *one woman to another,* but of one[133] *sister to another*. There being also the like reason to understand the word *sister* properly in this place, as the words *daughter* or *mother* in others, ver. 17, and chap. xx. 14. where he forbids a man to take a woman and *her mother*, or a woman *and her daughter*, as *Theodoric Hackspan* sufficiently notes.

The meaning therefore is, that though *two wives at a time, or more*, were permitted in those days, no man should take two *sisters* (as Jacob formerly did, before there was any positive law against it) begotten of the *same father*, or born of the *same mother*, whether legitimately or illegitimately, (which, though it may seem prohibited before, because the marriage of a *brother's wife* is forbidden) yet it is here directly prohibited, as other marriages are which were implicitly forbidden before; for ver. 7. the marriage of a *son* with his *mother* is forbidden, and ver. 10. the marriage of a *father* with his *daughter*."

To the above remarks of the learned and judicious *Bishop Patrick*, I will venture to add a conjecture of my own, the solidity of which must be submitted to the *reader's* determination. It is very certain that at ver. 16. the marriage of a *brother's wife* is forbidden, and as the *wife's sister* is thereby virtually or implicitly forbidden to marry the *sister's husband*, it might be supposed that there was little occasion to mention the *wife's sister* in direct terms afterwards, ver. 18. But the necessity of this is apparent, when we recollect the precedent of Jacob, which the *Jews* would probably have urged against an *interpretative* prohibition of such a thing, at ver. 16. It was certainly no *sin* in *Jacob*, because there was no *law* against it; but after this positive law, it could not be done *without sin*, for—*sin is the transgression of the law.*

As there was but *one* man and *one* woman at first, the peopling of the world must have been carried on between much nearer relations, and therefore there could be no law to forbid marriages of this sort. So after the flood, when but *eight persons*, and those all of one family, were left of mankind, we find, for many ages, no laws enacted against marrying within those degrees of relationship, which were afterwards expressly prohibited. But when the[134] *reason* ceased, the

---

133   It is to be observed that חיות is used *four* times in other parts of the chapter, and necessarily signifies, as our translators have rendered it—*a sister*. So Lev. xx. 17, 19.

134   After the *Exodus*, the *Israelites* were refrained from marrying within certain degrees of

thing itself was to cease, as demonstrably appears by God's enacting the positive laws against marrying within certain degrees of *consanguinity* and *affinity*; subject nevertheless, like all other of His general laws, to such exceptions, restraints, or qualifications, as He in His infinite wisdom should see expedient. Some of them carry their own reasons with them, others do not, but doubtless all equally wise, as equally the dispensations of *Omniscience*.

By the way, I cannot help observing it as a very extraordinary thing that the *Christian* churches should adopt one part of the law respecting marriages and pay no regard to the rest of it. They have made the *eighteenth* chapter of *Leviticus*, from ver. 6 to ver. 18, inclusive, a part of our religion; so Exod. xx. 14 and some other passages of the law. But why this and not the rest of the whole law of God, where marriage, as His ordinance relating to all mankind, is concerned? Is not this proceeding of *Christian churchmen*, like that of the *Jewish, Mal.* ii. 9, where God complains—*Ye have not kept my ways, but have been partial in the law?* The man who renders a solid reason for adopting *Exod.* xx. to ver. 17, inclusive, and Lev. xviii. from ver. 6 to ver. 18, inclusive, as well as many other parts of that chapter, and at the same time rejecting *Exod.* xxii. 16. and *Deut.* xxii. 28, 29, as touching the *moral* intendment of them, will perform a very difficult task, unless he can prove that marrying a *wife's sister*, for instance, is a greater crime, and of more evil tendency to mankind, as well as more inimical to the interests of *civil society*, than *enticing a virgin—debauching* her—and then[135] *abandoning* her to *infamy* and *prostitution*; or, that though this was a *sin* in the days of *Moses*, yet it is *no sin* now, and therefore the positive commandments which God enacted to prevent it, are

---

consanguinity, which had been, till then, permitted, to prevent their taking wives from among the idolatrous nations with whom they lived.

This was the reason which *Abraham* gave, for chusing a wife for *Isaac* from his own kindred (Gen. xxiv. 3 seq.), and his descendants for following his example, *Gen.* xxviii. 1, & alib. But which was now entirely ceased, by their being so multiplied; so that they could easily find wives, without being necessitated to marry their near relations, or to contract marriages with the *heathen*. See Ant. Univ. Hist. vol. Iii. p. 140.

135   This is what the *Jews* do not suffer to be done to this hour—if a *single man* debauches a virgin, he is obliged to *marry her*—if a *married man* does so, he is obliged to maintain her as long as he lives. This in countries where *polygamy* is not allowed; in others, where it is allowed, he must *marry her.* Surely, in this respect, they may *rise in judgment against this generation, and condemn it.*

no longer to be considered of any force or obligation.

It is true, that we do not keep *precisely* the[136] *seventh day*, as the *Christian Sabbath*, looking upon the *fourth* commandment, in that respect, as ceremonial, typical, or prefigurative of something else (whether rightly or not does not come within my present design to consider); but as to the *moral* part, which sanctifies a given *portion* of our time for the public worship of Him to whom we stand indebted for all, we very rightly look upon this as the bounden duty and service of *Christians*, as well as *Jews*, till time shall be no more. So with regard to the sum of *fifty shekels*, or the dower according *to the dowry of virgins* (see *Exod.* xxii. 16, *Deut.* xxii. 29), this may be set down among the ceremonial or temporary observances of what may be called, to this purpose, the *Jewish* law. But with respect to the *moral* intendment of those laws in *Exodus and Deuteronomy*, which was to establish, ratify, and confirm the *marriage-ordinance* in the fullness of its obligation—*they shall be one flesh*—to prevent men from abandoning women to whoredom and prostitution, and all the bitter consequences of seduction and dereliction, those laws ought to be as binding on the consciences of mankind, as the *morality* of the *fourth* commandment, or of any other law of God whatsoever. To these purposes, they are as much *moral laws as any of the ten commandments*. If this be not the case, why do we waste the time of public worship in causing these chapters to be read over to the people? *Deut.* xxii. is our first lesson for the *evening* service every 4th of *March*; as is *Exod.* xxii. for every 8th of *February* in the *morning*. But it would be very strange if the *minister* was to preface with—"Good people, ye are assembled here to hear the word of God; but ye are not to mind what ye hear, because the protection of females from the lust, villainy, treachery, and cruelty of men, is no

---

136   I have lately seen a MS. of that laborious calculator and chronologist, *Mr. Kennedy*, in which he would prove, that what we call *Sunday*, is the true original *Sabbath*. This is very clear, that the *week* was divided into *seven days*, so early as at the creation of the world (see Gen. i.); that each day is distinguished by the works which God wrought therein; that the day on which God is said to *rest from all His work that He had made*, is called the *seventh day*, which he *hallowed and sanctified* on that account; that the fourth commandment recites all this, as the reason for its being kept holy; that the *Jews* have at all times observed our *Saturday* as the *seventh day* or *Sabbath*; that its Greek name Σάββατον, and its Latin name *Dies Sabbathi*, always denoted the *Jewish* Sabbath; and that the day we call *Sunday*, is in the New Testament called Μια Σαββάτων, the *first day of the week*—ergo, it cannot be *the seventh*.

longer an object of the laws which I am going to read to you. They bound the *Jews*, but *we Christians* have nothing to do with them." Dreadful as such language would be to hear, it says no more than every man does, who contends for the obsoleteness and abolition of these wise, holy, and salutary provisions for *female* security.

With respect to the New Testament, the subject of *polygamy*, simply considered, is not so much as mentioned, either as good or bad. The more I have searched, the more I am convinced that it is not to be found, unless incidentally in the epistles to *Timothy* and *Titus*, and there only hinted at as the possible situation of certain people. Nor is there the least occasion it should be mentioned, as it was amply explained and determinately settled in the *law which was given by Moses* (see John i. 17.); where we do not find it said, that *one law* was given by *Moses*, and *another law* by *Jesus Christ*; but *Ο νόμος*, the law—which, in the connection it stands, must signify the *whole law*—all the law which God ever ordained or revealed to mortals—*was given by* Moses; *Grace*—to pardon the transgressions of that law; *Truth*—to fulfil and answer every demand of its *moral* requirements, as well as every ceremonial prefiguration—*came by* Jesus Christ. *Heb.* ix. 15. Col. ii. 17. So that Christ *is the end of* the law *for righteousness to every one that believeth.* Rom. x. 4.

However, as it is almost universally taken for granted, that "though *polygamy* might be *allowed* under the Old Testament, yet it is forbidden under the New Testament;" and as this opinion is as prevalent as that of *transubstantiation*, and the worship of the *Virgin Mary*, are in the church of *Rome*, and for centuries were in the church of *England*, let us proceed farther to examine the foundation upon which it stands.

In the first place, I cannot find, or even conceive, an instance in which the writings of the *apostles* of Christ contradict those of Moses and the prophets. If there could be such a thing, *both* must be *rendered suspicious—one* must be *false*—both sides of a contradiction cannot be *true*. The *adversaries* of revelation have long *tried*, as they have earnestly wished, to find such a thing, but in vain! God forbid that its *friends* should even imagine it possible! If it be true that the scriptures of the Old Testament *are able to make us wise unto salvation*[137], 2 Tim. iii. 15. it must be because they contain *the law* and the *gospel*; for no man can be *wise unto salvation* without the knowledge of these. They certainly contain *both*— the *gospel* was *preached unto* Abraham *Gal*. iii. 8; to the Israelites under the Old Testament, as *well as to us* under the New Testament Heb. iv. 2. We have *the same spirit of faith*, 2 Cor. iv. 13. and doubtless the *same object of faith* 1 Cor. x. 4. *Numb*. xxi. 9. with *John* iii. 14, 15. Wherefore it is not to be conceived, that God should leave the *heirs of salvation* in a state of ignorance touching the *original* institution of marriage, or of the meaning of those *positive* laws which were to enforce it (and this after the giving of the law for 1500 years together), any more under the Old Testament than under the New Testament. It must be as necessary for a *Jew*, in order *to be wise unto salvation*, to know God's mind and will on these interesting and important subjects as for a *Christian*. Each must be *judged* by the *same law*—each *saved*, though under different dispensations of it, by the *same gospel*.

As little probable is it, that He should allow His own beloved children to fly in the face of His authority and live in the breach of His *positive law*, for so long a period without the least check or reproof, when part of His gracious covenant runs in these words, Ps. lxxxix. 30. *If his children forsake my* Law, *and walk not in my* Judgments; *if they break my* Statutes, *and keep not my Commandments*; *then will I visit their offenses with the rod, and their sin with scourges*. There are instances enough of this for other things—*witness* David's *broken bones*, Ps. li. 8. for his *adultery* with Bathsheba, and murder of Uriah. But where is there one instance of it for *polygamy*? Wherein did God ever punish it? David died as really a *Christian believer* as St. Paul did; witness his *last words*, 2 *Sam*. xxiii. 5; and yet, amidst all the explicit confessions he made in the most solemn hours of his *repentance*, he does not once[138] bewail the *polygamy* he lived in; nay, almost the last act of his life was

---

137   The Apostle adds—διὰ πίστεως τῆς ἐν Χριστῷ Ἰησοῦ—*through faith which is in* Christ Jesus, *i.e.* believing Him to be the Messiah. For want of believing which, the apostate *Jews* were not made *wise unto salvation* by the scriptures of the Old Testament.

138   Which is very extraordinary, and indeed *unaccountable*, if to have more than *one wife at a time* be a *mortal sin*. The character also which we have of David, 1 *Kings xv*. 5. has, upon this principle, a

an act of *polygamy*, in taking Abishag the *Shunamite* to *lie in his bosom*, his wife Bathsheba being then living. For though it be said, 1 Kings i. 4. that *he knew her not*; yet it plainly appears, by what Solomon said, 1 Kings ii. 22, 23. that she was so *betrothed* or *espoused* to David, as to be looked upon as *his wife*[139]. Accordingly she belonged to the crown; was to be at the disposal of the *successor*; and therefore Adonijah, who was elder than Solomon, by asking for Abishag, the late king's widow, to wife, is treated as having a treasonable design against the crown itself, and is put to death as a *traitor*.

Is it then conceivable that *polygamy*, allowed of God uninterruptedly through so many ages and generations with impunity and even approbation, should all of a sudden start up into a *mortal sin*, by the *seventh* commandment's receiving a construction which it never before had—which was never before given to the words in which it was conceived? How could our lives and properties be secure, if time could alter the meaning of our penal statutes?—who will draw the line, and say how much or how little time is necessary to effect this? But if such can be the case with the *moral* law of God, then was the *Psalmist* mistaken in calling it *perfect* (Ps. xix. 7.) for it is *changeable*.

Then is it less to be depended on than the laws of the *Medes* and *Persians*. *Esth*. i. 19.—less sacred than the decree of an *earthly monarch*. *Esth*. viii. 8. *Dan*. vi. 15. If this be the case, what man can have any security for his *peace?*—In order therefore to avoid something worse than *absurdity*, we must conclude, that the original *institution of marriage*, and the *seventh* commandment of the *decalogue*, mean neither more nor less, where *Christians* are concerned, than where the *Jews* were—or, in other words, they mean precisely *one* and the *same* thing under the *New Testament as under the Old Testament*.

By taking texts here and there in the New Testament, and detaching

---

degree of *obscurity*, which must render it wholly unintelligible—for how can it be said of a man, who lived and died in an open, avowed, wilful, and continued course of deliberate iniquity, that *he did that which was right in the eyes of the Lord, and turned not aside from any thing that He commanded him all the days of his life, save* only *in the matter of Uriah the Hittite*?

139 Comp. Deut. xxii. 23, 24, where a *betrothed* virgin is called the man's *wife*, so as to make it *adultery* to defile her.

them from their reference to and connection with the Old Testament, many *heresies* have arisen; as *Arianism, Socinianism*, and perhaps most others. *Ye do err, not knowing the scriptures.* So with regard to *marriage*—because Christ said— *Some make themselves eunuchs for the kingdom of heaven's sake: he that is able to receive it, let him receive it* (Matt. xix. 12.); and St. Paul, 1 Cor. vii. 1. and in other parts of that chapter, speaks in favour of a *single life*, with respect to the then *distressed* state of the church (ver. 26) there were multitudes of people, in the early[140] ages of *Christianity*, who took these things in a wrong sense, and found out that "marriage was a *carnal* thing, and forbidden by the New Testament, as unbecoming the purity of that dispensation:" little reflecting, that the command of *increase and multiply*, and the institution of *marriage* as the means thereof, were the dispensations of God Himself to our *first parents* when they were in a state of perfect innocence, and therefore could not be incompatible therewith.

That venerable man *John Trapp*, on 1 *Cor.* vii. 8, says—"The blemish will never be wiped off some of the antient[141] *fathers*, who, to establish their own idol of I know not what *virginity*, which they themselves had not, have written most wickedly and basely of marriage." To say the truth, I cannot conceive any man's conscience to be more *taken captive by the devil* (2 Tim. ii. 26) than his is, who is brought under a persuasion that *celibacy* is more *pure* and *holy*, and, as such, more acceptable to God than *marriage*. Such a one, who, under this persuasion, abstains from marriage, lives in perpetual[142] opposition to that command which

---

140   "There arose in the *church* from *antient times*, sects of *heretics*, who condemned wine, and the use of animal food, and *marriage*; and not only *heretics*, but the *orthodox* also, ran into extravagant notions of the same kind, crying up *celibacy* and a *solitary life* beyond measure, together with rigid and uncommanded austerities and macerations of the body. (*Jortin*, Rem. vol. i. 278.)—*Christ* therefore, as we may conjecture, was present at a *marriage-feast*, and honoured it with the miracle of turning water into *wine*, that it should stand in the *gospel as* a confutation of these foolish errors, and a warning to those *who had ears to hear*, not to be deluded by such *fanatics*. St. *John*, who records this miracle, lived to see these false doctrines adopted and propagated." Ib.

141   *"Jerom, Ambrose*, and other *fathers*, have declaimed against matrimony and recommended monkish abstinence almost as much as *Manes*, and have employed almost as insignificant arguments." Id vol, ii. p. 69.

142   Dr. *Alexander*, Hist. Wom. vol. ii. p. 269, introduces what he says on the subject of *emasculation* on a religious account, with this pertinent and sensible observation:

was given with a *blessing* from God—*Increase and multiply, and replenish the earth, &c.* This was at the original creation of *male and female* upon earth (Gen. i. 27, 28). And again, at the renewal of the earth after the deluge, this commandment stands (Gen. ix. 1, 7), repeated *twice*. Now can an opposition to so positive, so expressed, so reiterated an ordinance of Heaven, be reckoned a constituent part of *righteousness* and *true holiness?* What is this, but to fly in the face of *divine wisdom* and *goodness*, and to esteem ourselves *wiser* and *holier* than the Lord of all? So those who prefer a life of *solitude* to matrimonial connection, as *better* and *better*; how much *better* and *better* do they make themselves than Him who said—*It is* Not Good *for man to be alone? It is* remarkable that the reiterated command for the propagation of the species stands, Gen. ix 7, in direct connection, as it were, and immediately following after the positive law against *murder*: as *prevention* of life is an offence against this, *prevention* of life is something very like it, and therefore fitly placed near it in the sacred code.

Some of the fathers were wild enough to say—*hoc dictum, ratione multitudinis liberorum, pertinere ad tempora ante* CHRISTUM, *non ad nos qui alio vivimus ævo—mundum jam non desiderare* ILLUD CRESCITE ET MULTIPLICAMINI. "This command, by reason of multiplying children, belonged to the *times before* CHRIST, not to *us*, who live in another age—the world does not now want that same—*Be fruitful, and multiply.*" Such were the delusions of *Jerom—Tertullian—Chrysostom—Cyprian—Oecume—nius*, &c. Bernard, in Cant. Serm. 59. thus glosses on the words—*The voice of the turtle is heard, &c.*; which he says is "the preaching of *continence*, respecting those who castrate themselves for the kingdom of heaven. At *the beginning* that voice was not heard, but rather *increase and multiply;* for barrenness was subject to a curse;

"The two sexes were evidently intended for each other, and *increase and multiply* was the first great command given them by the Author of Nature. But suppose no such command had been given, how it first entered into the mind of man that the propagation or continuation of the species was criminal in the eye of Heaven, is not easy to conceive. Ridiculous, however, as this notion may appear, it is one of those which early insinuated itself amongst mankind, and plainly demonstrated, that reasoning beings are most apt to deviate from nature; and not only to disobey her plainest dictates, but, on pretence of pleasing the Author of Nature, to render themselves forever incapable of obeying them."

polygamy was[143] allowed," &c. His words are—"*Vox turturis audita est,* quæ est predicatio continentiæ, eos, qui se *castrant* propter regnum cœlorum, spectans; cum ab initio vox ista non sit audita, sed magis—*crescite* & *multiplicamini,* fterilitas etiam maledictioni suit subjecta, *polygamia* concessa," &c.; but all this is now at an end, "quia hodie, repleto mundo, non tam sit necessaria quam olim"—"because now, the world being filled (with people) it is[144] not so necessary as formerly." If the reader has a mind to see how far folly and enthusiasm can carry people on these subjects, let him read *Tertullian's* epistles to *Eustachius*—to *Gerontius*—and against *Helvetius*; *Tertullian* on Chastity; *Chrysostom* on Virginity; *Cyprian* on the discipline of Virgins; and *Oecumenius* on 1 Cor. vii.—then he will begin to find out how MARRIAGE ITSELF was vilified, and of course, what gave rise to the condemnation of *second* marriages of all sorts, therefore of *polygamy*, in the *Christian church*, till the church of *Rome* had the impudence to *anathematize* the man who should say, that "it was *not forbidden by the law of* God," (see *Brent. Coun. Trent.* p. 784) "just as they did those who should affirm that for a *priest* to marry was *allowed* by the law of God". Ibid.

The consequences of all this unnatural plan of *celibacy* are too many to

---

143   This same *St. Bernard*, abbot of *Clairval*, from whom the *Cistercian* monks derived the name of *Bernardins*, was one of the most eminent among the Latin writers of the 12th century. He was a man of genius, taste, and judgement in some respects, and in others weak and superstitious. See Mosh. vol. i. 591. A pretty clear proof of the latter part of his character lies before us. His confining the command—*Be fruitful and multiply—to the days of the Old Testament,* is certainly a master-stroke of folly and weakness—however, his acknowledgment of the allowance of *polygamy* as a concomitant of that command, is much more scriptural and consistent, than the comments of some more modern expositors (or rather *exposers*) of the scriptures, who contend for the obligation and permanency of the command itself but deny the permanency and obligation of those laws which divine wisdom enacted for its regulation.

144   De liberis ferendis non ita solliciti erant *Christiani*, ut ob id solúm ducendæ uxoris necessitatem sibi imponerent; ideo quod finem seculorum de proximo instare suspicarentur. *Tertull.* de *Monogamia. Crescite & redundate evacuavit extremitas temporam.* See Pole Synop. in 1 Cor. vii. 1. "The *Christians* were not so solicitous concerning the propagating children, as if, on that account alone, they were to lay a necessity on themselves to marry, because they might suspect the end of the world was very near. *Tertull. de Monogamia.* The (supposed approaching) end of the times vacated the command of—*increase* and *multiply*." See *Pole Syn*
1 Cor. vii. 1.

enumerate, too[145] *horrible* to particularize. It fared with numbers of the *Christian*, who did not like *to retain* the *divine command* in their practice, as it did with the *heathens*, who did *not like to retain* God *in their knowledge*—God *gave them up to uncleanness, to dishonour their own bodies between themselves*: who changed the *truth* of God *into a lye*, &c. *For this cause,* God *gave them up*[146] *to vile affections,* &c. See Rom. i. 24-28. When we endeavour to stop the course of a river by laying a dam across the stream, the effect must be, that it will either make its way, bearing down all before it, or it will make a passage over its banks, and overflow and destroy the country. Such is the effect of endeavouring to stop the natural course of those desires which the Creator has implanted in us for the purpose of carrying His *primary command* into execution. They will bear down all before them, or be turned out of their course; and then follows what the history of the *Popish* celibacy abundantly acquaints us with. As this is a subject too indelicate to dwell on, I will only refer the reader to those books which treat thereof; such as *Foxe's Martyrology*—The *Packets* from *Rome*, collected and published in *two volumes* quarto, by a *set of gentlemen*, 1735, under the title of *The History of Popery*, vol. ii. p. 431. A work this, which is too valuable to be lost to the public; and therefore, as I fear it is near out of print, it were to be wished it should be reprinted in as handsome an edition as that above referred to. See also *Burnet Hist.* Ref. vol. i. p. 191.

As for those men who have the *gift of continency*, they, as it appears from

---

145   It is an observation of the excellent *authors* of the *History of Popery*, vol. i. p. 359, that "the first law against a certain *unnatural vice* in *England* was by *Anselm,* Archbishop of *Canterbury,* in the days of *William Rufus*; which said *vice* seems not to have been heard of here till *priests* were forbidden marriage. However, they treated it very gently, leaving it less penal in a *priest,* than to enjoy his lawful wife.—*Secular* men, guilty of this crime, were to be absolved only by the *bishop*; but the *monks* and *priests,* it seems, might civilly absolve *each other.* Yet even this *canon,* such as it is, was soon after recalled, and never published." Bernard, *Cent.* 12th, said, that sin was *frequent* among the *bishops* in his time, and that this, with many other abominations, was the effect of prohibiting marriage. BURNET *Hist. of Reform.* vol. ii. p. 91, 3d edit.

146   A thousand instances of which might be given—*sed ab uno disce omnes*—Pope *Sixtus* V. on the petition of *Peter Ricu,* cardinal and patriarch of *Constantinople,* of *Jeronymo* his own brother, and the cardinal of St. *Luce,* permitted "unto them and every one of them, *sodomy,* with this clause— FIAT UT PETITUR—Let it be done as it is desired." *History of Popery,* vol. ii. 292.

the scriptures, and all experience, are probably *very few*, at least comparatively; and those who received it in the days of *our* Lord and His *apostles*, seem to have received this for the particular purpose of keeping themselves *disentangled from the affairs of this life*, during the infancy and persecution of the church, 1 Cor. vii. 7, 17. Such do not want *cloysters* and *cells* for their security. As for those who have[147] it not, locking them up together in such places, and depriving them of the remedy which God *commands* in *marriage*, has been attended with a two fold wickedness; 1. in living contrary to the ordinance of Heaven; 2. in gratifying their desires contrary to the course of nature, or at least in some way which the *divine law* hath prohibited. Therefore the *Apostle* doth not say—if *they cannot contain*, let them shut themselves up, or pray that the order of nature may be inverted; but—*let them marry*; it is better *to marry than burn*: as if he had said—"*One* or *other* of these must be the consequence." So, when married persons have separated for a while or *season*, on some *religious occasions—come together again*, saith he, lest *Satan tempt you for your incontinency*.

From all which it may be gathered, that *celibacy* is not an ordinance of God, but a snare of *Satan*—that marriage *is* the ordinance of God; therefore, that a man who *may* marry, and doth not, has no more[148] warrant from God's word to expect that he shall be kept from *vice*, than that he would be kept from *starving*, if, instead of *eating* and *drinking*, he was to pray that the appetites of *hunger* and

---

147   These certainly constitute the bulk of mankind, as all experience throughout all ages sufficiently shews. The natural structure of the human body, its natural secretions, &c. which are carried on daily, not by any contrivance or management of the creature, but by the power of infinite wisdom, impressed, we know not *how*, on the wondrous mechanism of every part, afford us such *physical* reasons for this, as to amount to a demonstration of the necessity of marriage in the generality of men. This observation is abundantly verified by the manner of our Saviour's expression, Matt. xix. 11, 12, where He speaks of a power of total abstinence as the immediate and *special gift* of heaven, and this for a *special purpose*, unless in the cases, he puts off *accidental* imbecillity, arising, in some, from a defect in their constitution, being *born eunuchs*; in others, from external violence by the hands of men.

148   For, *continence* being none of those graces that are promised by God to all that ask it, as it was not in a man's power, without extreme severities on himself, to govern his own constitution of body, so he had no reason to expect God should interpose, when he had provided another remedy for such cases. *Burnet* Hist. Ref. vol. Ii. ii. 91, 3rd edit.

thirst might be totally annihilated.

The indiscriminate[149] and total prohibition of *polygamy*, as it has *no warrant* from the word of God, may also be the means of plunging many into the mischiefs of uncommanded *celibacy*; for many men there are, who very early in life marry, perhaps without all the consideration which ought to be exercised in so momentous an undertaking—many things may happen which may be very reasonable, and indeed unavoidable, causes of separation from their wives; as for instance—incurable disease of mind or body, unconquerable violence of temper, perpetual refractoriness[150] of disposition, levity of behaviour—which, though not

149   If the enacting part of 1 Jac. c. 11 had gone no farther than the preamble, and its severity been confined to—"diverse evil-disposed persons, who being married, run out of one county into another, or into places where they are not known, and there become married, having another husband or wife living, to the great dishonour of God, and the utter undoing of diverse honest men's children, and others"—it would have been a wholesome law and highly justifiable in its penalty on such miscreants; who are undoubtedly guilty of one of the vilest and most injurious frauds that can possibly be committed. It seems to fall within the equity of Exod. xxi. 16, for such persons are a sort of ἀνδραποδίσται or *man-stealers*.

150   It is to be feared, that there are not a few females who (like other monopolists) take advantage of the poor husband's situation, to use him as they please; and this for pretty much the same reason why the *ass*, in the fable, insulted and kicked the poor *old lion*—because it is not in their power to *resent* it as they ought.

The advice which King *Ahasuerus* received from his wife, men, the seven princes of *Media* and *Persia*, upon Queen *Vashti's* disobedience, would have had an excellent effect, could it be followed. Many a high-spirited *female* would have too cogent a reason against the indulgence of a refractory disposition, not to suppress it—her *pride*, which is now the husband's *torment*, would then become his *security*, at least in a great measure; for *pride* is a vice, which, as it tends to *self-exaltation*, maintains uniformly its own principle—not to bear the thoughts of a *rival*. See *Esther* i. 10, &c. As things are with us, the poor man must grind in *mola asinaria* during life.

It is certain, that nothing can be a release from the bond of marriage itself but *death,* or an act of *adultery* in the wife. But that a man is at all events bound to maintain the *external* bond by cohabiting with a woman, who, instead of being an *help meet for him* (as we say), becomes, by the violence and perverseness of her temper and disposition, a constant and increasing torment, and this after the most friendly, tender, and kind admonitions—is not consonant either to scripture or reason.

Some will tell us, that such a thing must be looked upon as happening by the will of PROVIDENCE, as a chastisement or visitation from Heaven, and therefore must be submitted to and endured.

So is sickness from the hand of God; so are afflictions of all kinds, and certainly to be submitted

amounting to such proof as to be the ground of utter *legal* divorce, yet such as may destroy the whole comfort of a man's life. By these and many other means, a husband may be reduced to the situation of an *unmarried* man, harassed by the same desires, subject to the same temptations; yet his condition is ten-fold worse; the one may *marry*, the other cannot: so he must remain hopeless and helpless, or plunge into *vice* and misery, because he is debarred of the remedy which God hath provided, stripped of that undoubted privilege with which God and nature have invested him, by the lies and forgeries of *fathers and councils*, &c. The *Romish* Catholic Church indeed, at the *Council of Trent*, anathematized all who should say, that "those who have not the gift of chastity might marry, in regard that God doth not deny the gift to him that doth demand it." This *anti-scriptural* decree, which directly gives the lye to the *Apostle*, 1 Cor. vii., is founded upon a *fallacy*, which

---

to with patience and resignation; yet to use means of recovery from sickness, and of deliverance from trouble and affliction, are apparent duties; and why not in the other case? The great *Milton* has some excellent and scriptural observations on these points in his *Tetrachordon*; to which I refer the reader.

It was proposed in the *book* for *reformation of the ecclesiastical law*, 1552, that "Desertion, long absence, capital enmities, where either party was in hazard of their life, or constant perverseness, or fierceness of an husband against his wife, might induce a divorce"—this fell to the ground by the death of Ed. VI. Burnet Hist. Ref. vol. ii. p. 198.

The whole analogy of scripture agrees with that saying of the *Apostle—Let not the wife depart from her husband; and again—Let not the husband put away his wife*—1 Cor. vii. 10, 11. But then these things must be construed agreeably to the analogy of that *wisdom which is profitable to direct*— Eccl. x. 10. They cannot mean, that *a wife is not to depart from her husband*, who threatens or endangers *her life*—nor that a husband may not separate from a wife who obstinately sets herself to be the plague and torment of *his*. Surely all this is within the equity of 1 Cor. vii. 15, and that persons are not *under bondage in such cases*.

This kind of things falls under a sort of *necessity*, which must always interpret the law in favour of self-preservation. *Thou shalt do no murder*—constitutes a capital offence in the man who wantonly or maliciously kills another—but if a man slays another in his own defence, it is an excusable homicide: this from the necessary care which every man has a right to take of his own life. The *ship-master* to whom I intrust my goods, is wicked and base, if he wantonly cast them into the sea; but if a storm arise, and he cast them out to save the ship from sinking, he is highly justifiable. I would therefore argue from *necessity* on the point of *separation*; for I cannot find any privilege conferred on one creature to make another wretched, and that without remedy. Of this *necessity* every person must judge at his peril; for—as the old *proverb* says—*None can tell where the shoe pinches, so well as he that wears it*; but then be it remembered—that *every man shall give an account of himself to God*. Rom. xiv. 12. If this were considered as it ought to be, it would certainly be the best means of binding both parties over *to their good behaviour*, in all conjugal disputes.

many fall into, from arguing without the necessary distinction between what God *can* do, and what He *will* do. That He *can* do everything is without a doubt; but that we are warranted to expect He *will* do what He hath nowhere promised, is not true. God *could* certainly have made us to live upon *air*; but He hath not: meat and drink are absolutely necessary for our subsistence; it would therefore be the highest presumption, nay even the madness of *enthusiasm,* for any man to pray that the natural appetites of *hunger* and *thirst* might cease, and that for the future he might live, not on meat and drink, but solely by respiration of *air.* So, to pray to Him whose command is—*Be fruitful and multiply, bring forth abundantly in the earth, and multiply therein* (Gen. ix. 7.) that the natural desire which is to lead to this may be *annihilated,* and the effect of it destroyed, is to *petition* against the *divine wisdom,* to *arraign* the *divine ordinances,* and to remonstrate, in effect, against having any share in an obedience to the *divine command.*—Where *is* there,—where *can* there be a promise, to warrant so unhallowed a proceeding? Surely no where, but in the imaginations of those who have deceived themselves, and who want to lead others into the *snare of the devil.* When we pray against what God has *forbidden,* no doubt we shall, in His own way and time, *obtain grace to help in every time of need;* but when we pray against what He has *commanded,* we tempt Him to deliver us up to the delusions of our own minds, and *our end will be* according *to our works*—what that end is likely to be, the histories before hinted at very sufficiently declare.

That there may be situations, and particular circumstances, under which it is not only *lawful,* but a *duty,* to pray for *continence*—I mean for entire subduction of, and power over, our natural desires—there can be no doubt; as where they would lead us to forbidden enjoyment: but then we must judge of this by the scriptures, not by the prejudices, folly, and superstition of men like ourselves; for, at this rate, we may be praying that God would alter His mind, change His will, and vacate His commands, in order to make way for our opposition to them. Whereas, *this is the confidence that we have in Him, that if we ask anything* ACCORDING TO HIS WILL, He *heareth us. And if we know that He hear us, whatsoever we ask* (i.e. according to His will) *we know* that *we* have *the petitions that we desired of* Him. 1 *John* v. 14, 15.

For a man to pray that he might never again feel the appetites of *hunger* and *thirst*, or, at least, be enabled to refrain entirely from satisfying them, would be deservedly reckoned madness—but to pray to be kept from *gluttony* and *drunkenness*, and all forbidden indulgence and excess, would be asking *according to the will of* God, and the man would have a *scriptural* ground and warrant to expect an answer of peace.

So, if a man takes it into his head that those other *desires*, which God hath, for the wisest purposes, implanted in our nature, are *sinful in themselves*, and, on *this footing*, prays against them, he is under a sad delusion, and every petition he utters is no less than an arraignment of the *wisdom* and *holiness* of the great *Creator* of all. Yet the *Popish* histories are replete with *miracles* wrought by *Christ* and the *Virgin Mary,* in answer to such petitions; and no doubt but these *lyes* are most *devoutly* believed by thousands, who make *men's*[151] *traditions*, and not God's *word*, the rule of their faith.

Besides the evils that have been noticed as the consequences of our *superstition* on the subject of *polygamy*, the utter extinction of *families* might also be mentioned; whereas, sooner than this should be the case in *Israel*, we find God enacting a peculiar *positive* law in order to prevent it; which said law was certainly a virtual command of *polygamy* in many, perhaps in most, cases, as it was very rare to find an *unmarried* man among the *Jews*. The law to which I allude is that of *Deut.* xxv. 5, where the *husband's brother* was to marry the widow of the deceased, if he died without children—*that his name might not be put out of Israel.* Though all the reasons for this law do not now subsist, therefore the law itself, as far as those reasons have ceased, hath itself ceased; yet it serves to show us that God did certainly allow *polygamy*, and even *command* it, sooner than suffer inheritances to

---

151   Among the fooleries of the *sixth century*, an entire abstinence from marriage was held the surest way to Paradise. Women were not even suffered to approach the altar, nor touch the pall which covered it, unless when, by the *priests*, it was delivered to them to be washed. The *eucharist* was too holy to be touched by their naked hands, they were therefore ordered, by the *canons* of the church, to have a white linen glove upon the hand in order to receive it. *See* Alexander's Hist. of Wom. vol. i. p. 166. The council of Auxerre, ann. 578, decrees, that *women* communicate with their *dominical,* which some suppose to have been a linen cloth, wherein they received the *species,* as not being allowed to receive them with the bare hand.

See Burnet Hist. Ref. vol. ii. p. 76. 3d edit. Also *Chambers*—sub voc. *Dominical.*

fail by the *extinction of families*.

The end of marriage, say some, is *society* and mutual *comfort*; but they are rather an *effect* of marriage, none of the *principal* end, which is the *procreation of children* and for the continuance of mankind, according to the first institution, Gen. i. 28. As for *comfort* and *society*, they may be between man and man, woman and woman, and therefore are not a *proper* end of marriage. That *conjunction* which cannot answer the great end for which marriage was ordained by God should not prevent or hinder that which *can*, nor does it appear from Scripture that it was ever intended it *should*.

Frigidity, or perpetual *impotency* of *generation* on the man's side, is held by our laws, as a cause of divorce a vinculo *matrimonii*; therefore, it is only reasonable that a perpetual *impotency* of *generation* (which at a certain time of a woman's life may be ascertained) in the woman, should be allowed as a reasonable and justifiable ground for *polygamy*. Folly and superstition may set up an objection to this, but *nature, reason,* and *scripture,* all unite in their suffrage for the truth of the position. See Gen. xvi. 2, 3. Gen. xxx. 1-9.

Among us, if a man is married to a *barren* woman, he cannot take another wife while she lives, but must content himself with letting his nobility, titles, honours, and family be annihilated, and his estates escheat to the crown, under pain and penalty of being adjudged a *felon* if he marries a *second wife* (living the first) who might be means of continuing and transmitting all these things to a long and numerous posterity.

This foolish superstition is like that of the *Jews* in the days of *Mattathias*, who suffered themselves to be slaughtered by the enemy without resistance, because it was the *Sabbath-day*, 1 Mac. ii. 32, 38; or like that of the *Carthusians*, who live entirely on *fish*, and would not eat a piece of other *flesh* (see 1 Cor. xv. 39.) even to save their lives.

The modern *Jews* are wiser, for though they in general coincide with the government where their lot happens to be cast, so that they are *polygamous* or *monogamous*, according to the laws of the country they live in; yet if a Jew be married *ten years* to a woman and has no child by her, he is at liberty to take another, that he may have an heir to his substance; and in so doing he certainly is justified by the law of God; which law we have set aside, and established our own superstition in its place, which not only tends to the annihilation and extinction of families, and of course to *depopulation*; but is, as elsewhere is more fully observed, the source of endless ruin and destruction to the weaker *sex*, whose *seducers*, if married men, are totally exempt from making them that amends, and doing them that justice, which God's law commanded, and which, among *us Christians*, is looked upon as a *duty* to withhold, or rather, as a *mortal*[152] *sin* to comply with.

As these points are fully treated in other parts of this book, I will now proceed to shew, that the wild notions about marriage, which were introduced into the church, bear an earlier date than the days of *Tertullian*, and those other fathers mentioned before.

"There were others," says Mr. *Broughton*—Hist. lib. tit. *Marriage*— "who simply exclaimed against marriage as *unlawful* under the *gospel*. This doctrine was first taught by *Saturnilus*, a scholar of *Simon Magus* and[153] *Marcion*, but afterwards better known amongst the[154] *Encratites*; to these may be added the *Apostolics* or *Apotactics*, the *Manichees*, *Severians*, and many others. The church had great struggles with these antient *heretics*, who inveighed bitterly against marriage under the *gospel-state*, and wrought upon many weak minds, to be guilty of great irregularities, under pretence of a more refined way of living.

The church had also another contest with the *Montanists* and *Novatians*, about *second* marriages, these *heretics* rejecting them as utterly unlawful.—And indeed, the ecclesiastical histories inform us, that this *madness* (for I can call it

---

152   *Bellermine*, that great champion *for The Man of Sin*, saith—Lib. 4. de Rom. Pontific, "Si Papa erraret præcipiendo vitia, & prohibendo virtutes, teneretur ecclesia credere vitia esse bona, & virtutes malas, nisi vellet contra conscientiam peccare."

"If the *Pope* should err in commanding *vices*, and in prohibiting *virtues*, the church would be bound to believe that vices are good, and virtues evil, unless he would sin against conscience." And again, *Cont. Barcl.* c. xxxi. "In bono sensu dedit Christus *Petro* potestatem faciendi de peccato non peccatum, & de non peccato peccatum. " "In a good sense—Christ gave *Peter*" (and of course the *Pope*) "a power of making that no sin which is sin, and to make that to be sin which is not a sin." What better principle do we proceed upon in the matters here mentioned?

153   *Marcion* prescribed to his followers an express *prohibition of wedlock*. See *Mosheim*, vol. i. p. 110. edit. *Maclaine*. One of *Marcion's* abominable tenets, which he laid down to his followers, was that they should "renounce the precepts of the God of the Jews." Ib.

154   See *Newton* on the Prophecies, vol. ii. pp. 442—3.

nothing else) was carried so far, that *second* marriages were styled no better than *whoredom*; and *ecclesiastical* persons were forbidden to be present at them on pain of *excommunication*. This in the very face of the scriptures of God, which declare just as much for *second* marriages as for *first*. Rom. vii. 2, 3. 1 Cor. vii. 39. By all this we see what work may be made with the scriptures, when the *imaginations* of men are let loose, instead of *comparing spiritual things with spiritual,* and making God the interpreter of His own word.

As for the practice of *polygamy* among the first *Christians*, it was probably very[155] frequent; if not—why did Paul (1 Tim. iii. 2. and Tit. i. 6.) recommend the choice of *Bishops* and *Deacons* from amongst those who had but *one wife*?—What occasion was there for this caution of the *apostle's* if none had *more than one*? That the *election* was to be made from amongst the *Christian believers*, there can be no doubt, that is to say, of such as had been admitted to *baptism* and the *Lord's supper*, and were enrolled as *members* of the *Christian* church. To suppose that none of these had more than *one wife,* is to suppose the *apostle* giving a needless rule in the election of *Bishops* and *Deacons*. To suppose that any who had *more than one wife* should be admitted to *baptism* and the *Lord's supper,* if Christ had forbidden *polygamy* as *adultery*, is to suppose a greater absurdity still, and that the great *apostle of the Gentiles* was less faithful to his trust, than those *Jesuits* who refused to admit the King of *Tonquin* into the Christian church unless he would put away *all his wives but one*: for which these *pseudo-apostles* were very justly driven out of the country.

The learned *Selden* has proved, in his *Uxor Hæbraica*, that *polygamy* was allowed, not only among the *Hebrews*, but among most other nations throughout the world; doubtless among the inhabitants of that vast tract of *Asia*, throughout

---

155 So it should seem to have been in times long after them, not only among the *laity*, but the *clergy* also, for Pope *Sylvester*, about the year 335, made an *ordonnance*, that every *priest* should be the *husband of one wife* only.

So in the sixth *century*, it was enacted in the canons of one of their councils, that if any one is married to *many wives*, he shall do penance. See Alex. Hist. Wom. vol. ii. 217, 272.

The case of *Philip* Landgrave of Hesse, as determined by the *six reformers*, is well known. But all these things prove nothing, with respect to the lawfulness or unlawfulness of the matter in the sight of God: I only mention them, to shew that *Christians* have, by no means, thought always alike on the subject. The *opinions* of an inspired *apostle* are certainly good evidence—to *these* let us attend.

which the *Gospel* was preached by the great *Apostle* of the *Gentiles*, where so many *Christian* churches were planted, as well as in the neighbouring states of *Greece*: yet in none of Paul's *epistles*, nor in the seven awful epistles which St. John was commanded to write to the seven churches in *Asia*, is *polygamy* found amongst the crimes for which they were reproved. Every other species of *commerce between the sexes* is distinctly and often mentioned, this not once, except on the *woman's* side, as Rom. vii. 31. But had it been sinful and against the law on the *man's side*, it is inconceivable that it should not have been mentioned on *both* sides equally.

When St. *Paul says* that a *Bishop* or *Deacon* is to be the *husband* of one *wife*, it certainly carries with it a tacit allowance of *polygamy*, as to the *lawfulness* of it with regard to[156] all other men; not that it was *sinful* in one more than in another; but this was a prudential caution in that distressed and infant state of the *church*, that those who were to have the management of it, should have as little avocation and distraction as the nature of things would admit of. Paul does not say that a *Bishop* or *Deacon* should not be *married*, as the Church of *Rome* says, but that he should be the *husband of one wife*; for however those who had *more* could find time to manage their *own* affairs, they could not be supposed to have leisure enough to attend the *church* and its embarrassed and various concerns, as they ought. Upon this principle, he seems to give the preference to those who had *no wife* 1 Cor. vii. 32, 33. *I would have you without carefulness. He that is unmarried careth for the things that belong to the* Lord, *how he may please the* Lord: *but he that is married, careth for the things that are of the world, how he may please his wife.* This certainly relates to all *Christians*, but especially to *ministers*. The *heretics* of old took it so strongly in the *former* sense, that they held marriage *unlawful* for *Christians*—the *Papists* take it so strongly in the *latter*, that it is one of the authorities on which they forbid their *clergy*[157] to marry at all.

---

156 Cardinal *Cajetan*, who disputed with *Luther* at *Augsburg*, and who is said to have given a brief, but judicious exposition of the *Old* and *New Testament*, writes thus: "*Pluralitatem uxorum nusquam a Deo prohiberi; adeoque Paulum cum Episcopum vetet habere plures uxores, reliquis concedere.*" "A plurality of wives is nowhere forbidden by God; so that Paul, when he forbids a *Bishop* to have *many wives*, allows it to others." Rainold de lib, Apoc. tom. i. præl. 4.

157 The celibacy of the *clergy* was among the errors of very early date, for *Paphnutius*, a venerable *confessor* and prelate, who assisted at the *Nicene* Council, which was held ann. 325, where there was

There are some who interpret the above *passages* (1 Tim. iii. 2. and Tit. i. 6.) to mean, that a *Bishop* or *Deacon* should, if a *widower*, have had but *one wife*, or have been *once married*; and this upon the ground of what is said in, 1 Tim. v. 9. concerning the *women* who were to be chosen for the office of *Deaconesses—Let not a woman be taken into the number under sixty years, having been the wife of one man.* There are also those, who, on the authority of these passages, hold it unlawful

---

a dispute, whether *ecclesiastics* should not separate from their wives, which they had married while *laymen*, said—"Satis esse ut qui in clerum xuissent adscripti, juxta *veterem ecclesiæ traditionem*, jam non amplius uxores ducerent.—" It was sufficient that they who were inrolled among the clergy, according to the *antient tradition of the church*, should no more marry." *Clerical celibacy*, and the condemnation of *polygamy*, stand on one and the same *footing*, and that a very *lame* one; that is to say, on the *antient tradition of the church*; so did the *religion* of the *Scribes and Pharisees*, and so do the *superstitions* of the *church of Rome* to this day.

Paphnutius's speech on the occasion is to be found in Jortin, Rem. vol. ii. p. 249. Though what *Papchnutius* says may rather apply against the *clergy* marrying a second time, yet those to whom he spoke must be supposed to have held it unlawful for the clergy to marry at all, else how could they be for their separating from the wives they took when *laymen*?

However, even the partial prohibition of wives to the *clergy* did not ripen into a *decree*, 'till about fifty years after, when *Siricius*, bishop of *Rome*, ordained, that if a *clerk* married a *widow*, or a *second wife*, he should be divested of his office. For many hundred years this was not observed, 'till Gregory VII. called *Hildebrand*, by cruel decree of excommunication, deprived ministers of their *lawful wives*, and compelled the clergy to the vow of *continency. Hist. of Popery*, vol. i. 21.

for a *minister*[158] to marry a *second* time on the loss of his[159] wife, and unlawful

---

158   Whether any carry this point so far as the anonymous answerer to Luther, Tr. *de digamia Episcoporus*, I cannot say; but he declares—"Mortaliter peccantqui bigamos (sacerdotes scil) ecclesiæ stipendio sueutant."—"They sin mortally who support clergymen that have been twice married, with the allowance or stipend of the church."—Again—"Peccant qui scientes ex bigami ore verbum Dei pollui audiunt."—"They sin, who knowingly hear the word of God polluted, by the mouth of a minister who has been twice married."—Again—"Bigamus censendus est, non solum is qui duas duxit virgines, sed & viduam aut aliter corruptam."—"He is to be reckoned a *bigamist*, not only who has married two *virgins*, but also he that hath married a *widow*, or a *woman* otherwise *corrupted*."

His conclusion breathes the true spirit of ignorance, superstition, and blind zeal.—"In summâ—quicunque proprias voluptates, & luxuriæ exactionem, *apostoli* verbis & *patrum* honestis præponit decretis, non tamen sacerdotis aut ecclesiastico stipendio cedere dignum putat, is non solum tolerandus non est, sed ad corvos abigendus, quò non ovis morbosa totum corrumpat ovile, & tam laudabilem, bonam, & longævam consuetudinem pestilenti suo defœdet exemplo."—"In fine, Whosoever prefers his own pleasures, and the requirements of luxury, to the words of the *apostle*" (we must here suppose 1 Tim. iii. 2: and Tit. i. 6. be meant) "and to the decent decrees of the *fathers*, and yet doth not think proper to depart from the ministry, or his ecclesiastical stipend, is not only not to be tolerated, but to be driven away to the crows" (we should say, *thrown to the dogs*) "that one scabby sheep might not mar the whole flock, and defile, by this own pestilent example, so laudable, good, and ancient a custom."

159   WILLIAM WHISTON, of famous memory, who, in the early part of the present *century*, was the great reviver and patron of the *Arian* hereby in this country, and might be called *Dr.* Clark's *master* in this branch of *blasphemy*; has left us some very remarkable matters on record.

One is, that the *New Testament* is the only rule of *faith*, and criterion of *truth* among *Christians*— and this to be interpreted by *apostolical tradition*. Another is, a *lesson* to all *Clergymen*, who are so profligate as to subscribe the doctrine of the *Trinity*, as held by the Church of *England*, though they do not believe it; and this, that they may gain admission to those preferments, which, on such terms, they have no right to hold—for *Whiston*, very fairly and honestly, gave up his professorship at *Cambridge*, sooner than dissemble, or give up his opinions; for which he is to be *honoured*, as an *honest* man, however mistaken he might be in his religious notions. *Dr. Samuel Clarke*, his pupil, died *Rector* of the *valuable* living of *St. James's*.

Another matter which *Whiston* left behind him, seems to be a *bone* for the *Clergy*, which those would do well to *pick*, who, with the ingenious *William Whiston*, are for setting up a new *Christian law*, or *law of the gospel*, of which *Christ* and *St. Paul* are the *legislators*.

Whiston's words are as follow—"It may not be amiss, here to take notice of that *Christian law*, for the marriage of the clergy but *once*; which is now so frequently broken by *Protestants*, and gives the *Papists* a great handle against them, as observing no rules for *restraining their inclinations* of that kind. I say, the *Protestants* do allow their clergy, not only to *marry more than once*, but to act as *Clergymen* after such *second* marriages, without the least permission under the *gospel* for so doing. Now, though the *law of Christianity* be plain, not only from copies of those laws of *Moses*,

also for *any* woman to *marry again* on the loss of her husband. These ridiculous opinions owe their birth to the before-mentioned cause, of taking words by the *sound*, instead of the *sense*—the usual consequence of detaching scripture from scripture, not comparing it with itself, by taking the whole together. By this, men may prove—*quidlibet ex quolibet*—"*what they please from what they please*;"—and this is the sheet-anchor of error, as well as of many monstrous practices, and so has been in all ages; they can be maintained no other way. The whole doctrine of *transubstantiation*, absurd as it is in all its parts, is held together by the sound of *Hoc est corpus meum*—This is my body.—The *sound of hæreticum devita*, in a Latin version of Tit. iii. 10. has authorized the most barbarous murders of thousands, who have been burned alive by the inquisition, under the denomination of *heretics*. It has been made to signify *hæreticum de vitâ*—*an heretic from life*; that is—*put him* from life—*kill him*.—Thus, by separating the word *devita*, and turning the last two syllables into the substantive *vita*, the preposition *de* just answered the purpose. A less *tragical* consequence of this method of interpretation is related by *Erasmus*. He tells of a friar preaching from those words of Christ, Luke xvii.

---

which oblige *Christians*; but from the present *New Testament*, the *apostolical constitutions*, and the known interpretation and practice of the *four first centuries*, that *Bishops, Priests and Deacons*, are allowed to *marry but once*; yet am I not sure, but they might marry a *second* time without reproach, if they voluntarily degraded themselves, and reduced themselves among the laity; in whom *second* marriages were not condemned; though I confess, I do not remember one example of such voluntary degradation and reduction in all *Christian* antiquity. I am confident our great men are, with *Grotius*, too good critics; and know *Christian* antiquity too well, to pretend that *St. Paul's* ordinances, that a *Bishop, Priest*, and *Deacon*, must be the *husband* of *but one wife*, signifies but *one wife at a time*; as some of our *weaker* authors are willing to interpret it. Nor was this constitution so severe as the moderns imagine; for almost all the *bishops* were originally *fifty* years of age, e'er they were ordained. The next order seems to have been in general considerably above *fifty*; which their very name *presbyter*, i.e., *elders* of the parish or diocese, directly signifies: and as for the *deacons*, they were, by parity of reason, to be supposed to be between *thirty* and *forty*; which ages, see these three orders, when we once restore, the objections of the *moderns* against this law will come to little. I mention this here because, I had once a discourse with *Dr. Clarke* upon this head, who looked upon that latter interpretation as ridiculous. Nor had he anything else to allege for the modern *Protestant* practice, but that this command might be supposed peculiar to the *first age of Christianity*; which yet, I dare say, was a secret to all those *first ages of Christianity*, which, so far as I have observed, always esteemed every *law of the gospel* to belong equally to all under the *gospel*, from the first 'till the *second coming of* CHRIST, our *legislator*." See Whiston,, Life of CLARKE, p. 140—142. 10

17. which stand in some *Latin* versions—*Nonne decem facti sunt*[160] *mundi*—who began to prove there are *ten worlds*. An arch fellow standing by, stopped his mouth with the following words—*Sed ubi sunt novem?*—*But where are the nine?*

It is said of *St. Francis*, that from the words, *Go you into all the world*, and *preach the gospel to every creature*, he thought himself bound to preach to *beasts* and *birds*, and accordingly did it very often, and with *wonderful success*, as they tell us in the legend of his life. Perhaps it was much on a like principle that *St. Anthony* of *Padua* went and preached to the *fishes*—whose discourse to them may be found in *Broughton* Hist. *Lib.* vol. i. p. 53.

Dr. *Hammond*, in his note on 1 *Tim.* iii. 2. says—"What is the meaning of μιας γυναικός ανηρ, *the husband of one wife*—both here and ver. 12, and *Tit.* i. 6. and of ενός ανδρός γυνὴ, *the wife of one husband*—chap. v. 9. will not easily be resolved." But surely all difficulty vanishes, when the whole is taken together; and it is observed from the *original* in what different *tenses* the verbs γινομαι and ἔιμι are used. This shews that the *apostle*, 1 Tim. iii. 2, and Tit. i. 6. was describing the situation of the men he was then speaking of, as what *it then was*—and in 1 Tim. v. 9. that of the *widows*, as to what it *had been*. 1 Tim. iii. 2. Δει ουν Τον Επίσκοπον ΕΙΝΑΙ μιας γυναικος Ανδρα—*A Bishop ought to* be (not to have been) *the husband of one wife*; and Tit. i. 6. Ει τις ΕΣΤΙΝ μιας γυναικος;—*if any be* (is) *the husband of one wife*. Ἔξιν being of the present tense, can signify only what a man *is* at *the time spoken of*: whereas the expression concerning the *women*, 1 *Tim.* v. 9. is widely different. The woman is called *Χηρα*, a *widow*; and it is observable, that the verb is not expressed as before, either in the infinitive or indicative mood of Ειμι, *to be*, but by the participle of the *præteritum*, or *past time*, of the verb γινομαι, *to be* or *become*—It is γεγονυῖα—which we have rightly rendered—*having been*—that is—in *time past having been*, or become the *wife of one man*—a *widow*, who never *had been* but once married; not—that had not had *two husbands* at a time; such a thing was hardly ever heard of, as lawful, even amongst the[161] *heathens*

---

160   I would just acquaint the *unlearned* reader, that the substantive *mundus* signifies *a world*— the adjective *mundus* signifies *clean*.

161   Never among *Jews*, or even *Turks*, was it permitted that the woman should have more than one husband at once. Only among the *barbarians* there is mention of the *Πολυανδροι*, a people so

themselves. I would therefore harmonize and paraphrase the whole as follows:—
"Forasmuch *as all things are to be done decently and in order,* (1 Cor. xiv. 40.)
but this cannot be, unless *some* proper form of government be established; it is
necessary that proper officers be appointed to administer that government. Some
who are to be—ἐπίσκοποι—overseers of the whole; others Διάκονοι—deacons, or
inferior serving *ministers* under them. The first order of men are to *overlook* the
clergy, as well as the *laity*—to *preach the word*—administer the *sacraments,* and
to have power to censure *evil doers,* even as far as *excommunication,* the *church*
agreeing thereto. 1 Cor. v. 4, 5. Such an office should, doubtless, be filled with
men of irreproachable characters, and of such conduct and dispositions as to be in
all respects *blameless,* not only for the better maintenance of their *authority,* but
also for the influence of their *example.* As such an office must moreover require
great attention, those should be chosen, who are entangled as little as possible in
the *affairs of this life,* 2 Tim. ii. 4. Therefore, though for this reason *single men*
might in general answer the purpose best, (1 Cor. vii. 33.) yet it may be expedient,
in some instances, to chuse *married men* into the offices of *Bishops* and *Deacons.*
Where this is the case, the election should not be made of such of the *Christians*
as have more than *one wife,* as such a situation must necessarily involve the person
in more *worldly care,* than can be consistent with a due attention to that *care,*
which must *come upon them daily,* respecting the *church.* Therefore, the having
more than *one wife* should always be considered as a bar to a man's election, either
to the office of a *Bishop* or of a *Deacon,* (1 *Tim.* iii. 12.); for though these last may
not have so extensive a jurisdiction, yet, what with preaching the word—assisting
the *Bishops* and *elders*—visiting the sick—and distributing the *church*'s alms to the
poor—*one wife* and family is as much as can be at all considered consistent with
any tolerable diligence in the duties of a *Deacon's* office.

But as the sick are to be visited and attended, as well as the poor relieved,

---

called, because the wife among them had *many husbands.* So among the *Medes,* that dwelt in the
mountains, it is said a woman was married to *five husbands at once.* See *Hammond* on 1 Tim. iii.
2. *Montesquieu* mentions the tribe of the *Naires,* on the coast of *Malabar,* where the women have
many husbands. Sp. of Laws, vol. i. p. 374, octavo. But all this is as contrary to nature itself, as the
custom of some of the *Indian* women's drowning their children in the *Ganges,* or exposing them to
wild beasts to be devoured.

it may be necessary also to appoint *women* for these purposes, especially as to attending and nursing the poor of their *own sex*. These may require many offices highly improper for *men* to be engaged in; though the nursing *sick men*, or visiting and relieving them, may very properly fall also under the care of *women*. These *women* may also be called Διάκονοι τῆς ἐκκλησίας (see *Rom*. xvi. 1.) *servants* or *ministers of the church*. Those who are to be deemed proper for these offices, must not be young, raw, unexperienced girls; nor *married women*, whose attention belongs to their husbands and families, 1 Cor. vii. 34: nor the *younger widows*, who are not arrived at a time of life suitable to such employments, 1 Tim. v. 11: let these *marry*, to keep themselves out of mischief, ver. 12, 13, 14. The only *women* who are fit to be chosen as *servants* or *ministers* of the church in the respects above mentioned, should be far advanced in years; that is to say, not less than *threescore years old*, who having buried their husbands and *brought up their children*, 1 Tim. v. 10. have time, as well as inclination, to devote themselves to the offices of the church. They should also be *sober* and discreet persons, who, by their conduct in their younger years, have shewn their temperance and sobriety, by having contented themselves with *one husband*, and who, ever after the death of that husband, have secluded themselves from any further worldly engagements of that sort, so as to be justly styled *widows indeed*; *though desolate, yet trusting in* God (1 Tim. v. 5.); and like ANNA, *Luke* ii. 36, 37. *continuing in supplications and prayers night and day*."—This I take to be a consistent and clear view of these passages taken together. As we may from hence infer, that there were women in the church younger than *sixty years*, by the Apostle's express exclusion of those *under* that age from those offices to which women were to be chosen; as also that there were many who had been *twice married*, by his designing those who had been but *once married* for the aforesaid offices; so we may as fairly conclude, from his saying a *bishop* δεῖ εἶναι—*ought to be*—and again, if any, ἔϛιν—*is* or *be the husband of one wife*—that there were many *Christians*, not who *had had*, but at that *present time* actually had *more than one wife*. If this had not been the case, it would have been as much out of the question to have mentioned the having but *one wife*, as to have said, that none should be chosen but those who had but *one head* or *one body*, when it was not to be supposed that any man had more.

As to the conceit, that, "what the *Apostle* says about the *bishops* and *deacons*, is to prove that no *minister* may marry a second time," it is all but as bad as saying, with the church of *Rome*, that he *ought not* to *marry at all*.

With respect to the business of *polygamy*, as to the thing itself, nothing that is here said proves it to be more or less sinful in one man than in another; that depends wholly on the law of God delivered by Moses. Therefore the *prudential* reasons, for which he evidently excepted against *polygamists* being elected to *church-offices*, no more affects the matter of *polygamy*, than the excepting against *women* under sixty years old, proves it *sinful* in a woman to be *younger*, or that, because no woman was to be chosen to the office of a *deaconess* who had been *twice married*, therefore it was sinful for the woman to marry again after the death of her husband, contrary to 1 Cor. vii. 39. and to the express advice of the *Apostle*, 1 Tim. v. 14.

As to the supposed unlawfulness of *second* marriages, or the notion, that if a man lost his wife, it was *sinful* to marry again; this began very early in the church, and spread itself even to this country. We find in the time of *Ed.* I.[162] about the year 1276, the parliament adopted a constitution made by the *Pope* at *Lyons*, to exclude *men* that had been *twice married* from all *clerks privilege*. So that if a man was convicted of *felony*, who would otherwise have had *his clergy*, and it appeared that he had been *twice married*, he was to be *executed like other lay-people*. A statute of 18 Ed. III. mitigated the rigour of this law with respect to clerks, by making a suggestion of *bigamy* triable by the *ordinary*, before the *justices* could proceed. But all were delivered from the bondage of such laws by 1 Ed. VI. c. 12. § 16. which enacts, that—"every person, who by any law or statute of this realm ought to have the *benefit of clergy*, shall be allowed the same, although he hath been *divers times married* to any single woman or single women, or to two wives or more, or to any widow or widows."

Among the six famous articles proposed by Henry VIII. to the *parliament* and *convocation*, one was—"whether *priests*, that is to say, men dedicate to God by priesthood, may, by the law of God, marry after or no?—After great, long, deliberate, and advised disputation and consultation had and made concerning the said article, as well by the consent of the *King's Highness*, as by the assent of

---

162   See Burnet Hist. Ref. vol. ii. p. 323.

the *Lords Spiritual* and *temporal,* and other *learned* men of his *Clergy* in their *convocations,* and by the consent of the *Commons,* in this *present parliament* assembled, it was and is finally resolved, accorded, and agreed—that *priests,* after the order of priesthood received as afore, *may not*[163] *marry by the law* of God. The enacting part of 31 Henry VIII. c. 14. goes on and says—If any person shall preach,—teach—or obstinately affirm and defend, that any man, after the order of priesthood received, may marry or contract matrimony, he shall be adjudged to suffer death, and forfeit lands and goods as a felon; and if any priest do actually marry or contract marriage with another, or any man that is or hath been a priest do carnally use any woman to whom he is or hath been married, or with whom he hath contracted matrimony, or openly be conversant or familiar with any such woman, both the man and the woman shall be[164] adjudged felons."

---

163   In the *eighth century,* some monks pretended, that the angel *Gabriel* had brought *twelve* articles from heaven, one of which was, that *ecclesiastics* must not *marry.* See Jortin Rem. vol. ii. p. 43.

In the *ninth century, Pope Nicholas I.* made a decree to restrain *priests* from marrying. The bishop of *Augsburg* wrote a pathetic letter to the *Pope,* setting forth the sad and mischievous consequences of taking their wives from the *priests.* The letter is at large in *Fox,* vol. ii. p. 392. and well worth reading. He tells Pope *Nicholas,* that his predecessor *Saint Gregory* (i. e. Gre gory IV.) made such a decree, but repented of it on this occasion; to use the old bishop's words as they are there translated—"Upon a certain day, as *St. Gregory* sent to his fish-pond to have some fish, his servants drained it, and found at the bottom 6000 infants heads, which were brought to him. Upon this he did greatly repent in himself his decree touching the single life of the *priests,* which he confessed to be the cause of that so lamentable murder." The letter in *Fox,* as above cited, is in Latin; the translation is referred to p. 393, as having been before inserted; which the reader may turn to. Whether the above letter was written by the *bishop of Augsburg,* according to Crit. Hist. *of England,* p. 83. or by *Volusianus bishop of Carthage,* as *Fox* seems to think, is very immaterial.

164   How ought the *clergy* of the church of *England,* some of whom are not only *married* men, but, having lost a *first,* are now living in comfort, honour, and reputation with a *second wife,* (see before, p. 190. n.) to bless the day when men *dared* to attack the reigning *superstition* of the times, and in the face of all manner of *reproach,* and even of the danger of *death* itself, boldly vindicate those rights of mankind, with which the Law Of God had invented them, but of which they had been deprived by the insolent tyranny of men like themselves?

It little concerned *Luther,* and his fellow *champions* for the honour of the divine law—that they were called *antichrists—scandals to religion—revivers and propagators of the laws of Mahomet*—or that the Popish *Cerberus,* with his *three heads* of ignorance, superstition, and blind zeal, threatened to tear them to pieces. They *persevered*—they were *successful*—and what they sowed in times of

That all this was contrary to the law of God is apparent; for the *priests* and *Levites* under the Old Testament, and the *apostles* and other *ministers* under the New Testament, who were respectively the *clergy* of the time, might marry, and many of them were actually married men. I therefore mention these things, to shew how we may be led into error, even to *putting men to death, thinking we do* God *service* (John xvi. 2.) when once the word of God is left for the inventions and *traditions of men;* and how far men may believe things which are *contrary* to scripture are *right* and *good,* and things *agreeable* to scripture are *wrong* and *abominable*—that this may become the *creed of a whole nation,* nay of a *whole church* including *many nations,* so as to gain the sanction of public *statutes,* the solemn opinions of *lawyers,* the most awful determinations of *courts of justice.* The condemnation of *polygamy* is equally an human device, and has no more authority from scripture for making a man *a felon and to suffer death* (see 1 Jac. c. 11.) for having *two wives,* than the stat. 31 Henry VIII. above mentioned, had for hanging a *priest* and the *woman* he had married. All these things are equally the inventions of men, or rather of[165] Satan *transformed into an angel of light;* but the scriptures are the true *Ithurel's* spear, the *touch* of which alone can make him appear in his own shape, of a *lyar and a murderer from the beginning.*

The first public[166] law in the empire against *polygamy* was at the latter

---

darkness and *persecution,* we are reaping in days of *light* and *liberty.*

Thank God, the aforesaid *Cerberus* is chained up. He now will *bark,* and *bark* he may 'till he be *hoarse;* the man who minds him can have but little else to do.

The *author* of this book pretends not to be a *prophet*—but judging from what *has been* to what *may be,* he entertains not the least doubt, that, a *century* hence, the world may either wonder at the *man* who had *wildness* enough to attack the *present system* of things with regard to *marriage,* or that there were found people who were absurd enough to abuse him for it.—This to those whom it may concern—Verbum Sat.

165   *Luther* saith well—"Satanæ commentum est, peccatum fingere ubi nullum est, & justitiam negare, ubi vera est."—"It is an invention of *Satan* to feign *sin* where there is none, and to deny *righteousness* where it truly is."

166   In the year 324, Christianity was by *law established,* when *Constantine,* after the death of *Licinius,* reigned, without a colleague, sole lord of the *Roman empire.* However favourable the protection of the *civil magistrate* was at that time, as well as in after times, to the *Christian religion,* yet from hence we must date the misfortunes which have attended the interference of human

end of the *fourth* century, about the year 393, by the emperor *Theodosius;* this was repealed by the emperor *Valentinian* about *sixty* years afterwards, and the subjects of the empire were permitted to marry as *many wives* as they pleased; "nor does it appear (says *Chambers,* tit. *Polygamy*) that the *bishops* made any opposition to this introduction"—(he should have said *restoration*; for if it had not existed before, no law would have been made against it by *Theodosius*)—"of *polygamy* into the empire." After all, no[167] human authority can decide upon the matter, as this has evidently given its suffrage *both ways* upon the same questions. But can the determinations of the *all-wise* God be thus precarious and contradictory? Can the Old Testament and New Testament be at as great a variance as the 31 Henry VIII. c. 14.—which makes it *death for both the man and woman,* in the case of a *priest,* to marry, or even to contract matrimony, or to affirm it lawful so to do—and the 5 and 6[168] Edw. VI. c. 12. which declares the marriage of *clerks* to be as lawful

---

power, in the establishment of *human systems of faith and ceremony;* the *former* of which have often been contrary to *God's* word, the *latter* utterly subversive of it. The advancement of the clergy in dignities, riches, and honour, under this *emperor* and his successors, proved so many pernicious baits to *sacerdotal* ambition, avarice, and pride; and introduced those scenes of vice and profligacy among the clergy, which occasioned it to be said—Mundus *per ostium,* pietas per *fenestram*—The *world* entered in at the *door—piety* flew out at the *window.*

167   For which reason, I forbear to lay any stress on the decisions of our chief *reformers, Luther—Melancthon—Bucer—Zuingleus,* &c. who, after a solemn consultation at *Wittenberg,* on the question—"whether for a man to have *two wives at once,* was contrary to the *divine law?*" answered unanimously, "That it was not"—and, on this authority, Philip the Landgrave of Hesse actually married a *second wife*—his *first* being alive. This proves *what they thought,* but, by no means, that they thought *right.*

168   The preamble to this law affords a most striking proof of the power of *superstition* and *error* over the minds of men: for though 2 and 3 Edward VI. c. 21. had made it lawful for *priests* to *marry,* yet far the greater number of people held such marriages "to be inconsistent with the law of God, and only to have been *tolerated"* by the former statute, "like *usury* and other unlawful things, to avoid greater inconvenience and evils," insomuch that they "accounted the children of such marriages to be *bastards,* as born in unlawful wedlock, and would hardly attend the ordinances of the church, if administered by *married priests."* Our prejudices against *polygamy* arise from the same source of error and superstition, and are equally unwarranted and groundless, as the law of God no more forbids this than it does the other. *Forbidding to marry,* where God has not forbidden it, is *the doctrine of devils* (1 Tim. iv. 1, 3.) however *holy, pure,* and *pious* it may be deemed, whether by *Protestants* or *Papists.*

as the marriages of other men?—Had the scriptures forbidden *polygamy,* all the human laws that ever could be enacted, and all the human authorities that ever could be produced, could not make it *lawful in the sight of* God—for that were to place men above God. On the other hand, if God hath not forbidden it, but even *allowed* it, all the men upon earth, though joined with all the *angels* in heaven, cannot make it *sinful*—for this were also to set the creatures above *their* Maker. Judging and determining on the matter either way, but on the authority of God's law, is a much more serious thing than is usually imagined; for there are as many *woes* pronounced on *those who call good evil,* as on those *who call evil good.* Is. v. 20.

The learned GROTIUS, in his book *De Ver. Christian. Rel.* lib. ii. § 13. note 12, seems to intimate, that 1 Cor. vii. 4. is to be relied on as a *text* full in point to prove the unlawfulness of *polygamy* amongst *Christians;* for that it was lawful amongst the *Jews,* he not only allows, but brings many authorities to prove, in *note* 7. on *lib.* ii. *sect.* 13. But there is another text, at ver. 2, which, as it has been looked upon as a conclusive argument against *polygamy,* I will first consider, and then proceed in order to the following verses, from ver. 2 to ver. 5, inclusive. The words of the text alluded to are—*Nevertheless, to avoid fornication, let every man have his own wife, and every woman her own husband.* The strength of the whole argument drawn from this passage consists in a sort of[169] quibble upon the word *wife,* that, as well as the word *husband,* being in the *singular number—wife,* not *wives.* But suppose it had been said, "Let every man have his *own* servant, and every servant his *own* master," would it afford a conclusive proof, that because *no man can serve two masters,* therefore no master could have *more than one servant?*

However, as this text has been, and is, looked upon as a direct proof of the unlawfulness of *polygamy* among *Christians,* let us give it a thorough consideration. In the first place, let us restore it to its own genuine words; for our *translators* have introduced something which is not in the *original.* The words in

---

169   I have elsewhere observed, on the danger of this method of interpretation, we have but to rely on the *sound* of words, and *all second* marriages are directly forbidden, ver. 27. *Art thou loosed from a wife? seek not a wife.* Again, the method of establishing doctrines by mere words or sentences detached from the context, might furnish us with as direct a prohibition of marriage to *Christians,* as ever was contended for in the primitive churches; for no words can be plainer than μὴ ζήτει γυναικα—*seek not a wife.*

the *Greek* are—*Δια δὲ τὰς πορνείας*—the verb *to avoid* is not there—the words *τας πορνείας*, which we translate *fornication,* are plural, not *singular,* and should be rendered *fornications,* or *the fornications*—they being in the *accusative* case, are governed, not by the verb *to avoid,* which is *not* in the text, but by the preposition *δια,* which is. This preposition *δια* has various meanings, according to the case it governs. Sometimes it governs a *genitive*—sometimes an *accusative,* and then it may signify—*for;*—so Dr. *Hammond* renders it here—*but for fornications;*—also—*with respect to*—*as to*—*with regard to*—*quod attinet ad:*—so ver. 26. *δια τὴν ἐνεστωσαν αναγκην,* may be rendered, *with respect to (in respect of*—Dr. *Hammond) the present necessity.* Many authorities might be cited for this use of the word, both in sacred and profane writers; and it so suits with the subject-matter of the verse in question, that I conceive this to be the sense of *δια* in this place.

The *context* shews very plainly, that what *St. Paul* says, is in answer to some *questions* put to him *by letter,* and sent to him at *Philippi,* where he appears to have been when he wrote the answer; and if we may judge of the *questions* by the[170] *answer,* which is surely a very fair way of judging, they probably concerned

---

170 This, in the instance before us, is the only way by which we can judge, as we have not the *Corinthians* letter itself to inform us of its contents; for want of which, there are some passages in the chapter *dark and hard to be understood.* Still a meaning they certainly must have; and our judgment, with respect to that meaning, should be directed—first, by a consideration of the manners, customs, dispositions, and characters of the *writers,* also of their situation with regard to time and place—secondly, of the character, situation, and office of the *answerer;* whose holy zeal, and consummate knowledge of the *divine law,* must render it impossible for him to write a syllable which doth not exactly harmonize with the Old Testament.

Both these I have endeavoured to keep in view, while I have been setting down my thoughts on this passage of scripture.

When the *Apostle* saith, ἕκαςος τὴν ἑαυτ8 Γυναῖκα ʹΕΧΕΤΩ, he certainly uses the verb ἔχω in a larger sense than merely *having.*—This verb signifies to *possess, retain,* which is to *continue the possession of.* So it is apparently used, Matt. xiv. 4. where *John the Baptist* tells *Herod,* concerning *Herodias* his brother *Philip's wife,* whom *Herod* had taken to himself—Ούκ ἔξεςί σοι ʹΕΧΕΙΝ αυτήν. So *Mark* vi. 18. Ούκ ἔξεςί σοι ʹΕΧΕΙΝ τὴν γυναῖκα τοῦ ἀδελφ8 σ8—where the *Baptist* cannot be supposed *merely* to condemn *Herod's having* her at first, but also to declare the unlawfulness of his *retaining,* or *continuing the possession of* her. So here—let every man *retain, continue the possession of*—γυναῖκα, the *wife*—τὴν ἑαυτ8, *of himself*—i.e. who is his own property—and not suffer her to go to other men, as the custom was, nor take other men's wives to himself.

The Apostle proceeds—καὶ ἑκάστῃ τὸν ʹΙΔΙΟΝ ἄνδρα ʹΕΧΕΤΩ.—Here is an evident variation in the phraseology, on which we shall take occasion to observe hereafter. At present, let it be noticed,

a very infamous, but common practice, that of *married men* lending out or even

---

that the introduction of the word *ΊΔΙΟΝ*, must affect, and materially, the meaning of the word *ΈΧΕΤΩ*, and make also the word *ἄνδρα* to be taken in an exclusive sense—as thus—*Let every* (wife) retain, possess (i.e. *keep to*, as we say) the man or husband *appropriated* to her *exclusively of all other men.*

Thus both parts of the verse are in the strictest analogy with the *divine laws,* and equally contribute to reprobate the breach of it by "community of women," which was a *Gentile*-custom.

As for the conclusion against *polygamy,* which is drawn from the word *wife,* as well as the word *husband,* being in the *singular* number, it will not hold; for the scriptures plainly shew us, that *wife* must frequently be understood in a *distributive* sense. A remarkable passage of this sort is in 1 Tim. iii. 12. Let *the deacons be the husbands of* ONE WIFE—*μιᾶς γυναικὸς ἄνδρες.* But can anybody suppose, that there was to be but *one wife* amongst them all?—So in the tenth commandment— *Thou shalt not covet thy neighbour's* WIFE—*This* (like *ox, ass, house, servant*) must be taken in a *distributive* sense, and mean any *married woman* or *women* whatsoever. So Exod. xxi. 33, 34. *If a man dig a pit, and not cover it, and an ox or an ass fall therein—the owner of the pit shall make it good,* &c. Are not *pits,* and *oxen,* and *asses,* to be here understood? So in the text, the word *wife* means any *woman* or *women* who may be married to the man.

The word *husband* must be understood in an *exclusive* sense, because the whole *Bible* shows that a woman could have but *one husband*—here well expressed by the *ἴδιον ἄνδρα.* In short, this scripture, like all others, must be interpreted according to the *analogy of the faith,* by taking a view of the *divine law* in all its parts, and not by confining ourselves to mere literal construction of a single word—or text—or passage; for, by this means, we might be brought into all the errors of the *church of Rome,* or into all the *heresies* that have been invented; not one of which is without some *text* of scripture for its support, which being *wrested* from all the rest, has been *wrested* from its meaning, and made to signify just what the fancies of men have applied it to. It is very truly observed by an ancient writer, "*Turpe est tota lege non inspecta, vel perlecta, de lege judicare.*" "To judge of the law, without reading over and examining *the whole,* is shameful.*"*—He proceeds—"Ita turpe etiam *theologo textum originalem* in scriptura sacra non inspicere, aut illum studio præterire, & tamen scripturam explicare velle."—"So it is shameful in a *theologist* not to inspect *the original text* in the sacred scripture, or purposely to pass it by, and yet pretend to explain the scripture." If this sentiment had had its due weight, it would have lessened the numbers of *expositors* and *commentators* on the BIBLE, in no inconsiderable degree.

The interpretation which the *Rhemists* give to this 1 Cor. vii. 2. is by no means to be despised—I will here set it down; for—

—*Fas est & ab hoste doceri.*—

"Let every one *have, keep,* or *use* his own wife, to whom he was married before his conversion; for the Apostle here answereth to the first question of the *Corinthians,* which was not—whether it were lawful to marry? but—whether they were not bound, upon their conversion, to abstain from the company of their wives married before in their infidelity? as some "did persuade them they ought to be." This would seem a good exposition of the place, if the *Apostle* had not so expressly treated *this point* in the following *verse.*

marrying their *wives* to other people, and of course the *married women* going from their *own husbands* to *other* men. That this was the case in *Corinth*, may well be taken for granted, when we consider that there were so many sources from which such practices were so easily derived. The *Corinthians* were a people lewd and[171] debauched to a proverb—Κορινθιαζειν, to *Corinthianize*, or play the *Corinthian*, was a *phrase* which expressed a man's being abominable:—add to this the fondness of the *Greeks* for the maxims of the *divine* PLATO, as he was called, one of which was—κοινὰς μὲν γυναῖκας, κοινὰ δὲ τέκνα παιδία, that "women and children ought to be common:"—add to this the sect of the *Gnostics*, those early *heretics*, who held "a community of women, and that all marriage was of[172] the devil;"—these spread their errors far and wide among the *Christian* churches:—and lastly—the horrid practice of *men's lending their wives to others*, was even a sort of[173] law in *Greece*; this originated first in *Sparta*, that famous city of *Peloponnesus*, on the edge of which *Corinth* stood; from thence it spread itself into the rest of the cities of *Greece, Corinth*, no doubt, as well as others. The following account of this vile custom is to be found in *Plutarch*'s life of the celebrated *Spartan* lawgiver *Lycurgus*. "He (*Lycurgus*) next bethought himself how to prevent that wild and womanish passion of *jealousy*, by making it a matter of reputation, not

---

171 See 1 Cor. vi. 11. former part. *Strabo* writes, that there was at *Corinth* a temple of *Venus*, so rich, that it maintained above a thousand harlots sacred to her services, ἱεροδέλες ἑταίρας, which were consecrated both by men and women to that goddess. See the advantage and necessity of the *Christian* revelation, by *J. Leland*, D.D. vol. i. p. 174. Others say, that the number of prostitutes in honour of *Venus* at *Corinth* was 2000. See *Lett. of Jews to Voltaire*, vol. ii. p. 53.

Strabo, Geog. lib. xii. speaking of the temple of the *moon* in *Comana* of *Cappadocia*, where all manner of the most horrid *impurities* were committed, as parts of *religious worship*, calls it—"*a little* Corinth."

172 Among the errors of the famous *Manes* or *Manicheans*, in the third *century*, this principle is found—he taught, that "all marriage is of the devil, invented by him to tie the souls to the flesh, and to retard their return to heaven." See *Jertin's Remarks*, vol. ii. p. 50.

173 *Grotius*, speaking of the *Jewish divorces*, saith—"Quod et hodie usurpant *Mahumetista*, & olim *Graci* ac *Latini* tanta licentia, ut & uxores ad tempus utendas aliis darent *Lacones* & *Cato*." "Which the *Mahometans often practise at this day, and formerly the Greeks and Latins, with such licentiousness, that they could grant the use of their wives to others for a* GIVEN TIME. *This was the case among the Lacedemonians, and Cato also did the same*." See Grot. de Verit. lib. ii. § 13.

only to banish from matrimony all violence and disorder, but also to allow men the freedom of *imparting the use of their wives* to deserving persons, that so they might have children by them. And he laughed at those who think the violation of the marriage-bed such an insupportable affront, that they revenge it by murders and cruel wars. *Lycurgus* thought a man not to be blamed, who, being in years, and having a young wife, should recommend some virtuous handsome young man, that she might have a child by him, who might inherit the good qualities of such a father, and this child the good man loves as tenderly as if he was his own getting.—On the other hand, a worthy man, who was in love with a *married woman* upon account of her modesty, and well-favouredness of her children, might, without formality, *beg of her husband a night's lodging*, that he might, like slips of a fine tree, planted in a goodly garden, have children of a good race, and well related. For *Lycurgus* was of opinion, that children were not so much the propriety of their parents, as of the *whole commonwealth*; and therefore he would not have them begotten by the *first comers*, but by the best men that could be found."

This custom was far from being reckoned *criminal*[174] or *adulterous,* it was applauded greatly; and "so far were women from that scandalous liberty which has been objected to them, that they knew not what the name of *adultery* meant." —A proof of this we have in *Geradas,* a very antient *Spartan,* who,

---

174   The *community of wives* cannot be conceived to have escaped the lewd *Corinthians,* when we consider how it spread far and wide among the *Gentiles.* This is said to have been the custom of the Troglodytes, Agathyrfi, the Maffagete, and Scythians, of whom *Strabe* saith— "they had their *wives in common,* agreeably to the laws of *Plato.*"

The natives of *Russian Lapland* were confusedly known to the ancients under the name of *Troglodytes* or *northern pigmies.* They are, for the most part, not above *four feet* and *an half* high, and dwell in caverns; they are just the same people they were formerly—they are said to intreat strangers to lie with their wives and daughters, as an *honour* done to them, and from a desire of amending, by their means, the defects of their own race. See *Volt.* Works. Transf. by *Franklin,* vol. xxviii. p. 10, 12.

Puffendorf has given a long list of other nations, which had the same custom among them, such as the ancient inhabitants of *Britain,* the *Sabeans,* those of the kingdom of *Calecut,* the antient *Lithuanians,* &c. See *Leland,* vol. ii. p. 129, note r.

Diogenes, whom *Epictetus* celebrates with the epithet of *divine,* held that "*women ought to be common*"—looking upon marriage to be nothing; "that every man and woman might keep company with whom they liked best, and that therefore children ought to be in common." Ib. 132. So the *Stoics* held that *women ought to be in common* among the wise, 133.

being asked by a stranger what punishment their law had appointed for *adultery?* answered—'My friend, there are no *adulterers* in our country.' 'But,' replies the stranger, 'suppose there were one, how would you punish him?' He answered— 'The offender must pay to the plaintiff a bull, with a neck so long, that he might drink out of the river *Eurotas*, from over the top of mount *Taygeta.'* 'Why, 'tis impossible to find such a bull, said the man.' *Geradas* smiling replied—''Twas just as impossible to find an *adulterer* in *Sparta.'* It is endless to observe on the total blindness of such people, with respect to the *law of* GOD: but when the *Corinthians* were awakened to a sense of *divine* things, though, as well as others in that part of *Greece*, they had been[175] infected with this *Spartan* leaven, and followed the *practices,* as they had imbibed the principles of their *neighbours*; yet neither custom, example, nor prejudice of education, could silence, or any longer satisfy their consciences, and therefore they seem to have written to the *apostle,* to know his sense of the matter; which he clearly gives them in the words of the text, and which evidently reprobate this horrid[176] custom. Having, in the preceding *chapter,* discussed at large the subjects of *whoredom* and *fornication*, and lewdness in general, he begins this seventh *chapter* with an answer to the *particular* questions proposed to him in the letter which he had received from them. The passage may be thus paraphrased—*Now concerning the things whereof ye wrote unto me*—"I say, first in general, though not for the reasons which some of your *philosophers* have given, nor for those of which the *Gnostics* have suggested, as if marriage was *wrong* or *sinful in itself,* but for *prudential* reasons, arising from the situation of things at this time (ver. 26.) *it is good,* καλὸν, *useful, profitable* (ver. 8 and 26.) *for a man not to touch a woman*—to have no dealings with the *other*

---

175   *Lycurgus* established his laws in *Lacedæmon* almost 900 years before CHRIST, so that they had full time to circulate and grow into customs, not only in *Greece*, but also in many other parts of the world.

176   By the manner of *St. Paul's* expressing himself, Cor. v. 1. he seems to insinuate, that, one man's taking or *having another's wife,* was a matter by no means *unheard of among the Gentiles;* though a man's *having his father's wife was.*
See an instance of this sort of degeneracy among the *Jews,* Amos ii. 7.

sex[177]. (See Matt. xix. 11, 12.) *But with respect to the*[178] *fornications* you mention, and concerning which you desire to know my sentiments; I answer, conformably to the law of GOD, which ordains, that a man *shall cleave to his wife,* &c. (Gen. ii. 24.) and that no woman shall *depart from her husband,* and *go to another man* (see Rom. vii. 1, 2, 3). *Let every man have his wife*—τηυ γυναικα ἑαυτῷ— the woman who belongs to him—and not lend her out, or suffer her to marry another, nor let him take a woman who is not γυνη ἑαυτ8, *his wife,* but another man's, to himself. *So also let every* married *woman have her own proper husband*— τον ἰδιον ανδρα—the man appropriated to her, exclusively of all other men upon earth, and not depart, or suffer herself to be *lent* or *given* to any *other man.*"

I would here observe, that there is a very remarkable difference of expression, which though preserved in many other translations, is not in ours. We render the two clauses just alike, whereas they are not so in the original, but—τηυ ΕΑΥΤΟΥ γυναικα, and τον ΙΔΙΟΝ ανδρα. The *Latin* translations preserve this difference of expression—*suam uxorem—proprium virum.* Leusd. ex Mont. So the old and new translations in *Beza's* Testament, and *Barker's* Eng. Test. 1615, and the *Geneva,* 1557. *Let every man have his* WIFE, *and every woman her own husband. If all scripture be given by inspiration of God,* (2 Tim. iii. 16.) and holy men *spake as they were moved by the Holy Ghost,* (2 Pet. i. 21.) I cannot but think that there is some weighty reason for the difference of expression, in giving the

---

177   Μη ἀπεχθεσθαι γυναικα is construed by some learned men, by *ducere uxorem*—to *marry a wife;*—but I rather think our translation right—*not to touch a woman*—for, as the word ἀνθρωπω denotes *man* in a *general* sense, so, to make both parts of the sentence correspond with each other, the γυναικα seems to be general also. The word ἀπεχθεσθαι answers to the Hebrew נגע, which sometimes means *to touch* or *meddle with,* in a *carnal* sense. See Gen. xx. 6.

178   There is no necessity to restrain the word πορνειας in this place, as our translators seem to have done, to the idea of what is usually meant by that term, that is to say, *commerce with harlots;* for it is a general word, expressive of *adultery,* as well as what is called *fornication.* Thus the *apostle* uses it but a little before in this very *epistle,* chap. v. 1. to denote not only *adultery,* but also *incest.* It is used as signifying *adultery,* Matt. v. 32. xix. 9; for though it may there signify lewdness committed before marriage, but not found out till afterwards, yet it must necessarily also be understood to mean such acts done after marriage; for our LORD cannot be supposed to mean that the *former* was a just cause of *divorce,* and not the *latter*—so that the word πορνεια must include both. Πορνειας, being plural, well denotes the complicated crimes of the husband's lending his wife to another man, and the wife's going to another man besides her husband, including also the crime of him who took her.

epithet Ἴδιον to the *husband*, with respect to the *wife*, and not to the *wife*, with respect to the *husband*. This is observable, not only in this place, but in[179] many others.

Leigh, Crit. Sac. observes this, as occurring every where in the sacred writings of the New Testament—*uxoribus sui ἴδιοι ανδρες tribuntur passim in sacris.* Leigh sub voc. *ἴδιος. Eph.* v. 24, 25. τοῖς ἰδίοις ἀνδράσιν, *their own husbands*—τὰς γυναῖκας εαυτων, *your wives;* and ver. 28, τας ἑαυτων γυναῖκας, *their wives*—την εαυτ8 γυναικα, *his wife.*—Again, Col. iii. 18, 19. τοῖς ἰδίοις ἀνδράσιν—*propriis viris—their* own *husbands*—τὰς γυναῖκας, *your wives* (ἑαυτῶν being understood). *St. Peter,* who was the *apostle of the circumcision,* uses the same mode of expression, 1 Pet. iii. 1. *Let the wives be subject,* τοις ἰδίοις ἀνδράσιν—*propriis viris—to their own husbands.* Comp. 1 Pet. iii. 5. The word ἴδιος has certainly an emphatical meaning wherever we find it, therefore must have its emphasis in this place, as well as in others. It seems to denote such an *appropriation* of the *husband* to the *wife,* as that she could not *have,* or *go to any other man.* This idea may be illustrated from Rom. xiv. 4. *Who art thou that judgest another man's servant?* τῷ ἰδίῳ κυρίῳ—*proprio domino—to his* own *master he standeth or falleth.* Here ἴδιος is used as an epithet to the *master* with respect to the *servant* (as 1 Tim. vi. 1. Tit. ii. 9.) and must denote such an *appropriation* of the master to the servant, as to exempt the servant from the authority, power, controul, command, or service of any other, but that of his own (ἰδι8) master; for, as was observed before, *no man can serve two masters,* though the master may have *many servants;* nor is any of his servants the less so, because he has others. So here, 1 Cor. vii. 2. and the other passages

---

179   Rom. viii. 32. we meet with a very material proof of the *emphatical* import of the word Ἴδιος, to denote Christ's being God's *own proper son,* in such a sense as no creature is or can be. So, in the passage under consideration, the word Ἴδιος denotes that the man is the woman's husband, in such a sense as no other man is or can be. Christ, John v. 18, is said to call *God Ἴδιον Πατερα—His own proper father:*—this must be in a sense as exclusive of *all other beings,* as the ἰδιος ανηρ is exclusive of *all other men.*

So 1 Cor. xv. 38. *God giveth it a body as it pleaseth Him, and to every seed*—το ἰδιον σωμα—*his* own *body,* i.e. so peculiarly appropriated to that sort of grain that it can pass into no other.—Thus hath *God* given to every *wife*—τον ἰδιον ανδρα—*her own—peculiar—appropriated*—husband—so that, *while he liveth* (Rom. vii. 3.) she can *pass* to no other man.

referred to, the husband is styled *ἴδιον,* to denote, that *no other* man can have any power, propriety, or interest whatsoever in the society of the wife, but the *ἴδιος ἀνήρ,* the proper and appropriated, peculiar husband. I own that I can account for this difference of expression in no other way, than by supposing the *scripture consistent with itself,* and that the distinction so evident in the Old Testament was to be preserved throughout the New Testament—that though a man might have *more than one wife,* yet a woman could have but *one husband;* had she more, neither could be styled properly *ἴδιος ἀνήρ,* for she would be as much the property of one as of the other, or rather be *in common* between, or among them, according to their number; whereas, doubtless, though a man has *two wives,* each can be properly styled *γύνη ἑαυτὸν—*[180] *his wife.*

No man may be said to have an *exclusive* property in, or appropriation of himself to, a person or thing, which others may share with him: therefore the word *ἴδιος* is peculiarly adapted to denote the *exclusive* appropriation of the *husband* to the *wife* to be, like the *exclusive* appropriation of the *master* to the *servant,* such a one as gives to him *alone,* exclusive of all others, the whole *attention, obedience,* and *service* of the party, so long as the relation which requires these shall continue. Whereas *γυνη, wife,* is never found with the *exclusive ἴδιος,* but coupled only with the pronoun possessive *ἑαυτ8.* To illustrate what has been said, we may observe as to *Jacob* and his two wives, *Leah* and *Rachel, Rachel* as well as *Leah,* with respect to *Jacob,* was *γυνη ἑαυτ8, his wife* (Gen. xxx. 26. xxxi. 50.) and he the *ἴδιος ἀνήρ,* the *husband,* exclusively of all other men, *appropriated to both,* insomuch that *neither* could have gone to any other man, without being an *adulteress:* but we no where find *Jacob,* nor any other *polygamist,* stigmatized as an *adulterer* or *fornicator,* on account of his having *two wives.* That such a custom as *Plutarch* shews to have originated from the famous lawgiver of *Sparta,* should reach *Corinth,* which stood at the edge of *Peloponnesus,* is not at all surprizing, when we find it had even reached to[181] *Rome. Numa Pompilius,* the famous successor of *Romulus,* anno

---

180   The propriety of this can hardly be disputed, when we reflect that it is the constant language of the Old Testament.

181   In short, this custom of *lending* wives to each other was so common among the *Gentiles,* that it is inconceivable such a practice should not be among the *Corinthians.*

715 before *Christ,* established this horrid practice among the *Romans.* He was a great reformer of *religion,* and improver of the *laws,* in which he is said "to have had a particular regard to the preserving of *modesty* in women. Nevertheless, he permitted husbands to lend their wives, after they had had children by them. This was a kind of temporary *divorce,* in favour of those men whose wives were barren; but the husbands still continued to have the same power over them, and could call them home, or lend them to others, as they pleased." Ant. Univ. Hist. vol. xi. p. 298.

That this practice long continued at *Rome,* there can be little doubt; for, about 700 years afterwards, we find, that *Cato* of *Utica* actually gave his wife *Marcia* to his friend *Hortenfius,* and himself affected at the wedding.

The words of the text clearly apply to the forbidding so monstrous a breach of the law of marriage, and apply equally to *polygamy* as to *monogamy.* *Abigail* and *Ahinoam* were, with respect to *David,* each of them γυνη ἑαυτ8, his *wife*—for the *Holy Ghost* saith, 1 Sam. xxv. 43: *they were both of them his wives:* and therefore he was the ἰδιος ἀνηρ, the peculiar, proper, appropriated husband to both. If David had taken *another man's wife,* or either of them had been lent out or given to another man, this would have fallen directly under the interdict of the *apostle,* who here says no more than is exactly consonant with the *law of Moses.*

Saying that this text forbids *polygamy,* because the word *wife* is in the singular number, is mere trifling; as much so, as contending that a man is to love but *one*[182] *neighbour,* because it is said, *Thou shalt love thy neighbour as thyself;* not

---

Cæsar tells us of the antient *Britons*—"*Ten or twelve* of them have wives in common amongst them—but every woman's children are accounted his, who first possessed her when a virgin; so many men, having each of them married his proper wife, afterwards agreed upon that friendly way of possessing them." De B. G. lib. v. Much more to the same purpose may be found in *Puffendorf,* book vi. c. 1. § 15.

182   We meet with numberless passages in the scripture, where the *singular* is not to be understood *exclusively,* that is, so as not to include the *plural,* but *distributively* so as to include it. Witness the passages referred to, as also the *fourth* commandment—"Thou shalt do no manner of work, thou, nor thy *son,* nor thy *daughter,* nor thy *man-servant,* nor thy *maid-servant,* nor the *stranger* that is within thy gates." Are we to gather from hence, that a man is to have but *one son, one daughter, one man-servant, one maid-servant,* &c.? So the ninth commandment—"Thou shalt not bear false witness against thy *neighbour.*"—Endless are the examples of this sort, which might be brought, to

neighbours; or that he shall keep but *one servant,* because it is said, Rom. xiv. 4. *Who art thou that judgest another man's servant,* in the *singular* number, not *servants,* in the *plural:* or to argue for *polygamy,* because it is said, 1 Cor. vii. 29, *they that have wives,* and not *every one that has a wife.* All such literal or verbal criticism is mere *word-catching,* far below the dignity of fair argument, and deserves nothing but contempt.

Those who represent the *apostle* as addressing himself to *single* persons, and advising them to marry, *to avoid fornication,* make him guilty of evident *tautology*—for the eighth verse is expressly addressed to the *unmarried* and *widows.* After wishing that all, like himself, could live *unmarried* (that they might have less distraction in their attendance on the service of God, ver. 35.) he adds—but *if they cannot contain let them marry, for it is better to marry than burn*—πυρουσθαι, to be *fired,* to be *on fire*—(comp. *Cant.* viii. 6. *Hos.* vii. 4.) that is, with *lust,* or unchaste desires, by which they might be driven into the commission of *fornication,* and all *manner of uncleanness*—which is, in effect, saying the same thing over again, as some would have him to say at the *second* verse, the very terms of which shew it to be addressed to *married persons;* for how could the apostle say to a *single man*—let him have—ἔχετω, retain—γυναῖκα ἑαυτοῦ, his *wife;* or to a *single woman*—let her have, i.e. *keep* to—τον ἰδιον ἄνδρα, her own *husband?* The immediate connection of this verse with the three following, which can belong to *married people only,* is another strong argument for the truth of this observation. Besides, if we understand the ἕκαςος, every man, and the ἑκαςη, every *woman,* to relate here to any but the *married people,* it may seem to make the *apostle* command *every one to marry,* whether they chuse it or not, contrary to ver. 7, 8. The word ἕκαςος is certainly *relative,* and must agree with some *masculine* substantive understood: this can be, (agreeably to the rest of the verse) nothing but ἀνηρ, which, in the last clause, must signify husband—τον ἰδιον ἄνδρα, her own *husband,* and so in the *four* times it is used in the two *following* verses. The word ἑκαςη is also *relative,*

shew that, in many instances, the *singular* number cannot be consined to an *exclusive* sense, but must, of necessity, be extended *distributively,* so as to include *many,* and indeed *all* of the kind which is spoken of: and in this sense the word *wife* must be understood, 1 Cor. vii. 2. in order to make the text harmonize with the Old Testament.

and must agree with some *feminine* substantive understood; this can be no other than γυνη, which, in this verse, is rendered *wife*; and so the *four times* it is used in the following verses. If the ανηρ and γυνη which are *understood,* had been rendered as they are uniformly in the rest of the *context,* all difficulty in understanding, and all disputes about, the *apostle's* meaning had been saved, and the *evil alluded to* reproved in as plain terms as the *apostle* intended it should; for the verse would have stood thus—*Let every husband* (or married man) *have his wife*—γυναικα εαυτ8, the wife that belongs to him—*and every wife* (or married woman) *have her own husband.*

When he addresses himself to *single persons,* and advises them to *marry* to *avoid fornication* (which is certainly the meaning of ver. 9.) he does not use a *doubtful*[183] *periphrasis,* but speaks the matter in the common usual phrase—γαμησάτωσαν—*let them marry.* There is something remarkable also at the tenth and eleventh verses, where, in answer to some questions put to him in the *Corinthians* letter, probably about *married persons,* who were in a state of *separation,* he says—*Let not the wife depart from her husband, but if she depart*—μενέτω άγαμος—*let her remain unmarried.* Comp. Rom. vii. 3. and 1 Cor. vii. 39. This is said to be the *command of* God, ver. 10; how is it that it is not extended *to the husband?* It is only said—*Let not the husband put away his wife.* Had he construed Matt. xix. 9. by the *sound* instead of the *sense,* he most probably would have said of the *husband* also, μενέτω άγαμος—*let him remain unmarried,* in case of *her departure,* or of his *putting her away.*

But as those *false apostles, deceitful workers, transforming themselves into the apostles of* Christ, 2 Cor. xi. 13. had, by their *erroneous* and monstrous doctrines, saying, "that *all* marriage was of the *Devil*" (for such was the doctrine of the *Gnostics*) sadly distressed the consciences of weak people, and led them to think, that, as *marriage* was a *sinful* thing, therefore all conjugal intercourse

---

183 Which seems not conformable to the *idiom* of the *Greek language* itself, for I do not recollect, that, in any *Greek author,* any more than in the *scriptures,* εχειν γυναικα, or εχειν ανδρα, ever signifies to *marry,* or stands as a phrase for γαμειν or γαμηθηναι.

between married people must be[184] *sinful* too, we find the *apostle* proceeding, ver. 3. to answer that part of the *letter* which related to their distress on this account. But, so far from deeming the intercourse of married persons wrong, he says— "Let the husband render unto the wife due benevolence, Ὀφειλομενην εὐνοιαν (which answers to the ענה of *Moses*, Exod. xxi. 10. and which we decently render *duty of marriage)* and likewise the *wife unto the husband. The wife has not power over her own body*, so as to withdraw herself entirely from the *conjugal debt, but the husband* may, as a matter of right, have access to her at all proper times and seasons. Likewise the *husband has not the power* (8κ ἐξ8σιαζει) *of his own body*, so as to withdraw from the conjugal intercourse with his wife, *but the wife,* as a debt due from the contract which the man is under to her, by the very terms of their union, has a right to his *society.*

Therefore, *defraud ye not one the other*—μὴ ἀποςεριετε ἀλλκλους—do not *deprive* or *wrong* each other in these respects, under a false notion of its being sinful to come together as man and wife. There may be *times,* indeed, when both may find it expedient, and therefore both consent to separate for a while; as on occasion of particular abstinence and devotion: but let not even this exceed the bounds of prudence, lest, if it should, *Satan* should take the advantage of you, and tempt you to gratify, in an unlawful way, those desires which may lawfully be satisfied between married persons. However, I do not insist upon the matter of your parting, even for a season, by way of *commandment*, κατ> ἐπιταγην, but by way of *permission*, κατα συγγνώμην. See 2 Cor. viii. 10.

I take the Ὀφειλομενην εὐνοιαν of *Paul* to answer exactly to the word ענה, which is rendered *duty of marriage.* This is mentioned by *Moses* to be still due to the *first wife,* though a man take a *second.* Exod. xxi. 10. Therefore this passage of *St. Paul* no more concludes against *polygamy,* than that of *Moses,* which actually supposes it. The root ענה, means to *act upon some person or thing*—and, in *Kal, to lie with a woman,* Gen. xxxiv. 2. Deut. xxi. 14. Deut. xxii. 24, 29: so that by comparing scripture with scripture, we shall find one part explain the other.

---

184   In the 4th century there were a set of people who censured *matrimony,* and said, that "wives and husbands *cohabiting* together cannot be saved." These were condemned by the council of *Gangara,* anno 369. *Fortin* Rem. vol. iv. p. 43.

There is a similarity of expression between *Moses* and *Paul,* which, I own, makes me think that the *latter* copied the sentiments of the *former,* upon the subjects before us. *Moses* saith ויענתה לא יגרע—*her duty of marriage he shall not withhold—subtract—withdraw—keep back from her.* Paul says—*let the husband render to the wife due benevolence—*Ὀφειλομενην Ευνοιαν—which is saying the same thing, in other words indeed, but with the same meaning. To *render* to another their due is not to *withhold* it, and not to *withhold* it is to *render* it. Paul says, μὴ ἀποστερεῖτε— *Moses* says: לֹא תִגְרָע, which the LXX actually translate ἀν ἀποστερεῖτε. This is the very identical verb which we translate *defraud not.* גָּרַע signifies to *subtract* or *withdraw—*to *withhold* or *keep* back;—the Greek ἀποστερεῖτε has the *same meaning—*so that *Paul* may be said to translate, just as the LXX have done, the גָּרַע of *Moses.* The only shadow of difference between the *Jewish lawgiver,* and the *Christian apostle,* consists in the explicitness of the *latter* and the conciseness of the *former. Moses's* words imply what *Paul's* declare, and, *vice versa, Paul* declares what is implied by *Moses.* If the *husband* is not to withhold the *marriage-duty* from *the wife,* this must imply that the *wife* is not to withhold it from the *husband.* There must be a parity of reason in both cases. Neither *husband* nor *wife* can have *any such power over their own bodies.* This is plainly *said* by *Paul,* and, in consistency with the *law of marriage,* must evidently be *meant* by *Moses.* For my own part, I as much believe that *Paul* had the doctrine in Exod. xxi. 10 in his mind when he[185] wrote that part of the answer to the *Corinthians* letter, wherein he solved their difficulties about the *intercourse* of married people, as it is now in my mind, while I am writing these words; and thus, upon good authority, even that of the mind of GOD as delivered by *Moses,* he could be so peremptory in declaring that *such intercourse* was *duty* on both sides, and therefore could not (as the *Gnostic* doctrine might have led them to suppose) be *a sin.*

---

185   On looking into *Pole Syn.* in 1 Cor. vii. 3: I find him of the same opinion—"Respexit hîc *Paulus* locum illum, Ex. xxi. 10. ibi enim idem quod hîc marito præcipitur." "*Paul* here looked back to that place in Exod. xxi. 10. for there the same thing is commanded to the husband as here."

St. Paul, who, before his conversion, *had profited in the Jews religion above many of his equals in his own nation, Gal.* i. 14, could hardly, after his conversion, be ignorant of the law of *Moses*; so far from it, he was undoubtedly, a most accomplished teacher of it. Witness the masterly manner in which he explains the sense and meaning of the *moral* law, and unfolds the whole design of the *ceremonial* law. By the first, he demonstrated the necessity of the *gospel* for salvation—by the *second,* he shewed the *gospel* to have been one and the same, though under different dispensations, from the fall of *Adam* to the coming of *Jesus Christ.* Now to set *Paul*, as a law-giver, in *Moses'* seat, and to represent him as condemning that which was not condemned by the *law of Moses*, is to make him act inconsistently with his own declaration, Rom. iii. 31. *Do we make void the law through faith?—God forbid! Yea—we establish the law.* It is to make him transgress the law, by despising that solemn sanction, which equally forbade *adding to it or diminishing from it;* and to put him in much the same situation with those, whether *men or angels,* who preached *any other gospel* than *that which he preached;* for to preach any *other law* than that *which was given by* MOSES, is as great an offence as to preach any other *gospel* than that which *came by* JESUS CHRIST. This we may learn from the very words of the law itself. Deut. iv. 2. xii. 32.

Dr. Whitby, a very laborious and learned commentator, in his comment on—*the husband,* εἰς ἐξουσιάζει, *hath not power of his own body, &c.* says—"Here is a plain[186] argument against *polygamy.*" That here is a plain argument to prove that he shall not withhold the *duty of marriage* from the wife, and that, in this respect, *neither* shall *defraud* or withhold from the other, on proper occasions, the *conjugal debt,* is very certain. But as what is here said, is founded in the very *nature* and *essence* of the *marriage-relation,* it must equally concern all that ever have married, or shall marry, to the end of the world, as well under the Old Testament

---

186 "Sane *patres Tridentini*," saith one, "si adhuc in vivis essent, ipsis immortales agerent gratias, quod a scripturis anathematis in polygamos vibrati justitiam atque aequitatem defenderint, eaque praestiterint quae ipsi ne quidem audire voluerint."

"Truly the *fathers* of the *council of Trent,* if they were yet alive, would give immortal thanks to those who should defend, out of the holy scripture, the justice and equity of their *curse* brandished against *polygamists,* and who should do that, which they themselves would not even dare to attempt."

as the New Testament; it bears equally hard, if it be an argument against *polygamy*, on the man who, having *one* wife, *took another*, in the days of *Moses*, as on any one who should do so at this hour (for certainly the marriage-relation must always be the same) and will prove much more against certain *distinguished characters* under the Old Testament, than I dare say the author meant it should. For this we have his own word— "Nor can I think" (says he) "that *Abraham, Jacob, David*, and other pious men, would have had *more wives*, or *wives* and *concubines*, had this been a plain violation of the *law of nature*; nor would GOD have so highly approved of them, had they lived in *adultery*." Note on *Matt.* xix. 7, 8.

When learned and pious men find out "plain arguments" against things which are not mentioned, or even hinted at, in the *text*, it is a shrewd sign that[187] *prejudice*, and not *judgment*, dictates the *comment*. The *Corinthians* had a very "plain argument" against their fears about married persons *cohabiting* together; and if they compared this scripture, ver. 3, 4, with what *Moses* so positively laid down in Exod. xxi. 10. the *polygamists* among them were no more to forsake the company of *their wives*, so as to withhold the *duty of marriage*, than those who had but *one wife* were to withdraw themselves from *her society* in the *same* respect.

That there were many *polygamists* among the *Gentile* converts, as well as among the *Jewish*, there can be but little doubt; for, as[188] *Grotius* observes—

---

187 How this learned man's *prejudices* warred against his *judgement* (like many others who want to support a preconceived opinion, against the *truth* which would overturn it) may be seen from the concession he falls into, in his note on Mark x. 11. in the following words— "Since to commit adultery is to violate the bed of another person, he that commits adultery against his wife, must violate her bed, which no husband can do only by doing that which an husband lawfully might do. Since then a right to *polygamy*, is a right to marry more wives than one, he that hath this right, cannot violate the bed of his first wife, by assuming another to it. It *therefore must be acknowledged*, either that the husband, under CHRIST's institution, and by the original law of matrimony, had no such right, or that he that marrieth another cannot, by that, commit adultery against his first wife." Here is a fair ISSUE IN LAW joined—and must be tried by THE LAW—for CHRIST made no *institution* whatsoever on the subject of *marriage*, but only *declared, explained,* and *inforced* those already made and recorded in the LAW *which was given by* MOSES. This LAW, like all other RECORDS, is to be tried by ITSELF—taking the WHOLE TOGETHER.

188 *De Verit.* lib. ii. § 13. So *De Jure,* lib. ii. cap. 5. § 9. he says—"Sed & apud *Græcos*, CECROPS primus, teste *Athenæo*, μιας εστι συζεσι, *unam feminam uni marito attribuit:* quod tamen ne Athenis quidem diu observatum Socratis & aliorum exemplo docemur. " *But among the Greeks,* CECROPS

Inter Paganos paucæ gentes una uxore contentæ fuerunt.— "Among the *Pagans*, few nations were content with one wife;" and we do not find the *apostle* making this any bar to *church-membership*, though he expressly does to *church offices*. See before, p. It can hardly be supposed, that if *polygamy* were sinful, that is to say, an offence against the law of GOD, the great *apostle* should be so liberal and so particular, in his epistle to the *Corinthians*, in the condemnation of every other species of illicit *commerce between the sexes*, and yet omit this in the black catalogue, chap. vi. 9, &c. or that he should not be as zealous for the honour of the *law of marriage*, and of the *seventh commandment*, which was evidently to maintain it, as *Ezra* was for that positive law of Deut. vii. 3, against marrying with *heathens*. *Ezra* made the *Jews put away the wives* which they had illegally taken, and even the very *children* which they had by them; How is it that *Paul*, if *polygamy* was sinful, did not make the *Gentile* and the *Jewish* converts put away *every wife*, but the *first*, and annul every *polygamous contract*? Why not say, that being the *husband of one wife* was as necessary to being a *Christian*, as to be chosen a *Bishop* or *Deacon*? for it certainly was, if *polygamy* be *sinful*. *John the Baptist*, at the expense of *his liberty*, and afterwards of his life, honestly and openly, in words that it was out of the reach of all commentators to sophisticate, or give more than one meaning to, told

---

first, as *Athenæus witnesseth, allowed one woman to one man; which, nevertheless, was not long observed, even at* ATHENS, *as we are taught by the example of* SOCRATES *and others.*

Παλαι γαρ ειωθεσαν και—Ελληνες, και Ἰσδαιοι, και δυο ἠ τρισι, ἠ πλειστοι γυναιξι νομιμ γαμη καλει ταινον συνειοικεν. Theodoret—cited by *Whitby*, on 1 Tim. iii. 2. "*Formerly the Jews and Greeks were wont to be married to* TWO *or* THREE, *and even* MORE *wives together.*" *Stanley*, Hist. of Philosophy, Tit. Socrates, p. 53, says—that "the occasion whereupon the *Athenians* (who from the time of *Cecrops* had strictly observed single marriage) allowed *bigamy* in the time of *Socrates*, was, that in the second year of the 87th Olympiad, and the 3rd of the 88th, *Athens* was visited extremely by the *pestilence*, which, attended by war and famine, occasioned so great a scarcity of men, that they made an edict, for any that would, to take *two wives*. *Euripides* made use of this indulgence, and that *Socrates* also did so, is attested by *Satyrus* the *Peripatetic* and *Hiernonymus* the *Rhodian*, who recorded the order; to which *Athenæus* imputes the silence of the comic poets in this particular, who omitted no grounds of reproach."

However, it is much to be doubted, whether *Cecrops* did any more than institute *marriage* itself among the *Grecians*, who, before his time, lived promiscuously, and coupled as their fancy led them. See Ant. Univ. Hist. vol. vi. p. 175.—After all, as CECROPS is supposed to have been *cotemporary* with MOSES, it is not very probable, that we should meet with any accounts of him, which can be depended upon.

Herod, with respect to *Herodias*, his *brother Philip's wife—It is not lawful for thee to have her.* But how could *Paul*, with truth, say to the *Ephesians*, the *Corinthians*, or any other people amongst whom he ministered—*I have not shunned to declare unto you*, πᾶσαν τὴν βουλὴν, All (the whole) *counsel of* GOD—if *polygamy* were a sin, and he did not as openly and plainly declare against it, as he did against every other fleshly transgression of GOD's *pure and holy* law? That he has no where done this, I may say—*res ipsa indicat.*

As for taking a *text* here or there, detaching it from the *context*, and the *context* itself from the rest of the *Bible*; then chusing out a single *sentence*, or *word* in a *sentence*, this too without any reference to the original *Hebrew* or *Greek*, and because it seems to *sound that way*, to make it a proof of some opinion we have been taught to hold; it is that sort of criticism which may make the scripture prove any thing, and every thing, just as fancy leads, and, in short, must render the scriptures themselves as vague and indeterminate as the minds of men are.

Wetstein, Prol. p. 146, speaks of "certain *doctors—qui, neglecta connectione contextus sacri, singulas pericopas tanquam singulas sententias, & quasi totidem aphorismos considerant; ut ita liberius suæ phantasiæ indulgere, atque quidlibet ex quolibet efficere possint.*"—Who neglecting the connection of the sacred context, consider all the several verses, as single sentences by themselves, and as so many *aphorisms*, or general maxims, so that they may the more freely indulge their own fancy, and make what they please from what they please.

Whoever has read the history of that *renowned* worthy, Alderman *Whittington*, whose *biographer* tells us that he was twice *Lord Mayor of London*, may recollect a circumstance in that *great* man's life, which affords an exemplification of the aptness which possesses the human mind, to interpret *sounds* into that particular *sense* which its own prejudices, however imbibed, wish to put upon them. It is said that *Whittington*, being an apprentice in the *city*, left his master with an intent to go into the *country*. It being about the time of evening, he sat himself down somewhere in the skirts of the town; his ear was caught with the ringing of *six bells*, he listened attentively to them, 'till at last he persuaded himself that they proclaimed his future greatness in the following *sounds*:

1 2 3 4 5 6

"Turn again *'Whittington,*

123456

Lord Mayor of *London.*"

He was so captivated with the conceit, that he not only imagined the *bells*[189] said this to him, but that all who heard them must give their *peal* the same interpretation; and, no doubt, under such a prepossession, it would have been almost impossible to have persuaded him to the contrary.

So, when men have been brought up under the prejudices of *vulgar opinion* and *common error,* and have their minds swayed and biassed by long custom to one certain train of thinking, they have but to meet with a text in scripture which seems to echo to their *sense* of things, that *sense* will immediately chime in with the *sound*, and both together, almost beyond the power of conviction to the contrary, confirm them still more strongly in their sentiments. What these may happen to be, makes very little difference—whether it be *transubstantiation*—praying to saints—worshipping images—the doctrine of *purgatory*—or, "though *polygamy* was *allowed* under *the law,* it is forbidden *under the* gospel"—or, in short, any other popular prejudice: they will always act towards scripture as *Whittington* did with *the bells,* till that liberality of mind, which ought to possess us, as the privilege of thinking and reasonable beings, opens the way to *free enquiry*—then, and not till then, we shall be *noble* like the *Bereans,* Acts xvii. 11, who would no longer be led by their own prejudices, or prejudiced by other people's opinions, but *received the word of* GOD *with all readiness of mind, and searched the scriptures daily, whether those things* (which they heard preached by *Paul*) *were so.* The scriptures which these *Jews* at *Berea* searched *diligently,* must have been the scriptures of the Old Testament; no others, if written, could then have come to their hands; but they compared the New Testament as preached by *Paul,* with the Old Testament of *Moses and the prophets,* that they might judge whether the things he declared to them were of divine authority, answerable to former revelations of GOD's mind and will, or not. This is the method which I have endeavoured to observe throughout this book, and which I most sincerely recommend to every reader, as

---

189 "We have an homely English proverb, which says—As the fool thinks, the bell clinks—A proverb applicable, in our opinion, to all arguments founded on the *sound,* and arbitrary meaning of words." Lond. Review for 1778, p. 75.

well as to every person who wishes to *know* and to *do* the will of GOD. If once we detach the New Testament from the Old Testament, there is not a single *heresy* that will not find something to say for itself, perhaps more than we may be able very easily to answer. But let us carry what we hear to the Old Testament; if it exactly[190] tallies with that, we may be sure it is a right interpretation of the New Testament; if otherwise, it must be false, because the mind and will of GOD can never vary, disagree with, or contradict itself. I do not say these things with regard to any particular doctrine of the New Testament, but with respect to the whole.— The doctrine of a *Trinity in unity*—the *incarnation—birth—life—teaching— miracles—sufferings—death—burial—resurrection—ascension—glorification,* and *intercession* of *Jesus Christ,* together with the aspect these things bear towards the salvation of mankind, if only related in a book, no single article of which was ever heard or thought of for *four thousand* years together, would challenge little more of my assent or belief, than the *Koran* of *Mahomet,* the *Zend,* or *Zend-avesta* of *Confucius,* or the *Shaster* of the *Bramins.* But when I compare these things with what is contained in the Old Testament, to which the New Testament so often refers for their truth, I then can no more support them to be false, than I can suppose it possible for men to see into futurity, exactly delineate what is to happen ages before it comes to pass, and so exactly, as that the event shall be a literal fulfilment of all that is foretold, unless *He* who is *perfect in knowledge* hath made a revelation or discovery of things which no mortal wisdom or foresight could have ever otherwise been acquainted with. Therefore, when we compare the New Testament with the Old, we may be assured that it is as impossible to be false, as that a *dozen dice* should be thrown the same number for a[191] million times running; no hazard or casualty could bring such a thing within the most acute calculation of chance; therefore I conclude, that nothing short of *infinite wisdom* and *divine contrivance* could ever first *declare,* and then *fulfil,* the wondrous things which are written in *Moses* and the *prophets.* When therefore I hear of a doctrine as taught in

---

190   "The gospel is the best comment upon the *law,* and the *law* is the best expositor of the gospel: they are like a pair of indentures, they answer in every part: their *harmony* is wonderful, and is of itself a conviction. No human contrivance could have reached it." *Lesue's* Works, vol. i. p. 75.

191   For which reason, AN INFIDEL may be styled, the most CREDULOUS OF MORTALS.

the New Testament, I am certain, if it be true, it must accord with the scriptures of the Old Testament. Thither I carry it; if I find it does not exactly *tally* with what I find there, I am certain it is false, and must arise from some misconception, and, of course, some misinterpretation of the passage where it is supposed to be found. I am told that *sin is a transgression of the law*; when I hear it asserted that *polygamy* is *sinful*, I consult *the law*; if it be forbidden *there*, I agree to the *sinfulness* of it; if not forbidden there, but[192] *allowed*, I find myself reduced to this *dilemma*—either the asserter of such a proposition, who says he takes it from the New Testament, is *mistaken*, which is probable, or the New Testament must *contradict the law*, which is *impossible*.

With respect to what is frequently urged against *polygamy* among *Christians*, that "tho it was allowed by the *law of Moses*, yet it is *forbidden by the law of christ* "—by which CHRIST is made a repealer of the *old*, and a giver of a *new law*—it so affects His character as the *Messiah*, as to render Him, if it be true, *not* the person which *Moses* and the *prophets* represent Him, or what He represented Himself to be. The discussion, therefore, of this *horrid position* requires, and shall have, a *chapter* by itself.

At present, I will advert to an argument taken from the New Testament, to prove the unlawfulness of *polygamy* among *Christians*, though *allowed* to the *Jews* under the Old Testament. *St. Paul*,[193] Eph. v. 31, 32. and in some other passages, represents marriage as a figure or representation of *Christ* and *His church*, which is but *one*: whereas, having *more wives* than one at a time, destroys the *analogy* which the marriage-state bears to CHRIST *and His church*. In answer to which, I would ask, If CHRIST *and His church* were not as much *one* under the Old Testament as under the New Testament? Is. liv. 5. *Thy Maker is thine husband, the* LORD

---

192 "*Lex Hebræa omnem spurcitiem inhibet, sed plures uni concedit uxores.*" GROTIUS.— "The *Jewish* law restrains all filthiness, but allows a plurality of wives to one man."

193 That *marriage* may be looked upon in a *typical* view, with respect to the union of CHRIST with the church, appears very clearly from this scripture, and the others referred to—but in this view of the matter, *polygamy* and *monogamy* were equally *typical*—the *former*, of the *church*, as consisting of *Jews* and *Gentiles*, and of the many and various individual believers among them—the *latter*, of the whole company of *believers*, collectively considered, as making but *one body*, of which CHRIST is the head. Comp. Rom. xii. 5. 1 Cor. xii. 2. with Eph. i. 23. ii. 21, 22.

of Hosts is his name; the GOD *of the whole earth shall He be called.* See also Jer. iii. 14, 20. The *church,* taken *collectively,* is but *one;* but *distinctively,* it consists of *many.* Rom xii. 5. *We being many, are one body in* CHRIST—and 1 Cor. xii. 12. *For as the body is* ONE, *and hath many members, and all the members of that one body being many, are one body, so also is* CHRIST. So that the argument against *polygamy,* taken from the *union* and *unity* of CHRIST and *His church,* rather leans the other way; unless, contrary to scripture and fact, it could be proved that the *church* consisted but of *one member;* whereas it consists of *many,* and yet is but *one body—one household*—Eph. ii. 19. *One family,* even though the *saints in heaven* be also taken into the account. Eph. iii. 15. The *bride* or *spouse* of CHRIST is but *one*—i.e. *one church;* yet every member of that *church* is as distinctly the *spouse of* CHRIST, as really *married to Him that rose from the dead* (Rom. vii. 4.) as the *whole* is, collectively considered. Surely these scriptural illustrations of the nature of the marriage-bond, afford a complete answer to that question, "If a man hath *two wives,* how can he be *one flesh* with *both*—or *each one flesh* with him?" See Eph. v. 30.

We also read not only of the *church of* CHRIST in the *singular* number, but of the *churches of* CHRIST in the *plural,* about forty times in the New Testament; which, by the way, is at least as conclusive an argument for *polygamy,* as the other is *against* it.

From the making CHRIST and *His church* an emblem of *marriage,* or *marriage* an emblem of CHRIST *and His church,* some have looked upon it as a *sacrament.* There is certainly an *outward sign* of something *spiritual;* but as there wants that which is essentially necessary to make it a *sacrament,* which is GOD's own appointment of it as such, the more scriptural professors of *Christianity* reject it. For the same reason I would reject those arguments against *polygamy,* which are drawn from the *union of Christ and His church,* because GOD has no where established their authority, (that I can find) either in the Old Testament or the *New.* These arguments would have been just as conclusive under the *former* as under the *latter.* The *church* is called the *married wife.* Is. liv. 1. *Her* REDEEMER, *the* LORD *of hosts,* is called *her Husband,* ver. 5; but never did *Isaiah,* nor any other of the *prophets,* use this as an argument against the *polygamy* of the people. If this was not done, or so much as hinted at, under the Old Testament, why are we to conceive it to be done under the *New*, when the same things and persons are equally represented under both?

Had *polygamy* been intended to have been condemned under the New-Testament dispensation, I should humbly suppose that OUR LORD would have put the matter out of question by words too plain to admit of the least dispute: that He *whose loins were girt about with faithfulness* (Is. xi. 5.) would have been at least as *faithful* to His hearers of *the lost sheep of the house of* ISRAEL, to whom He was so immediately sent (Matt. xv. 24) and spoken to them in as *plain* and *unequivocal terms as John the Baptist* did to *Herod,* upon the subject of *his brother Philip's wife (Matt.* xiv. 4.) There cannot be the least doubt, that numbers of our LORD's *multitudes of hearers* were *polygamists—all* in *principle—many* in *practice*; nor can it be doubted, that if this was against the *law of marriage*, the law of the *seventh* commandment, or any other *positive law* of GOD, it must be a mortal, damnable[194] sin, involving the *man* as well as the *woman* in destruction

---

194 *St. Augustine*, lib. xxii. c. 47. against *Faustus*, says of *polygamy—"Quando mos erat crimen non erat."—*"When it was a custom, it was no crime."—How this great man could be capable of such an absurdity is astonishing.—The idea of a *sinful act* losing its *criminality* from *custom*, or the frequency of the commission of it, leaves little room for GOD's command, Exod xxiii. 2. *Thou shalt not follow a multitude to do evil. Nunc proprterea crimen est,* saith he, *quia mos non est.—* "Now it is a crime, because not customary."

St. *Chrysostom*'s account of the matter is much more consistent with scripture and common sense, when, speaking of *Abraham* and *Hagar*, he says—ὃδεπω γαρ ταύτα τοτε κεκωλυτο—*These things were not then forbidden.* Indeed *Augustine*, in other parts of his writings, speaks much in the same manner. "There was (says he) a *blameless* custom of one man having many wives—for there are many things which at that time might be done in a way of *duty*, which now cannot be done but *licentiously*—because, for the *sake of multiplying* posterity, *no law forbade a plurality of wives.*" See Grot. de Jur. vol. i. p. 268. note[h].

St. *Austin*, like others of the fathers, seem to have supposed that the command, *Be fruitful and multiply*—and the allowance of *polygamy*, as a means of fulfilling it, went hand in hand together:— that as that command—"Ratione multitudinis liberorum, pertinuit ad tempora ante CHRISTUM: non ad *nos* qui alio vivimus ævo—quia hodie, repleto mundo, non tam necessarium sit quam olim— mundum non desiderare illud *crescite & multiplicamini"*—therefore the allowance of *polygamy* ceased with the necessity of the *command* which it accompanied.

Thus, as is usual, one absurdity begat another. Those who could be persuaded, that the command for the propagation of the human species was only obligatory on former ages, might very consistently suppose, that even *marriage* itself had very little to do with *Christians*, and that therefore *polygamy* became an *evil*, which they allowed to have been a *lawful* thing, and even *duty*,

and perdition. *Paul* could declare openly, that if *a woman, living her husband, be married to another, she shall be called an adulterer,* and vouches the *law of* GOD for his authority, *Rom.* vii. 1, 2, 3. How is it that *CHRIST* did not openly say the same thing on the part of the man?—Because, if He had, He could *not have vouched the law of* GOD for his authority; and for the same reason, that he could not *say* it, he could not *think* it, for GOD's *law was within his heart*, Ps xl. 8. and no *thought* could ever be in the *pure* and *perfect* heart of CHRIST, but what was exactly conformable, *in all things,* to the *pure and perfect law of* GOD. Let us then carry what OUR LORD saith against *divorce,* Matt xix. 9. to the *law and to the testimony,* and it can no more conclude against *polygamy,* simply considered, than it concludes against *bigamy,* or a man's marrying a *second* wife after the death of his *first,* and being *twice married.* Some of the primitive fathers cited it, to prove that *every second marriage was adultery;* but here their learned and pious advocate, *Dr. Cave,* does allow, that "they stretched the string till it cracked again."

I might also observe, that, if *polygamy* was a sin, and even a *national* sin, an *epidemical* transgression of the law of *GOD,* it is very extraordinary that OUR LORD's *fore-runner, John the Baptist,* who came to *preach repentance,* should not mention, nor even hint at it; for his commission ran thus—Luke i. 17. *To turn the hearts of the fathers unto the children, the disobedient to the wisdom of the just; to make ready a people prepared for the* LORD. It is said of him, Matt xvii. 11. that he should *restore* or *reform* (αποκαταςῃσει) *all things.*

No man could have a fairer opportunity to bear his testimony against a *national sin* than the *Baptist* had; for it is said (Matthew iii. 5.) *Then went out to him Jerusalem, and all Judea, and all the region round about Jordan;* and among the numbers *who were baptized by him in Jordan, confessing their sins* (ver. 6.) there were *many harlots* (chap. xxi. 32.). So that it is evident he had not spare to inveigh most sharply against the sin of *fleshly uncleanness;* had *polygamy* been of this kind, he doubtless would have preached against it, which, if he had, some trace would most probably have been left of it, as there is of his preaching against the sin of

---

in times past. Such are the γραωδεις μυθοι—the *aniles fabella*—the *old women's stories*—which the *fathers* told, till they believed them, and, on their authority, they are believed to this hour!

whoredom, by the harlots (αἱ[195] πορναί) being said to *believe on him*; which they certainly would not have done, any more than the *Scribes* and *Pharisees* (Matt xxi. 32.) if the preacher had not awakened them to a deep and real sense of their guilt, by setting forth the heinousness of their sin. He exerted his eloquence also against *public grievances*, such as the extortion of the public officers of the revenue—the *publicans*—τελωναι—*tax-gatherers*—likewise against the oppressive methods used by the *soldiery*, who made it a custom either to take people's goods *by violence*, or to *defraud* them of their property, by extorting it under the terror of *false accusation*. These were *public grievances*, against which the *Baptist* bore so open a testimony, that the *publicans* and *soldiers* came to him, saying— *What shall we do?* This being the case, is it conceivable that a man of the *Baptist's* character, who was so zealous for the honour of the law, as to reprove even a *king* to his face for *adultery*, should suffer, if *polygamy* be *adultery*, a *whole nation*, as it were, of public *adulterers*, to stand before him, and not bear the least testimony against them? I do not say this is a *conclusive*, but it is surely a very strong presumptive argument, that in the *Baptist's* views of the matter, *polygamy*, *whoredom*, and *adultery* were by no means the same thing.

Having finished, for the present, what I had to say on the subject of *polygamy*, as supposed to be condemned by the New Testament, I must return back to the Old Testament, to shew that *polygamy* was not only *allowed* in *all cases*, but in some *commanded*. The first instance of this which I shall mention, is with respect to the law, *Deut.* xxv. 5—10. *If brethren dwell*[196] *together, and one of them die, and have no child, the wife of the dead shall not marry without unto a stranger: her husband's brother shall go in unto her, and take her to him to wife, and perform the duty of an husband's brother unto her. And it shall be that the firstborn which she beareth, shall succeed in the name of his brother which is dead, that his name be not put out of Israel*, etc.

This law must certainly be looked upon as an *exception* from the general law (Lev. xviii. 16.) and the reason of it appears in the law itself, viz. "To preserve

---

195   The word πορναί may signify *lewd women* of all sorts.

196   They are said to *dwell together*, not only who were in the *same family*, but in the *same country*. Gen xiii. 5, 6.

inheritances in the families to which they belonged." Therefore all lands which had been mortgaged, were to return back to the owner at the year of *jubilee*. See Lev. xxv. 25, 28. See also a special provision against the alienation of lands from the tribe to which they belonged, Numb. xxxvi. 2-9. This was of the utmost consequence in the designs of *Providence* respecting the MESSIAH, whose *genealogy*, with respect to his being of the *seed* of *Abraham—the tribe of Judah—the family of David*, was not more ascertained by his lineal descent, than by the preservation of *Bethlehem Ephrata* in the *tribe of Judah*, and *family of David*. By which it came to pass, that the prophecy concerning the very *place* of the MESSIAH's *birth* was literally fulfilled (Comp. Mic. v. 2. with Matt. ii. 4, 5, 6, and Luke ii. 3, 4, 5, 6, 7.) The *Jewish*[197] *doctors*; as Mr. *Selden*, in his *Uxor Hæbraica*, and others after him, observe, made several exceptions to this law; but as the *text* makes *none*, I know not that we are warranted in making *any*. Bishop *Burnet* seems to have had a right view of the matter, in his observation on the *generality* of this law. His words are—"Yea, *polygamy* was made, in some cases, a *duty* by *Moses's* law; when any died without issue, his brother, or nearest kinsman, was to marry his wife, for raising up seed to him; and *all were obliged* to obey this, under the hazard of infamy if they refused; neither is there any exceptions made for such as were married; from whence I may faithfully conclude, that what God made *necessary* in some cases, to any degree, can in no case be *sinful in itself*; since God is holy in all his ways. And thus far it appears that *polygamy* is not contrary to the law and nature of marriage."

I am indebted for the above quotation to the[198] before-mentioned reverend *Dean's* book on *polygamy*, wherein the *Dean* seems a little comforted by the *Bishop's* having said, that "he was at a distance from his books and papers, when he gave his opinion on this point."—"This," adds he, "was the best excuse that could be given for so rash a decision, which it would have been for the honour of his reading to have retracted, and which, I sincerely wish he "had retracted, when he returned to his books."

The good *Dean*, in his zeal against *polygamy*, don't give himself time to

---

197   Their comments on the *Old Testament* are about as much to be depended upon, in general, as the *Popish* comments upon the *New*. See *Fulk* on *Rhemish Testament*—per tot.

198   See before, p. 116

consider the soundness of the learned *prelate's* opinion.

As there was *no law* against *polygamy*, there was nothing to exempt a *married man* from the obligation of marrying *his brother's widow* on this account; for if so, things might have been so situated, that *Bethlehem* might have gone away into some other family than that of *David*, into some other tribe than that of *Judah*, and, of course, *Joseph and his wife Mary* have gone elsewhere to *be taxed*; for this might evidently have been the consequence of the *widow and the inheritance* going into the hands *of a stranger*. But GOD says—*The wife of the dead shall not marry without unto a stranger—her husband's brother shall go in unto her*, &c. Here is a *negative* clause, positively declaring whom she shall *not* marry, and an *affirmative clause*, as positively declaring whom she *shall*. Now let us suppose, that not only the *surviving brother*, but all the near *kinsmen*, to whom the marriage of the widow, and the redemption of the inheritance belonged, were *married men*; if that exempted them from the obligation of this law—as they could not *redeem the inheritance*, unless they *married the widow* (Ruth iv. 5.)—the end of this important law must in many cases be defeated—the widow be tempted to marry a stranger—to put herself and the inheritance into his hands—and the whole reason assigned for the law itself, that of *raising up seed to the deceased,* to preserve the inheritance in his family, that *his name be not put out of Israel*—fall to the ground. For which *weighty* reasons, as there was evidently no law against *polygamy,* there could be no exemption of a man from the positive duty of this law *because he was married*. As we say—*ubi eadem ratio ibi idem jus*.

But the learned *Dean*, in order to overthrow all the *Bishop's* reasoning on the subject, observes from *Selden's* Ux. Heb. that "the *Chaldee* paraphrast, the *Midrash*, and *Josephus,* agree, that this was the reason why *Mahlon's* next kinsman refused to redeem *Ruth*, his widow, viz.—Because it was *not lawful for him to marry her, having a wife of his own."* That people should invent reasons for men's actions, where none are given, is not so surprising as overlooking the reasons that are given, and substituting others which do not appear to be so much as thought of by the parties themselves. This is the case here—*Mahlon's* next *kinsman* is applied to, as by law he ought to have been, to buy *Mahlon's* inheritance, and to marry *Ruth* his widow: his answer is neither more nor less than this—"I cannot redeem it for myself, *lest I mar my own inheritance.*"—How these words relate to the *lawfulness* or *unlawfulness* of the matter, was reserved for the ingenuity of modern interpreters to make out—that they may, and most probably do, relate to the *expediency* or *inexpediency* of such a step, the *kinsman's* present circumstances considered, may be easily inferred from the *words* of the *reason* given. The *kinsman* might be married, perhaps have many children, and but a small provision for them—therefore, when he hears of not only disbursing the redemption-price for *Mahlon's* parcel of land, but that this could not be done, without marrying a very poor young woman, by whom he might have another numerous family of children, which he could not maintain, educate, or provide for, out of the small parcel of land which was[199] *Elimelech's*, but must diminish his own inheritance of which he was possessed, to the damage of his other family, he prudently declines the *kinsman's part*—*lest*, said he, I *mar mine own inheritance.* Such a sense as this the words will most certainly bear; but as to their meaning that the man would not marry *Ruth*—"because it was not lawful for him to marry her, *having a wife of his own"*—it is a conceit, fetched even farther than, one would think, the utmost unfairness of prejudice itself could reach.

Since I wrote the above, I have looked into *Bishop Patrick*, on *Ruth* iv. 6. who mentions the passage alluded to in the *Chaldee paraphrast*, and *the Midrash*; and so far from their appearing to say what the *Dean* would make them, there is not a word of any such thing; they put quite a different sense upon the words. As for *Josephus*, I would almost venture to affirm, without looking into the book, that he cannot so grossly contradict himself; for when he is writing that part of the *History of David*, where he speaks of his *polygamy*, he says—δοντος δε αυτω και ἁς δικαιως νομιμως ηγάγετο—(GOD) "giving him *wives*, which he *justly and lawfully married."* However, having consulted *Josephus* on the subject, I find no such reason assigned by the *kinsman*, for refusing to redeem *Mahlon's* land, and to marry his widow, as the *Dean* asserts.—*Josephus*, Antiq. lib. ix. c. 5. § 4. speaking of the *kinsman's* refusal, says, that he rejected the offer—Ειναι δε καί γυναικα λεγων ἁυτω και παιδας ηδη—"Saying, he had already a wife and children;" but not a word that it was *"unlawful to marry another woman."* Not that *Josephus* represents

---

199 *Elimelech* was the father of *Mahlon;* therefore the land is called *Elimelech's*, it descending to *Mahlon* from him.

the matter as the *Bible* does, any more than the learned *Dean* rightly represents the sentiments of *Josephus*. It might not be expedient for the *kinsman* to marry *Ruth*, as he was circumstanced; but this has nothing to do with the *lawfulness* or *unlawfulness* of the matter, with respect to the law of God. *Lawfulness* and *expediency* are very distinct and different considerations. See 1 Cor. vi. 12. 1 Cor. x. 23. As for Mr. *Selden*, he, in the very passage which the *Dean* quotes, resolves the kinsman's refusal to marry *Ruth* into a matter of *prudence*, and that for much the same reasons which I have assigned above.

The law itself on which we have been discoursing, was only a *local* and *temporary* institution, and, in the very nature of it, could only concern the *Jews*, and that only with regard to their peculiar situation before the coming of the *Messiah*, when so much depended on the clearness of *family descent* and *inheritance*. It is observable that this law, though not reduced to writing and published till the time of *Moses*, yet existed among the *patriarchs*, as we learn from Gen. xxxviii. 8.

I now shall observe on some laws of more extensive import, the obligation of which must concern *every man*, and that at all times and places, because the evident purpose for which they were ordained, and the reasons on which they are apparently founded, must equally concern all mankind. The *laws* I mean, are those already spoken of, as made for the preservation of the *female sex* from *ruin and prostitution*, by compelling every man to marry the *virgin* he *lies with*. The first of them is to be found *Exod.* xxii. 16; the other *Deut.* xxii. 28, 29. These *laws* must in some cases[200] *command polygamy*, and therefore, in such cases, make it a *duty*; for they are so framed as to admit of no other construction, consistently with the terms in which *Moses* hath recorded them. The terms in which these laws are enacted, with respect to the *men seducing* or *taking virgins*, &c., are as *indefinite* as words can possibly be: *If a man*, says our translation.—This must, *ex vi termini*, mean *any man* whatsoever, be his situation what it may—which is exactly the sense of the *Hebrew* כי איש—As the right understanding of this comprehensive and unlimited word איש is of the utmost importance to the point in question, I will lay

---

200   Luther, de Digam. Episcoporum, § 65, says—*"Nota sunt jura Mosaica de fratris defuncti uxore, & filia corrupta invito patre, quæ cogunt plurium uxorum esse virum."*—"The Mosaic laws concerning the wife of a deceased brother, and concerning a daughter defiled against the father's consent, are well known, which *compel* a man to have a *plurality of wives*."

a full and clear explanation of it before the reader.

יִשׁ "This word has no relation to *kind* or *species,* though, according to its different genders, it has to *sex;* but is applied to almost any distinct *being* or *thing;* as, for instance, to *man.* &c. " See *Parkhurst's* Heb. Lex. sub voc. יִשׁה—"which," saith he, "denotes *existence, subsistence, reality.* "

I will next subjoin the interpretation of *Calasio,* who, in his valuable *Hebrew Concordance,* gives us some *hundreds of texts* in which this word occurs.

אִישׁ "*Persona, creatura*—nomen generale quod essentiam rei non distinguit"—A *person, a creature—a general name, which doth not distinguish the essence of the thing spoken of.*

אִישׁ "Homo generaliter complectens masculum & fœminam."—Man *generally, including male and female.*

אִישׁ "Quis—quilibet—aliquis—unusquisque—quisque—alter."— *Who—whosoever—any one—[201]every one—every man—any other—*

"*Unus*   *ullus*"

some one   *any one.*

אִישׁ "Sexus masculus in qualibet animantium specie" cum "mentio fœminæ additur." Ut Gen. vii. 2. (xxiv. 16.)—The male sex *in any species of animals where the female is also mentioned.*

אִישׁ "Vir—maritus—si cum uxore conferatur. Gen. iii. 6. *An husband, a* married man, *where joined with* wife.

The reader has now before him the meaning of the word, אִישׁ wheresoever it may be used, as applicable *to,* or significant *of,* mankind; and by this may see the use of it throughout the Bible where *man* is mentioned. He may also see that the phrase כִּי אִישׁ—*If a man,* &c. so far from carrying any exception with it, as to a man's situation of being *married* or *unmarried,* excludes all exception whatsoever wherever we meet with it; therefore as much in the texts of *Exodus* and *Deuteronomy* as elsewhere. Let the *reader* take the *Hebrew,* or even the *English* concordance, and try the experiment: he will find that כִּי אִישׁ in *Hebrew,* and *If any*

---

201   Thus it is rendered, Job. xliii. 11

man in *English*, are in the scriptures, as in every other book I ever met with, as *indefinite* as words can be, with relation to the subject in question.

But if no exception as to the *situation of the man* is *expressed*, is it not *implied?*—So far from that, the *Holy Ghost* (in this passage particularly) has demonstrably guarded against any such implication, and this by adding the words *not betrothed* to the description of the *virgin* or *damsel*, which is done in both places. *Expressio unius est exclusio alterius*—the *expressing* an *exception* with regard to the *woman*, but *none* with respect to the *man*, proves, as far as the soundest rules of construction of all laws can prove, that *none* was intended.

Had any restriction of this law with regard to the *situation* of the *man* been intended, it might easily have been expressed, by only adding some *restrictive* expression or[202] epithet to the description of the *man* as to that of the *damsel*. But, instead of any thing of this sort, we find the indefinite איש; and therefore our translators have rightly rendered it *a man* indefinitely;—so the LXX—*ἐαν δε τις*—but if any man;—the *Latin*—*si vir*—*if a man*—the *French* of D. Martin— *si quelqu'un*—*if any one*. Though all the *translators* of the *Bible* which I have met with, have modestly, humbly, and faithfully represented the mind of God as He has been pleased to reveal it, yet some expositors have ventured to interpret כי איש—*If a man*—by *If* an *unmarried man*—thus corrupting the passage by an interpolation, not only unwarranted by the *Hebrew text*, but by every translation of it extant. This method of interpreting scripture, not by scripture, but by our

---

202   The restrictive description of the *damsel* is לֹא אֲרָשָׂה—*non desponsata*—*not betrothed*. But no אלש is added to the *description* of the *man*. And it is very remarkable, that though *betrothing* is used so often in the *Bible*, it always relates to the *woman*, never to the *man*, as the *person betrothed*. The *man* is said to *betroth a woman*, as Deut xxviii. 30. Deut xx. 7. & al.—so when *betrothing* is figuratively used, as Hos ii. 19, 20. But in neither sense is it once used in all the scriptures *passively on the man's side*.

This distinction is also maintained in the New Testament. See Matt i. 18. Luke i. 27; ii. 5. *2* Cor xi. 2. This can make no difference with regard to DIVORCE; but it seems to make a *considerable* one in certain other respects.

Agreeably to the above remarks, *Gronovius* on *Grot. de Jure*, lib. ii. c. 5. § 8. n. 20. observes, that where *Grotius* speaks of the woman's contracting herself to the man, there is "tacitly implied, that the contract on the man's side is not by *nature*, but from *positive institution*." See before, p. 22. n. This must mean *human institution*, for there is no trace of such a thing in the *Bible*, as the confinement of the word אלש to the side of the woman sufficiently demonstrates.

own prejudiced imaginations, is making the word of God mean *any* thing and *every* thing which fancy may invent; and rendering it—instead of a *sure word of prophecy, to which we do well to take heed, as unto a light that shineth in a dark place,* 2 Pet. i. 19.—a sort of *ignis fatuus,* by no means to be depended on for a director and guide, in so awful a concern as therein is proposed to every man to whom that word shall come.

The only shadow of excuse for such an interpretation, or rather *corruption* of the passages above mentioned, is being able to produce some *positive law* against a man's *having more wives than one at a time*; and then, in order to make GOD's laws agree together, it may be thought reasonable to restrain the indefinite expression כי איש—*if a man*, in *Exodus* and *Deuteronomy*, to *unmarried men only*. But as the *first* is impossible, the *second* is without, and indeed against, all authority from the law of GOD; for that it allowed *polygamy*, is just as clear as that it allowed *marriage*. Therefore the consequence is, that the expression in question being *general*, without *limitation* or *exception* with respect to the situation of the man, as *married* or *unmarried*, it must in some cases command *polygamy*, and therefore make it a *duty*. This consequence must be *allowed*, if we let scripture speak for itself; it could not be avoided by any other means than a *man's* refraining entirely from the *other sex*, or, if he married, contenting himself with *one wife*. If a man went farther than this, he must take the consequence.—But as God would not suffer *a whore of the daughters of Israel,* so he made these laws to prevent their being exposed to prostitution by men's *taking* them, and then *putting them away*. This was just as likely to be the case where *married* men were concerned, as where *others* were; therefore positively forbidden as to *both* alike.

That there were some ingredients in these laws, of the ceremonial, local, or temporary kind—as the payment of *the fifty shekels to the father*—we do not deny; but that the *morality* of these laws must survive as long as *morality* itself exists, is as clear, as that exposing a woman to *prostitution* and *ruin* must at all times be equally hateful in the sight of God, and therefore at all times equally provided against by these humane and salutary laws.

In confirmation of what is here said, I would lay it down as a rule in all cases, that wherever a *moral* intendment appears to be involved in the words of a *ritual, ceremonial,* or *local* and *temporary* institution, there, though the *letter* of the law itself can have no place among us, yet the *spirit* and *moral intention* must survive as long as the world endures. For instance, it is written, *Deut.* xxv. 4. *Thou shalt not muzzle the ox when he treadeth out the corn.* By this we must suppose, that it was the custom in *those days,* and in *that part* of the world, to lay the *heaves on the floor,* and to get the corn out by the *treading* or trampling of[203] oxen. We get the corn out of the *sheaves* by *threshing with flails;* therefore the *letter* of the law above mentioned has nothing to do with us. But the *spirit* of this law being of a *moral* nature, and to teach us, that *those who labour in the word and doctrine* are *to live of their labours,* for that *the labourer is worthy of his reward*—this law is itself quoted by *St. Paul,* 1 Cor. ix. 9; 1 Tim. v. 18. *as a* proof that *they who preach the gospel should live of the gospel.* 1 Cor. ix. 14. From whence, as from other instances which might be mentioned, I infer, that though a *law itself,* or *some part* of it, may have vanished as to the *letter,* yet it *may,* or rather *must,* survive as to the *spirit* of it.

Shall we say, that we must construe the words—*if any man*—to mean *unmarried* men only, because, though God's laws do not forbid *polygamy,* yet *ours* do? To imagine that our laws are to control the laws of God, is a blasphemous arrogance, in comparison of which Cardinal *Wolsey's*—Ego ET REX MEUS—is *humility* itself in the very abstract. The law of the land is such, that a *married Englishman* cannot publicly and openly marry *the virgin he has seduced or taken;* he cannot obey the *letter* therefore of these laws of God, as the *Jews* could have done; but he can and ought to make them the law of his conscience; and if he has *taken a virgin,* &c. he can, according to the *spirit* of these laws, *maintain, protect,* and *provide* for her, and, if he survives his present engagement, marry her publicly in preference to all other women upon earth.—Thus would one great end of this law be answered, and millions be preserved from destruction. If indeed the woman is profligate enough to forsake the man, and voluntarily unite herself with another, she is guilty of transgressing these laws of God, as in other cases of *adultery:* for, the same reason which is given why the man *shall not put her away all his days,* viz. *because he hath humbled her,* goes to what is also said of the

---

203   *Kolben* tells us, that this practice is observed at the *Cape of Good Hope,* (vol. ii. p. 73) *and* adds— "'tis most certain, that corn is much more expeditiously got out of the ears by the treading of *horses* or *oxen,* than it is by threshing. A team of *eight horses* or *oxen* will tread out more corn in a few hours, than a dozen men can thresh out in a whole day."

woman—*she shall be his wife*—the certainty therefore is his wife in God's sight, and *whoever touches her shall not be innocent.* Prov. vi. 29.

I some time ago met with two sermons, which were preached, and afterwards printed, on occasion of passing the *marriage-act.* The learned author, speaking of *polygamy,* expresses himself as follows:—"We find likewise in those early times, and afterwards, that *polygamy* was partly indulged, but only upon certain *typical* occasions, and then only among the *patriarchs* and some of the *kings,* who were all express types of Christ in their several marriages; and in this respect they each typified and prefigured CHRIST's marrying the *Jewish* church, and the several churches of the *Heathen* nations, which, under the gospel, were all designed to make but *one church* or one *spouse;* therefore, under the *gospel, polygamy* ceases, and but *one wife* is allowed."

If this author will examine his *Bible* a little more closely, he will find himself mistaken both in his *premises* and in his *conclusion.* In the first place, it cannot be true that "*polygamy* was partly indulged, only upon some typical occasions, and then only among the *patriarchs* and some of the *kings.*"—This appears from the law, Deut. xxi. 15. which was enacted after the *patriarchal* age had ceased, and many ages before there was a *king in Israel.* That law is framed in general terms, so as to include *any* and *every* man—that has *two wives:*—it does not say, *if a patriarch* or *king hath two wives—but—*כי תהיין לאיש שתי נשים*—literally—*if there be to a man*—or—as we translate it—"*if a man have—two wives*" See Taylor Concor. sub voc. היה, N° 82. It is apparent, then, that the law being *general,* it was meant to regulate a *general* practice. It is also *untrue* in point of *fact,* that "*polygamy* was partly indulged only to patriarchs and some of the *kings;*" witness *Elkanah,* who was neither *patriarch* nor[204] *king,* but a *Levite,* descended from *Kohath,* the son of *Levi,* 1 Chron. vi. 27; 28, and yet we find, by his history, 1 Sam. i. 1, &c., that *polygamy* was *indulged* to him as evidently as to any *patriarch* or *king* that ever lived. From all which it appears, that our *author's* conclusion—"therefore, under

---

204   So it is said of *Gideon—He had seventy sons of his body begotten, for he had many wives.* Judg. viii. 30. Of Jair, he had thirty sons. Judg. ix. 4. *Ibzan of Bethlehem had thirty sons and thirty daughters.* Judg. xii. 9. *Abdon had forty sons,* ver. 14. There were neither *patriarchs* nor *kings,* but all *judges* of *Israel,* and must, by the numbers of their children, be concluded to have been *polygamists* as well as *Gideon.*

the *gospel, polygamy* ceases, and but *one wife is allowed*"—falls to the ground. But let us look back again to Deut. xxi. 15.—That law was evidently made to regulate the disposal of a man's *inheritance* who had *two wives,* and to prevent the *disinheritance* of the *first-born* through favour and affection towards the child who was not so, because born of the *favorite wife.* This could not concern the *patriarchs,* who had all been long dead—nor (immediately at least) the *kings,* who did not exist till near *four hundred* years afterwards—nor the *priests* and *Levites,* who could have no *inheritance* to dispose of. *Numb.* xviii. 20, 21. Deut. x. 9. xii. 12. latter part. Deut. xviii. 1, 2.—If then it did not concern the *people at large,* it was *nugatory,* for it concerned *nobody* at all. This is surely a very sufficient proof that *polygamy* was an allowed practice of the *Jews*[205] in general. The *all-wise* God cannot be supposed to enact so positive a law, if there were no persons who could be objects of it; and this law to regulate *certain circumstances* which did not exist; nor is it easy to imagine, that if those *circumstances* were *sinful,* they would not have been as explicitly *condemned* as they are here plainly allowed and regulated. What has been observed above, concerning the law of *Deut.* xxi. 15 holds equally true of *Exod.* xxi. 10. which had as little to do with *patriarchs* and *kings* as the other had.

I cannot conclude this part of my subject without mentioning a case, which those would do well to consider, who confound *polygamy* with *adultery,* and plead the authority of the *great* and infallible *interpreter* of God's mind and

---

205   The modern *Jews* forbid *polygamy* among the people, and this from the authority of some passage in the *Talmud*; but the reasons assigned to me, on discoursing with a learned *Jew* on this subject, were of the prudential kind; such as the people in general being too *poor to maintain more than one wife, the quarrels it occasioned,* and the like. I asked him if he looked upon it as forbidden by the law of God?— "No, God forbid," replied he earnestly; "what then must be the case of *Abraham, Jacob, David,* &c.?" He likewise told me, that this prohibition was "not *universal,* for that in some countries *polygamy* was still practiced among the *Jews.*" He added "that even *here,* if a *Jew* married a woman, and had no children by her, after *ten* years he might marry *another wife.*" So, where a man defiles a *virgin,* "*she shall be his wife,* agreeable to Exod. xxii. 16 and Deut. xxii. 28, 29." I take the truth to be, that the *Jews,* as to the business of *polygamy,* usually conform to the custom of the country where they live. "As for the modern *Jews,*" says *Leo Mutinensis,* "those of them who live in the *East* still keep up their ancient practice of *polygamy;* whereas in *Germany* they are not allowed this privilege, and in *Italy* very rarely, and only in case a man has lived *ten* years with his wife without issue." See *Puffend.* book vi. ch. 1. § 16.

will for so doing; I mean the case of *Abimelech*, King of *Gerar*; who, having already a *wife of his own*, sent and took *Sarah*, the wife of *Abraham*, Gen. xx. 2. *But God came to Abimelech in a dream by night and said to him—Behold, thou art but a dead man, for the woman which thou hast taken—for she is a man's wife.* Here God plainly set forth *His* thoughts of *adultery*, or *taking a man's wife;* that it is a *sin* to be punished with *death.*—However, *Abimelech* had not actually *defiled* her, and shews that, if he had not been deceived by *Abraham's* saying that *Sarah* was *his sister*, he would not have taken her at all.—*Said he not unto me, She is my sister? and she, even she herself said, He is my brother. In the integrity of my heart, and innocency of my hands, have I done this.* And God said unto him in a dream, Yea, I know that thou didst it in the *integrity* of thine *heart, for I also withstood thee from sinning against Me, therefore suffered I thee not to touch her.* The sin of *adultery* is certainly marked very strongly, but here was a fair opportunity to have as strongly marked *polygamy*, if that was a sin also. How could *Abimelech*, having a wife, ver. 17, take *any other woman innocently*? and yet God allows this to have been done, in his answer to the plea of *Abimelech*. Though he was innocent as to an intentional *adultery*, being ignorant that *Sarah was Abraham's* wife, yet *Abimelech must know* that he had a *wife of his own*, and therefore could not *innocently*, and in the *integrity of his heart*, take any other woman of any kind, if *polygamy* was a *sin*. But supposing this poor[206] *heathen* was *ignorant*, and therefore said this knowing no better, yet God could not be *ignorant* of His *own mind and will*, when he said— *Yea, I know that thou didst this in the integrity of thine heart, for I also withheld thee from sinning against Me.* Rather, why did he not say,—"Thou wicked wretch, how canst thou dare to talk of the *innocency of thine hands*, and of the *integrity of thine heart?*—supposing thou didst not know *Sarah* to be *another man's wife*, yet the taking *any woman*, as thou hast already a *wife of thine own*, is against the *law of marriage*, and therefore a *mortal sin*." Instead of this, God allows his plea, and the moment *Abimelech* restored *Sarah* to her *husband*, God graciously removes

---

206 "It appears by this whole history of *Abimelech*, that he was a man of great virtue in those days; not an *idolater*, but a *worshipper* of the *true* God, as *Melchizedeck*, the *high-priest* of that country, was." *Patrick on* Gen. xx. 7.

every mark of his displeasure, ver. 17, 18. *So Abraham*[207] *prayed* unto God, and God *healed* Abimelech, *and his wife, and his maid-servants*—ואמהתיו (which seem to have stood in the same relation to *Abimelech*, as the אמה—*Hagar* (See Gen. xxi. 10. Comp. Judges viii. 31. with ix. 18. did to *Abram*, chap. xvi. 3. 4) *and they bare children*—וילדו—*pepererunt*, Mont.—*they brought forth: for the* Lord *had fast closed up all the wombs of the house of* Abimelech, because of Sarah, Abraham's *wife*. It should seem by the context, that God had *withheld Abimelech from sinning against Him*, in a criminal access to *Sarah*, by inflicting a *judicial disability of* some kind upon him; also, to mark the more strongly His holy indignation against him, for taking *another man's wife*, He rendered *Abimelech's* wife, then *great with child*, (as also such of his *maid-servants*, who it should seem, from what is said, ver. 17, 18, were probably his *concubines*, and some of them also *great with child*) unable *to bring forth*—but when *Sarah* was restored, *Abimelech* was restored to his own women, and they to him.—All this by the *immediate* hand of God.

I would only say, that any person who can attentively consider the several circumstances of this history of the divine interposition, and talk of the sinfulness of *polygamy* in the sight of God, even putting it on the same footing with *adultery*, will appear to differ very widely, in his judgement of the matter, from this authentic record of the *mind* and *will* of the Most High.

How early an abhorrence of the sin of *adultery* was impressed on the minds of men, and of the *punishment* which awaited it, may likewise be gathered

---

207   Who was himself at that hour a *polygamist*. See Gen. xvi. 3, 4. It is likewise to be observed, that *Abraham was a Christian* believer, as much so as *Paul was*, who tells us, *the gospel was preached to Abraham*—that *he believed it*—*was justified by faith*—and that they which *be of faith, are blessed with faithful Abraham*, who is (spiritually) *the father of all believers* in Christ. Comp. Rom. iv. 16, &c. with Gal. iii. 9, 14. and John viii. 56. *Abraham* would have been exceedingly puzzled, to have found out what the *gospel which was preached to him* (and in which he *believed* and *rejoiced*) had to do with *polygamy*, or to have accounted for the possibility *of the children of his faith*, in future ages, finding out that it was the same thing with *adultery*; when *Abraham's* own *eyes* and *ears* were witnesses of there being put as great a difference between *polygamy and adultery*, as could possibly exist between any two things in creation; and this, by the determination of *that* God, who afterwards gave the law to *Moses* at *Mount Sinai*—and who bore testimony concerning *Abraham*—that he had *obeyed His voice*—*kept His charge*—His commandments—His statutes—and His laws. See Gen. xxvi. 5.—But how is this consistent with *truth*, if *Abraham's* polygamy was an open and continued violation of God's *primary law of marriage*? or if, as St. *Ambrose speaks*—he was living in *adultery*?

from the history of *Isaac* and *Abimelech king of Gerar,* which is recorded Gen. xxvi, particularly at ver. 10, 11.

It is to be remarked also, that throughout the whole scripture, the same approbation; many like circumstances which evidenced that approbation; also, like *answers to prayer,* and like *miracles,* in token of that approbation, attended equally on a *second, or after-taken wife,* under a *polygamous* contract, as on a *first* or *only wife.* This may be said to be uniformly the case, as may appear from the following

PARADIGM

Sarai was barren—she had no child—Gen. xi. 30.

And *Abram* said, Lord God, what wilt thou give me, seeing I go childless?—Behold to me thou hast given no seed.—And He brought him forth abroad, and said, Look now towards heaven, and tell the stars, if thou be able to number them; and He said unto him—So shall thy seed be. Gen. xv. 2, 3, 5.

And God said unto *Abraham*, As for *Sarah* thy wife, I will bless her, and give thee a son of her. Yea I will bless her, and she shall be a mother of nations; kings of people shall be of her. Gen. xvii. 15, 16.

GOD said—*Sarah* thy wife shall indeed bear thee a son, and thou shalt call his name Isaac. Gen. xvii. 19.

And *Sarai* said unto *Abram*, Go in unto my maid; and she gave *Hagar* to her husband *Abram* to be his wife. And he went in unto *Hagar*, and she conceived—and the angel of the Lord said, I will multiply thy seed exceedingly, that it shall not be numbered for multitude. Gen. xvi. 2, 4, 10.

God said, As for *Ishmael*, behold I have blessed him, and will make him fruitful, and multiply him exceedingly; twelve princes shall he beget, and I will make him a great nation. Gen. xvii. 20.

And the angel of the Lord said unto *Hagar*, Behold thou art with child, and shalt bear a son, and shalt call his name *Ishmael*,

And *Hagar bare Abram* a son, and *Abram* called his son's name, which *Hagar* bore, *Ishmael*. Gen. xvi. 11, 15.

And *Sarah* conceived and bare *Abraham* a son in his old age—and *Abraham* called his name *Isaac*. Gen. xxi. 2, 3.

Isaac was forty years old when he took *Rebekah* to wife—and *Isaac* intreated the LORD for his wife, because she was barren; and the LORD was *intreated* of him, and *Rebekah* his wife conceived. Gen. xxv. 20, 21.

Manoah's wife was barren and bore not; and the angel of the Lord appeared unto the woman, and said unto her, Behold, now thou art barren and barest not, but thou shalt conceive and bear a son—and the woman bare a son, and called his name *Samson*; and the child grew, and the Lord blessed him. Judg. xiii. 2, 3, 24.

From henceforth all generations shall *call me blessed*. V. M. *Luke* i. 48.

Jacob took *Leah* and *Rachel*—but *Rachel* was barren. Gen. xxix. 31. And she gave him *Bilhah* her handmaid to wife; and *Jacob* went in unto her, and *Bilhah* conceived and bore *Jacob* a son. And *Rachel* said, God hath judged me, and hath also *heard my voice*, and hath given me a son. Gen. xxx. 4, 5, 6.

And Bilhah, Rachel's maid, conceived again, and bare *Jacob* a second son, and *Rachel* said: יתלחפנ םיהלא ילותפנ "By the agency (Heb. twistings) of the *Aleim* I am in twisted with my sister—*i.e.* my family is now interwoven with my sister's, and has a chance of producing the promised seed." See Park. Heb. Lex. לתפ

When *Leah* saw that she had left off bearing—she took *Zilpah* her maid, and gave her to *Jacob to wife*. And *Zilpah*, *Leah's* maid, bare *Jacob* a son.

And *Zilpah, Leah's maid*, bare *Jacob* a second son.

And *Leah* said—Happy am I, for the daughters will *call me blessed*.

And God *hearkened* unto *Leah*, and she conceived and bare *Jacob* a sixth son. And *Leah* said, God hath given me my hire, *because I have given my maiden to my husband*. And God remembered *Rachel*, and God *hearkened to her, and opened her womb*, and she conceived and bare a son, and said, God *hath taken away my reproach*. And he called his name *Joseph*, and said, The Lord shall add to me another son. Gen. xxx-24 - See also Gen. xxxv.9-12.

There was a certain man of *Ramathaim Zophim* (a *Levite* of the family of the *Kohathites*, see 1 Chron. vi. 33, 34, &c.) and his name was *Elkanah*. And he had *two wives*—the name of one was *Hannah*—and of the other *Peninnah.—Peninnah* had children; *Hannah* had no children—the Lord had shut up her womb.—And her adversary also provoked her sore for to make her fret, because the Lord had shut up her womb. And she was in bitterness of soul, and *prayed* unto the Lord, and wept sore—and she vowed a vow, and said, O Lord of Hosts, if thou wilt indeed look upon the affliction of thine handmaid, and remember and not forget thine handmaid, but wilt give unto thine handmaid a man-child, I will give him unto the Lord all the days of his life-&c. Then *Eli* (*the high priest*) answered, and said—Go in peace, and the God of *Israel* grant thee thy petition that thou hast asked of Him, &c. Wherefore it came to pass, when the time was come about, after *Hannah* had conceived, that she bare a son, and called his name *Samuel*, saying, Because I have *asked* him of the Lord, &c.

There was a certain *priest* named *Zacharias*, and his wife's name was *Elizabeth*—and they had no child, because *Elizabeth* was barren, and they both were well stricken in years. And the *angel* said unto him, Fear not, *Zacharias*, for thy *prayer is heard*, and thy wife shall bear thee a son, and thou shalt call his name *John*—and he shall be great in the sight of the Lord, &c. And his wife *Elizabeth* conceived, and said— Thus hath the Lord dealt with me in the days wherein he looked on me to take away my reproach among men.

And she brought forth a son, and his name was called *John*, &c. Luke 1. 5, 7, 13, 25, &c.

And *Hannah* said—For this child I *prayed*, and the LORD hath given me my petition that I *asked* of Him. 1 Sam. i. 1, &c. See also chap. ii. 20, 21, 26

Song of the Virgin Mary.

My soul doth magnify the Lord, and my Spirit hath rejoiced in God my Saviour.

For he hath regarded the low state of his handmaiden.

He that is mighty hath done to me great things, and holy is his name.

And His mercy is on them that fear Him from generation to generation.

He hath shewed strength with His arm, He hath scattered the proud in the imagination of their hearts.

He hath put down the mighty from their feats, and hath exalted them of low degree.

He hath filled the hungry with good things, and the rich He hath sent empty away.

He hath holpen His servant *Israel*, in remembrance of his mercy, &c.

Hannah's Song.

Mine heart rejoiceth in the Lord, mine horn is exalted in the Lord, my mouth is enlarged over mine enemies, because I rejoice in thy salvation.

There is none holy as the Lord.

He will keep the feet of His saints.

The bows of the mighty men are broken, and they that stumbled are girt with strength—the wicked shall be silent in darkness.

The adversaries of the LORD shall be broken to pieces—the LORD maketh poor and maketh rich, He bringeth low and lifteth up.

They that are full have hired themselves out for bread, and they that were hungry ceased.

He shall give strength unto His king, and exalt the horn of His anointed.

The conclusion of all which appears to be, that either we do not worship the same God which the *Jews* did, or the God we worship doth not disallow nor[208] disapprove *polygamy.* Miraculous blessings bestowed of God, in answer to the prayers of people living in open breach of His law, are totally contradictory to the whole scripture-character of God. *The way of the wicked is an abomination to the* Lord, *but the prayer of the upright is His delight. Prov. xv. 9. He that turneth away his ear from hearing the law, even his prayer shall be abomination. Prov. xxviii. 9.* Comp. Ps. lxvi. 18, 19, 20.

In what has been said on the subject of this *chapter on polygamy,* I should think arguments enough have been brought to prove that it was not *sinful* in the sight of God, under the Old Testament, and that the *blessed* God, by *becoming man* (1 Cor. xv. 47) and condescending to appear on earth for us men, and for our salvation, *in the likeness of sinful flesh,* Rom. viii. 3; *made of a woman made under the law,* Gal. iv. 4; *came not to destroy the law,* by lessening the *security* which it was evidently made to afford the *weaker sex* against the *stronger.* That the *treachery* which was so positively forbidden, and so amply provided against, among the *Jews,* should be *allowed* to *Christians* (who *are children* of the same *Heavenly* Father, *subjects* of the same *Almighty* King) and even *commanded* them in some cases, is a monstrous supposition!—repugnant to the positive institution of God, *They shall be one flesh*—contradictory to all *sound* reason—and abhorrent from every *generous, honourable,* and *humane* principle. Whatever the *situation* of the *man* may be, the danger arising to the *woman* from the consequences of *seduction* and *dereliction* is *equal,* therefore *equally* provided against by the law of God.

How *polygamy* became reprobated in the *Christian church* is easily accounted for, when we consider how early the reprobation of *marriage itself* began to appear. The *Gnostics,* whom *Epiphanius* derives from *Simon Magus,* condemned *marriage* in the most shocking terms, saying that it was "of the *Devil,*" but this was to support themselves in their horrible tenet, that "*all women should be common* amongst them." Better people soon afterwards condemned

---

208   To say that He once did not disallow or disapprove it, but that He has *changed His mind* upon the subject—is one of those assertions which are diametrically opposite to the attribute of *unchangeableness,* so strongly marked out in scripture, and which *is,* and must be, of the very *essence* of an All-Perfect Being.

marriage as *unlawful to Christians*, and this under a wild notion of greater *purity* and *perfection*, in keeping from all intercourse with the other sex. This opinion divided itself into many sects, and gave great trouble to the *church* before it was discountenanced. Still *second marriages* were held *infamous,* and called no better than *lawful whoredom.* Nay, they were not ashamed to write that, "*a man's first wife being dead, it was adultery, and not marriage to take another.*" Amidst all this, *polygamy* must necessarily receive the severest *anathema*—for if it could be supposed *unlawful for Christians to* marry *at all*, and then so detestable to marry a *second time*, after the death of a wife, having *two at once* must be, a *fortiori*, accounted more horrible than all the rest. All these several opinions had texts of scripture pressed into their service, by the *ingenious zeal* of their several abettors: the Old Testament was of no authority in the matter; the New Testament was made to *speak* what it did not *mean,* concerning what it *does* mention; and construed so as to condemn what, when rightly understood, it *does not* mention. The two first of these conceits about marriage have been long exploded, except with respect to the *Romish clergy*, who, to this hour, are *forbidden to marry*. But *polygamy* throughout the *Christian church*, the *western* part of it at least, is looked upon as a sin against the *seventh* commandment, though there is not a syllable in the *whole Bible* which makes it so. When I mention *polygamy*, I would always be understood to mean on the *man's side*, for on the *side of the woman*, the whole scripture shows it to be a *capital offense.*

Why this distinction should be made, He best knows who made it; but, in part, we may suppose, from the consequences attending on *one side*, which cannot be on *the other*; these are finely touched by the strong and masterly pen of the *son of Sirach—Ecclus* xxiii. 22, 23. Having spoken of the *adulterer*, he says, (agreeably to Lev. xx. 10.) *This man shall be punished in the streets of the city,* (see also *Deut.* xxii. 24.) *and where he suspecteth not, he shall be taken.* He then proceeds—*Thus shall it go also with the wife that leaveth her husband, and bringeth in an heir by another—For, first, she hath disobeyed the law of the Most High—secondly—she hath trespassed against her own husband—and thirdly—she hath played the* whore in adultery, *and brought children by another man. She shall be brought out into the congregation, and inquisition shall be made of her children.—Her children shall not take root, and her branches shall bring no fruit. She shall leave her memory to be cursed, and her reproach shall not be blotted out.* Though these be the words of an *apocryphal* writer, they deserve the highest regard because they are exactly consonant with the law of God. But it is very extraordinary that in a discourse against *fornicators, whoremongers,* and *adulterers* (which commences, ver. 16, and is continued to ver. 26, inclusive) not a word should be said against *polygamists,* if *polygamy* were a sin as much on the *man's* side as on the *woman's.*—He most likely would not have passed it over in silence had there been *any law* against it.

His description of the *adulteress* is very fine, and the aggravations of her offense, by bringing forth a spurious issue, strongly marked; but they are such as cannot exist on the man's side, and therefore, hence, in part at least, arises the difference.

What he says of the *adulterer* is also remarkably striking, and evidently taken from *Job* xxiv. 15. We lose much of its propriety, from our mis-translation of 'Ο' Ἄνθρωπος παραβαίνων απο της κλίνης αυτ8—*A man that breaketh wedlock,* we call it; but this is not a translation of the words—they literally are—*the man who transgresseth from out of his bed*—like the *murderer,* Job xxiv. 14. *who, rising with the light, is in the night as a thief*—So the *adulterer.* Saith *Job*—the eye of the *adulterer waiteth for the twilight, saying, No eye shall see me, and disguised his face.* The *son of Sirach* represents the adulterer as "*leaving his bed,* stealing out of it, as it were, to execute his plans of wickedness, at a time when he thinks the unseasonableness of the hour, and the darkness of the night, will conceal him from the eyes of all." This man is, in *Job,* called נאף—an *adulterer,* or *defiler of other men's wives.*—That the same character is meant by the son of *Sirach,* is evident from comparing *Ecclus* xxiii. 18. with *Job* xxiv. 15, and the punishment said to await him, *Ecclus* xxiii. 21. with that assigned to *adulterers,* Lev. xx. 10. Deut. xxii. 22, 24.

Another reason of the difference, that is to say, why *polygamy* should be allowed to the *man,* and no such liberty belong to the *woman,* arises also from the *inferiority* evidently stamped upon the *woman* by the God *of nature,* by whom she is placed under the absolute *power* of *her husband,* so that she cannot dispose of her *person,* on any occasion, or to any purpose whatsoever, to any other but to himself, as may appear from Gen. iii. 16. She is not at liberty to make any *contract* whatsoever, without her *husband's* consent—even *religious vows* are utterly void; she cannot *perform* them if the *husband* disagrees thereto. Num. xxx. 8. *The wife* is—ὑποτασσομένη τω ἰδίω ἀνδρι—*subjected to her own proper husband*, 1 Pet. iii. 1. The apostle *Paul* uses the same expression, when he says, Rom. xiii. 1. *Let every soul be subject (ὑποτάσσεσθω) to the higher powers.* But none of these things are said on the *side* of the *man*—even in teaching in the congregation, the *apostle* marks out the woman's in*feriority*—1 Tim. ii. 11. *Let the woman learn in silence with all subjection—I suffer not a woman to teach, nor to usurp authority over the man, but to be in silence.* Again, the same *apostle* saith—*The head of the woman is the man—the man is not of the woman, but the woman of the man; neither was the man created for the woman, but the woman for the man.* 1 Cor. xi. 3, 8, 9. It appears then from the *nature of things,* as constituted by the *Creator* himself, that the *man* hath powers which the *woman* hath not, and therefore may use a freedom of action which the[209] woman cannot. The *apostle's* saying, *the man was not created for the woman, but the woman for the man*, reminds me of the manner in which Christ vindicated his disciples, when they were accused by the *Pharisees* of breaking the Sabbath, because *they plucked some ears of corn on the sabbath day—He said unto them, The Sabbath was made for man, and not man for the Sabbath, wherefore the Son of Man is* Lord *also of the Sabbath.* The reader may transfer this argument, by parity of reason, to the other subject which we have been speaking of; and it furnishes a proof, by no means inconclusive, why a *man* may be a *polygamist*, but a woman not.

But we may go farther, and observe, that without *this difference*, the grand ends of God's *moral government*, with respect to the *commerce of the sexes,* would not have been provided for. The very *laws* themselves, which were made to secure *those* ends on *both* sides, must have become mere *cyphers*. If *polygamy* had been *permitted* on the *woman's side*, what must become of that law—Deut. xxii. 22: *If a man (כי איש—if any man whatsoever) be found lying with a woman married to an husband, then they shall both of them die, both the man that lay with the woman, and the woman. So thou shalt put away evil from* Israel? If the having

---

209   Besides all this, it may be said, that the more wives a man hath, the more children he is likely to have; but this cannot be on the woman's side; for she cannot breed the oftener by having more men than one.—Such a mixture is known to be even destructive of *conception*, so that the more men a woman may have, the less likely is she to breed at all. This surely affords a strong proof that *polyandry* (as it is called) is contrary to nature.

more wives than one at a time had been *forbidden the man,* what, in numberless instances, must have become of Deut. xxii. 28, 29. *If a man (* כי איש *as before—if any man whatsoever) find a damsel that is a virgin which is not betrothed—and lie with her—she shall be his wife; because he hath humbled her, he may not put her away all his days?* The *first* of these laws (as that of Lev. xx. 10) was apparently to secure the man against the *treachery of the woman*—the *second* (*as Exod.* xxii. 16) to secure the woman against the *treachery* of the man—and *both* to secure the world from that confusion and mischief which must be brought upon it (and are daily brought upon it by our disregard of these laws) by the *treachery* of either.

As the *woman* had the business of *parturition* allotted to her, she must necessarily be looked upon as the *repository* of those bonds and cements of human society, without which it cannot[210] subsist; such as family descents, pedigrees, genealogies, inheritances, and all communications and distinctions of relationship. Therefore the *Creator* did, in his infinite wisdom, set bounds to the *commerce of the sexes,* on the part of the *woman,* which could not be passed under pain of death.

Whoredom and *fornication* are, for the same reasons, also inimical to those *bonds* of human society above-mentioned, introductory of all manner of confusion and wickedness, inconsistent with the law of marriage, and the probable causes of ruin and destruction to the *female sex.*—Therefore, as *seduction* and *dereliction* must, in the very nature of things, lead to these, the positive law of God

---

210 The *rabbinical* explanation of the word וְנֹאֵף—in Exod. xx. 14 has something very striking in it. *R. Levi* saith, that "this word, absolutely and simply, denotes *congress* with *the wife of another man.* Nor is it used but where a *married woman* is concerned. The reason for this precept is, that the world should be peopled agreeably to the will of God. The blessed God willed, that all creatures of the world should bring forth fruit according to their respective species, and that one species should not be mixed nor confounded with another. He willed that the same should obtain with respect to the human offspring, that it might appear whole child every man was, and that the seed of *one* should not be confounded with that of *another.* Moreover, many corruptions are found in *adultery,* which occasion the breach of many commandments. God commanded to *honour parents;* but in case of *adultery,* they cannot be known. So we are forbidden any intercourse of marriage with *sisters* and *other relatives;* but adultery tends to destroy these laws; for, where this is, men cannot know their own relations."Thus speak the *Rabbins,* agreeably to the scriptures, and matter of fact, therefore are worth attending to in this point. The *reader* must surely see, very evidently, reasons for the *seventh* commandment on the *woman's* side, which cannot apply on the *man's,* and why *adultery,* or *defiling* a man's wife, was made so *penal* to *both parties* concerned.

forbids *any man* to take *a virgin,* and then abandon her.

As to what has been said touching the harmony of the *Old* and *New Testaments,* and the perpetual obligation of the *moral law* as to its *immutability,* so that what it once *forbad* it always *forbids,* and what it did *not forbid* can never be *forbidden*—it is a point of such infinite consequence, as to deserve a recapitulation—and as I cannot sum up the matter in words more clear and forcible, than our *church* has done in her seventh *article,* I will introduce the conclusion of this *chapter* with that sound and scriptural account of the matter:—

"The *Old Testament* is not contrary to the *New;* for both in the *Old* and *New Testament* everlasting life is offered to mankind by Christ, who is the only mediator between God and man. Wherefore they are not to be heard, which feign that the *old fathers* did only look for *temporary* promises. Although the law of God, given from God by *Moses,* as touching *ceremonies* and *rites,* do not bind *Christian* men; nor the *civil* precepts thereof ought, of necessity, to be received into any commonwealth—yet, notwithstanding, no *Christian* man whatsoever is free from the obedience of the commandments which are called *moral.*"

No one can consider aright the *divine institution of marriage,* and not see that it is founded in the very *nature of things,* and that by the God of nature. This is as self-evident, as that if mankind were to *increase and multiply, and replenish the earth,* there must be an appointed means by which this was to be brought to pass. Therefore the laws concerning *marriage* cannot be reckoned a mere object of those *rites and ceremonies* which were to *vanish away.* Heb. viii. 13

Nor can they be reckoned among the objects of that *civil polity,* which was only calculated for the government of a *particular* people, in a *particular* part of the world, and that under *particular* circumstances, such as never were or can be known to any other people on the earth—unless *marriage* itself can be supposed to be confined to them, and not equally to concern the whole human race.

The *moral* law hath therefore *marriage* as its object, as concerning, in the highest and most material points, the *moral* actions of men. This clearly appears, not only from the very nature of the thing itself, but from the very words of the *seventh commandment—Thou shalt not commit adultery;* and again of the tenth—*Thou shalt not covet thy neighbour's wife.* These are *moral* laws, equally binding at *all times*—in *all places*—over *all persons*. And as the *seventh* commandment is a *moral* law founded on the divine institution of *marriage itself*, are all the expositions of it which are to be found in the scripture, unless we can be absurd enough to imagine, that the *letter* of a law can be of a *moral* nature, and that the sense, meaning, and intendment of it are only of a *ceremonial* or *civil* tendency.

What is meant by the word נאף—*adultery*, is not to be determined by the conceits, inventions, customs, or laws of men, but by the mind and will of God, as revealed to us in the *precepts* and *examples* which are recorded in *His word* for our instruction; and especially from the uniform and unvaried idea annexed to the use of that word throughout the writings of *Moses* and the *prophets*. If these have failed in giving us the true sense of it, then is it not true that their writings *are profitable for doctrine, for reproof, for correction* (ἐπανόρθωσιν—the amendment of what is wrong), for *instruction in righteousness*, so that *the man of God* (i.e., the believer) *might be perfect, thoroughly furnished* (both as to *knowledge* and *practice*—nothing *left* can be the sense of ἄρτιος) *unto all good works*, 2 Tim. iii. 16, 17. The scriptures which are spoken of in this passage are the scriptures of the Old Testament, or *those holy scriptures* which Timothy had *known from a child*—before a single line of the New Testament was written, ver. 15. If therefore *polygamy* does not stand recorded as a *sin against* the law of God, either by *Moses* or the *prophets*, but as a matter *owned, blessed, allowed* of God, we must say, unless we pretend to be wise above what is written, that it is *no sin, for sin is the transgression of the law.* As to the common notion, that it was made sinful by some *new law* of Christ, and absolutely forbidden in the New Testament, it is one of the *three pious*[211] *lyes* which owed

---

211 "*It* was a maxim avowed in the 4th century, that—it is *an act of virtue to deceive and lye, when, by that means, the interest of the church might be promoted.*—This horrible maxim was indeed of long standing, and had been adopted for some ages past, to the unspeakable detriment of that glorious cause in which they were employed. And it must be frankly confessed, that the greatest men, and most eminent saints, were more or less tainted with this corrupt principle. We would willingly except *Ambrose* and *Hilary, Austin, Gregory Nazianzen*, and *Jerome;* but TRUTH, which is more respectable than these venerable fathers, obliges us to involve them in the general accusation." *See Mosheim, vol. i. p. 200.*

"Though the primitive *Christians* (says *Moyle*) lived up to the full rules of their religion with the utmost probity and innocence of manners, yet it is too certain, there were some persons among them, who, through a mistaken zeal, made no scruple of *lying* for the sake of their religion. Their

their invention to the *ignorant zeal* of some professors and writers in the very early ages of *Christianity*. *One* was—"that marriage was a carnal thing, inconsistent with the purity and perfection of a *Christian*, and therefore[212] unlawful under the gospel."—Another was—that "if a man, on the death of his wife, married again, it was no better than *adultery*."—The *third*, begotten between the other two, was—that "*polygamy*, though allowed to the *Jews* under the Old Testament, is forbidden to *Christians* under the *New*." The two first (among the *Protestants* at least) *are come to nought*—the *last* is as generally believed among *Christians* of all sorts, as the lie of *transubstantiation* is in the *Romish church*. And there can be little doubt, but that a man who has *two wives*, under whatever circumstances they might be taken, would be looked upon to be as *impious*, and as much a *child of the devil*, among us, as a person would be among the *Papists*, who *wickedly* refused to give up his outward senses, and to believe that a small piece of *wafer*, after certain words said over it by a *priest*, is the body, flesh, blood, and bones, of a man six feet high—or as a *priest, bishop, or pope*, who married at all.

As these things will be farther considered under the head of *Superstition*, I will now hasten to the examination of a *notion*, which I fear is *too common* among us, and on which what is usually said and thought on the subject of *polygamy*, is for the most part built; I mean that of representing Christ as appearing in the world, as "*a new lawgiver*, who was to introduce a *more pure and perfect system of morality*, than that of the *law which was given by* Moses."—This horrible blasphemy against the *holiness* and *perfection* of GOD's law, as well as against the truth of Christ, who declared that *He came not to destroy the law, but to fulfil it*—this utter contradiction both of the *law* and the *gospel*—was the foundation on which the heretic *Socinus* built all his other abominable errors. From whence he

---

fictions found an easy reception in a credulous age, and were conveyed down to posterity as certain truths." *See Fortin, Rem.* vol. i. p. 299.

Du Pin owns, that *St. Hilary* seems to think "a lye necessary upon some occasions." Vol. ii. p.76.

212   *Epiphanius*, Hæres. 58, speaks of the *Valesians*, who castrated themselves, and also their *guests*, that by this means they might introduce themselves into the kingdom of heaven— "*Se & hospites suos castrârunt, ut ita secum introducerent in regnum cælorum.*"—They held that none but *eunuchs* could be saved.

Nifi quis eunuchus fieret, salvari non posse.

had it, will appear in the sequel. In the mean time, I cannot help stopping a while to lament the progress which *Socinianism* is daily making among us—with many, among the *Dissenters* especially, it is called *new light*—but, thank God! there are yet some remaining, who call it by its true name—*old darkness*—and as such oppose it.—As it is coincident with the main subject of the following *chapter*, it will fall in my way to say something, which I hope will thoroughly apprise the *reader* of the mischiefs which must result from *Socinianism* in all its shapes.—In the course of what I shall have to say, it will appear, that, so far from Christ's ever condemning *polygamy*, which, as a new *lawgiver*, he is supposed to have done, He never mentioned it during the *whole course of His ministry*, but left that, as He did all other *moral* actions of men, upon the footing of that law under which *He was made,* and to which He, *for us men*, and for *our salvation*, became not only *subject*, but even *obedient unto death*. Phil. ii. 8.

Upon the whole, I take the truth to be, that the first *general institution of marriage*, accompanied with the first *general blessing*, is to be found in those words of Gen. i. 28, *Be fruitful, and multiply, and replenish the earth.*—The special manner of this, together with the indissolubility of the obligation created by it between the parties, is revealed, Gen. ii. 24, where it is said—*A man shall be joined*—רבק—προσκολληθησεται—agglutinatus erit—to *his woman*—and *they*, as in consequence thereof, *shall become one flesh*, i.e., *inseparable* from each other. Gen. iii. 16. reveals the entire subordination and subjection of the *wife to the husband*—and the rest of the *Bible* shows us, that *virgins* could not be *seduced*, and *taken as appetite* might *prompt*, and then abandoned and forsaken as licentiousness might *incline*—but that *monogamous and polygamous* contracts were equally valid and binding, equally lawful as to the inheritability of the issue, and all other marks of legitimacy, that is to say, on the *man's* side; but that, on the *woman's*, polygamy was, for the most apparently-wise reasons, forbidden under pain of death.

While this system was reverenced and observed, we read of no *adultery, whoredom*, and *common prostitution* of women among *the daughters of Israel*: no *brothels, street-walking,*[213] *venereal disease*: no CHILD-MURDER, and those

---

213 Much has been said concerning the antiquity of this disease. The subject is ably handled, and indeed exhausted, in that learned and laborious work of *Johannes Astruc,* de Morb. Ven. lib. i. I will

other appendages of female ruin, which are too horrid to particularize. Nor were these things *possible*, which, since the revocation of the divine system, and the establishment of human systems, are become *inevitable*. The supposing our *blessed Saviour* came to destroy the *divine law,* or alter it with respect to marriage, is to suppose Him laying a foundation for the misery and destruction of the weaker sex; whereas no *being* less wicked than *Satan* himself, could ever have devised the almost total departure from God's Law, which, from even the earliest ages of *the church*, since the Apostles' times, is to be found among the *Christians*.

I now put an end to this long chapter, in which *polygamy*, divested of all the nonsense of human reasonings, is set in its true *scriptural* light, as not *sinful in itself*, but, in some cases, highly *expedient*—in others—*duty*; and in this last view of it, forming one *link* in that divine chain of *heavenly legislation*, on which the security and protection of the *weaker sex* is suspended; it being, upon the footing of God's law, as highly criminal for *one man* as *another,* to *seduce* and abandon to prostitution and ruin, those who have a most indefensible claim upon him for their safety and support.

If among us, as among the *Jews*, and as formerly in *France*, and now in some other parts of the world, a *single man*, be his rank and station what they may, was constrained to[214] marry publicly the woman he seduces; and if the *spirit* of the *divine law* was so far complied with, as to compel the *man already married*,

---

only here observe, that as the *divine law* punished *adultery*, or the defilement of another's wife, with death in both parties—and *whoredom* was, on the part of the woman, also a *capital offence*— the consequences of *prostitution* must of course be prevented, by the prevention of the thing itself. Besides, the almost universality of marriage among the *Jews* (for *celibacy* was a disgrace) and the fixing the virgin on the man who first *took her*, so that he could not *put her away all his days*, left little room for *prostitution*, had their laws been even less severe against it.

214   In the book for the *reformation* of the *ecclesiastical laws*, in the time of *Edward* VI, it was proposed "that those who corrupted *virgins*, were to be *excommunicated* if they did not *marry* them, or, if that could not be done, they were to give them the third part of their goods, besides other arbitrary punishments." See Burnet, Hist. Ref. vol. ii. p. 198. This, and many other salutary proposals, fell to the ground by the death of that excellent young *prince*, *Edward* VI.—Had Queen *Elizabeth* paid attention enough to the mischiefs accruing to her sex from the want of some such regulation, to have had it passed into a *law*, it might justly have been reckoned one of the glories of her *reign*.

to give security for the maintenance and provision of such a woman as he seduces, and, if his present *engagement* shall determine, to *marry publicly* her whom, in God's account, he has *married privately*—it would be such a check upon the licentiousness of mankind—such a restraint upon what is called *gallantry*—such a security for female chastity—and such a preservative against *prostitution*, as might make those who live to see it say—

Jam redit & virgo, redeunt Saturnia Regna.

VIRG.

Now *Justice* and the *Golden Age* again return.

Doubtless, *irregularities* there always *were*, and always *will be*, while *human nature* is *human nature*. Still, a vast difference there must be found, between a *system* which is formed as a check to the lust, treachery, and cruelty of mankind, and *one* which, in *numberless* instances, lets them loose to act without control.

APPENDIX TO CHAP. IV.

Since the preceding *chapter went to the press*, the *author* has been favored with a transcript from a tract in the *British Museum*, which contains the whole of[215] *Bishop Burnet's* opinion on *polygamy*. The *reader* has before seen it partially quoted; but the whole is here inserted *verbatim*.

"IS *polygamy* in any case *lawful* under the *gospel*?

For Answer. It is to be *considered*, that *marriage* is a *contract* founded upon the *laws "of nature*, its end being the *propagation of mankind;* and the *formality of doing it by churchmen, is only* a supervenient benediction, or pompous solemnising of it; and therefore the *nature of marriage*, and not any *form* used in the celebration of it, is to be *considered*. It is true, the case is harder, when any is married by such a[216] *form*, as binds him to one *woman*, than where he is bound

---

215   *Bishop Berkely* thought *polygamy* agreeable to the *law of nature*. Sec Lond. Mag. for *June* 1754, p. 267.

216   The *Bishop* here doubtless alludes to that part of our *form*, where the priest is to ask the man— "Wilt thou have this woman to thy wedded wife—&c—and, forsaking all others, keep thee *only unto her*, so long as ye both shall live?"
> "*The man shall answer*,
> I Will."

Here is no *decent* qualification, as in the *ordination* of ministers—"I will endeavour so to do, the LORD being my helper"—"I trust so"—"I think so"—"I have so determined, by God's grace"—or the like; but, with the peremptoriness and confidence of a *Stoic*, who held—ἐφ' ἡμῖν ὅσα ἡμέτερα ἔργα—"*all our own actions are in our own power*"—ill suited to a frail and fallible creature, who knows *not what a day may bring forth—(see Prov. xxvii.* 1; comp. *Jer.* x. 23) the *answer* is to be—I Will—I—Rex Dominusque Mei—I will.

The man is afterwards to take her—"*for better and for worse*"—but, be she ever so much *worse than he took her for*, short of actual *adultery*, still he is to groan under the sore bondage of what is called a *vow*; which his fellow-creatures have just as much right to impose upon him, from any authority in scripture, as another set of people had, to make a man *vow* voluntary *poverty*—perpetual *chastity*—and *implicit obedience* to a fellow-mortal—on becoming a monk.

There was a time when, if *such a man* had *married*, the *Law* (see 31 Hen. VIII. c. 14) would have sent him to the *gallows*, and no doubt the *church* would have sent him to *the devil*. Tempora Mutantur—well if we could say—as touching *all* the foolish and unscriptural *snares* which mankind

only by the *tie of marriage,* conceived in *general terms.*

The *case* of mankind, since the *fall,* varies very much from what it was in *innocence*; for then the soundness of their *bodies,* and purity of their minds, did keep out of the way all the hazards of *barrenness, sickness, uncleanness,* or *crossness* of *humours,* which made the former law not so proper for mankind; yet still a *single* marriage was the preferable, as being[217] nearer the original. Before the flood, we find *Lamech* a *polygamist*; such were *Abraham* and *Jacob* after it; not that this was not indulged by *Moses*; for all that he did relating to these affairs, was only to allow a Divorce, which was a *provison* for the hardness of the hearts of the *Israelites.* Every man was bound to maintain whom he had first married; lest, therefore, such as designed another wife, and could not maintain a *former,* might use *indirect* ways to be rid of them, this *fair one of divorce* was allowed[218] by God; and their *polygamy* was practised, without either *allowance* or *control,* as the *natural privilege* of mankind. Neither is it any where marked among the *blemishes* of the patriarchs; David's wives, and the store of them he had, are termed by the prophet, God's *gift to him*: yea, *polygamy* was made in *some cases* a duty by *Moses's* law;—when any died without issue, his brother, or *nearest kinsman,* was to marry his wife, for raising up seed to him; and all were obliged to obey this, under the *hazard of infamy,* if they refused it; neither is there any exceptions made for *such as were married.* From whence I may *faithfully* conclude, that what God made necessary in some cases to any degree, can in *no case be sinful in itself*; since God is *holy in all His ways.*

But it is now to be examined, if it is *forbidden* by the gospel. It is certain that our Lord designed to raise mankind to the highest degrees of purity and chastity; and therefore Our Lord and St. Paul do prefer a *single life to a married*

---

have invented, and laid for one another's consciences—ET NOS MUTAMUR IN ILLIS. We may observe that the aforesaid *vow,* exacted by the *priest* in the marriage ceremony, is a *corruption* of Gen. ii. 24.—*Therefore shall a man leave his father and his mother, and shall cleave unto his wife.*

217   *See Burnet* on the Articles of the Church of *England, 3d edit. fol. p. 288*

218   I just take the liberty to observe that it is best to keep to the expression of scripture. Our Blessed Saviour doth not say, that God *allowed divorce*—but—*Moses allowed or permitted* it;—so the Bishop expresses himself a few lines higher.

state[219], as that which qualifies us for the kingdom of heaven, and was loaded with the fewest incumbrances; and by this rule, a *single* marriage being next to none at all, was certainly more suitable to the *gospel*", [he means the times of the *gospel*.] "But a simple and express *discharge* of *polygamy* is nowhere to be found.

It is true, our Lord discharges *divorces*, except in the case of *adultery*; adding, that whosoever *puts away his wife* upon any other account, commits *adultery*: so St. *Luke* and St. *Matthew* in one place have it—*or commits adultery against her*: so St. *Mark* has it—*or causes her to commit adultery: so* St. *Matthew* in another place.

'If it be *adultery* then to take another woman after an *unjust divorce*, it will follow that the *wife* has *that right* over the *husband's* body, that he must *touch no other*,'— This is indeed *plausible, and it is all that can be brought from the New Testament*, which seems convincing; *yet it will not be found of weight.*

For it is to be considered, that if our Lord had been to *antiquate polygamy*, it being so deeply rooted in the men of that age, confirmed by such fashions and *unquestioned* precedents, and riveted by so long a practice, he must have done it *plainly* and *authoritatively*, and not in such an involved manner, as to be *sought* out of his words by the *search of logick*.

Neither are these *dark words* made more clear by any of the *apostles* in their *writings*: words are to be carried no farther, than the *design* upon which they were written will lead them to; so that our Lord being, in that place, to strike out divorce so *explicitly*, we must not, by a *consequence*, condemn *polygamy*; since it seems *not to have fallen within the scope* of what our Lord does there disapprove.

Beside, the term *adultery* may be taken in general, for such a *breach* of *wedlock* as is equivalent to *adultery*; and such is an *unjust divorce*. This may be the importance of the phrase used by St. *Mark*, viz.—*he committeth adultery against her*; or all may be better explained by the phrase St. *Matthew* uses about it, in one place—*he causes her to commit adultery*; since he that *exposeth* or *tempteth* to sin, shares in *the guilt* with the person that succumbs: and from this it appears, that *polygamy* is not declared *adultery*, neither in the place cited, nor any other that I

---

219 "This was meant only with respect to *particular* persons in *particular* circumstances, such as an *apostle*; which is the reason why St. *Paul* applies it chiefly to himself." 1 Cor. vii.

know of.

But it is true that *polygamy* falls short of the intendment of marriage, in *innocence*, to which state, we that are *under the gospel* must return *as near as it is possible.*—It is to be confessed that *polygamy* was much condemned by the ancients, though I think I have met with something about it, that is little noticed; but of that I can adventure to say nothing at this[220] distance from my books and papers.

But all that being granted, it is to be considered that the *antients* were *unjust* and *severe* against *marriage* (itself), and did excessively favour the *celibate*, or single (life); so that in some places, they who married a *second* time, were put to do *penance* for it; and, indeed, both *Jew* and *Gentile* had run into such *excess* by their free commixtures, that it is no wonder if the holy men of those ages, being provoked to a just zeal, against such unjust practices, must have been carried, through immoderate swaying of the counterpoise, into some extremes on the *other hand*.

Therefore, to conclude this *short answer*, wherein many things are hinted, which might have been enlarged into a volume, I see nothing so strong against *polygamy*, as to balance the *great* and visible *imminent* hazards that hang over so many *thousands*, if it be not *allowed*."

The *author* cannot help expressing the highest satisfaction in finding, that in what he has written on the subject, he has had the honour of coinciding in so many points, with the sentiments of this learned, judicious, and excellent *Bishop*. But, on the other hand, he must express his sorrow, that his *Lordship* was so far "distant from his books and papers," otherwise, it is most probable, that he would have produced some valuable testimonies from the *antients,* concerning what he hints at as—"*little noticed.*"

Another thing is also to be lamented, which is, that the good *Bishop* did not proceed to explain what he meant by those "great and visible imminent

---

220   How unfairly *Dean Delaney* represents this passage in the *Bishop's paper*, may be seen before, p. where we are to suppose his *Lordship* making "the best excuse" he could, for giving a *rash opinion*—whereas, he seems to give the circumstance of being at "a distance from his books and papers," as a reason for not producing testimonies from the *ancients* "little noticed," but which, if produced, would tend to show, that some of them thought as his *Lordship* did upon the subject.

hazards," mentioned in the last paragraph.

If so small and inconsiderable a person as myself may venture to guess at the meaning of so considerable and great a man as *Bishop Barnet*, I should suppose, that his *Lordship* has here a reference to his observation before made, concerning the difference between the state of *innocency,* and that of mankind since the *fall,* and to those *evils* which he mentions as the consequences of the *latter*—which could not exist during the *former*. Such as *"barrenness, sickness, uncleanness, or crossness of humour."* What "great, imminent, and visible hazards hang over *thousands*," from these causes, has been observed before,   p.   To vindicate, therefore, the lawfulness of *polygamy* is, as the world is now constituted, in *such cases* at least, to act as a good *citizen* of the *world*, by vindicating the "natural privileges," and necessary *rights* of mankind; and it is, at the same time, to act as a sincere believer of *divine revelation,* to set forth, openly and without disguise, that Heavenly System, by which those *rights* are established and secured. To vindicate also that *universal law,* which had the good of the Whole for its object—to show that its *wisdom* and *beneficence* are too Vast to be confined to a *single people,* or a single period of *particular dispensation*—to free it from that obscurity which *monks* and *priests*, and other *enthusiasts* and *fanatics*, have involved it in, to the distress and destruction of millions—is a task reserved *alone* for those who, for the sake of *truth*, are willing to sacrifice their ease and *reputation* to the malevolence of *ignorance* and *prejudice*.

APPENDIX TO CHAP. I.

Containing FARTHER THOUGHTS

on Exod. xxii. 16, 17.

This scripture is usually understood very evidently to contain a law, that he who *enticed*, &c. a young woman, should be obliged to marry[221] her. To understand it in any other light is to divest the most intelligible and plain words of their certain and obvious meaning. But it is to be observed, that the *damesel* must be entirely disengaged from any *betrothment* to another man; for if she were betrothed to another, then the man who defiled her could not marry her, but both he and she, if she consented to the defilement, were to be put to death, according to Deut. xxii. 23, 24; otherwise it is here *said*, ver. 16, *he shall surely endow her to be his wife, or for a wife to himself*, as—לו לאשה—may be more literally rendered. So *Josephus*—'Ο φθείρας παρθένον, &c. αυτός γαμείτω. He "who defiles a virgin, the same shall marry her." That is, shall pay the *dowry*, and so recognize and confirm the *marriage-obligation*, which had been created by his antecedently taking possession of her person.

From the 17th verse, it is usually understood, that, *if the father refused to give her to him*, the man was to pay a satisfaction in money for the injury and disgrace he had done her: Although the law, in ver. 16, appointed the marriage, both as a punishment to him who had done the wrong, and as a recompense to her who had suffered the wrong: there was an express reservation of the father's power (ver. 17). If he refused his consent, it must be no marriage; only the money to be

---

221 I would here be understood to take the word *marry* in its *popular* sense, as denoting some outward act of public recognition of the *marriage-obligation,* such as the payment of the *dower* among the *Jews.*

paid as τὴν τιμὴν τῆς ὕβρεως—a satisfaction for her reproach, as *Josephus* speaks.

The *Jewish* doctors were very lax in their interpretation of this passage of scripture, who would not have it to be a command (ver. 16) that he should marry her (though that was best), but only that he should make satisfaction for taking away her virginity; which was by paying so much in the nature of *dowry* as would render her fit to be his wife if *both* of them could agree.

This interpretation of the 16th verse is one of those arbitrary expositions of the *Talmudists*, which by robbing the text of its plain meaning, leave us to the uncertainty of human imagination, which being various in various men, must render the scriptures totally uncertain as to any determinate meaning whatsoever.

The 17th verse says nothing of the *marriage*, whether *it shall* or *shall not be binding*, on the *father's refusal*; but only—"*If the father utterly refuse to give her unto him, he shall pay money according to the dowry of virgins.*" Here I take the words according to translation—"*If*," &c. And supposing it (for argument's sake) to include a reservation of the father's authority, so that he might, even where matters had gone so far as described in verse 16, *invalidate* the contract by withholding his *consent*—which, though insisted on by the *Talmudists*, is hardly reconcilable with the peremptory and positive command of verse 16.—yet this does not affect the principal point which I contend for, and which is contained in verse 16; namely, that it is the taking *possession* of the woman's *person* which creates the *contract* or *marriage obligation*. Therefore, no man, agreeably to the divine law, can entice a *virgin*, *defile* her, and then *forsake* her at his *own will and pleasure*, as is done every day among us in this *Christian* land, where the law of God is supposed to be the rule of right and wrong but is, in truth and in fact, put entirely out of the question.

I thought fit to lay these several expositions of this scripture before the *reader*, that he might the better judge how far I may be right in my views of it, which are before submitted to his consideration, p. 25-28; and, at the same time, form his own judgment of the matter, from that which appears to him to be most agreeable to the context, as well as to the rest of the scripture.

The *apostle* tells us, *Rom.* iii. 19. *Whatsoever things the law saith, it saith to those who are under the law; therefore no Jew, who by circumcision was a debtor to do the whole law (Gal. v. 3.) could be exempt from any part of it.* For a like reason, the believing *Gentiles*, who are compared to *the olive-tree wild by nature, but grafted into the good olive tree* (see Rom. xi. 24.) and become members of God's church by the *circumcision made without hands* (Col. ii. 11) are certainly *under the law* as a rule of life, and therefore subject to its *moral* precepts in every instance. From this, it ought to be concluded that *Christians* are as much bound by Exod. xxii. 16, and Deut. xxii. 28, 29, as the *Jews* are. No reason can be given to the contrary that will not equally apply to their exemption from the *ten commandments*; for these were at first delivered, and *immediately* and *particularly* addressed to the *Jews*, as appears from the short preface, Exod. xx. 1, 2. But can there be found a man, *mad* enough to suppose that because they were emphatically addressed to the *people* which God *brought out of the land of Egypt, out of the house of bondage,* no others have any thing to do with them?

APPENDIX TO CHAP. II.

The celebrated *Martinus Bucerus*, one of our excellent and learned *Reformers*, in enarrationibus ad cap. 19. *Libri Judicum*, has left us the following observation concerning *concubinage*; which seems to throw much light on the subject.

"*Concubinæ* erant *legitimæ etiam uxores*: sed hoc a *matronis* differebant, quod sine dote et sine solenni sanctificatione recipie bantur: & erant ferè ex ancillis, & servilis conditionis: & non erant adjutoria illius præstantioris gradus, ut omni rerum communione gauderent sed humiliore gradu, & quæ haberentur humiliore loco, quod ad administrationem domus attinet, et ad filiorum successionem.— Legitimum verò genus concubinatum est, quum habentur conjunctæ copula matrimoniali, ne abjici temere possint: tametsi non habeant communionem plenam omnium rerum cum marito, ut matres-familias: nec convenerunt pactis dotalibus, unde & nati ex illis non habent successionem in hæreditate paternâ cum natis ex matre-familias: sicut *Abraham* ex concubinis *veris uxoribus*, sed non matribus-familias, dona quædam deputavit, portionem hæreditatis nullam addixit.—Ex *legitimo genere concubinarum* fuerunt concubinæ sanctorum patrûm. Et quia Dominus dignitates et patrimonia quæ suis contulit, conservari vult, optandum omninó ut hoc genus uxorum, uti apud sanctissimos olim Patres observatum est, rursus apud Christianos, & maximè in præstantibus families observateur, &c."

"*Concubines* were also *lawful wives*; but in this they differed from the *matrons*, that they were received without dowry and a solemn sanctification. They were usually from maid-servants, and of a servile condition; and they were not *help-mates* of that superior degree, as to enjoy a communion of things in every respect, but in a lower degree, and were reckoned in a lower sphere, as to the administration of the house, and the succession of their sons.—They are a lawful kind of *concubines*, who are joined to their husbands by a *matrimonial* tie, so that they cannot rashly be put away; although they may not have a full communion of all things with their husbands, as *mistresses of the family*, nor did they agree [or come together] by *dowry-contracts*; wherefore the sons born of them have not a succession in the heritage of the father, with the sons of the *mistress* of the house. Thus *Abraham* gave gifts to the sons born of his *concubines*, who were *true wives*, but gave them no portion of the inheritance.—The concubines of the holy fathers were of the lawful kind. And because the Lord wills, that the dignities and patrimonies which He has conferred on His people, should be preserved, it is altogether to be wished, that this kind of *wives*, as observed among the holy *patriarchs*, might be again observed among *Christians*, and especially in great and illustrious families, &c."

There is much good sense in what *Bucer* says, not only as tending to give a scriptural and proper idea of *concubinage*, but also as pointing out a convenient *medium* between men of *family* and *fortune* being obliged to match with *inferior* women whom they may happen to *take*, so as to put them upon a footing with themselves and families, and the liberty of abandoning them to prostitution and ruin.

This hint of *Bucer's*, with respect to *Christians*, seems to have been taken in some parts of *Germany*, where we are told of *wives* of a sort of *second degree*, which they call *left-handed wives*; these are indeed taken with more ceremony, but, in other respects, differ little in their situation from the antient *concubines*. See *Chambers*, Tit. Hand—and Marriage.

Dr. Alexander Hist. Wom. vol. ii. p. 267, writes thus concerning this custom in *Prussia*—"Though their code of laws seems in general to be as reasonable, and as consistent with sound policy as any in *Europe*, yet we still find in it an allowance given for a species of that *concubinage* which has long since been expelled from almost all the *western* world. A man may there marry what is called a *left-handed wife*, to whom he is married for life, and by the common ceremony—the only difference is, the bridegroom gives her his *left* hand instead of his right—but with this express agreement, that neither she nor her children shall live in the house of her husband, nor shall take his name, nor bear his arms, nor claim any dower or donation usually claimed by every other wife, nor dispose of any part of his property, exert any authority over his servants, nor succeed to his estates or his titles; but shall be contented with what was agreed on for their subsistence during his life, and with what he shall give them at his death. This privilege, however, is always in the power of the *king* to deny, and is seldom granted to any but such of the nobility as are left with large families, and, from the smallness of their fortunes, cannot afford to marry another legal wife, and rear up another family of the same rank with themselves."

There are certainly in the above very strong traces of the antient *concubinage*, which was allowed and practised under the *divine law*. If such a custom as this prevailed among us, and was inforced on men of *rank* and *fashion*, who are now turned loose on the *lower order of females*, and debauch them at *free cost*, without being under the least responsibility towards them—it would not only prove a happy check to the most mischievous licentiousness in many instances, but be also a means of preventing the utter ruin of *thousands*, who, under the present *system* of things, are seduced, abandoned, and destroyed, without any *remedy* whatsoever, or almost any possibility of *escape*.

END OF THE FIRST VOLUME.

Book IV

The History & Philosophy Of Marriage Or,

Polygamy & Monogamy Compared

James Campbell (A Christian Philanthropist)

1869

JAMES CAMPBELL

- The Christian Philanthropist

Almost nothing is known about this individual outside of the book he wrote, titled, "The History And Philosophy Of Marriage; Or Polygamy And Monogamy Compared;" published in 1869. Now, before anyone panics over the date, you can rest assured that I, too, was very hesitant to even give this book a try, seeing as how it was published during the rise of Mormonism in America. One could easily (and very reasonably) assume that this "Christian" philanthropist was actually a Mormon in disguise. That's what I assumed at first, but I went against my gut and gave the book a chance to speak for itself; or, more accurately, a chance to be non-Mormon. A couple of things I found initially concerned me. The first was a web page dedicated to James Campbell on the Latter Day Saint's website. The other was future publishers of his book being based in Salt Lake City. These are serious red flags, so I approached the book prayerfully and with caution; and boy, am I glad I did! The author noted his orthodox Puritan upbringing and never once insinuated a departure from his Puritan faith. He also made no mention of Mormonism or Utah in any way, which, coupled with his accurate use of the Bible, led me to conclude that he was indeed a Christian. Being from Europe, he seemed totally unaware of the rising Mormon movement in America. The subsequent publications were likely done by Mormons but their re-printing of his work has nothing to do with him or the original. Also, for what it's worth, after examining the Mormon's web page about him, it turned out there was no information other than the dates of his birth and death, which demonstrates how little they know about him. It would appear that James Campbell was nothing more than what he claimed to be, a Christian philanthropist, writing for the benefit of all women everywhere.

I couldn't be happier about purchasing an original copy and reading it. It's not as Biblically thorough as Madan's Thelyphthora, but it's certainly just as accurate and impactful. In my estimation, it is tied with Thelyphthora for the greatest work on polygamy ever published. It's not quite as big as Madan's treatise, but it's still bigger than any other theological work on the subject in English. He argues from Scripture, nature, statistics, and history with striking precision, leaving any critics with no choice but to completely abandon logic if they're to refute him. I only read one point that I disagreed with, but in the book's appendix, he responded to a critic who addressed that very point and cleared up the confusion. It truly is an incredible work.

The only problem James Campbell had was circulation. Though just as good as it was controversial, it received only a fraction of the attention that Madan's did. This was because Campbell was like me; a nobody. He was an evangelist, but not a famous one. Madan had already established himself as a mighty evangelist for decades before writing his treatise, but Campbell emerged from what appeared to be nowhere. Unfortunately, as is usually the case with more obscure authors, his book remained almost as obscure as him.

THE

History and Philosophy

OF

MARRIAGE

OR,

POLYGAMY AND MONOGAMY
COMPARED

BY A CHRISTIAN PHILANTHROPIST

"There shall be no widows in the land, for I will marry them all; there
shall be no orphans, for I will father them all." –OLD PLAY

SECOND EDITION, REVISED AND ENLARGED

PREFACE

TO THE

SECOND EDITION

This little book disdains disguise, and paints humanity as it is. As the artist delineates the exact forms of Nature, although his living models are never perfect, either in feature or in attitude, so should the moral writer portray both the beauties and the blemishes of social life, without omitting even those which are most repulsive. It is an axiom of prudence, never to shut our eyes against a painful truth, but to know the worst, and to provide for it. In the following pages, I have depicted some of the evils of society, but only in order to demonstrate them to be evils, and to point out a remedy for them which is desirable, practicable, and beneficent. Some eminent critics have suggested that I have drawn the picture with so great freedom as to be offensive, especially to the ladies; and I began to think of preparing an expurgated edition for their reading, which should advocate the same principles, but in which many of the historical facts upon which those principles depend should be suppressed. On further reflection, however, I am ashamed to have yielded to such suggestions even for an hour. If we treat the sex like fools, and they submit to such treatment, neither they nor the men can justly complain if they are somewhat foolish. It is a just cause of complaint against the men, that they have too long kept the women in subjection and ignorance; first withholding: from them the key of knowledge, and then charging them with incapacity for many responsible duties and employments, for which an equal share of knowledge would have qualified them. This sin shall not be justly imputed to my account. I cordially welcome them to every branch of learning and of industry. I have written nothing that I shall blush to have my sisters or my daughters read. I blush for humanity that so many debasing crimes against the laws of chastity should ever be committed; but I do not blush to know when and by whom they have been committed, nor to know what are their terrible consequences. This knowledge has become a part of human experience and history, which it is not only proper, but important, for everyone to know; for this knowledge is my heritage and my children's heritage, that we may take warning from the calamities of others, and guard ourselves against them.

That a second edition should be called for, of a philosophical treatise so generally regarded as heterodox in its social opinions, and so avowedly opposed to the fashionable vices and prejudices of the times, is a sufficient vindication of the importance of the subject, and the candor of the public. The author gratefully acknowledges his obligations to those gentlemen of the press who have condescended to notice the work. These notices, some extracts from which are appended to this edition, are all that could be expected. While most of the reviewers are very conservative upon the main question, they very generally express some graceful compliments to the author's earnestness and ability, which are equally creditable to him, and honorable to them. Some have given a full analysis of the argument and done ample justice to the work; some have condemned it without reading it; and a few have made the most gross misstatements of its scope and design. There has been much contradiction, but no rebutting testimony. Not one historical or statistical fact stated in the book has been disproved, not one proposition claimed to be demonstrated has been shown to be fallacious. The only critique worthy of reply is from the pen of J. A. H., Esq., of Springfield, Mass., which is quoted in full in this edition, with the author's reply; and each one can now judge for himself of the merits of the respective arguments. Some other additions to this edition will further enhance the value of the work.

CHAPTER I:

INTRODUCTORY

Audi Alteram Partem

Philosophy takes nothing for granted. It doubts all things that it may prove all things. The marriage question is a proper subject of philosophical inquiry, involving an examination and analysis of both polygamy and monogamy. Of the latter form of marriage the Christian world has known too much, and of the former too little, to have felt, hitherto, the need of any analysis of either. We have inherited our monogamy, or the marriage system which restricts each man to one wife only, and have practiced it as a matter of course, without any special examination or inquiry: so that we really know but little concerning its origin or its early history; while we know still less of the system of polygamy. We read something of it in the Bible and in the history of Eastern nations, and we learn something more from the reports of modern travellers; and it cannot be denied that what we know of it has come to us in such a form as to prejudice our minds against it. This prejudice is unfavorable to a just and candid philosophical inquiry; and while pursuing this inquiry, let us hold this prejudice in abeyance. Let us not forget that what we have seen of this system is in its most unfavorable aspects. Most travellers carry their native prejudices abroad, and look upon the customs of distant countries with less astonishment than contempt. And they remember, when writing up their accounts of those countries, that their books are made to be sold at home; and they must not institute comparisons unfavorable to their own land, but must flatter the conceit of their fellow-countrymen by assuring them that their own social and political institutions are vastly better than those of other lands. So, also, with history: it presents human affairs in a perspective view, painting its roughest mountains with distinct exactness, but casting its peaceful plains quite into the shade. It devotes a hundred pages to the details of wars and intrigues, illustrating the crimes of men, in proportion to a single page of descriptions of common life and domestic tranquility, illustrating their virtues.

If the writer, on the contrary, shall seem prejudiced in favor of polygamy, let it be attributed to his love of fair play, and his desire to let both sides be heard, rather than to any undue bias of mind preventing him from doing equal justice to the arguments in favor of either system.

It is attested and proved by competent authority, which no one doubts, that polygamy, or that social system which permits a plurality of wives, has always prevailed in most countries and in all ages of the world, from time immemorial; but this form of marriage, being foreign to the customs of modern Europe and her colonies in America, is very naturally regarded throughout these enlightened regions as something heathenish and barbarous. And modern writers, whose works are the exponents of European civilization, have hitherto said everything against it, and nothing for it. But they have condemned it almost without examination or debate, rather because it is strange than because they have proved it to be at fault. No one has given to the subject the time and research necessary to its fair elucidation. But as a venerable institution the social system of polygamy does not deserve such supercilious treatment. Such treatment, besides being unjust, is unphilosophical, and unworthy a liberal and an enlightened age. Its great antiquity alone should entitle it to sufficient respect to be heard, at least, in its own defence. It constitutes an important part of human history. It is a great fact that cannot be ignored; and as such, it must be studied and known. To insist upon the condemnation of this system, without hearing its defence, is oppression. It is even the worst kind of oppression; for, in such case, it must be allied with ignorance and bigotry. But if there ever was a time, when polygamy could properly be thrust aside with a sneer, and it was satisfactory to Christian justice to condemn it unheard and unexamined, it can be so no longer; for, with the general diffusion of knowledge and the increased facilities of modern intercourse, our speculative inquiries are seeking a range of cosmopolitan extent, and we are brought into daily contact with the opinions and the practices of the antipodes. If we disapprove of their practices we should be prepared to make substantial objections to them; and if we wish to teach them our own, we should be able to give equally substantial reasons. If the advocates of polygamy are in the minority in the Christian world, let the common rights of the minority be granted them, – freedom of debate and the privilege of protest; and let their solemn protest be listened to with respect, and be spread upon the current records of the day. And, on the other hand, if those who practise this ancient system do constitute the majority of mankind, it cannot be either uninteresting or unimportant to inquire what has made it so nearly universal, and caused it to be adopted by so many different nations, and even different races of men, among whom are, no doubt, some persons who are justly distinguished for their wisdom, their piety, and their humanity.

The writer is not aware that any former attempt has been made in this country to analyze and explain the social system of polygamy, or that any works written abroad for this purpose have ever been current here; at least, he has not been able to obtain any,[222] and thus to avail himself of their assistance. While, therefore, the subject matter of this essay is of the most venerable antiquity, the manner of its discussion must be entirely new; and not only can the author claim the singular merit of originality, but the reader can be assured of the no less singular zest of novelty.

SOME ACCOUNT OF THE AUTHOR

Almost everybody who takes up a new book is curious to know something of the writer; of his special qualifications for his work, of his opportunities of acquiring a thorough knowledge of his subject, and of the standpoint from which he views it. He will, therefore, proceed at once to give some account of himself, and how he came to write this work. And the courteous reader will now please permit him to drop the indirect style of address so common among writers, and to introduce himself by speaking in the first person. I am a native of New England and was brought up a strict Puritan. My father always declared his intention to educate me for the law, and I took to learning as readily as most boys of my age. I was graduated from college almost forty years ago, and had nearly completed my

---

222   See Appendix

professional studies, when my health suddenly broke down; and I then discovered that I had been bestowing all my care upon the improvement of the mind, to the total neglect of the healthfulness of the body. And this, I fancy, was only a common defect at that time, in our American, or, at least, our New-England, system of education. The physicians having prescribed a voyage at sea and a residence of some months in a tropical climate, the influence of my friends obtained a foreign situation for me in one of our Boston houses having an extensive business in India; and I became their clerk, and afterwards their factor. The engagements then entered into could not easily be broken off, and I have continued in them many years; and having seen all the continents of the globe, and many islands of the sea, and having observed human society in every climate and in every social condition, I have at length returned to my native land, an older, and, I hope, a wiser man. Having become an active member of the church in my youth, I did not renounce my Christian character abroad, but have always afforded such encouragement and assistance as I was able, to our American and English missionaries, whenever I fell in with them. In fact, I had long cherished a profound respect and admiration for the missionary and, notwithstanding my father's wish to educate me for the law, I had, during my course of study, seriously offered myself as a candidate for missionary labor; and, had I been deemed worthy of that honor, I should, no doubt, have devoted my life to that service. But Providence did not so order it. Yet when I went abroad, my early predilections easily reconciled me to the pain of leaving my native land, to the disappointment which I experienced in renouncing a career of professional and literary honors, and readily introduced me to the society of those devoted missionaries whom I would fain have chosen for my fellow-laborers and life-companions. I was very much surprised, however, soon after my first acquaintance with them, to learn that, under certain circumstances, they allowed the members of the native Christian churches a plurality of wives. As I had been educated a strict monogamist, in New England, I had never once dreamed that any other social system than monogamy could be possible among Christian people, anywhere; and I remonstrated with the missionaries for permitting polygamy among their converts, under any circumstances whatever.

WHAT THE MISSIONARIES SAY ABOUT POLYGAMY

I was answered by them that the Bible has not forbidden it, but, on the contrary, has recognized it, as sometimes lawful and proper; and although they themselves did not encourage it, they could not positively prohibit it. I then endeavored to recollect some prohibition in the Bible, but could neither recollect nor find one there. On the contrary, to my own astonishment, after a careful examination of the Sacred Scriptures, I did find therein many things to favor it. The missionaries also said that their experience had taught them that the converting grace of God was granted to those living in polygamy as often as to others; the natives themselves attach no moral reproach to it; "and," said the missionaries, "if such persons give evidence of genuine conversion, 'Can any man forbid water, that they should not be baptized, who have received the grace of God as well as we?' Besides," they added, "if they are not received and recognized as Christians, how shall we dispose of them? Shall we refuse them our fellowship, and send them back again to their idolatry? This would be no less unchristian than unkind. Shall we compel them to put away all their wives, but those first married, and then receive them into the church? But in many cases this would be impracticable, in others unjust, in all cruel. For the chastity of the women hitherto irreproachable would be tarnished by their repudiation: they would often be left without a home and without support; and, like other disgraced and destitute women of all lands, they would be thrust upon a life of infamy and vice. Who," continued they, "shall dare assume the responsibility of separating wife from husband, and children from parents? since the Bible expressly forbids a man to divorce his wife, for any cause, except unfaithfulness to her marriage vow: God is not said in the Bible to hate polygamy, but it says there that '*he hateth putting away.*'"

I need not say that I was completely disarmed and silenced by this array of "the law and the testimony;" and was compelled, by their arguments, to admit that their course was one of equal justice and mercy. I soon learned, however, that the rules of the missionaries are by no means uniform upon this question. Many of them, particularly those who possess a great regard for the authority and the dogmas of the church, and who reason rather from the "tradition of the elders," than from the laws of Nature or of God, have rigidly enforced monogamy among their converts; and if any one becomes a Christian while living in polygamy, such missionaries require him to repudiate all his wives but one. It was not many months after the conversation above related that one of the missionaries called my attention to a religious journal that he had just received from Boston, containing the report of certain missionaries among the North-American Indians, giving an account of the conversion of an old and influential chief.

THE INDIAN CHIEF AND HIS TWO WIVES

This chief at the time of his conversion to Christianity was living with two wives. The one first married was now aged, blind, and childless. The other was young, attractive, healthful, and the mother of one fine boy. One of these wives the missionaries required him to put away, as an indispensable requisite to baptism and church-membership. The old chief, after careful deliberation, could not decide which one to repudiate. The first he was bound by every honorable motive "to love and to cherish," especially on account of her age and infirmity; while the other was devotedly attached to him, and was the mother of his only child and heir, which he could not give up, and from which he could not separate the mother. He, therefore, submitted the case to the missionaries to decide which one of them he should put away. They decided against the younger one. And as he was old himself and his other wife was barren, that she must also give up her child. This mandate was obeyed with martyr-like fortitude, which nothing but the strongest religious motives could have inspired; opposed, as it was, to every natural sentiment of love and honor. And thus, in one hour, was that young wife and mother deprived of her husband, her child, her character, and her home; and sent away a bereaved and lonely outcast into the wide world. The report which the missionaries themselves gave of this affair closed by saying that the repudiated wife and bereaved mother soon died inconsolable and broken-hearted.

MY OWN REFLECTIONS UPON THIS REPORT

On reading this report, I could not forbear contrasting their mode of treating polygamy with that of the missionaries in the East, which had come under my own observation there, and which I had, at first, so severely criticised. I now began to blush at my own late ignorance and bigotry. And the more I thought of the ecclesiastical tyranny of the North-American missionaries, the higher rose my indignation against it. I could not fail to see that their narrow attachment to their own social system had made them judicially blind to the merits of any other; and that they were more ignorant of the true spirit of Christianity as well as of the natural rights of man concerning the laws of marriage, than even the poor savages themselves. Yet they undoubtedly supposed they were doing God essential service by this act of inhumanity; just as our fathers did when they hanged and burned honest men because they worshipped God in a different manner, and entertained different views of divine truth, from themselves. Their mistake is one which has always been too common, and from which no one, perhaps, is altogether free. It consists in assuming that because we are honest in our belief, and mean to be right, others who essentially differ from us are dishonest and wrong; and in presuming to judge the conduct of others by what we *feel to be right,* i.e., by our own standard of morality, instead of judging them by what we *know to be right,* according to the infallible standard of divine truth.

These reflections led me to give the whole subject of marriage, in respect to its divine and natural laws, as thorough and as critical an investigation as my abilities and advantages enabled me to do; and to inquire into the origin and the moral tendencies of the two social systems of monogamy and polygamy.

I have now pursued this investigation many years, and have become convinced that polygamy is not always an immorality; that sometimes a man may innocently have more than one woman; and then that it is their right to be married to him, and his duty to love and cherish them for better for worse, for richer for poorer, in sickness and in health, till death shall part them.

WHY I HAVE WRITTEN THIS BOOK

I am unwilling to leave the world without having given it the benefit of these reflections. All truth is important. If these views are true, they ought to be known; if they are not true let them be refuted. If the prejudices of modern Christians are opposed to the social system which their ancient brethren, the earliest saints and patriarchs, practised in the good old days of Bible truth and pastoral simplicity, I believe that these prejudices are neither natural nor inveterate; but that they have been induced by the corrupted Christianity of the mediaeval priesthood, and that they will be removed when Christian people become better informed; and if it be necessary for me to sacrifice my own ease and my own credit, in attempting to remove them, I shall only suffer the common lot of all reformers before me. Yet I scarcely expect to see any immediate result of my labors. It is a melancholy and a humiliating fact that the opinions of most people are determined more by what others around them think and say than by what they believe themselves. They are not accustomed to the proper exercise of their own reason, and do not follow the convictions of their own minds. Yet there are some who dare to think and act for themselves; and into the hands of a few such I doubt not these pages will fall: and to all such I most heartily commend them. To an active and an ingenuous mind there is no pursuit more fascinating than the pursuit of knowledge, no pleasure more exquisite than the discovery of truth. All those who would enjoy this pleasure in its highest sense must love Truth for herself alone; they must emancipate themselves from the trammels of prejudice and public opinion, and dare to follow Truth wherever she may lead. And I make no further apology for calling the attention of an intelligent age to a new examination of an old institution. Truth dreads no scrutiny; shields herself behind no breastwork of established custom or of respectable authority, but proudly stands upon her own merits. I will not despair, therefore, of gaining the attention of every lover of the truth while I attempt to develop and demonstrate the laws of God and of nature upon the important subjects of love and marriage, and to apply those laws to the two systems of monogamy and polygamy.

THE LAWS OF GOD AND OF NATURE; THE TERMS DEFINED

To prevent misconception of the meaning intended to be conveyed by these terms, it is proper to state, that, by the laws of God, I mean the written laws contained in the Holy Bible; which I believe to be the most perfect revelation of the divine will and God's inestimable gift to man. The laws by which the universe subsists, embracing those of mind as well as those of matter, are undoubtedly the laws of God also; but we call them, by way of distinction, the laws of nature; because it is only by a diligent study of nature, and by reasoning from cause to effect and from effect to cause, that they can be determined, yet when determined they are always found to harmonize with each other and also with the written law, which they may safely and properly be employed to illustrate and explain.

Both these classes of law differ materially from the civil law, or the laws of States and nations; especially in these respects: the former are always harmonious with each other, and equally valid at all times and places, and are, therefore, infallible and unchangeable. The latter are always conflicting with and often contradictory to one another and are constantly being altered, amended, and repealed; and, although founded upon truth, in general, and intended for the public good, and therefore entitled to our respect and obedience, they are so only in a qualified sense, far inferior to that profound respect and implicit obedience due to divine and natural law. In my analysis of the laws of love and marriage on which depends the mutual relation of the two sexes, I shall be obliged to speak of that relation with unusual familiarity; even though I may sometimes offend our modern notions of modesty and propriety – notions which I shall not now stop to discuss, whether they be true or false; it matters not. Truth rises superior to every consideration of fastidiousness, and it is high time that these truths should be demonstrated. Yet it shall be my care so to treat them as not to offend true modesty unnecessarily: *puris omnia pura*.

NOTES TO THE SECOND EDITION

1. The term "monogamy" is used throughout this volume to denote *enforced* or *restricted monogamy*, or the system which allows each man but one wife; and a monogamist is one who supports this system, whether he be married or unmarried. The term "polygamy" denotes *freedom to marry either one wife or more*; and a polygamist is one who maintains this freedom, whether he has one wife or many, or is unmarried.

2. This treatise is restricted, as its former title indicates, to the history and philosophy of polygamy and monogamy exclusively; and attempts no discussion of any other form of marriage so called, or of any other social system whatever. The curious reader will find many important facts concerning the history of marriage, and other systems of social life, in a new and valuable work entitled "Medical Common Sense and Plain Home Talk." By E. B. Foote, M.D., 120 Lexington Avenue, New York, 1870.

CHAPTER II:

THE PRIMARY LAWS OF LOVE

LOVE LIKE ELECTRICITY

Among all the inherent properties of mankind, none is more important than that of love; and no one more clearly evinces the wisdom and benevolence of his Creator. Love, in its primary sense, to which it will be restricted in this treatise, is the mutual attraction of the two sexes. It exists in all persons, either as a sensibility or a passion. It is a sensibility when in a state of rest, or when exercised towards the whole of the opposite sex indiscriminately; but it is a passion when strongly excited and when exercised towards particular individuals. And it is as truly and fundamentally a law of human nature as electricity is of material nature, – to which it bears a curious analogy. We can scarcely reason with more certainty upon the laws of electricity than upon those of love, for we have the assistance of consciousness in one case which we want in the other. But note the analogy: it has been demonstrated that all bodies possess electricity in a greater or less degree; and that some are positive when compared with others, and some are negative. They are usually at rest; but when two bodies of different electrical states approach each other, they at once become highly excited, and continue so till brought in contact with each other, when the positive charges or impregnates the negative. So it is found that love exists in different states in the two sexes, and in different degrees of intensity in different individuals of the same sex. Males are positive, and females negative; and while the latter differ less from each other than the former do, being nearly all of them susceptible to the proper proposals of genuine love, yet they are not so much affected by spontaneous passion as the former are, who usually experience it with great intensity, and are impelled to make the first advances. But there are always some individuals among them who need a great deal of encouragement before they will advance and propose; and others who are almost destitute of the common sensibility of love, and who will neither make proposals nor receive them.

LOVE REFINES AND ENNOBLES

Love sheds on earth something of the beauty and the light of heaven. Love develops the noblest traits of humanity; and often brings them out from those persons who had given little promise of possessing them, until they were brought under the influence of this master passion. There is nothing so great, so difficult, or so self-sacrificing that love will not inspire men to dare and to do. But it is not more in splendid achievements or wonderful adventures, than it is in the innumerable little things, which conspire to make up the happiness of social life, that the greatest victories of love are won. We cannot love any person, without seeking his or her benefit; and in endeavoring to benefit and please the object of our affection, we are impelled to improve and beautify ourselves, in order to become more worthy of our beloved one's affection in return. And this leads us not only to adorn our persons but to polish our manners and cultivate our minds. Hence, we are deeply indebted to this sentiment for those qualities of mind and person which combine to constitute us social beings; since it does not more certainly impel us to the acquisition of what is beautiful and becoming in dress and deportment, than to the attainment of intelligence and politeness, and to surround ourselves with all the embellishments of civilization. Love refines all that it touches. Under its influence the rough boy becomes the respectful young gentleman, and the awkward girl assumes the innate refinement of the lady. Love paints the cheek with roses, adds new lustre and intelligence to the eye, imparts strength and elasticity to the step, grace and dignity to the mien, courage to the heart, eloquence to the tongue, and poetry to every thought. In fact, love is at once the poetry of life, and the life of poetry. Love has inspired, in every age, the brightest dreams of fancy and the noblest conceptions of literature and of art, constituting the perpetual theme which animates the writer's pen and tunes the poet's lyre. Love reposes in the sculptor's marble; love blushes upon the painter's canvas. And all these various embodiments of love by literature and art are universally appreciated and admired; for the pen, the chisel, and the pencil have only given expression to the general sentiment of mankind. The poet and the artist have only wrought out what everyone else had already thought: and have only given speech, form, and color to the silent, shadowy images of the common heart of man.

LOVE INHERENT IN ALL

That the language of love is universally understood, and that its varied delineations by the inspiration of art are always and everywhere delightfully recognized, is sufficient proof that the sentiment is universally experienced. It is not confined to the gifted, the highborn, or the rich, nor is it peculiar to any period of the world, or to any condition of life. All have possessed the sensibility, if they have not experienced the passion; they have felt the want of love, if they have not enjoyed its fruition.

It is our birthright. We have no sooner passed the period of adolescence than we inherit the power and the inclination to love. We then feel an instinctive yearning of the heart for a kindred heart. We are each of us conscious of being incomplete alone, and incapable of enjoying alone our fullest happiness, and we intuitively seek that happiness by linking our destiny in life with some dear one of the opposite sex. It is there only that our natural wants can be supplied. One sex is the complement of the other. Each is imperfect alone, and each supplies what the other lacks. Self-reliant as man may suppose himself to be, yet divine wisdom has said, "It is not good for the man to be alone;" he needs a "helpmeet" in woman. Still less is it good for the woman to be alone, for "she was created for the man," and every woman wants a man to love; for love is her life, and it is only while she loves, or hopes to love, that she lives to any happy or useful or honest purpose. It has been said that as woman was taken out of man in her creation, so it is man's instinctive desire to seek her and to reclaim her as his own counterpart, or that portion of himself is required to complete the symmetry of his nature and the happiness of his life. For this love the youthful heart longs and pines until it attains the object of its desires, or until it has become so sordid, so hard, and so profligate, as to be, at once, unworthy of possessing it, and incapable of enjoying it. This susceptibility of the youthful heart has been faithfully portrayed by a youthful poet, in the following lines, which are at once recognized, as expressing the common sentiment of humanity:

> "It is not that my lot is low,
> That bids the silent tear to flow,
> It is not grief that bids me moan,
> It is that I am all alone.
>
> In woods and glens I love to roam,
> When the tired hedger hies him home;
> Or by the woodland pool to rest,
> When pale the star looks on its breast.
>
> Yet when the silent evening sighs.
> With hallowed airs and symphonies,
> My spirit takes another tone,
> And sighs that it is all alone.
>
> The woods and winds with sudden wail
> Tell all the same unvaried tale;
> I've none to smile when I am free,
> And when I sigh, to sigh with me.
>
> Yet in my dreams a form I view.
> That thinks on me and loves me too;
> I start! and when the vision's flown,
> I weep that I am all alone."

H. K. WHITE

Another poet has expressed the same sentiment in the following impassioned lines:

"Give me but
Something whereunto I may bind my heart;
Something to love, to cherish, and to clasp
Affection's tendrils round."

Now, if any one should be inclined to call all this but love-sick sentimentality, unworthy our serious consideration, I shall only answer him in the words of Dr. Johnson, the English moralist: "We must not ridicule the passion of love, which he who never felt, never was happy; and he who laughs at never deserves to feel, – a passion which has inspired heroism, and subdued avarice; a passion which has caused the change of empires, and the loss of worlds."

Shall these heaven-born impulses of nature be regarded, or must they be repressed? Shall we permit these tendrils of our love to bind themselves around some kindred heart, or shall we suffer them to be rudely torn asunder, and cast aside to wither and decay? Implanted for the noblest purposes within our breasts, interwoven with the very fibres of our being, the laws of God and of nature unquestionably demand their indulgence.

LOVE IS THE RIGHT OF ALL

In plainer terms, the laws of God and of nature clearly indicate that every man and every woman, possessing sufficient health and vitality to experience the passion of love, is benefited by its proper gratification; and those laws both allow and invite everyone to enjoy it in its full fruition. A man is not wholly a man, nor a woman wholly a woman, who has never experienced the ecstasies of gratified love. And those men and women who are spending their most vigorous period of life in cold and barren celibacy, without ever having yielded to the warm desires of reproduction, are living, every moment, in debt to their Creator and to the commonwealth of mankind. They have never fulfilled some of the most important purposes of their being.

"Torches are made to light, jewels to wear,
Dainties to taste, fresh beauty for the use,
Herbs for their smell, and sappy plants to bear;
Things growing to themselves are growth's abuse:
     Seeds spring from seeds, and beauty breedeth beauty.
     Thou wast begot – to get it is thy duty.

Upon the earth's increase why shouldst thou feed,
Unless the earth with thy increase be fed?
By law of Nature thou art bound to breed,
That thine may live, when thou thyself art dead;
     And so in spite of death thou dost survive,
     In that thy likeness still is left alive."

             SHAKESPEARE (Venus and Adonis)

LOVE MUST BE PROTECTED WITHIN THE LIMITS OF CHASTITY

Yet men and women must not rush into sensual pleasure like brutes, for we are moral beings, as well as corporeal beings, and, as such, the subjects of moral law, which requires us to govern our passions, and circumscribe them within the limits of purity. But, even in this respect, there is no real disagreement between the laws of morality and those of Nature: when they are properly understood, they are each equally explicit in forbidding every form of licentious impurity. The most loathsome and incurable diseases are the penalties imposed by natural law, and the severest retributions of eternity, the penalties imposed by divine law, upon the promiscuous and unrestrained indulgence of the amorous propensity. Nor are these penalties unnecessary. No passion of our nature is more vehement, and no one more liable to be tempted and led astray from the path of rectitude; and we should, therefore, attend the more carefully to those laws and limitations which God and Nature have imposed upon its indulgence. And I cannot doubt that they have limited its indulgence strictly to the marriage relation. Some well-defined limit there must be between chastity and unchastity, and vice and virtue, or else the laws which define them and which punish transgressors must be unjust and oppressive.

MARRIAGE CONSTITUTES THAT LIMIT

Here there is no oppression and no injustice. Everybody is born with a propensity to love, and everybody that is willing to marry may marry, and indulge that propensity in innocence and purity. Within this limit the gratification of love affords us the most exquisite pleasure, promotes health, conduces to longevity, and is entirely consistent with the rules of morality and religion. But when it oversteps this limit prescribed by our Creator, and bursts the barriers of chastity, it then assumes the form of unprincipled lust, and inflicts upon its miserable votaries the utmost torture of body, degradation of mind, and remorse of conscience.

"Marriage is honorable in all, and the bed undefiled; but whoremongers and adulterers God will judge." – Heb. xiii. 4.

> "Hail wedded love, mysterious law, true source
> Of human offspring, sole propriety,
> In Paradise, of all things common else.
> By thee adulterous lust was driven from man,
> Among the bestial herd to range; by thee
> Founded in reason, loyal, just, and pure
> Relations dear and all the charities
> Of father, son, and brother first were known.
> Far be it, that I should write thee sin or blame;
> Or think thee unbefitting holiest place;
> Perpetual fountain of domestic sweets,
> Whose bed is undefiled and chaste pronounced,
> Present or past, as saints and patriarchs used.
> Here Love his golden shafts employs, here lights
> His constant lamp, and waves his purple wings."
>
> PARADISE LOST, Book iv.

CHAPTER III:

PRIMARY LAWS OF MARRIAGE

Since the infallible and unchangeable laws of God and of Nature have limited the indulgence of love to married persons only, it becomes necessary to inquire into the laws and limitations of marriage itself. What is marriage? and who are entitled to its rights and benefits?

MARRIAGE DEFINED

The proper definition of marriage is the main point at issue between the social system of polygamy and that of monogamy, which it is the object of this treatise to examine and compare. One system defines marriage to be the exclusive union of one man to one woman until separated by death or divorce; the other defines it to be the union of one man to either one woman or more, until separated, in like manner, by death or divorce.

It now remains for us to determine which of these definitions is most in harmony with the laws of God and of Nature. And we shall be better able to do this, by considering carefully the beneficent purposes which marriage is designed to subserve.

MARRIAGE BENEFICIAL

Marriage is the first and best of all human institutions, if it can properly be called human, since it was first solemnized in Paradise, by the Creator himself, who then said, "It is not good that the man should be alone; I will make him a help meet for him." And he made a woman, and brought her unto the man. "And God blessed them, and God said unto them, Be fruitful, and multiply, and replenish the earth, and subdue it."

It is impossible to enumerate all the benefits of marriage, since there is no vital interest of mankind which it does not affect favorably. Marriage perpetuates the human race; lays the foundations of organized society; promotes industry; accumulates wealth; cultivates the arts, and maintains religion. It builds the house, tills the soil, supports the family, and fosters every charitable and benevolent enterprise.

ALL ARE ENTITLED TO ITS BENEFITS

As the word of God has declared marriage to be honorable in all, so we must infer that his laws have made provision for the honorable marriage of all; and that every person of each sex is equally entitled to its rights and benefits. These rights should no more be restricted to the rich and the fortunate than are the susceptibilities of love, upon which marriage properly depends, and from which it derives its only proper warrant and authority.

"Love, and love only, is the loan for love."

Marriage, when authorized and warranted by the promptings of an honest love, is a pure and blissful consummation of all that is divine in humanity; but when it is contracted from mercenary or ambitious motives, it becomes a most unholy profanation. Love was not made for marriage, but marriage for love. Love is an inherent and a necessary attribute of humanity; marriage a subsequent relationship instituted to minister to love's wants. Love is the mistress, marriage the handmaid. Marriage must wait the demands of love, and not love the demands of marriage. It is, therefore, equally disrespectful to our Creator, and dishonorable to man, to require that love should be suppressed because marriage is inconvenient, and still more dishonorable and disrespectful to require any one to be deprived of the rights of love on account of the impossibility of marriage; for marriage ought to be possible to all. If love be refining and ennobling, if it be the spontaneous, instinctive birthright of all, and if our Creator has restricted its indulgence to the marriage relation, then marriage must be the right of all, or else God is not a benevolent being. But all nature and all revelation have demonstrated that he is a benevolent being, and it is both impious and absurd to believe that his laws have made no adequate provision for everyone to be married who wishes to be. We may waive our rights, and live in celibacy, if we prefer to; but no one who *loves* and who wishes to marry ought to be compelled to remain unmarried. It is, therefore, demonstrated that any form of society which fails to provide for the marriage of all is a defective system, and opposed to the natural, inherent, and inalienable rights of man.

THESE RIGHTS ARE DENIED TO MANY

Yet we well know that there are very many persons, especially many women, who are neither married nor have an opportunity to marry. By some means they have been deprived of their right. The fault is not theirs; they would, in almost every instance, prefer wedded life if it were in their power to attain it; but it is not. They possess the same susceptibilities of love, the same yearning for intimate companionship, that others do, but these tender sensibilities they are obliged to repress. The fault is not in nature, nor in the laws of God, but it is in the tyrannical laws and fashions of the artificial system of social life which now obtains among us. This system must be at fault, for it does not and it cannot provide for the marriage of all; and many who desire to marry are forever deprived of husbands and homes: while the system of polygamy does provide for all, and is, therefore, the only system which is in harmony with divine and natural laws.

This proposition is further demonstrated by the simple fact that the number of marriageable women always exceeds the number of marriageable men.

MORE WOMEN THAN MEN

The statistics of all States and nations agree in this fact,[223] except,

---

223   The censuses heretofore taken of more than one hundred million of the population of Europe exhibit the remarkable fact, that in those countries, during the first fifteen years of life, the males uniformly exceed the females in number, but that, subsequently to this age, the females become most numerous, and increasingly so with increase of age. The same is true with regard to the proportionate numbers of the sexes in Massachusetts and the other New-England States.

occasionally, in those States in which the population is very largely made up by foreign immigration. Most of these immigrants are men; and many of them have left their wives and families in the mother-country, and do not intend to become permanent citizens, but hope to make their fortunes and return home to enjoy them. Yet many persons who have never examined statistical tables, nor taken any other accurate means of informing themselves, suppose the number of the men to be equal to that of the women; and it has been a plausible objection to polygamy, that if some men have a plurality of wives, some other men must thereby be deprived of any, and the system must be unequal and unjust. The objection would be valid were it based upon valid facts: but it is all an error; and it is one which a little observation would enable almost any one readily to correct. One has only to count up the persons of each sex of marriageable age in all the families of his own acquaintance to satisfy himself that the females will outnumber the males. It is true, that, at birth, the number of each sex is nearly equal; that of the males being slightly in excess, but a much larger proportion of the males die in childhood, than of the females.[224]

"During the ten years 1856-65, the total number of births registered in Massachusetts was 334,493, of which 171,584, or 51.29 percent, were males; 161,715, or 48.35 percent, were females; and of 1,194, or 1/3 of one percent, the sex was not stated. During the first ten years of life, the deaths of males exceeded those of females in a ratio beyond that of the relative number of the sexes at birth. In 1855, there were 32,301 more females than males in Massachusetts; in 1860, 37,640 more females; and the excess of females in 1865 was 63,011." – *Census of Massachusetts for* 1865, pp. 286, 287.

"Ever since the first census of 1765, there has been found an excess of females over males in Massachusetts; the disparity has increased somewhat rapidly since 1850." – *Massachusetts Registration Report of Births, Marriages, and Deaths for* 1866.

224   In Massachusetts the percentage of the deaths of male children under one year of age during the year 1866 was 22.25, that of female children during the same year was 17.42. See Massachusetts Registration Report for 1866, p. 44.

Generally, about fifty percent of all male children die before the age of twenty-one years; while only about thirty-three percent, or two-thirds as many females, die during the same period.[225] And then, as they grow up to manhood, the

---

225   STATISTICAL TABLES

POP OF MASSACHUSETTS, June 1, A.D. 1860

	Male	Female
Under 1 year	15,809	15,666
1 and under 5	60,059	59.695
5 and under 10	64,476	64,080
10 and under 15	57,544	56,804
15 and under 20	57,070	63,730
20 and under 30	63,070	132,106
Total	596,713	634,353

COLORED POP. N.Y. CITY, 1860

	Male	Female
Under 1 year	82	114
1 and under 5	410	453
5 and under 10	566	574
10 and under 15	565	531
15 and under 20	446	648
20 and under 30	1,120	1,655
Total	5,468	7,106

WHITE POP. OF SUFFOLK CO., (City of Boston), Mass., 1860.

	Male	Female
Under 1 year	2,707	2,743
1 and under 5	9,358	9,334
5 and under 10	9,730	9.945
10 and under 15	8,224	8,313
15 and under 20	19,805	23,906
Total	91,015	99,234

POP. OF PENNSYLVANIA, 1860

	Male	Female
Under 1 year	44,167	42,704
1 and under 5	179,253	176,115
5 and under 10	194,258	191,094
10 and under 15	171,162	167,025
15 and under 20	149,531	160,357
20 and under 30	246,343	263,931
Total	1,454,419	1,451,796

POP. OF N. YORK STATE, 1860

	Male	Female
Under 1 year	52,175	51,257
1 and under 5	216,112	210,591
5 and under 10	232,426	227,413
10 and under 15	203,453	197,884
15 and under 20	188,803	205,604
20 and under 30	341,037	386,141
Total	1,933,532	1,947,203

POP. OF PHIL. CO., PENN., (White), 1860

	Male	Female
Under 1 year	7,829	7,475
1 and under 5	30,864	30,533
5 and under 10	31,981	31,737
10 and under 15	26,135	27,113
15 and under 20	23,425	29,294
20 and under 30	49,667	61,380
Total	260,156	283,188

boys and young men are constantly exposed to hardships and dangers, from which the softer sex is exempt; and hence the excess of the females goes on continually increasing, as we see by the statistical tables, from the beginning to the end of the marriageable age. All this in times of peace: the excess must be much greater than usual after a destructive war; for during the late civil war in America there were

WHITE POP. OF N.Y. CITY, 1860			POP. OF PHILADELPHIA (Colored), 1860		
	Male	Female		Male	Female
Under 1 year,	12,247	12,072	Under 1 year,	187	209
1 and under 5	47,074	46,025	1 and under 5	809	1,065
5 and under 10	46,380	45,452	5 and under 10	1,019	1,195
10 and under 15	36,233	34,936	10 and under 15	996	1,199
15 and under 20	33,344	39,628	15 and under 20	915	1,452
20 and under 30	77,747	97,627	20 and under 30	1,875	2,864
Total	391,521	409,567	Total	9,177	13,008

The foregoing statistics are compiled from the United-States Census for 1860. The following are from the Census of Massachusetts for 1865, published under the supervision of O. Warner, Secretary of the Commonwealth. Table I. p. 2.

POP. OF MASSACHUSETTS, June 1, 1865.			POP. OF SUFFOLK CO., MASS. (City of Boston), June 1, 1865.		
	Male	Female		*Male*	*Female*
Under 1 year	11,974	11,745	Under 1 year	2,145	2,017
1 and under 2	12,808	12,431	1 and under 2	2,003	1,819
2 and under 3	13,643	13,516	2 and under 3	2,288	2,255
3 and under 4	14,161	14,188	3 and under 4	2,205	2,233
4 and under 5	14,735	14,653	4 and under 5	2,280	2,301
5 and under 10	71,777	71,614	5 and under 10	11,267	11,627
10 and under 15	63,853	62,838	10 and under 15	9,848	9,971
15 and under 20	55,281	61,890	15 and under 20	8,527	10,267
20 and under 30	96,027	129,497	20 and under 30	17,601	25,618
Total	91,015	99,234	Total	96,529	11,683

In the above table the excess of females between the ages of 15 and 20 is 6,600, or about 1/8 of the number of males; between 20 and 30 it is 33,452, or more than 1/3 of the number of males.

lost from both parties nearly a million of men in the most productive period of life.

WOMEN MATURE EARLIER THAN MEN

Young women become marriageable at a much earlier age than young men do. There is a natural or constitutional difference of several years, and prudential considerations cause the difference to become practically greater. But few young men are born to large fortunes, which these times of extravagance require for the fashionable maintenance of a family; and those who are rich are not always the most prompt to marry. They prefer to spend their early manhood in dissipation, and are unwilling to bow to the yoke of wedlock till they begin to feel the infirmities of age; while the poor man must devote several years of his majority to toil before he becomes able to assume matrimonial expenses. The result is that most men do not marry until between twenty-five and thirty-five years of age, and many at a later period; while a large majority of women who marry at all are married between the ages of fifteen and twenty-five. On the whole, therefore, women are practically marriageable ten years younger than men are, a period which constitutes a third part of the average duration of adult life. From these two causes alone, – the greater number of women, and their being marriageable so much younger, – the proportion of marriageable women to marriageable men would be about two to one.

MANY MEN REFUSE TO MARRY

But the practical difference is still greater. For after men have arrived at adult manhood, and have acquired the means of supporting a family, many of them refuse marriage. Some have out-lived their youthful desires, and have acquired decided habits of celibacy; some are too gay and too profligate; others too busy and too selfish; others so broken down by early dissipation and diseased by the contagious poison of low vice, that they are totally unfit to marry: while there are many others whose occupations (such as sailors and soldiers) most commonly prevent marriage. From these disabilities the other sex is much more exempt. They are exposed to fewer temptations; they are more susceptible to religious impressions; they are more immediately under the control of parents and guardians, and are saved from many of those enervating and degrading habits which beset young men, rendering them either disinclined to marriage, or unfit for it, or both.

FEW WOMEN DECLINE MARRIAGE

There are, on the other hand, few women who are unwilling to marry. They are naturally dependent upon their male friends; and, after the period of childhood, this dependence is seldom happy or even tolerable, except in the marriage relation. The former is a dependence of necessity, the latter is, or ought to be, a dependence of love; and this distinction makes all the difference in the world. Hence it needs no argument to prove what is so universally admitted, that women fulfil their highest destiny in life only by becoming wives and mothers. I will cite a woman's testimony, and submit the case, quoting the earnest words of Gail Hamilton: "There is not one woman in a million who would not be married if . . . she could have a chance. How do I know? Just as I know that the stars are now shining in the sky, though it is high noon. I never saw a star at noonday; but I know it is the nature of stars to shine in the sky, and of the sky to hold its stars. Genius or fool, rich or poor, beauty or the beast, if marriage were what it should be, what God meant it to be, what even, with the world's present possibilities, it might be, it would be the Elysium, the sole, complete Elysium, of woman, yes, and of man. Greatness, glory, usefulness, happiness, await her otherwheres; but here alone all her powers, all her being, can find full play. No condition, no character even, can quite hide the gleam of the sacred fire; but on the household hearth it joins the warmth of earth to the hues of heaven. Brilliant, dazzling, vivid, a beacon and a blessing her light may be; but only a happy home blends the prismatic rays into a soft, serene whiteness, that floods the world with divine illumination. Without wifely and motherly love, a part of her nature must remain enclosed, a spring shut up, a fountain sealed."[226]

---

226   New Atmosphere, p. 55

MONOGAMY PREVENTS MARRIAGE

But under the system of monogamy it is impossible for half the women to live in the enjoyment of the married state. This cruel and oppressive system is compelling them either to repress the fondest sensibilities and the most imperative demands of Nature, and to renounce their dearest rights, or else to assert them in a clandestine and forbidden manner, and thus to abandon themselves to a life of infamy and an eternity of shame and woe.

In older and more wealthy countries practising monogamy, the comparative number of unmarried to married women is even greater. The statistical tables of England show that less than one-third of the marriageable women of that country were living in marriage at the time of the last census.

At the period of the highest glory of the Roman empire, and also during its long decline, while wealth and luxury increased, and the artificial conventionalities of society were greatly multiplied, it was observed, with alarm, that marriages became less and less frequent, and were consummated later and later in life: and all the power of the government was exerted in vain to arrest the growing evil. Heavy fines and special taxes were levied upon old bachelors, and high premiums paid to persons having numerous families; but the evil continued to increase till the empire was dismembered.[227]

---

227   "But neither rewards nor penalties proved effectual to check the increasing tendency to celibacy; and at the period of the Gracchi an alarm was sounded that the old Roman race was becoming rapidly extinguished...When the legislation of Julius Caesar was found ineffectual for controlling the still growing evil, it was re-enforced by his successor with fresh penalties and rewards." – *Merivale's Hist. of the Romans*, chap. 33, vol. 2, pp. 37, 38.

"But upon this one point the master of the Romans [Augustus] could make no impression upon the dogged disobedience of his subjects: both the men and the women preferred the loose terms of union upon which they had consented to cohabit, &c". – *Ibid*.

"Augustus most anxiously, both by law and precept, encouraged marriage; but the profligacy of the manners which then prevailed was such that all the honors and rewards and immunities which he prepared were of but little avail." – *Keightley's Hist. of the Roman Empire*, chap I. p. 11.

"The principal cause of the prevalent aversion to marriage was the extreme dissoluteness of manners at that time, exceeding anything known in modern days...The first law on the subject was the Julian *'De Maritandis Ordinibus'* of 736; and this having proved ineffectual, a now and more

THE MARRIAGE CEREMONY

In respect to the mode of performing the marriage ceremony, the divine law does not prescribe any: and nothing more was necessary, in ancient times, to constitute a valid marriage than a mutual agreement, or actual cohabitation. The ancient Romans had three different modes of tying the hymeneal knot, each with a different degree of looseness, but none of them so firm as it should be. The ceremony has always varied in different States, and at different times in the same State, and should never be regarded as anything more than a public recognition of a relationship already formed and completed between the parties. Yet as marriage is a matter of important consequence to the friends and kindred of the parties, and also to the whole State, involving public as well as private obligations, it is eminently proper that some appropriate ceremony should be performed, and that it should be sufficiently public to leave no doubt as to its reality. Yet marriages are made in heaven; the claim of the Romish Church to make and unmake them is a blasphemous assumption. No ceremony can add to their religious validity; and it can only be necessary to their legality and publicity.

---

comprehensive law, embracing all the provisions of the Julian, and named the *'Papia-Poppaea,'* was passed in the year 762." – *Ibid.*, chap. 2, p. 34.

CHAPTER IV:

ORIGIN OF POLYGAMY

PREJUDICES TO BE OVERCOME

Having thus fulfilled my promise to analyze and demonstrate the fundamental laws of love and marriage, I shall now attempt, with equal candor and simplicity, to trace the origin and indicate the moral characteristics of the two social systems of monogamy and polygamy, and to apply to them the same tests of philosophical analysis and comparison. And here allow me again to say that it is necessary to arm ourselves with patient candor, or we cannot appreciate the truth and justice of any fair analysis of these systems. As we have been brought up under the system of monogamy, we have inherited the prejudices of that system and, having been taught to look upon the opposite one with detestation and contempt, we are, on that account, but ill qualified to judge between them. Let us remember that, whether our prejudices are right or wrong, they are prejudices only. We have not stopped to reason; we have been content to cherish our opinions on this subject without examination and without reason. We have always accustomed ourselves to believe that polygamy originated in barbarism; that it is perpetuated by barbarians only, and that it panders to the basest and most depraved of human passions. But let us now think for ourselves. For one, I claim that right. I dare to question the superior purity of monogamy; and on behalf of the despised and persecuted system of polygamy, I venture to appeal from the rash decisions of prejudice to the solemn tribunals of divine and natural law; and in support of this appeal I cite the facts of sacred and profane history, and plead the inalienable rights of man.

POLYGAMY IS NOT BARBARISM

If European monogamists have hitherto surpassed all other men in civilization and social happiness, it is not on account of their monogamy, but, no doubt, on account of their Christianity. Even a perverted Christianity, a corrupted Christianity, a Roman Christianity, is better than idolatry or Mohammedanism. What, then, may we not hope when Christianity shall become free and pure, and restored to its pristine simplicity and glory?

An idolatrous nation practising monogamy has never been able long to exist. History does not furnish one example. Such nations soon become so incurably corrupt as to incur the wrath of God, and are swept from the face of the earth. Neither civilization nor barbarism; military power or pusillanimity; tyranny or freedom; monarchy, aristocracy, or democracy; literature, art, wealth, genius, or stupidity has ever been able to save them. Many such States and nations have started in the race of glory and perpetual empire; but each of them has come to premature decay. Such were the different States of ancient Greece and ancient Italy, many of them distinguished for having produced men of the most brilliant genius and the most renowned experience in the various arts of peace and war, and several of them achieving extensive conquests and becoming vast empires; yet they very soon collapsed and went to ruin. And such was the fate of the many scores or perhaps hundreds of the petty States of all Europe before the establishment of Christianity. They rose, they flourished, they became licentious, they fell. Wave after wave of the purer races of the polygamists of Asia rolled over them, and assumed their places; and as these, in turn, fell into their social habits, and adopted their monogamy, and became corrupt, they also became extinct, and were succeeded by newer and purer immigrations. On the other hand, the polygamists of Asia have preserved their social purity, and along with it many of their nationalities, through every age, notwithstanding their idolatry and Mohammedanism. Such are the nations of China, Japan, Persia, and Arabia, whose living languages and existing laws date back to the very earliest records of antiquity. An intelligent Christian nation practising polygamy has never yet existed, simply because the two institutions have hitherto been falsely deemed incompatible and irreconcilable. The Gnostic heresy had so soon corrupted the springs of Christian learning, and the Grecian and Roman hierarchies had so soon usurped the seats of Christian authority, that the freedom and simplicity of the pristine faith were perverted, even before such an experiment could be made, as I shall fully demonstrate in the next chapter; and now it is most probable that if such an experiment shall ever be made, it will be somewhere upon the continent of free America.

"Westward the course of empire takes its way;
The four first acts already past,
A fifth shall close the drama with the day, –
Time's noblest offspring is the last."

Polygamy is not barbarism, for it has been maintained and supported by such men as Abraham, Moses, David, and Solomon; whose superiors in all that constitute the highest civilization – knowledge, piety, wisdom, and refinement of mind and manners – the world has never known, either in ancient or modern times. Yet polygamy, though it be not barbarism, has almost always and everywhere prevailed, where a simple, natural, and in artificial state of society subsists. Its origin is coeval with that of the human race. It is mentioned before the flood. It is mentioned soon after the flood. As soon as mankind were multiplied upon the earth, it was discovered that the number of the women exceeded that of the men; and also that the amorous passions of the men were stronger than those of the women. Polygamy brings both these inequalities together, and allows them to correct each other. It furnishes every woman who wishes to marry, a husband and a home; and gives every man an opportunity of expending his super-abundant vitality in an honest way.

WHY GOD MADE BUT ONE WOMAN

If it be objected that God created but one woman for Adam, it is a sufficient answer to reply, that both the man and the woman were also created perfect. They were perfect in health, and perfect in morals. But we are now imperfect in both respects; and we now need a social system adapted to men and women as they are. If humanity shall ever be restored to its pristine strength and beauty, the equality of the sexes will also be restored, and there will be a man for every woman, and a woman for every man; a true woman without imperfection, whose accomplishments will not be superficial, nor whose attractions artificial; but whose rosy cheeks and pearly teeth and swelling breasts and clustering ringlets shall be all her own. God speed the day! Should I live to see it; I would become an advocate for monogamy. But, as it now is, there is not a man for every woman; and either some women must remain unmarried and "waste their sweetness on the desert air," and be entirely deprived of their birth right, and denied all matrimonial advantages, or they may, several of them, agree to share those advantages in common with each other, by having a single husband between them. Polygamy does not compel them to do this; it only permits them to do it in case they have no opportunity to do better. On the other hand, it does not compel a man to marry even one woman, much less to have more; but, if the intensity of his passion urges him to such lengths that he must have and will have more than one, it requires him to take them honestly and honorably, and to support them and be a true husband to them.

POLYGAMY TAUGHT IN THE BIBLE

The Sacred Scriptures represent the wisest and best men that ever lived, as practising polygamy with the divine blessing and approval. David had seven wives before he reigned in Jerusalem, "and he took more concubines and wives out of Jerusalem, after he was come from Hebron," for God "gave him the house of Saul and the wives of Saul into his bosom."[228] When God reproved Abimelech, king of Gerar, for his intended adultery with Sarah, wife of Abraham, he did, at the same time, approve of his polygamy; for Abimelech said, "In the integrity of my heart and innocency of my hands have I done this." "Said he not unto me, She is my sister? and she, even she herself, said, He is my brother." And God said, "I know that thou didst this in the integrity of thy heart:" "now, therefore, restore the man his wife." "And God healed Abimelech and his wife and his maid-servants." God could allow him to live in open polygamy, without reproof, and

---

228   2 Sam. iii. 2-5, 14; v. 13; xii. 8

"in the integrity of his heart," but could not allow him to commit adultery, even ignorantly.[229] Solomon was reproved for multiplying the number of his wives to an unreasonable and ostentatious degree, but more especially for having taken them from heathen nations; for "they turned away his heart after other gods:" but these are the only reasons assigned for his reproof, there being no intimation that polygamy was wrong in itself. But it is unnecessary to cite other examples from the Bible. No one familiar with that book has ever denied that polygamy is taught in the Old Testament, and yet most Christians suppose it to be forbidden in the New. Have we any right to such a supposition? Are we right in entertaining *any supposition* on this subject? If it is forbidden in the New Testament, have we not a right to demand the most unequivocal and undoubted proofs of such prohibition? Is the God of Abraham and Isaac and Jacob the Christian's God, or is he not? Is it not possible that this supposition is an error? And, if it be an error, is it not possible that it has been one means of lessening our reverence for the Old Testament, and thereby undermining our confidence in the Bible as a whole? If this supposition be an error, has it not been tending to make infidels of us all? I copy the following paragraph from an essay of the Rev. S. W. Foljambe, recently delivered by him, at a Sabbath-school Teachers' Convention at Boston, with my most hearty commendation: –

"It is sad to believe that infidelity in some form prevails throughout our State, yet we cannot doubt that it is even so, generally covert with an outward profession of regard for Christianity, but nevertheless real, accompanied by a disregard and disbelief of the scriptures of the Old and New Testaments. I refer to this not as any proof that Protestantism or Christianity is or can be a failure, or that the Scriptures are in any real danger, but as indicating a responsibility resting on us to maintain and defend the equal authority and inspiration of the Holy Scriptures; that "all scripture is given by inspiration of God;" that its writers, whether Moses or David, Isaiah or Paul, Ezekiel or John, were 'holy men of God who wrote as they were moved by the Holy Ghost.' Is it not true, that, among many who hold to the truth and reality of a divine revelation, there has come to be a feeling that in some way the New Testament has superseded the Old, and that

---

229   Gen. xx

the Old has ceased to be 'profitable for doctrine, for correction, for reproof, for instruction in righteousness'? Now, if this can be demonstrated, what is there to prove that in a still more advanced stage of spiritual life, as is claimed by many, the New Testament itself may not be superseded by some wiser interpretations of the meaning and purpose of Christ's life, and the Gospels of Matthew and of John be superseded by the gospel of Strauss or Renan; or the interpretations of Paul as to the person and work of Christ be superseded by the interpretation of Parker and of Music Hall?

"It seems to me that our Lord is explicit on this point, that the Jewish Scriptures were not and could not be superseded by any later revelation even by himself: 'Think not that I am come to destroy the law, or the prophets: I am not come to destroy, but to fulfil;' and again – 'Had ye believed Moses, ye would have believed me, for he wrote of me;' and he is continually quoting them as authority, showing that there is no inconsistency between the two revelations. Together they form one continuous and connected divine word. True, the Scriptures are composed of books that are cumulative and progressive, but they are interdependent. The internal meaning of the two parts is entirely harmonious. The divine Spirit is in them both. They never contradict, but always interpret, explain, and illustrate each other."

But let the inspiration and perpetual authority of the Old Testament be fully admitted, yet the modern Christian may say, "We do not live under the First Covenant, nor observe the ceremonies of Moses; but we live in the New Dispensation, under the full light of the gospel: Christ has fulfilled the ritual and emblematical ordinances of the law, and set them aside; and it is presumed that the ancient marriage laws have been set aside among the rest, and superseded by the purer system of monogamy." But this assumption cannot be supported either by sufficient testimony or by valid reasoning. The social system of polygamy had existed before the time of Moses, and had no dependence upon the ceremonial law which was instituted in his day. That law only confirmed it as a pre-existent institution. Marriage laws cannot be regarded as merely ritual and emblematical: they are moral and fundamental, guarding the dearest rights and punishing the deepest wrongs of mankind. They are, therefore, equally permanent with those laws protecting life and property, those inculcating obedience to parents and rulers, and those maintaining the sanctity of oaths. All these, together with the marriage laws, existed before the time of Moses, and have survived the time of Christ. They are among those "laws" that Jesus came not to *subvert* but to *ratify* as Dr. George Campbell of Aberdeen has, in Matt. v.17, very exactly translated the terms καταλῦσαι and πληρῶσαι. Hence the marriage system of polygamy never formed a part of that ceremonial dispensation which was abrogated by the New Testament; nor has it ever been proved that the New Testament was designed to affect any change in it; but the presumption is that this new dispensation has also left it, as it found it, – abiding still in force. If any change were to be made in an institution of such long standing, confirmed by positive law, it could obviously be made only by equally positive and explicit ordinances or enactments of the gospel. But such enactments are wanting. Christ himself was altogether silent in respect to polygamy, not once alluding to it; yet it was practised at the time of his advent throughout Judaea and Galilee, and in all the other countries of Asia and Africa, and, without doubt, by some of his own disciples.

The Book of the Acts is equally silent as the four Gospels are. No allusion to it is found in any of the sermons or instructions or discussions of the apostles and early saints recorded in that book. It was not because Jesus or the apostles durst not condemn it, had they considered it sinful, that they did not speak of it, for Jesus hesitated not to denounce the sins of hypocrisy, covetousness, and adultery, and even to alter and amend, apparently, the ancient laws respecting divorce and retaliation; but he never rebuked them for their polygamy, nor instituted any change in that system. And this uniform silence, so far as it implies anything, implies approval. John the Baptist was thrown into prison, where he was afterwards beheaded, for reproving King Herod on account of his adultery and we cannot doubt, that, if he had considered polygamy to be sinful, he would have mentioned it; for Herod's father was, just before that time, living with nine wives, whose names are recorded by Josephus, in his "Antiquities of the Jews;"[230] but John only reproved him for marrying Herodias, his brother Philip's wife, while his brother was living. He administered the same reproof to Herod that Nathan had formerly done to David, and for similar reasons. The apostles always

---

230   Antiq. Jud., book 17, chap. 1 & 3

denounced the sins of fornication and adultery, but never denounced polygamy, nor intimated in any way that it was a sin. In all the long and painful catalogues of sins enumerated in the first, second, and third chapters of Romans, many of which relate to the unlawful indulgence of the amorous propensities, polygamy is not once named. It is the very place where it is morally certain that it would have been named if it were sinful; and, that it is not there named, we are fully warranted to believe that it is not sinful.

MONOGAMY OF BISHOPS AND DEACONS

The only portions of the Sacred Writings which seem to disapprove of polygamy are found in the epistles of Paul concerning the qualifications of bishops and deacons. These passages have been variously interpreted by various commentators. Some suppose that it forbids these officers of the church from contracting a second marriage after the death of the first wife; others that it forbids any but married persons being inducted into these sacred offices – that they must be the husbands of one wife, at least, – but that it does not forbid them taking more. But the commonly received opinion, and the one to which I am myself inclined, is, that in choosing men for these offices, such men should be chosen who are not much inclined to amorous pleasures, and each of whom has one wife only. They should be men of peculiar temperance and sobriety. This implies that polygamy was still practised in the primitive Christian churches; for otherwise it would have been superfluous and irrelevant to mention this as a special qualification in a candidate for one of those offices. And even this recommendation applies only to candidates, and not to those who have been already ordained. In confirmation of these views I here cite the authority of James McKnight, D.D., one of the most learned commentators on the New Testament.

DR. MCKNIGHT'S COMMENTARY

"As the Asiatic nations universally practised polygamy, from an inordinate love of the pleasures of the flesh, the apostle ordered, by inspiration, that none should be made bishops but those, who, by avoiding polygamy, had showed themselves temperate in the use of sensual pleasures. ... It may be objected, perhaps, that the gospel ought to have prohibited the people, as well as the ministers of religion, from polygamy and divorce, if these things were morally evil. As to divorce, the answer is, all, both clergy and people, were restrained from unjust divorces by the precept of Christ. With respect to polygamy being an offence against political prudence, rather than against morality, it had been permitted to the Jews by Moses, and was generally practised by the Eastern nations as a matter of indifferency; it was, therefore, to be corrected mildly and gradually, by example rather than by express precept, without occasioning those domestic troubles and causeless divorces which must necessarily have ensued, if, by an express injunction of the apostles, husbands, immediately on their becoming Christians, had been obliged to put away all their wives except one." – *Commentary on* 1 *Tim.* iii, 2.

This testimony is especially valuable as being extorted, by the force of truth, from an avowed advocate of monogamy. Although it is highly colored by that system, yet these *four points* are distinctly admitted. 1. That polygamy was commonly practised by the primitive Christians. 2. That it had been expressly permitted in the Old Testament. 3. That it was not prohibited in the New Testament. 4. That it was from political and prudential considerations, and not from any immorality in it, that candidates for the ministry were recommended to abstain from it. Hence, we conclude that this recommendation of the apostle was made out of respect to the prejudices of the Greeks and Romans, under whose laws they were then living, and who practised a corrupt and licentious monogamy, which I shall describe in the next chapter. It was doubtless for similar reasons that the same apostle recommended to the Corinthian Christians not to marry; but no one except a Shaking Quaker or a Roman Catholic can believe that such a recommendation was intended to apply to all persons, at all times and places, or that it was proper then, on any other ground than the notorious corruption of Corinthian morals. See Appendix, page 253.

Now polygamy is either right, or it is wrong. If it is wrong, it is contrary to the will of God. If it is contrary to the will of God now, it always has been, ever since the fall of man; for God has not changed, human nature has not changed, and the mutual relation of the sexes has not changed. If it is contrary to the divine will, God would certainly have expressed decided disapprobation of it in his word, and denounced those who practised it. But on the contrary, it was, by the Mosaic law, expressly sanctioned, and, under certain circumstances, expressly commanded, as fully appears from Deut. xxii. 28, and xxv. 5. In the former passage it was commanded that if any man (whether married or unmarried) had had illicit intercourse with an unbetrothed virgin, then he *must marry* her, and must not put her away all his life. In the other passage it was commanded that when a married man died without issue, his brother *must marry* his widow. And this command is positive, whether the surviving brother have a wife already, or not; and even if several such married brothers should die, and leave no offspring, the surviving brother would be obliged, by this law, to marry all the widows; and in each case, the first-born children would succeed to the inheritances of their mothers' first husbands, but the younger children would belong to their own father. This was a law in Israel long before the ceremonial law of Moses, as we learn from the 38th chapter of Genesis, where it is stated that Onan the son of Judah was required to marry the widow of his brother Er, and because he took a wicked course to prevent having offspring by her, he was put to death by the immediate act of God. The entire Book of Ruth, also, constitutes a beautiful illustration and commentary of this ancient law; and it is mentioned in the New Testament in such terms as to imply that it was still in force in the time of Christ (Matt. xxii. 24-28).

POLYGAMY APPROVED OF GOD

I sum up the divine testimony thus: If polygamy is now a vice and a sin, like adultery or lying or stealing, it always has been and always will be a sin; and God would never have approved or commanded it: but we have seen above, that he has commanded it in two cases at least, viz., in case of the married man's illicit intercourse with an unbetrothed virgin, and in case of the married man's brother's widow; and in these cases, therefore, it cannot be a sin. In further proof of its innocence, let it be remembered that it was practised without rebuke by Abraham, when he was styled "The Friend of God;" by Jacob, when his name was changed to Israel on account of his piety and his faith; by David, when God himself "gave testimony, and said, I have found David the son of Jesse a man after my own heart;" and by many others whose names will be held in everlasting remembrance, being preserved in Holy Writ, long after those of modern pseudo-religionists, who now denounce polygamy as barbarous and sinful, shall have perished in oblivion.

CHAPTER V:

ORIGIN OF MONOGAMY

MONOGAMY IS THE DISSOLUTE DAUGHTER OF PAGANISM AND ROMANISM

I have demonstrated that monogamy is not commanded in the Bible, and that it is not the doctrine of Christianity. I shall now account for its origin, by proving that it is the joint offspring of paganism and Romanism. The social system of European monogamy is proved to be derived from the ancient Greeks and Romans (especially from the latter), by the early histories of the nations of Europe, and by an uninterrupted descent of traditional customs from them to our own times. It is one of those pagan abominations which we have inherited, which the Roman Church has sanctioned and confirmed, and from which we find it so difficult to emancipate ourselves.

IMPURITY OF ANCIENT GREEK AND ROMAN MORALS

The ancient Greek and Roman notions of marriage and of chastity were in some respects different from ours, but only as Christianity has made them different. We are ready to admit, at least in theory, what Christianity requires, that the laws of chastity are binding upon men and women equally, and that no person can innocently indulge in amorous pleasure except with his own wife or her own husband. But among them this rule of chastity applied to the female sex alone. The other sex claimed and exercised their freedom from it, without concealment or palliation, and at the same time without the loss of moral character or of public estimation. To be grossly addicted to whoredom and seduction was no dishonor: it was only when convicted of Sodomy that they were pronounced unchaste.

Marriage was not expected or intended to preserve the public purity, or to secure domestic happiness, but was rather designed to perpetuate their heroic races, to preserve their rich patrimonial estates, and to maintain the ascendency of their aristocratic families. For these purposes they guarded the chastity of their wives with vigilant jealousy and punished their adultery with severity; but the men placed themselves under no such restrictions either in law or in fact, but they habitually sought their own pleasures away from home, in the public haunts of impurity, at the house of an Aspasia, of a Leona, or of a Messalina, or at some other establishment of their numerous Cyprian and Corinthian dames; or, if they could not pay the extravagant prices demanded by these celebrated beauties, they could at least resort to their public temples, and gratify their lust among the prostitutes kept there.[231]

THEIR MARRIAGES NOT PERMANENT

The monogamy of the ancient Romans, from and after the time of two hundred years at least before the Christian era, did not require their marriages to be permanent. The principle of a life-long relationship between the husband and wife, which both Moses and Christ have insisted upon, formed no part of

---

231   "The Greeks had but little pleasure in the society of their wives. At first, the young husband only visited her by stealth: to be seen in company with her was a disgrace." — Bulwer's Hist, of Athens, book i. chap. 6.

"In the times of Corinthian opulence and prosperity, it is said that the shrine of Venus was attended by no less than one thousand female slaves dedicated to her service as courtesans. These priestesses of Venus contributed not a little to the wealth and luxury of the city." — Anthon's Classical Dict., art. "Corinthus."

Strabo, in his great work on Geography, in speaking of the temple of Venus in Corinth says, "There were more than a thousand harlots, the slaves of the temple, who, in honor of the goddess, prostituted themselves to all comers for hire, and through these the city was crowded, and became wealthy." — Book 8, p. 151.

"Gravely impressing upon his wife and daughters that to sing and dance, to cultivate the knowledge of languages, to exercise the taste and understanding, was the business of the hired courtesan, it was to the courtesan that he repaired himself for the solace of his own lighter hours." — Merivale's Hist. of the Romans, vol. ii., chap. 33, p. 32. D. Appleton & Co., 1864.

their social system. Marriage, among them, was not so much a religious ceremony inculcating and requiring solemn vows of binding obligation, as a civil compact, instituted for purposes of mere present convenience or family aggrandizement. It originated in policy rather than in love. They were not, of course, destitute of the passion of love, for they were human beings; but that passion was permitted to influence them but little in contracting their marriages. They systematically degraded their love into lust. Their monogamy required it. Whenever they loved a woman they would manage to enjoy her favors without marriage. Seduction, adultery, and whoredom were rather the rule than the exception among them; but marriage was for other and more important purposes than those of love. It was rather an alliance of interests than of affections, and an affinity of families rather than of hearts.

And as policy made marriages, so policy often unmade them. If a man could, at any time, form a new alliance which would give him more wealth or influence, he always felt himself at liberty to divorce his wife, and form that new alliance. It was not uncommon, among them, for a man to have had half a dozen different wives, in, perhaps, as many years.

CONSEQUENCES OF THEIR FREQUENT DIVORCES

Imbecility and barrenness, the usual penalties which Nature inflicts upon the violators of the marriage laws, came upon them. Their children were few and short lived, and in order to maintain their family influence, and transmit their names and their wealth to future generations, which it was their great ambition to do, they were obliged to resort to the expedient of very frequent adoptions, by taking the children of distant relations, or of those allied to them by marriage, and calling them their own. And such were the frequency of their divorces, and the intricacy of their relationships caused by their numerous adoptions, that it has been almost impossible for the best historians and biographers to give us any intelligible account of their families. Such authors as Gibbon, Anthon, Keightley, and Merivale, who are usually accurate in other respects, are found utterly at fault, when they undertake to state the relationship which the most eminent personages of Roman history bear to one another.[232]

---

232 *Contradictions and Inaccuracies of Eminent Historians*

ANTHON — In art. "Drusus," in his Classical Dictionary, Dr. Charles Anthon says that Drusus "was born three months after his mother's marriage with Augustus;" but in art. "Livia" he says, "She had already borne two sons to her first husband, viz., Tiberius and Drusus, and was six months gone in pregnancy with another child, which was the only one she ever had after her union with Augustus, and which died almost at the moment of its birth."

In art. "Julia II.," he calls her the mother of Augustus; and in art. "Augustus," he says his mother was Atia, the daughter of Julia.

In art. "Julia IV.," he calls Scribonia the first wife of Augustus; but in art. "Augustus," he calls her his third wife.

In art. "Messalina," he says she was the first wife of Claudius; and in art. "Ælia Paetina," he says Ælia was the former wife of Claudius, and that she was repudiated to make way for Messalina. And, according to Suetonius, Ælia was, in fact, the fourth, and Messalina the fifth, of his wives.

In art. "Julius Caesar," he says his first wife was divorced in consequence of the affair of Clodius; but in art. "Clodius," he says it was against Pompeia that Clodius had illicit designs, and in art. "Pompeia," he says she was Caesar's third wife, &c.

KEIGHTLEY — In his Hist, of Rom. Empire, p. 11, he says, Scribonia was the first wife of Augustus; but she was his third. On the same page he says Tiberius married Agrippina, who was the younger daughter of Agrippa: but Tiberius did not marry her, but he married Vipsania, her older sister; and his brother Drusus married Agrippina, and he was the only husband she ever had, which was a remarkable circumstance for Roman ladies in those days.

On the same page he repeats the error of Anthon mentioned above, – that Drusus was born after his mother's marriage with Augustus. Two similar errors occur on p. 13.

LIDDELL — On p. 726 of Dr. Liddell's Hist. of Rome, there are three errors of this kind within the limits of twice as many lines, viz., he calls the name of one of Augustus's wives Clodia for Claudia; he says Scribonia was his second wife, for his third; and says that Livia, at the time of her marriage to Augustus, was pregnant of her second child instead of her third. Thus it is demonstrated that very respectable modern historians are accustomed to perpetuate error by compiling and copying from each other, when they should, every one of them, go back to the original and exact authorities, and thus eliminate the truth.

Messrs. Harper & Brothers, New York, have republished the above work of Dr. Liddell, so faithfully as to give us page for page, line for line, and word for word, an exact reprint of the English edition by John Murray; reproducing not only such historical blunders as those above noticed, but even the most obvious typographical errors; e.g., on p. 250, under the bust of Scipio there is L., for Lucius Scipio Africanus, instead of P., for Publius Scipio Africanus; and on p. 453, footnote, we are referred to the end of chapter 37, for the bust of Ennius, when it is not there, but at the end of chapter 50,

THE MONOGAMY OF THE CAESARS

In order to give some just conception of Roman monogamy at that time when it first came in contact with Christianity, and when it began to impose its social system upon the other nations of Europe (for these two events are quite synchronous), I will now, as briefly as possible, give some account of the domestic life and manners of the six imperial Caesars, who governed Rome at that period. In this account I shall enumerate their many marriages, and their numerous divorces and adoptions, and state their exact relationship to each other. By this means, I hope to be able to explain the complexity of Roman affinities, which has baffled the apprehension of so many acute and learned historians, and at the same time to exhibit the original nature and true spirit of Roman monogamy. "Ex pede Herculem;" from the Caesars let us learn the Romans.

I should hesitate to pollute my pages with these delineations of Roman manners, if the nature of my treatise did not require it. But it is necessary to the plan and scope of this work that the analytical examination of the origin and early history of our present marriage system should be conducted with philosophical exactness, – an exactness that requires explicit facts, which I have spared no time nor labor to search out, and which I am not at liberty to withhold, however revolting they may be. In order that modern monogamists may clearly see the justice or the injustice of the boasted claims of their system to superior purity and virtue, it is very proper that they look to the rock whence they were hewn and to the hole of the pit whence they were digged.

The single family of the Caesars is selected as an example, not because it is the worst example which those times produced, for, on the contrary, there is abundant evidence that Sylla and Catiline and Clodius and Sejanus, and the emperors Domitian and Commodus and Caracalla, and many others of their contemporaries, exceeded the Caesars in profligacy; but the domestic history of

---

&e. Such exact faithfulness in following copy is worthy of the well-known skillfulness of the Chinese tailor, who, when about to make a new garment in European style, took home an old one for a pattern, which he succeeded in imitating with exactness, even to the patches.

the latter family is given, because it is the most authentic, and the most familiar to all classical and historical scholars. Caius Suetonius Tranquillus, commonly called Suetonius, is the principal authority for the facts cited; and his testimony is confirmed by all the other authorities of his own age, and fully allowed by those of every subsequent age. As he was born A.D. 70, very near the time of those whose lives he records; as he has maintained a reputation for candor and impartiality; as he was private secretary to the Emperor Hadrian, and had access to the secret archives of the Caesars, and often alludes to their handwriting, – no one has ever questioned either his authenticity or his credibility.

1. JULIUS CAESAR —Caius Julius Caesar, the dictator, married successively four wives, whose names were, 1. Cossutia, 2. Cornelia, 3. Pompeia, and, 4. Calpurnia. Cossutia was a wealthy heiress, and was married for her money; but she was divorced before Caesar was eighteen years of age (which was, according to Roman law, during the first year of his majority), upon the occasion of the triumph of the party of Marius, to which Caesar had attached himself; when the ambitious youthful politician and future conqueror Avas permitted to marry Cornelia, the daughter of Cornelius Cinna the consul, and the friend and colleague of Marius by which alliance Caesar brought himself at once into public notice, and began to aspire to the highest offices of state. Cornelia died young, after having given birth to Caesar's only legitimate child, a daughter named Julia; who was married to Pompey the Great, at the formation of the first Triumvirate, but who died without issue. Pompeia, Caesar's third wife, was divorced, in favor of Calpurnia, who survived him. He repudiated Pompeia in consequence of the affair of the infamous Clodius, who had introduced himself into Caesar's house, disguised in female apparel, for the purpose of assailing the virtue of Pompeia, at the festival of the Bona Dea, when, by law and by custom, it was deemed the greatest sacrilege for any male to be found upon the premises. Caesar at once divorced his wife, but brought no charge against Clodius; but he was tried for the sacrilege upon the accusation of Cicero. When Caesar was called as a witness, and was asked why he had put away his wife, he answered with the proud remark, that his wife's chastity must not only be free from corruption, but must also be above suspicion. Yet Caesar himself, who made this memorable remark, was excessively addicted to gross sensuality, and was the father of several illegitimate children. Suetonius

says that he committed adultery with many ladies of the highest quality in Rome; among whom he specifies Posthumia the wife of Servius Sulpitius, Lollia the wife of Aulus Gabinius, Tertullia the wife of Marcus Crassus, Mutia the wife of Pompey the Great, Eunoe the wife of Bogudes, Cleopatra Queen of Egypt, and Servilia the mother of Marcus Brutus, to whom he presented a pearl costing six millions of sesterces (equal to two hundred thirty-two thousand, one hundred and seven dollars); at the same time seducing her daughter Tertia. Yet in another paragraph Suetonius says the only stain upon Caesar's chastity was his having committed Sodomy with Nicoraedes, King of Bithynia; which proves what has before been said, that the Romans did not consider fornication, or even adultery, as constituting unchastity in men, but only in women; and that they expected and permitted licentiousness in the most respectable men, as a necessary part of their social system of monogamy. It is evidently with similar opinions of their social system that Dr. Liddell thus sums up the character of Caesar: — "Thus died 'the foremost man in all the world,' a man who failed in nothing that he attempted. He might, Cicero thought, have been a great orator: his 'Commentaries' remain to prove that he was a great writer. As a general, he had few superiors; as a statesman and politician, no equal. His morality in domestic life was not better or worse than commonly prevailed in those licentious days. He indulged in profligate amours freely and without scruple; but public opinion reproached him not for this. He seldom, if ever, allowed pleasure to interfere with business, and here his character forms a notable contrast to that of Sylla," &c.[233]

2. AUGUSTUS —He was the grand-nephew and adopted son of Caesar, being the grandson of his sister Julia, wife of Marcus Atius. Their daughter, named Atia (sometimes written Attia or Accia), married Cains Octavius, and became the mother of Augustus and his sister Octavia. His name, at first, was identical with that of his father, Caius Octavius; but Julius Caesar, having failed of any direct male heir, adopted him in his last will and testament, as his son; and, upon the publication of the will, he assumed his adopted father's family name: twenty years afterwards the additional name or title, Augustus, was conferred upon him by

---

233   Suet. Vit. Jul. Caesar, par. 40-50. Liddell's Hist. Rome: London, 1857; book 7. Anthon's Class. Dict., art. "Caesar, Mutia," &c.

vote of the Senate, and then his full name became Caius Julius Caesar Octavianus Augustus.

Like his great-uncle, Augustus had four wives, named, 1. Servilia; 2. Claudia; 3. Scribonia; and, 4. Livia Drusilla, whom he successively married and successively divorced, except the last, who survived him. And like Caesar he had but one child – a daughter – also named Julia, who was the daughter of his third wife Scribonia. This wife he divorced soon after he obtained supreme power, and at the same time married Livia Drusilla. She was already married to Claudius Nero: she had borne her husband two sons, and was then six months advanced in pregnancy with her third child; but Augustus demanded her on account of her beauty and accomplishments, and her husband durst not refuse the demand. She was therefore divorced from Nero, and married to Augustus. Her child was born not long afterwards, and died at birth. She was at this time twenty years of age, and highly educated. She had already travelled in foreign countries, and, to the fascinations of rare personal beauty, she added the charms of a cultivated mind.

Augustus's only child, Julia, was married three times. Her first marriage was to Marcellus, her cousin, only son of Octavia, her father's sister. Marcellus died young, much lamented, and left no issue. Augustus had, some time before, compelled Agrippa, commander-in-chief of the army, to divorce his wife Pompeia, and marry Marcella, his sister Octavia's daughter; but now, on the death of Marcellus, he commanded Agrippa to divorce his niece, Marcellus's sister, and marry his daughter, Marcellus's widow. By this second marriage, Julia had five children, three of whom were sons, the youngest of which was born after his father's death and his mother's third marriage, and was named Agrippa Posthumus: the other two sons were called Caius and Lucius. This final marriage of Julia was to Tiberius Nero, the stepson of Augustus, and was without issue: it will be alluded to again under the notice of Tiberius. Julia was one of the most dissolute women of that dissolute age. And there can be no doubt that the age and the monogamous system were even more dissolute than the women, and caused them to become so when they were not so. The chastity of the Roman matrons and virgins was prized and honored as highly by themselves, and by their husbands and fathers and brothers, as it has ever been among any people in the world; as the legends of Lucretia and of Virginia and others can testify. The ordinances of

God and of Nature in behalf of female purity were enforced among them, both by their ancient traditions and by their current laws; and all combined to cause them to preserve their chastity to the last possible extremity. But that extremity had, with many of them, been reached. The unbounded license of the other sex, permitted by public opinion to be practised with the utmost impunity; the scant and insufficient opportunities for lawful marriages, and the frequent, unjust, and arbitrary divorces from those marriages; in fine, the whole theory of monogamy, – finally drove the women to desperate recklessness and ruin. It had been Julia's happy lot to be the wife of two honorable men, both eminent for their manliness, – Marcellus and Agrippa. She had also been the happy mother of five healthful children. And now, while still young, she found herself hastily and forcibly united to a man against his will; and that man a monster and a beast. It is not strange that she fell, nor that, in her fall, she dragged down many others with her. Her exalted rank easily seduced some of the noblest men of Rome to become her paramours. "And she became at length so devoid of shame and prudence as to carouse and revel openly, at night, in the Forum, and even on the Rostra. Augustus had already had a suspicion that her mode of life was not quite correct, and when convinced of the full extent of her depravity, his anger knew no bounds. He communicated his domestic misfortune to the Senate; he banished his dissolute daughter to the Isle of Pandateria, on the coast of Campania, whither she was accompanied by her mother Scribonia. He forbade her there the use of wine and of all delicacies in food or dress, and prohibited any person to visit her without his special permission. He caused a bill of divorce to be sent her in the name of her husband Tiberius, of whose letters of intercession for her he took no heed. He constantly rejected all the solicitations of the people for her recall; and when, one time, they were extremely urgent, he openly prayed that they might have wives and daughters like her." Her confidential servant and freedwoman, Phoebe, having hanged herself when her mistress's profligacy was made known, Augustus declared that he would rather be the father of Phoebe than of Julia. This treatment of his daughter, and this remark concerning her, is another confirmation of the different regard had in those times to the unchaste conduct of women and of men; for Augustus himself was a seducer and an adulterer, and was as profligate as his uncle Julius. Suetonius declares, that he constantly employed men to pimp for him, and that they took such freedom in selecting the most beautiful women for his embraces, that they compelled "both matrons and ripe virgins to strip for a complete examination of their persons." He also says, upon the authority of Marc Antony, that at an entertainment at his house, "he once took the wife of a man of consular rank from the table, in the presence of her husband, into his bedchamber, and that he brought her again to the entertainment with her ears very red and her hair in great disorder," plainly implying that every one could see that he had ravished her.

But it is the judgment of that distinguished scholar and historian, Dr. Liddell, that in these "and other less pardonable immoralities there was nothing to shock the feelings of Romans;" and Keightley thus sums up his character. "In his public character, as sovereign of the Roman empire, few princes will be found more deserving of praise than Augustus. He cannot be justly charged with a single cruel, or even harsh action, in the course of a period of forty-four years. On the contrary, he seems in every act to have had the welfare of the people at heart. In return, never was prince more entirely beloved by all orders of his subjects; and the title 'Father of his Country,' so spontaneously bestowed upon him, is but one among many proofs of the sincerity of their affection." "He was surrounded by no pomp; no guards attended him; no officers of the household were to be seen in his modest dwelling; he lived on terms of familiarity with his friends; he appeared like any other citizen, as a witness in courts of justice, and in the senate gave his vote as an ordinary member. He was plain and simple in his mode of living, using only the most ordinary food, and wearing no clothes but what were woven and made by his wife, sister, and daughter. In all his domestic relations he was kind and affectionate; he was a mild and indulgent master, and an attached and constant friend."[234]

3. TIBERIUS —Tiberius was the son of Claudius Nero and Livia Drusilla. He was not at all related by blood to the Julian family, but belonged by birth to the ancient Claudian gens; being allied to the former family only by marriage and adoption. His mother married Augustus when he was five years of age; he himself married Julia, Augustus's only daughter, when he was thirty; and Augustus adopted him as his son when he was forty-five: so that he was at once the step-son,

---

234   Suet. Vit Ang. par. 60-69; Liddell's Hist. of Rome, book 7; Keightly, chaps. 1, 2.

the son-in-law, and the adopted son of Augustus. His name, at first, was Tiberius Claudius Drusus Nero; to which, after his adoption by Augustas, he added simply Caesar. Augustus, with his characteristic prudence, as soon as he perceived that direct heirs in the male line were likely to fail him, began to make provision for the perpetuation of his name and fortune, as well as for the preservation of the peace of the empire, by making sons by adoption. He first adopted his two oldest grandsons, Cains and Lucius Agrippa, in their early childhood; but they both died during the lifetime of Augustus, and left no issue, – Lucius at the age of nineteen years; and two years afterwards, Cains, at the age of twenty-four.[235] Drusus Nero, the younger brother of Tiberius, and the favorite step-son of Augustus, had also died before them; but he had left two sons, Germanicus and Claudius. These with Tiberius, and his only son Drusus, by his first wife Vipsania, and Agrippa Posthumus, the only remaining son of Julia, were all the males allied to Augustus. Upon the death of Caius, therefore, A.D. 6, Augustus adopted both Agrippa Posthumus and Tiberius, and caused Tiberius at the same time to adopt Germanicus: so that all the males of the family then became Caesars, except Claudius Nero; but he was considered foolish, and was not included. Tiberius, as has been observed, was, at this time, forty-five years of age; and each of the three young men, Agrippa, Germanicus, and Drusus, was about nineteen.

Tiberius was married twice; first to Vipsania, eldest daughter of Agrippa, and after divorcing her, as usual, he married Julia, Agrippa's widow. It is but justice to Tiberius, to say that both the divorce and the marriage were hateful to him, and were consummated only upon the order of Augustus. He had lived happily with Vipsania, who was the mother of his only son, and who was then pregnant with her second child, while Julia was also pregnant with her fifth child by Agrippa.

Upon the death of Augustus, Tiberius commanded his step-brother Agrippa Posthumus to be put to death, and assumed sole command of the empire. His first order was but a sample of his government for he soon became one of the most odious tyrants that ever cursed the world. His vices were of the most

---

235   Caius married Livilla, sister to Germanicus, and grandniece to Augustus, but had no offspring; his widow afterwards married Drusus, son of Tiberius, by whom she had two children, Tiberius and Julia.

infamous character, and comprised all that are alluded to in the first chapter of Paul's Epistle to the Romans, and for which the ancient city of Sodom was destroyed by fire. In order to give loose rein to his worse than beastly propensities, he retired from Rome to that lovely sequestered island in the Bay of Naples, which was then called Capreae, and which in modern Italian is now named Capri. "But," says Keightley, "this delicious retreat was speedily converted by the aged prince into a den of infamy, such as has never, perhaps, found its equal and it almost chills the blood to read the details of the horrid practices in which he indulged amid the rocks of Capreae." Like all the other Caesars, Tiberius left no son. His son Drusus was married, and had a son and a daughter; but he was poisoned by his own wife Livilla, and died during his father's lifetime. The grandson named Tiberius, and the grand-daughter named Julia, both survived him. His adopted son Germanicus, after achieving an excellent reputation as a man and a military commander, had also died, about five years after the accession of Tiberius, at the age of thirty-four years, attributing his death to slow poison secretly administered by the command of his adopted father. Germanicus left nine children; but all the sons were destroyed before the death of Tiberius, except one, named Caius, but commonly called Caligula. Tiberius therefore left two male heirs only, – Caius Caligula, his grandson by adoption, and Tiberius, his grandson by birth.[236]

4. CALIGULA —Tiberius, by his last will, had appointed his two grandsons his joint and equal heirs; but Germanicus, the father of Caligula, had always been greatly beloved by the people, while Tiberius had been hated. The will was therefore unanimously set aside, and the sole power conferred upon Caligula. Thus was the line of the Caesars still continued by adoption. Caligula was born A.D. 12, and became emperor at twenty-five years of age, A.D. 37. He was married four times. His wives' names were, 1. Junia Claudilla; 2. Livia Orestilla; 3. Lollia and, 4. Milonia Caesonia. The first died, the next two were divorced, the last survived him. Soon after the death of Junia, which was some time before he attained the supreme power, he took Ennia, the wife of Macro, as his favorite mistress, promising to procure a divorce from her husband, and to marry her himself when he should attain the empire; and Macro appears to

---

236   Suet.; Keightley; Anthon

have acquiesced in this arrangement, selling his wife's virtue and the honor of his house for such rewards and emoluments as Caligula was pleased to accord to him. But in the second year of his administration, instead of fulfilling his engagements to Ennia and her husband, he neglected and disgraced them; so that they both committed suicide.

Caligula then took his own sister Drusilla, and lived in incest with her, having forced her husband, Lucius Cassius, to divorce her for that purpose but, in order to cover the affair, he caused her to be married to one of his attendants, Marcus Lepidus, his cousin, with whom he was at the same time practising the still more horrid and unnatural crime of Sodomy. Upon the death of this sister, which occurred during the same year, he mourned for her with the most extravagant grief, and caused her henceforth to be worshipped as a goddess; building a temple and consecrating priests in her honor. His own solemn oath ever after was, "By the divinity of Drusilla."

He next married Livia Orestilla; and in this strange and cruel manner. He had been invited to the wedding-feast of Caius Piso, a man belonging to one of the noblest families of Rome, whose bride was this same Livia. Caligula accepted the invitation; the marriage ceremony took place, and the feast was at its height, when, struck with the beauty of the bride, he resolved to appropriate her to himself, and saying to Piso, "Do not touch my wife," he took her home with him. The next day he caused proclamation to be made for the information of the Roman public, that he had purveyed himself a wife after the manner of Augustus. It is not strange that under such circumstances he did not find her an agreeable consort, for her affections had been given to Piso, and with him only could she be happy. He therefore divorced her again, within three days of her marriage, but would not permit her to have her former husband.

The occasion of his marrying his next wife, Lollia Paullina, was equally strange, but quite different. He heard someone extol the beauty of her grandmother, and was inflamed with passion to enjoy hers. She was already married to Memmius Regulus, and was then away from Rome, in a foreign province, with her husband; but Caligula sent orders to Regulus to divorce his wife, ordered her home and married her. He lived with her about a year, when he divorced her for her barrenness; and then married his last wife, Caesonia, with whom he had already been having illicit intercourse for many months, and who was now far advanced in pregnancy. She was a woman of infamous character, and had had three illegitimate children before; but he married her, and she was very soon delivered of a daughter, which was Caligula's only child.

During most of this time, since the death of Drusilla, he was living in incest with both his other sisters, Agrippina and Livilla, while at the same time he would prostitute them to his male favorites, the ministers of his more heathenish lusts. Suetonius says, that, in addition to these incests and adulteries already specified, he debauched nearly every lady of rank in Rome; whom he was accustomed to invite, along with their husbands, to a feast: he would then examine them, as they passed his couch one after another, as one would examine female slaves when about to purchase; and after supper he would retire to his bedchamber, and then send for any lady present that he liked best.

During his administration public prostitutes paid twelve and a half percent of their fees into the imperial treasury; and in order to increase this branch of the revenue he opened a brothel in his own palace, filled it with respectable (?) women, and sent out criers into the forum to advertise it, and invite the people to resort to it.

Caligula was slain by the officers of his own guard, in the twenty-ninth year of his age, after governing the Roman world less than four years. During the first year of his administration he had first adopted and then murdered the younger Tiberius Caesar, then about seventeen years of age, who left no issue; and a few hours after his own death his wife Caesonia was slain, and also their infant daughter, who had its little brains dashed out against a wall: so the last of the Caesars seemed to have perished. But there was one old man left, who, if he was not a Caesar, was certainly related to all the Caesars, and it was determined to make him a Caesar, and raise him to the supreme power. This old man was Claudius Nero.

5. CLAUDIUS —He was the uncle of Caligula, and the nephew of Tiberius. His name at first had been Tiberius Claudius Drusus Nero, to which he now added that of Caesar. He was married six times. His wives' names were, 1. Aemilia Lepida; 2. Livia Medullina Camilla; 3. Plautia Urgullinilla 4. Aelia Paetina; 5. Valeria Messalina; and 6. Agrippina. Of these, the first, third, and fourth were

divorced, the second died, the fifth was executed, and the last survived him. Aelia Paetina, the fourth, was divorced soon after Claudius obtained the empire, in order to make way for Messalina, whose principal recommendation was that she had already become pregnant by him. They were accordingly married: the child was born and was a boy, whom they named Britannicus. She afterwards bore him a daughter called Octavia. Messalina's lust and cruelty were so unbounded, that her name has become the synonym of everything most vile and detestable in the female character. She has been called the Roman Jezebel; but the comparison is an injustice to the Samaritan queen. She was as much more wicked than Jezebel as Roman monogamy is more impure than Jewish polygamy. Her husband's chief officers became her adulterers, and were allied with her in all her abominations. She cast an eye of lust on the principal men in Rome, and whom she could not seduce to gratify her vile propensities she would contrive to destroy. She was so excessive in her sensuality, that she often required the services of the strongest and most vigorous men to satisfy her lusts; and often for that reason chose gladiators and slaves: but such persons would not always venture to incur the risk of discovery, and then she would make her stupid husband the unwitting broker of her adulterous pleasures. As an example of this mode of procedure, in such cases, it is recorded that "when Mnester, a celebrated dancer, refused to yield to her solicitations or her threats, she procured a written order from Claudius, commanding him to do whatever she should require. Mnester then complied. The same was the case with many others, who believed they were obeying the orders of the prince when they were yielding to the libidinous desires of his wife."

But she was not content with being infamous herself, she determined to make others so; compelling many respectable married women to prostitute themselves, even in the palace, and in the presence of their husbands, who were powerless to prevent it, for she brutally destroyed those who would not acquiesce in their wives' dishonor. Meantime her own excesses were unknown by Claudius; for she caused some one of her maids to occupy her place in his bed, and purchased by rewards, or anticipated by murder, those who could give him information. At length her enormities were discovered and brought to light in this manner, – a manner so strange and unnatural, that the grave historian Tacitus expressed his doubts whether posterity could be made to believe that any woman could be so wicked. Messalina had set her heart upon Caius Silius, the consul elect, who was esteemed the handsomest man in Rome. In order to obtain sole possession of him she drove his wife Junia out of his house; and Silius, knowing that to refuse her would be his destruction, while by compliance he might possibly escape, yielded to his fate. But the infatuated adulteress became so reckless that she disdained concealment and came openly to visit him, heaping wealth and honors upon him, and transferring the slaves and the treasures of the prince to his house. Silius then saw that he was so deep in guilt that either he or Claudius must perish, and proposed to Messalina to murder her husband and seize the supreme power. She hesitated; not from regard to her husband, but from the fear that when Silius should be invested with the empire he would cast her off. She therefore proposed, as an amendment to his plan, that they should be married first, and then murder the prince and seize the empire afterwards. This plan was agreed to; and while Claudius was absent from the city to perform a sacrifice at Ostia, when he was building the new harbor there, they were publicly married, in due form, and with much ceremony. But their own attendants were shocked. They informed the prince; and the whole plot was discovered and the guilty parties put to death.

Claudius then took for his sixth and last wife his brother's daughter Agrippina; and as such a union was regarded as incestuous by the laws and customs of the Romans, Claudius first repaired to the senate-house, and caused a new law to be passed legalizing marriages between uncles and nieces, and then formally espoused her. Agrippina, the new imperial consort, was sister to the late emperor Caligula; and besides having lived in incest with him, she had been married twice before. By her first husband, Cneius Domitius Ahenobarbus, she had had a son, named Lucius, who was nine years of age at the time of her marriage with Claudius, and three years older than his only son Britannicus. To promote the interests of her own son Lucius, and to destroy Britannicus, was now the ruling passion of Agrippina; to gratify which she paused at nothing. Yet she was not, like Messalina, naturally inclined to licentiousness; but in order to win the influence and assistance of powerful men for promoting her ambitious designs in behalf of her son, she stooped so low as to prostitute herself to their lusts, when they could not be purchased by any other means at her command. At first she managed to have Octavia, the sister of Britannicus, divorced from Silanus, to whom she had been betrothed, and married to her son Lucius, and, in a year or two afterwards, to have Lucius adopted by Claudius as his son. Three years afterwards she procured poison from the notorious Locusta, and put her husband, the Emperor Claudius, to death, in the sixty-fourth year of his age after he had governed Rome a little less than fourteen years.[237]

6. NERO —Agrippina carefully concealed the death of Claudius until secure measures had been taken for setting aside Britannicus, and for the succession of her son; when the death was announced and the new emperor proclaimed. Nero was successively the grand-nephew, the step-son, the son in-law, and the adopted son of Claudius; and, by adoption, the great-grandson of Tiberius; being son of Agrippina, daughter of Germanicus, adopted son of Tiberius. He was also, by birth, the grandnephew of Augustus, by the collateral female line; his father, Domitius Ahenobarbus, being son of Antonia Major, eldest daughter of Octavia, sister of Augustus. His name, at first, was Lucius Domitius Ahenobarbus; but upon his adoption by Claudius, into the Julian family, he took the name of Nero Claudius Caesar.

He was married seven times. The names of his consorts were, 1. Octavia; 2. Poppaea Sabina; 3. Octavia again; 4. Poppaea again; 5. Statilia Messalina; 6. Sporus; and, 7. Doryphorus. It will readily be seen, from this list, that his marriages and divorces were more numerous than his brides, and that the last two names are those of males.

Nero had no affection for his first wife, the chaste and modest Octavia, whom he had married from policy, and not for love: and his mother, the ambitious Agrippina, who loved power so much, was pleased with this indifference; for she hoped to maintain an undivided influence over him, and through him to rule the world. But in the second year of his administration he conceived a violent passion for an Asiatic freedwoman named Acte; a passion which his preceptor, the celebrated philosopher Seneca, and his other councillors of state encouraged, permitting him to take her as his acknowledged mistress, without rebuke, hoping that this attachment would keep him from a life of promiscuous licentiousness and from debauching women of rank. But Agrippina was furious; not because

---

237   Suet. Vit. Claud.; Tacitus Ann.; Keight.; Anthon.

Acte was a low-bred woman (though this was the excuse for her opposition), but she felt that her own power would be diminished by her: and she threatened that if he did not give her up, she would herself abandon him, and would set up Britannicus; and, as the daughter of the beloved Germanicus, would appeal to the army against her son, in Britannicus' behalf. This was a powerful argument, and Nero knew that his mother was capable of anything to maintain her power; but he resolved, that, instead of giving up his mistress, he would murder his innocent brother. He procured poison from Locusta and gave it him, but it proved too weak; he then sent for Locusta again, and reproached her and beat her, and bade her prepare a stronger dose. She obeyed him; and, having proved the potency of the venom upon a kid and a pig, he had it given to Britannicus, in some cold water, at dinner. Its effect was instantaneous, and the poor boy dropped down dead. Nero carelessly remarked to the company that he had been subject to fits from infancy, and would soon recover. Agrippina and Octavia were struck with terror, and said nothing; the latter, young as she was, having learned to suppress her feelings, and the former perceiving that her son was fast becoming her superior both in cruelty and in craft.

Nero next became enamored of Poppaea Sabina, a lady of great beauty and of noble birth, who had been divorced from her first husband, Crispinus, and was then married to her second, Marcus Otho; but Otho was sent out as governor of the distant province of Portugal, and Nero gave himself up to the enjoyment of his adulterous passion. Then Agrippina became more furious than ever, for she saw, that if he should divorce Octavia, and marry Poppaea, her own influence would be gone forever. But she set at work in a different manner than before; for such was her insane love of power, that, in order to retain her influence over her son, she began herself to pander to his vices, diverting and distracting his mind with a succession of beautiful ladies, offering her purse, and the use of her own apartments for his private assignations, and even attempting to seduce him to unnatural incest with herself; and nothing but the fear of the army and of the people prevented them from the consummation of that abominable crime. Still the influence of Poppaea increased; and so did Agrippina's hatred and jealousy of her, until at length Nero resolved upon the crime of matricide, which he effected in the most barbarous manner. He first attempted to drown her, in a manner that might appear accidental, by sending her to sea in an unseaworthy vessel laden with lead; the deck of which was to give way at the proper time, and the vessel itself to fall in pieces. She went on board, and the deck fell, with its freight of lead, as was expected; but she was saved by the devotion of her attendants. He then sent assassins to shed her blood. When they entered her apartment, and one of them drew his sword, she exposed her womb, and cried out, "Strike here:" he obeyed, and thus she perished. But it was only after the lapse of three years more, that he divorced the virtuous Octavia, by whose alliance he had obtained the empire, and who was greatly beloved by the people. He effected her divorce, however, and married Poppaea; but the murmurs of the people were so alarming, that, in a short time, he divorced Poppaea, and married Octavia the second time. But his affections were still unchanged, and he at length induced Anicetus, the assassin that had slain his mother, to make oath that Octavia had committed adultery with him; and, although nobody believed the wretch, this served as a pretext for divorcing her again. She was then banished to the usual place, the Island of Pandataria, where she was soon afterwards put to death, at twenty-one years of age, and her head sent as a present to Poppaea; to whom Nero was then married the second time. Soon after this marriage, to his great joy, she bore him a daughter, his first and only child, which lived, however, but a few months.

It was the next year after the birth of this infant, that Rome was burnt [A.D. 65]. The loss of lives, as well as of property, was very great. The streets of the city were narrow and crooked, and the flames spread so rapidly, that escape was difficult. The fire raged six days. Five-sevenths of the city was laid waste. Nero has often been charged with having caused the fires himself; but the charge has never been proved. He was strongly suspected at the time, and, in order to divert suspicion from himself, he laid the blame upon the innocent Christians. They had become already numerous in the city, and were generally hated and despised. They were put to death, upon this suspicion; with torture and insult; some torn to pieces by dogs, after being sewed up in the skins of wild animals, some crucified, and some wrapped in pitch and set on fire, to serve for lamps in the night. Two years after the great fire, Poppaea came to her death in as brutal a manner as mother, sister, and brother had done before. She was killed by Nero, in a fit of anger, by a violent kick when in an advanced state of pregnancy.

He then celebrated his fifth marriage, with a lady named Messalina; with whom it happened to be her fifth marriage also. Her last husband was Atticus Vestinus, whom Nero put to death in order to obtain possession of his wife. But he soon divorced her, yet that did not break her heart, for she outlived him, and preserved her beauty to captivate the fancy of another emperor, in future years.

Nero was married the sixth time to a boy. His name was Sporus. Nero fancied that his beauty resembled that of his slain Poppaea, whose death he repented and bewailed. He caused Sporus to be made a eunuch, and exhausted the powers of art in trying to make him a woman. He then espoused him, with the most solemn forms of marriage; and it was cleverly remarked by the people, that it was a great pity that his father Domitius had not had such a wife.

His seventh and last marriage was to Doryphorus, his own freedman; but in this case Nero himself was the bride, and his manumitted slave the groom. Nero was a musician and a comedian, and was accustomed to spend a great part of his time in rehearsal and in public performance, as an actor. He chose the crowded theatre as the place in which to celebrate this marriage. He first covered himself with the skin of a wild beast, and in that dress, before thousands of assembled men and women, committed rapes upon persons of both sexes, who were tied to stakes for that purpose. Having thus demonstrated his manhood, he appeared as the bride in his marriage to Doryphorus, to whom he was married in the same solemn form that Sporus had been married to him; finishing the representation by consummating the marriage in the embraces of Doryphorus, himself imitating the cries and shrieks of young virgins when they are ravished.

Nero died by his own hand, A.D. 68, in the thirty-first year of his age, and the fourteenth of his imperial power. He left no child, either by birth or by adoption. He was the last of the Caesars. That name was henceforth only an honorary title. Can any one regret the extinction of, the dissolute and degenerate race? Is it not a happy provision in the laws of God, that "monsters cannot propagate"?[238]

Such was monogamy at the commencement of the Christian era; for it was during the reign of Augustus that Christ was born, and during that of Nero

---

238   Sueton. Vit. Neronis, par. 20-29.; Tac. Ann.; Keight. Hist. Rom. Emp.

that Paul was beheaded. Such was the social system imposed by Rome upon the nations of Europe. This is no fancy sketch, nor have the facts here cited been herein exaggerated. My authorities are accessible to every scholar, and I invite criticism and investigation. The question now arises. How was Roman monogamy affected by its contact with Christianity? And this question I shall proceed to discuss in another chapter.

CHAPTER VI:

HOW WAS ROMAN MONOGAMY AFFECTED BY THE INTRODUCTION OF CHRISTIANITY?

The introduction of Christianity effected no violent revolutions of any kind in the social relations of men and women, except by purifying these relations, and enforcing the duties dependent upon them. Christianity did not dictate any particular form of government, or any code of laws, but enjoined obedience to the existing laws, when they were not inconsistent with the laws of the gospel. The first Christians, while they were themselves scarcely tolerated, were not inclined to attempt a social revolution by opposing the established system of monogamy; but they attempted to oppose only its vices, and to remove them. They insisted, from the first, upon purity and chastity in men and women equally. They denounced prostitution, adultery, and frequent and capricious divorces, and did what they could to eradicate their practice. But before they attained any degree of civil or religious freedom, or were in any situation to introduce the purer system of polygamy, they had themselves become thoroughly Romanized; and the errors of Gnosticism, Platonism, and Montanism had then prevailed so extensively as to impel them, at last, to attempt a social reformation in a direction quite contrary to polygamy, by discouraging marriage, and by introducing asceticism, monasticism, and celibacy.

GNOSTICISM IN THE FIRST CENTURY

Christianity was not fully tolerated in Europe till the time of the Emperor Constantine the Great, in the former part of the fourth century and was not established by law as the religion of Rome, till the reign of Theodosius, in the very last part of that century; while Gnosticism and its cognate errors began to be disseminated even in the first century, in apostolic times: they prevailed extensively in the second century, and had permanently corrupted the church in the third and fourth. While the different Gnostic writers and teachers differed greatly from one another on many points of belief, they were generally agreed in their fundamental doctrines, which sprung from the ancient Persian or Magian system of religion, and which taught the existence of two eternal beings, – Ormuzd, or God, the author of good, and the creator of light, which is his emblem; and Ahriman, or the Devil, the author of evil, and the creator of darkness, his emblem. They believed that the world consisted of spirit and of matter, both being eternal; the latter, essentially evil, formed or moulded by the Devil from the eternal substance of chaos, and the former, essentially good, proceeding out of God, and still forming a part of God: hence, that the body is vile, wicked, and dark; while the soul is pure, holy, and light. The body, therefore, with its appetites and passions, should be despised and subdued; while the soul, with its superior attributes, should be cherished and obeyed. The principal Gnostic teachers of the first century were Simon Magus, Menander, and Cerinthus. They all studied at Alexandria, and all became Christians. Cerinthus taught that the man Jesus was born of Joseph and Mary in the natural way that the εἰων, Christ, descended on him at his baptism, in the form of a dove; and, previous to the crucifixion, that the εἰων returned to God, leaving the man to suffer on the cross.

GNOSTICISM AND PLATONISM OF THE SECOND CENTURY

In the second century, the Gnostic Christians became much more numerous and influential. Among the writers and teachers whom historians particularly mention were Saturninus, Basilides, Carpocrates, Valentine, Bardesaues, Tatian, Marcion, Montanus, Tertullian, and Origen. Saturninus (A.D. 115) taught that Satan, the ruler of matter, was coeval with the Deity; that the world was created by seven angels, without the knowledge of the Deity, who, however, was not displeased when he saw it, and breathed into man a rational soul. Satan, enraged at the creation of the world and the virtue of its inhabitants, formed another race of men out of matter, with malignant souls like his own;

and hence arose the great moral difference to be observed among men. The moral discipline of Saturninus was ascetic and severe: he discouraged marriage, declaring it to be the doctrine of the Devil;[239] he enjoined abstinence from wine and flesh, and taught to keep under the body, as being formed from matter, which is in its essence evil and corrupt. Bardesanes wrote about A.D. 170, in the time of the Emperor Marcus Aurelius. "His moral system was ascetic in the extreme; he enjoined his disciples to renounce wedlock, abstain from animal food, and live in solitude on the slightest and most meagre diet, and even to use water instead of wine in the Lord's Supper."[240] Montanus (A.D. 175) insisted upon more frequent and more rigorous fasts than had yet prevailed in the church, for they had hitherto fasted only during the passion-week; he forbade second marriages; taught the absolute and irrevocable excommunication of adulterers, murderers, and idolaters; required all chaste women to wear veils; and forbade all kinds of costly attire and ornaments of the person. His most distinguished disciple was Tertullian, bishop of Carthage, a very learned and voluminous writer, whose works have been held in the greatest estimation in every age. Origen, a still more learned and more voluminous writer, and a very eloquent preacher, embraced the Gnostic errors when a young man, and carried his principles of subduing the passions of the body to such an extent, that he made a eunuch of himself: but in after-life, when he had spent many years in studying, translating, and expounding the Holy Scriptures, and understood them better, he regretted the rash act of his youth, and greatly modified his Gnostic sentiments; so much so, that many have accused him of teaching different views of the same subject, and of contradicting himself.

The first Platonic philosopher who joined the Christians was Justin Martyr, who was beheaded at Rome A.D. 155; followed by Clement of Alexandria, A.D. 192, who had a school in that city called the Catechetic School, which attempted to harmonize the philosophy of Plato with the materialism of the Gnostics by means of the common medium of Christianity. This scheme was called the New Platonism; and a long contest prevailed between the followers of this system and

239   Mosheim, Ecc. Hist., vol. 1, p. 246

240   Keightley's Hist. Rom. Emp., part 2, chap. 7

the Advocates for gospel simplicity. But the victory appeared to be on the side of the Platonists, which assured the lasting corruption of Christianity; for learned Christians now began to maintain that the Scriptures have a double meaning; one literal and plain, and the other latent and symbolic: the literal or exoteric sense to be taught to the people, and the latent or esoteric sense to be communicated only to the initiated and the faithful. A similar distinction in morals followed. There was one rule for the multitude, and another for the aspirants to higher sanctity. These were to seek retirement and to mortify the flesh, avoiding marriage and all indulgence of the senses. Hence originated the austerities of religious hermits; hence the celibacy of priests, monks, and nuns.

RELATION OF MONOGAMY TO CHRISTIANITY IN THE THIRD AND FOURTH CENTURIES

At the council of Caesarea, A.D. 314, it was decided and decreed, in the first canon, that, if a priest should marry after his ordination, he must be deposed from office. The seventh canon forbids a priest to be present at the marriage of a bigamist.

At the council of Ancyra, in the same year, it was ordered, in the tenth canon, that those deacons who expressed their intention to marry at the time of their ordination might innocently do so; but, if they should marry without having expressed such intention, they must be deposed from office.

At the first council of Carthage, A.D. 348, by the second canon, it was ordered that all Christians who had violated their vows of virginity by subsequent marriage should be excommunicated; and, if they were priests, they should be deposed from office. Siricius, Bishop of Rome, in 385 ordered that every priest and every deacon within his diocese who should marry a second wife, or a widow, should be deposed from office.

While these Gnostic and Platonic sentiments were at work corrupting the church within, the state of social life without the pale of Christianity was much the same as it has been described under the first six Caesars; or, if the testimony of all the contemporary writers can be believed, it was becoming more and more corrupt. The Christians formed but a small minority of the whole population, and they were generally hated, and often persecuted. It is scarcely possible for us to conceive of any greater depravity than that of the age of Caligula and Nero; and we do not wonder to learn that in the succeeding century the once mighty Roman empire was beginning to totter to its fall. But before it fell it was destined to be upheld a while by the fortitude of Christian patriots; and, in turn, the purity of Christianity was to become more and more sullied by its long contact with Roman depravity, and its intimate complicity with Roman monogamy.

CONSTANTINE AND THEODOSIUS

In the former part of the fourth century, the two joint emperors were Constantino and Licinius. They agreed, at first, to tolerate Christianity; but Licinius violated his agreement, and commenced a persecution. Then Constantine, who had himself been a pagan hitherto, resolved to favor the Christians more than he had done already, and thus attach to himself the most industrious and peaceable citizens, and the most brave and loyal soldiers of the empire. In the year A.D. 324 the cross appeared for the first time upon his banners; his rival was defeated, and he became sole emperor. Then Constantine issued circular letters, announcing his conversion to Christianity, and inviting the people to follow his example. This call of the powerful monarch was not unheeded. The Christian faith spread rapidly: ministers of religion thronged the royal court, and offices of honor and profit were conferred upon Christians. Yet Constantine himself, through all his subsequent life, was only a catechumen or inquirer, and was not baptized, and received into full membership in the church, until he was near his end. And, in the meantime, he left the ancient system of the Roman state undisturbed; and paganism, with its corrupt monogamy, was still the law of the land. At length Theodosius, his grandson, required the Senate, a majority of whom had hitherto remained pagans, to choose between the two religions; and they were finally induced to vote in accordance with his wishes, in favor of Christianity. He soon (A.D. 392) published a severe edict against paganism; and "then pretended conversions became numerous, the temples were deserted, and the churches filled with worshippers, and the religion under which Rome flourished for twelve centuries ceased forever."[241]

ASCETICISM AND MONASTICISM

And then at length, when Christianity became paramount in the State, a permanent and decided social reform might have been possible, had they tolerated polygamy, as the first Christians had done in Judaea and other Asiatic countries; for they would thus have made it possible for all to be married that wished to marry, and thus have guarded themselves from the terrible licentiousness of the pagans, by the influences of which they were surrounded on every hand. But, on the contrary, impelled by the prevailing influences of Gnosticism, they not only retained their former monogamy, but they made it more strict and ascetic than before, and attempted an impossible reform by suppressing the amorous propensities, and vainly endeavoring to eradicate them. The bishops and doctors of the church had already done what they could to discourage marriage, and bring it into disrepute, especially with the ministers of religion; but now they forbade it to them altogether.

At the council of Toledo, in A.D. 400, it was ordered, by canon seventeenth, that every Christian that had both a wife and a concubine should be excommunicated; but he should not be excommunicated who had only a concubine without a wife.

At the fourth council of Carthage, A.D. 401, it was ordered, by canon seventieth, that all bishops, priests, and deacons, who had wives, must repudiate them, and live in celibacy, under penalty of deposition from office.

Pope Innocent I., about A.D. 412, in his official letter to the two bishops of Abruzzo, orders them to depose those priests who had been guilty of the crime of having children since their ordination.

Thus the seeds of Gnostic error, that had been sown in the church during the former periods of its history, now sprang up anew, and bore a plentiful harvest. "Nothing," says Keightley, "is more characteristic of the corruption which Christianity had undergone than the high honor in which the various classes

---

241   Keightley Rom. Emp., part 3, chap. 6

of ascetics were held. These useless or pernicious beings now actually swarmed throughout the Eastern empire, and were gradually spreading themselves into the West. We have shown how asceticism has been derived from the sultry regions of Asia, and how it originates in the Gnostic principles. It had long been insinuating itself into the church; but, after the establishment of Christianity, it burst forth like a torrent." "The hope of acquiring heaven by virginity and mortification was not confined to the male sex: woman, with the enthusiasm and the devotional tendency peculiar to her, rushed eagerly towards the crown of glory. Nunneries became numerous, and were thronged with inmates. Nature, however, not unfrequently asserted her rights; and the complaints and admonitions of the most celebrated fathers assure us that the unnatural state of vowed celibacy was productive of the same evils and scandals in ancient as in modern times."[242]

MEDIEVAL SUPERSTITION AND IMMORALITY

"And then," says the learned ecclesiastical historian, Mosheim, "the number of immoral and unworthy Christians began so to increase, that the examples of real piety and virtue became extremely rare. When the terrors of persecution were totally dispelled; when the church, secured from the efforts of its enemies, enjoyed the sweets of prosperity and peace; when the major part of its bishops exhibited to their flocks the contagious examples of arrogance, luxury, effeminacy, animosity, and strife, with other vices too numerous to mention; when multitudes were drawn into the profession of Christianity, not by the power of conviction and argument, but by the prospect of gain or by the fear of punishment, – then it was indeed no wonder that the church was contaminated with shoals of profligate Christians, and that the virtuous few were, in a manner, oppressed and overwhelmed by the superior numbers of the wicked and licentious." "Nor did the evil end here; for those vain fictions, which an attachment to the Platonic philosophy and to popular opinions had engaged the greatest part of the Christian doctors to adopt before the time of Constantine, were now confirmed, enlarged, and embellished in various ways. Hence arose the extravagant veneration for

242   Hist. Rom. Emp., chap. 6

departed saints, the celibacy of priests, the worship of images and relics, which, in process of time, almost totally destroyed the Christian religion, or at least eclipsed its lustre, and corrupted its essence." "A preposterous desire of imitating the pagan rites, and of blending them with the Christian worship, and that idle propensity which the generality of mankind have towards a gaudy and ostentatious religion, all combined to establish the reign of superstition on the ruins of Christianity. Accordingly, frequent pilgrimages were undertaken to Palestine and to the tombs of the martyrs, as if there alone the sacred principles of virtue and the certain hope of salvation were to be acquired. The public processions and supplications, by which the pagans endeavored to appease their gods, were now adopted into the Christian worship, and celebrated with great pomp and magnificence. The virtues that had formerly been ascribed to the heathen temples, to their lustrations, to the statues of their gods and heroes, were now attributed to the Christian churches, to water consecrated by certain forms of prayer, to the images of holy men; and the worship of the martyrs was modelled according to the religious services that were paid to the gods before the coming of Christ."[243]

Similar testimonies could easily be cited from Gibbon's "Decline and Fall of the Roman Empire," from D'Aubigne's "History of the Reformation," from the ancient works of Eusebius, and the modern ones of Neander, and from hundreds of others; but I will not weary my readers with them. Thus it appears from the testimonies of all the historians, ecclesiastical and civil, sacred and profane, that the doctrines and practices which distinguish the Roman-Catholic Church today were most of them derived from a very early age, anterior to the civil acknowledgment and legal establishment of Christianity. Keightley says, "The Church of Rome is, in fact, very unjustly treated when she is charged with being the author of the tenets and practices which were transmitted to her from the fourth century. Her guilt or error was not that of invention, but of retention."

---

243   Mosheim, Ecc. Hist. Cent. 4, part 2, chap. 3

IMMUTABILITY OF THE ROMAN CHURCH

Her boasted claim of immutability is well sustained, as far back, certainly, as the commencement of the fifth century. The Western empire survived till the close of that century; and as the power of the emperors continued to decline, that of the bishops of Rome, who were afterwards called popes, continued to increase, till at length they attained monarchical as well as hierarchical power, and governed the religious and the social affairs of the European world. And as the dogmas of the Roman Church are now maintaining monogamy with many of its attendant vices, and are now prohibiting marriage to its clergy, and discouraging it in all its more earnest religious devotees, of both sexes, so they always have done. And we have the testimonies of all modern historians, all modern travellers, and of modern statistics, that the vices of old Rome that then attended its social system of monogamy are still the vices of modern Rome, and of all the countries under the sway of the Roman Church; the most recent statistics of the Catholic countries of Europe giving the number of illegitimate children born there each year, as greater than the number of those of legitimate birth. And it is not only on the corrupt soil of old Europe that the licentiousness of ancient Roman monogamy still prevails, but also in the Catholic countries of new America. In proof of this I will cite only one testimony, where thousands might be cited, from a recent work entitled "What I saw in South and North America." By H. W. Baxley, M.D., Special Commissioner of the United-States Government. D. Appleton & Co., New York, 1865. This is his description of "what he saw" in Lima, the capital of Peru: —

"It is rarely the case that one walks in any part of the city, during the day or night, without being shocked by sights of indecency, immodesty, and immorality, too gross even to be hinted at, and disgraceful to the arrogant civilization of the nation. If one thousand seven hundred and ninety-three priests, exercising ecclesiastical authority and performing religious functions in this city, as published in its statistics, with seventy churches, forty-two chapels, six hundred and twenty-eight altars, and vast power of influence and enforcement, cannot produce a better state of morals and manners, it shows either a defective system of religion, or incapacity and faithlessness on the part of the executors of the holy trust. The statements of candid citizens and of foreign residents of many years compel the belief, that the general demoralization is mainly clue to a depraved clergy. If priests taking vows of chastity and devotion alone to God, perjure themselves, obey the lusts of the flesh, and scatter their illegitimate offspring abroad, it is to be expected that they will find imitators among those whose temporal purity they should guard, and whose eternal welfare they should promote. The unblushing boldness with which clerical debauchery stalks abroad in Lima renders it needless to put in any saving clause of declaration. The priest may be seen on the sabbath day, as on others, in bullring and cock-pit, restaurant and tavern, with commoner and concubine, joining in noisy revel, or looking on with complacent sanction. Nor does the going-down of the sun arrest his wayward peregrinations for he may be seen at that hour, at corners, with *tapadas*, in gay and lascivious conversation, or threading by-ways in fulfillment of a lustful assignation. If the bishop of Arequipas will turn to the 'weak and beggarly elements of the world,' if he cannot, like his great predecessor St. Paul, 'contain,' but must obey the carnal desires, 'let him marry,' as he is commanded by the apostle, like an honorable man and a consistent Christian; and let him not encourage the frailty of depraved disciples by a shameless example of licentiousness made public by his procurement of separate apartments in Lima for his seven concubines and his thirty-five illegitimate children.

"The streets of this capital were yesterday the scene of a procession which was a disgrace to its professed enlightenment, and an idolatrous violation of its boasted Christianity. A gorgeously gilded throne, borne on the shoulders of negroes, who were partially concealed by a deep valance, supported the pontifically-attired effigy of St. Peter; its right arm, moved by secret machinery, being occasionally raised in attitude of blessing the throngs of deluded worshippers who bowed their heads for its benediction. Another similarly decorated dais bore a life-size graven image of La Merced, the patron saint of Peru; elegantly arrayed in curls, coronet, richly-embroidered crinoline and robe, pearl necklace, and earrings, brooch and bodice; and holding in its uplifted jeweled fingers a silver *yoke*. These effigies were escorted by prelates and other ecclesiastics and that of La Merced was preceded by six pert-looking mulatto girls, – designed to represent virgins, – carrying incense upon silver salvers, from which numerous censers, swung by priestly hands, were kept supplied, and rolled upward their clouds of perfume, to tell of the adoration of her votaries. The whole procession moved to the sound of measured chants sung by hundreds of the clergy, who often bowed; behind whom followed the civic dignitaries of the nation and city, bareheaded and reverential; and after these came the plumed warriors, on horse and foot, with breastplate and helmet, lance, sabre, musket, and cannon, flaunting banners, and martial music, guarding the saints through the city, and back to the altars of the Church of La Merced, whence they came, and where they will receive hereafter, as heretofore, the petitions and vows of thousands of misguided religionists. Can popular regeneration be rationally looked for when examples of ecclesiastical profligacy are patent to the public eye, and when such violations of divine precepts are practised, and such delusions devised to mis-lead the ignorant?

"No one can scrutinize the social habits in Lima, without becoming sensible of the fact that women are probably 'more sinned against than sinning.' For they not only have provocations to faithlessness, and opportunity afforded for its indulgence by sanctioned customs, but they are taught by the universally-recognized dissoluteness of the men not to place any confidence in them, and not to contemplate marriage as a means of happiness beyond its power to furnish an establishment, and make a woman mistress of her own actions.

"In the street called San Francisco, opposite the monastery of that name, a kind of barracks is found, containing quite a population apart from the rest. There lives a class of women and children whom one would think came in a direct line from the gypsies, if their complexion did not 'show a variety of a thousand shades, from white to black. These women are the acknowledged mistresses, and the children the progeny, of the monks, who visit them at all times, and pay them a regular stipend. 'La casa de la monjas,' – the house of the nuns, – as the people ironically call it, is a real Gomorrah. The clerical protectors of the tenants that inhabit it willingly mistake the chambers, not having the weakness of the laity of being jealous of each other. Do not suppose that we are amusing ourselves in speaking ill of the monks of Lima. These abominations among themselves they are the first to expose; for in their stated elections for superiors, such is the bitterness of rival aspirants, that they publicly charge against each other these infamous transactions, making known the number of their concubines and illegitimate children."

Thus have Dr. Baxley and others cast the principal reproach of this frightful immorality upon the poor priests; but does it not belong rather to their entire social system? The priests in assuming the vows of perpetual celibacy, and the people in supporting the old Roman monogamy, which their Gnostic views of Christianity require, have assumed more than human nature is able to bear, and more than it ought to bear and there must be constant transgression and immorality as long as their present system prevails.

And now I think I have fairly demonstrated that the European social system of monogamy had its origin in Roman paganism, and has been perpetuated by Roman Catholicism.

CHAPTER VII:

MONOGAMY AS IT IS AMONG PROTESTANTS

MONOGAMY IS ROMANISM STILL

Take monogamy as it is today, in Protestant countries, and we see that the old Roman leaven is still in it. Christianity has not reformed and purified that system so much as that has corrupted Christianity. Most of us in these countries are accustomed to congratulate ourselves upon our happy escape from the bondage and the bigotry of the Papal Church. But we are mistaken. We have not escaped. Rome binds us in stronger shackles than the iron chains of the holy Inquisition. Her shackles are upon our consciences: they are intertwined with every fibre of our social life. Much of her intolerant spirit, many of her questionable doctrines and practices, and her traditional forms and ceremonies, are still common to the nominally Christian world. In respect to a few of them, we have discovered that they are unscriptural, and unsupported by divine authority, and are therefore of no binding obligation; but, by many other traditional doctrines and practices of that hierarchy, we are unconsciously, and therefore so much the more securely fettered. We boast of our Christian freedom, while we are, in fact, but little better than slaves; for if we are nominally free, yet we are bound by an apprenticeship to Rome more degrading than our former slavery itself: and our boasted emancipation is but a miserable farce. We are too servile and timid in our interpretation of the Bible, and in our examination of the divine and natural laws. We hesitate to follow the simple truth to its legitimate and logical conclusions. We stand aghast at the radical changes which severe truth requires in our religious and social systems. We shrink from exploring the profound labyrinths to which truth attempts in vain to lead us; while we look anxiously around for clews and leading-strings by which to trace our way. We dare not go forward without example and authority; and authority and example are reconducting us to Rome. Our great champion, Dr. Martin Luther, made a few bold steps in the right direction, but stopped far short of the ultimate results to which his own principles were leading. A Protestant in theory, he was, in practice, essentially a Romanist. He insisted much upon justification by faith alone, and declared personal piety to be necessary to true Christianity; and yet he admitted all citizens, irrespective of their faith or their want of it, to the most solemn and most esoteric ordinances of the Christian Church. He repudiated the authority of earthly potentates to compel men's Christian belief, but retained the union of Church and State in order to compel their Christian obedience. He denied the infallibility of the pope, and the miraculous power of the priesthood, and yet believed in the Real Presence, if not the adoration of the host. His disciples are today imitating his example rather than promoting his principles and possess little more evangelical faith than the Romanists themselves.

Henry the Eighth, the founder of the Church of England, was even less a Protestant than Luther and the present tendency of many of the most influential doctors and dignitaries of this Church is in the same retrograde direction as that of the Lutherans. Yet these two churches, the Anglican and the Lutheran, are the main pillars of Protestantism – the Boaz and Jachin of the porch of the new temple. I have not lost my hope that the truth of gospel simplicity will ultimately prevail over ecclesiastical bigotry; but it may require as many centuries for the Christian world to unlock the trammels of the Roman hierarchy, and to escape from its thraldom, as it originally required to fix those trammels upon the consciences of Christian freemen.

But the Romans are more consistent in their system of monogamy than we are; for while the dogmas of the Church forbid polygamy and even single marriages to the ministry, they provide for the surplus women, by having numerous societies of nuns and sisters of charity, who make a merit of necessity, by assuming the vows of perpetual celibacy, to serve the Church, and acquire religious merit. As Protestants, we have been taught to believe that these monastic institutions have proved to be schools of vice, and that the vows of perpetual chastity assumed in them are unnatural and wicked, and that they are often violated under the detestable hypocrisy of sacerdotal sanctity.[244] For these reasons, we have suppressed the nunneries, but we have made no provision for the nuns, and those who would have become nuns. In those institutions they were, at least, assured of a home and a support, even if they did learn vice; but now, when thrown upon the world, they are still more exposed to vice, and are without a home and without support. Under Catholic monogamy, if a young woman made a false step, she could hide her shame in a convent, and devote her future life to penitence and prayer; but, under Protestant monogamy, the frail fair sinner has no such refuge. Her first lapse from virtue shuts her out forever from the respect and sympathy of the world, and from the hope of future reformation; and her downward career

---

244   The following citations are from Froude's Hist. of Eng., vol. ii., chap. 10.

"Only light reference will be made in this place to the darker scandals by which the abbeys were dishonored. Such things there really were, to an extent which it may be painful to believe, but which evidence too abundantly proves."

Among other specifications, Mr. Froude cites the letter of the Archbishop of Canterbury (written A.D. 1489) to the Abbot of St. Albans, wherein he accuses him thus: "'Not a few of your fellow monks and brethren, as we most deeply grieve to learn, giving themselves over to a reprobate mind, laying aside the fear of God, do lead only a life of lasciviousness, – nay, as is horrible to relate, be not afraid to defile the holy places, even the very churches of God, by infamous intercourse with nuns. You yourself, moreover, among other grave enormities and abominable crimes whereof you are guilty, and for which you are noted and defamed, have, in the first place, admitted a certain married woman named Elena Germyn, who has separated herself, without just cause, from her husband, and for some time past has lived in adultery with another man, to be a nun, or sister in the Priory of Bray; and . . . Father Thomas Sudbury, one of your brother monks, publicly, notoriously, and without interference or punishment from you, has associated and still associates with this woman, as an adulterer with his harlot. Moreover, divers other of your brethren and fellow-monks have resorted and do resort continually to her and other women at the same place, as to a public brothel or receiving house. Nor is Bray the only house into which you have introduced disorder. At the Nunnery of Sapwell, you depose those who are good and religious, you promote to the highest dignities the worthless and the vicious.'"

In the year 1536, the Report of Special Commissioners appointed to inspect the Monasteries of England was laid before parliament, by which it appeared, says Mr. Froude, that "two-thirds of the monks in England were living in habits which may not be described. . . . The case against the monasteries was complete; and there is no occasion either to be surprised or peculiarly horrified at the discovery. The demoralization which was exposed was nothing less and nothing more than the condition into which men of average nature compelled to celibacy, and living as the exponents of a system which they disbelieved, were certain to fall."

to the gates of hell is so generally taken for granted, that it becomes almost a certainty. The only safe and proper provision for homeless women is marriage. An early marriage will usually save them from the dangers to which they are exposed. Monogamy cannot secure their marriage; but polygamy can: yet we are taught to look with horror upon polygamy as one of the "relics of barbarism," although it is plainly taught in the Bible, and is the only social system which provides marriage for all, and which secures the honest and lawful gratification of those impetuous passions which must be and which will be indulged in some manner, if not by marriage, then without it; while we wink at all the disgusting abominations of prostitution, divorce, adultery, and other vices, which are the well-known and the inevitable results of restricted marriage. Monogamy, in "forbidding to marry," assumes all the curses which this prohibition entails. We must choose between the system which provides marriage for all, with comparative purity, or the system of restricted marriage with inevitable impurity.

IMPURITY OF MODERN MONOGAMY

The Bible forbids prostitution, but permits polygamy. The ancient Greeks and Romans forbade polygamy, but permitted prostitution. Modern monogamy pretends to forbid both, but really permits prostitution also. Our monogamous morality is, therefore, that of ancient paganism, and not that of the Bible; and prostitution is as much a necessary part of our social system as it was of that at Athens, at Corinth, or at Rome. Our magistrates are not ignorant of the extent of public licentiousness, but they do not attempt to suppress it. They only seek to conceal it, and confine it, if possible, within its present limits, requiring its votaries to keep it in the dark. Our police officers know almost every prostitute that walks the street, and allow her to ply her nefarious trade unmolested, so long as she is polite and unobtrusive. As the Spartans are reputed to have said to the youth of their state, in respect to theft, *"Steal, but do not be caught at it,"* so the guardians of our public morals say, "You may be as licentious as you please, only make no public display of your immorality." The reason of this connivance at prostitution must be because our legislators and judges believe its suppression to be impossible; and, with our system of monogamy, it is impossible. If there must be a multitude of women unmarried and unprovided for, there will be a multitude of prostitutes and, if there are a multitude of prostitutes, there will be a multitude of men, who, like Shakespeare's Falstaff, will decline marriage, because they can be "better accommodated than with a wife:" and so the evil will go on continually increasing and propagating itself. The Foundling Hospital, the Five Points House of Industry, and the Home for Friendless and Abandoned women, must be built alongside of the brothel; and their numerous inmates must be maintained either by public tax or by Christian charity (most frequently by the latter): so that honest men must support their own wives and children and also the cast-off drabs and bastards of unprincipled libertines. If we must have public prostitutes, let us have them openly and boldly, as the ancient Greeks and Romans did; and let them be publicly licensed, as they were under Caligula, and as they are said to be still in France; and let the state derive, at least, sufficient revenue from them to bury their murdered infants, and to bring up their abandoned foundlings.

THE HIGHER LAW OF CHRISTIAN PHILANTHROPY

Let me not be misunderstood in what I have just said. I do not depreciate that form of charity which seeks out the victims of licentiousness, and makes them the special objects of its beneficence. I would not say one word in its disparagement. On the contrary, I acknowledge its genuineness. Such charity is worthy of great commendation: it is in a special sense true Christian charity, for it is eminently Christ-like; since he came to seek and to save the lost, and disdained not to be called the Friend of publicans and sinners. But what I demand is this, that this form of Christian charity should so expand its efforts and its aims as fully to meet the case, and yield a permanent and radical relief to that class of the poor and miserable which it has taken under its charge. Let its aims be so comprehensive, so high, so broad, and so deep, that it cannot be satisfied with anything less than a prevention of the "social evil" which it has hitherto attempted only to alleviate. And it is certainly no slander to our present charities of this kind, to say that the alleviation which they have effected is altogether inadequate. The miserable victims of this vice are increasing faster than the ability or the disposition to relieve them. The most enthusiastic philanthropists have already become disheartened in vainly endeavoring to furnish sufficient relief, and they can see no means of prevention. They are at their wits end; and some of them have become fully aware, that, under our present social system, no prevention can be possible. "While sin is in the world," some say, "we cannot prevent men and women from sinning: they will sin, in spite of us and in spite of everything; and the world itself is growing more and more depraved and wicked every day. All that we can do is to show Christian mercy, and grant some present relief."

But the true Christian philanthropist does not rest satisfied in such conclusions. He knows that it is not true that the world is growing worse and worse, but that facts and statistics prove the contrary. He believes in the "good time coming," and that the world is actually growing better and better. Many causes of human misery have been discovered and removed, or greatly diminished, and he hopes that more will be. The average duration of human life is actually being prolonged. The average state of health is incontestably being improved. Christianity has not been instituted in vain. It has already accomplished wonders of mercy and grace, and its blessed work of reform is still going on. The true philanthropist, therefore, must not and will not despair. If no preventive of licentiousness has hitherto been found, and if it be impossible to find any under our present social system of marriage, we must look for it under some other system. Marriage was made for man, and not man for marriage.

IS THE "SOCIAL EVIL" PREVENTABLE?

But perhaps some may suppose that sincere and genuine piety is a sufficient preventive of licentiousness, and that, when all the people become truly converted, and well instructed in religious knowledge, then they will be secure from this vice. I have great confidence in genuine piety, and believe that it is indeed the best antidote to all the ills that flesh is heir to; but the difficulty is, that it is this very licentiousness which is hindering people from becoming pious. And, besides this, it is not from want of religious knowledge that people become licentious: they have already had line upon line, and precept upon precept, for many successive generations. They know that licentiousness is a sin; and they know, that, when they fall into it, they become liable to the most fearful punishments, both in this life and in the world to come: but the tyranny of monogamy has left them no alternative; they have no other available means of gratifying the wants of nature. Marriage is impossible to half the women, and a single marriage is inadequate to the requirements of half the men. Pious exhortation is but idle talk to those who are sinning from the excitement of amorous desire of which there is no possible gratification except a sinful one. If the philanthropist who is giving them these exhortations cannot point out a lawful means of meeting those natural wants, of what profit can his exhortations be? "If a brother or a sister be naked, and destitute of daily food, and one of you say unto them, Depart in peace, be ye warmed and filled; notwithstanding ye give them not those things which are needful to the body; what doth it profit?" It is not instruction which our "destitute and abandoned women" want; they want marriage; they want homes of their own to shelter them, and husbands to love them and to provide for them. And I have already demonstrated that it is their right to have them; their natural and unquestionable right, of which the injustice and tyranny of monogamy has cruelly deprived them. Society has wronged them; and with their own peculiar, intuitive instinct they feel it, though they cannot tell exactly how. Society, somehow, has made war upon them, most unjustly; and, when they become licentious, it is from an instinctive feeling of self-defense; it is only to take such justifiable revenge upon society as a state of warfare authorizes, and has, in a manner, rendered necessary.

Now, let this warfare cease. Let the women have their rights. Let every woman have a husband and a home; and let every man have as many women as he can love, and as can love him, and as he is able to support, until all the women are provided for: then, and not till then, will prostitution cease; and then the happy time that the poet dreamed of, when he put the apparently extravagant sentiment into his hero's mouth, which I have placed upon my titlepage, will have come at last, and

"There shall be no more widows in the land."[245]

---

245   "No man who loves his kind can in these days rest content with waiting as a servant upon human misery, when it is in so many cases possible to anticipate and avert it. Prevention is better than cure, and it is now clear to all that a large part of human suffering is preventable by improved social arrangements. Charity will now, if it be genuine, fix upon this enterprise as greater, more widely, and permanently beneficial, and therefore, more Christian, than the other. It will not, indeed, neglect

the lower task of relieving and consoling those, who, whether through the errors and unskillful arrangements of society, or through causes not yet preventable, have actually fallen into calamity. Its compassion will be all the deeper, its relief more prompt and zealous, because it does not generally, as former generations did, recognize such calamities to be part of man's inevitable destiny. When the sick man has been visited, and everything done which skill and assiduity can do to cure him, modern charity will go on to consider the causes of his malady, and then to inquire whether others incur the same dangers, and may be warned in time. When the starving man has been relieved, modem charity inquires whether any fault in the social system deprived him of his share of Nature's bounty, any unjust advantage taken by the strong over the weak, any rudeness or want of culture in himself, wrecking his virtue and his habits of thrift." [I continue this quotation with a reservation; applying it to the first *Roman* Christians, but doubting its truthfulness in respect to the "apostolic," Jewish Christians.]

"The first Christians were probably not so much hopeless of accomplishing great social reforms, as unripe for the conception of them. They did not easily recognize evil to be evil, and did not believe, or rather had never dreamed, that it could be cured. Habit dulls the senses, and puts the critical faculty to sleep. The fierceness and hardness of ancient manners is apparent to us; but the ancients themselves were not shocked by sights which were familiar to them. To us it is sickening to think of the gladiatorial show, of the massacres common in Roman warfare, of the infanticide practised by grave and respectable citizens, who did not merely condemn their children to death, but often in practice, as they well knew, to what was still worse, – a life of prostitution and beggary. The Roman regarded a gladiatorial show as we regard a hunt; the news of the slaughter of two hundred thousand Helvetians by Caesar, or half a million Jews by Titus, excited in his mind a thrill of triumph; infanticide committed by a friend appeared to him a prudent measure of household economy. To shake off this paralysis of the moral sense produced by habit, to see misery to be misery, and cruelty to be cruelty, requires not merely a strong, but a trained and matured compassion. It was as much, probably, as the first Christian could learn at once, to relieve the sick, the starving, and the desolate. Only after centuries of this simple philanthropy could they learn to criticize the fundamental usages of society itself, and acquire courage to pronounce that, however deeply rooted and time honored, they were in many cases shocking to humanity.

"Closely connected with this insensibility to the real character of common usages is a positive unwillingness to reform them. The argument of prejudice is twofold. It is not only that what has lasted a long time must be right, but also that what has lasted a long time, right or wrong, must be intended to continue. We are advanced by eighteen hundred years beyond the apostolic generation. Our minds are set free, so that we may boldly criticize the usages around us, knowing them to be but imperfect essays toward order and happiness, and no divinely or supernaturally ordained constitution which it would be impious to change. We have witnessed improvements in physical well-being which incline us to expect further progress, and make us keen-sighted to detect the evils and miseries that remain. Thus ought the enthusiasm of humanity to work in these days, and thus, plainly enough, it does work. These investigations are constantly being made, these reforms commence." —Ecce Homo

MONOGAMY OCCASIONS SEDUCTION AND RUIN

If any of my readers have failed to see that there is any necessary connection between monogamy and female ruin, I beg them to examine carefully the following observations. It has been demonstrated, in a former chapter, that monogamy leaves a multitude of women unprotected, and unprovided with the privileges of marriage. It does not and it cannot furnish half of them with husbands and homes of their own: hence the galling bondage of female dependence; hence the difficulty of woman's finding her "sphere." Yet there is nothing mysterious or doubtful about what constitutes her sphere; for it is defined by the simple term "home," – that word, above all others, so charming, and so suggestive of every excellence in the female character, and of all the sweet memories which cluster round the blessed names of mother, sister, and bride. But, alas! the practical mystery with an immense number of women still remains; and that is, how to find a home. A father's house is no longer a home to many a young woman; perhaps that father is poor, and the burden of years is at last superadded to that of poverty. He cheerfully toiled for his child while she was young and necessarily dependent upon him; and, as she grew up to womanhood, he stinted not to bestow upon her such learning and such accomplishments as his scanty means could command; and his heart was often cheered by the hope of seeing her well married and well settled in life: but, as these hopes are not realized, he begins to feel the burden of her maintenance. "She is old enough to provide for herself," and "Why doesn't she get married?" Sure enough! poor thing, why doesn't she? But oh! how cruel to reproach her with her involuntary dependence and her miserable lot! And it is an immense relief to her, when it is at length decided that she must go out to service. And so she goes to toil for bread among strangers. Her frail form is overburdened, and often broken down, by unremitting and ill-requited labor, and her young heart not unfrequently corrupted and hardened by unavoidable contact and contamination with vice.

THE HARLOT'S PROGRESS

What wonder is it, then, that, under such circumstances, the unprotected, wearied, homesick girl should yield a reluctant ear to the seductive flatteries of the profligate libertine, who scruples not to utter vows of constancy, and draw fond pictures of future affluence, to be shared with her; but who, having accomplished his fiendish purpose, and stolen from her, forever, her only dower of innocence and purity, now ignores his vows and promises, and casts her off, to seek and ruin another victim! What shall become of that poor, desolate, guilty, heart-broken wretch thus ruthlessly abandoned? Alas! the result is scarcely doubtful: it is too often experienced. Despised by herself no less than by the world, driven in anger from the paternal threshold, the gates of honest toil and the doors of Christian charity closed against her, she yields to hopeless despair, and, even for the miserable purpose of prolonging a wretched existence, she abandons herself at length to a life of open shame; becoming herself the means of propagating that misery of which she is such an unhappy victim.

The artificial system of monogamy offers up other sacrifices on the unholy altar of abandoned lust, besides those furnished from among the daughters of toil or the victims of seduction. The accomplished, the refined, the proud, and the wealthy have furnished their full proportion to swell the aggregate number of the lost. We hope, of course, that much the larger portion of women who have been well brought up, and have failed to marry, have lived and died honest old maids. They never quite lost their hope. Poor, simple souls, they had always been told that their husbands would come for them by and by; that there is a Jack for every Gill, as many men as women in the world; and so they sat and waited, —

> "Rusticus expectat, dum defluat amnis; at ille
> Labitur et labetur in omne volubilis aevum."

And thus the ceaseless tide of human life rolls on and on, the number of competitors among marriageable maids abates not, the number of men who are ready to marry augments not. Some, therefore, among the higher and the middling ranks of life, who ought to die old maids, according to the system of monogamy, do not so die. The very pride and spirit of accomplished women have sometimes proved their ruin. When they have discovered that real men are comparatively rare in the matrimonial market, and that there are more rakes and triflers than honest lovers in society, and that there cannot be husbands and homes provided for more than half the women, – being unable to suppress all their strong susceptibilities of love, and unwilling to surrender all their rights to its enjoyment, – they have deliberately determined to enjoy what they can without marriage; and thus to defy the scorn of men and the wrath of God.

But passion does not impel so great a number of intelligent women to self-abandonment, as a desire of self-support and a dread of being an intolerable burden to others. Under such apprehensions, many unhappy women, who had been nursed in the lap of luxury, and accustomed to every indulgence during childhood, have found, after coming of age, that as year after year passed round, and no eligible opportunity of marriage occurred, their presence at home was becoming more and more unwelcome, and their formidable bills of expenses more and more reluctantly allowed, till they have at last fled from those halls of wealth, and from an intolerable dependence on churlish relatives, to a still more wretched existence in the haunts of public vice.

How great is the injustice and oppression of the social system which makes no other provision for so many of its most beautiful and originally innocent daughters than this! Well may the poet thus rave against the social tyranny of our system.

"Cursed be the social lies that warp us from the living truth;
Cursed be the social wants that sin against the strength of youth:
Cursed be the sickly forms that err from honest Nature's rule."

TENNYSON

MONOGAMY CAUSES CHASTITY AND RELIGION TO BE HATED

Monogamy being partial in its privileges, and oppressive in its prohibitions, like every other oppressive and unjust thing, provokes resentment and enmity, and cannot be thoroughly maintained and honestly observed. Human nature is constantly rebelling against it, and is persistently asserting its inherent and inalienable right to all the benefits of love and marriage, of which this system has deprived it. These struggles for freedom from the oppression of monogamy, being made in ignorance of the privileges of polygamy, have assumed the form of defiant transgression against the laws of chastity itself; for the popular conscience is so depraved by the erroneous education of our social system, as to regard the restrictions of monogamy as identical with those of religion. And, finding them too hard to be borne, instead of resorting to the just and proper alternative of polygamy, many persons have broken away from all moral restraint whatever, have given loose rein to impetuous passion, and have become lost to every sentiment of virtue and to every hope of heaven.

As Christianity itself was outraged and repudiated at the period of the French Revolution, on account of the abuses of Roman Catholicism, with which the popular mind had confounded it (Romanism being the only acknowledged form of Christianity then known in that country, so that, when they rose against it, they rose against Christianity itself, and became raging demons of barbarity and crime), so now, throughout Europe and America, is chastity outraged and religion repudiated on account of the unjust restrictions which monogamy has instituted in their names. But neither religion nor chastity is the real object of this hatred. All men sincerely respect the one and revere the other. Yet many cannot see how to assert their natural rights and achieve their long-lost freedom without destroying both. Polygamy alone solves the problem how those rights can be enjoyed while chastity is preserved and religion maintained; for polygamy alone can honestly furnish sufficient indulgence of love to all the men, and sufficient protection of marriage to all the women. Monogamy says to half the women, "Ye cannot marry, and hence ye shall not love;" and to every man it says, "Thou canst marry but one woman, and one only shalt thou love," without regard to the condition of that woman, or her ability or inability to meet his conjugal wants.

It is a physical fact that women are not only less inclined to amorous passion than the men, at all times, but they are also subject to interruptions and periodical changes, which men do not experience. During the long period of lactation, or nursing, most women have a positive repugnance to the embraces of love, as well as during the progress of certain nervous chronic disorders peculiar to the sex, which are aggravated, if not caused, by frequent connubial intercourse; so much so, that some medical men insist upon entire separation from the marriage-bed during the continuance of these disorders, and also during the period of lactation. At such times, one would suppose that no civilized man, or at least that no Christian man, could be so brutal and so cruel as to force his wife to yield to his propensities against her own inclinations and in spite of her repeated and earnest remonstrances: but nothing is more certain than that there are many thousands of just such Christian men; for what can the poor monogamist do? The healthful currents of vigorous life impel him to amorous desire; and he cannot afford to shut down the gates or to shut off the stream. To do so would involve immense loss of pleasure and of power. The passions furnish the only streams to turn the machinery of action; and love is the strongest of them all. While there is the hope of indulgence, the machinery runs smoothly, and the whole man is full of life and buoyancy and power but, if this master-passion must be repressed, its unnatural restraint absorbs all the remaining strength of the man, and he is no better than a hermit or a monk. Hence no vigorous man is willing to endure this restraint. Yet the Christian monogamist has been taught that it is both a sin and a shame to look for the gratification of his desires away from home; so the poor heart-broken and back-broken wife must submit to torture, and so the otherwise kind and honorable husband must commit violence upon his dearest friend, whom he has most solemnly promised to love and to cherish, in sickness and in health, till death shall part them. Many a poor wife then prays for death to part them soon. But other men, at such times, disdaining to avail themselves of extorted pleasures, which can afford so little satisfaction, and despising that religion which will justify or allow such cruel brutality, then steal away from their unwilling wives, and, in defiance of the most solemn obligations and sacred laws of God and man, go and do worse; defiling the beds of virgin innocence, or wasting their health and strength upon vile prostitutes. Which horn of this trilemma should the vigorous husband of this invalid woman choose; imbecile continence, wicked licentiousness, or matrimonial brutality? Would not polygamy be an alternative preferable to either? would it not be more just and more merciful than either? It is just and merciful to both the men and the women; it preserves the marriage-bed undefiled; it provides husbands for all the women; and it allows each man to take more than one wife when circumstances warrant and require it. And they often do require it. The extraordinary vehemence and intensity of the amorous propensity which some men experience is sufficient of itself to require it. Such men can no more restrain this desire than that for their necessary food. They may call to their assistance every motive to continence that can be drawn from heaven and earth and hell, but they often call in vain; for the intensity of this passion sweeps down every barrier, and rushes to its gratification. If, then, there will be and there must be indulgence, let it be such as is regulated and controlled by divine and natural law. God who made man, and who knows what is in man, has provided sufficient means to supply his natural amorous wants. Marriage is that means; and, as one wife is not always sufficient, he has provided more. There are women enough, and no man need be either pining or sinning for the want of them.

"Take the good the gods provide thee:
Lovely Thais sits beside thee,
Blooming like an Eastern bride,
In flower of youth and beauty's pride.
Happy, happy, happy pair!
None but the brave,
None but the brave,
None but the brave deserves the fair."

GREAT MEN ARE ALWAYS POLYGAMISTS

And it is the brave, the gifted, the talented, that deserve the fair, who have always desired the fair, and won the fair. "Lovely Thais" never refuses to unveil her charms to the true hero. Great men always recognize the voice of God in the voice of Nature, no matter under what social system they may live. They yield to the natural and the divine behests, even though they transgress the laws of ordinary social life. They obey God rather than men; and this obedience is the first element of their greatness. Ordinary laws may be sufficient to restrain ordinary men; but when a Samson is within their bonds, those bonds are snapped asunder like the green withes and the new ropes of Delilah. Yet, were not our social laws so manifestly arbitrary and oppressive, such eminent philosophers as Plato, Aristotle, and Bacon, such noble heroes as Alexander, Caesar, Napoleon, and Nelson, such divine poets as Goethe, Burns, and Byron, and such enlightened statesmen as Pericles, Augustus, Buckingham, Palmerston, and Webster, and many thousands more, would never have incurred the odium of libertinism as they have. Although they lived under the system of monogamy, they would not and did not submit to it. Their noble natures required a larger indulgence, and they took it, law or no law, like brave men as they were. And there are many more such men than the world dreams of in its narrow monogamous philosophy and yet it is a shame and a pity that our social laws cannot be so amended, and brought into harmony with those of God and Nature, that our noblest men would yield them the most prompt obedience. And is it not a sad pity, a burning shame, and a fearful wrong that our laws are such, that such men cannot acknowledge their mistresses, and avow their children? The wrongs of these women and children are crying to God from the ground, and he will hear and judge. These great men are brave; but they are not brave enough. They have no just right to practise their polygamy in the dark. Let us have either an honest monogamy or an avowed polygamy. Hence it is that I am called by the justice of God and the sufferings of humanity to appeal to every honorable sentiment in mankind in behalf of a greater freedom to marry, and a greater purity of the marriage relation. Let us have such marriage laws, that whatever relations any honorable man shall determine to form with the other sex can be honorably formed and honorably maintained.

HYPOCRISY OF MONOGAMY

But an honest monogamy is an impossibility. Wherever it is practised, it is a system of hypocrisy. It is a veil of abstemiousness assumed to conceal a mass of hidden corruption. Its direct tendency is to stimulate the contemptible vices of intrigue and lying, as well as the equally detestable ones of prostitution and adultery. By attempting to deprive one-half the women of any lawful and honorable means of amorous pleasure, and by allowing the men only partial and inadequate means, it impels a multitude of each sex to secret transgression, or else to open profligacy; and thus the laws of chastity are violated on every hand, and truthfulness, integrity, purity, and honor are becoming but unmeaning terms.

No one familiar with social life in Europe will dare to dispute that a large proportion of the upper classes of society there are addicted to some form of licentiousness. It is often observed there, that, as soon as the women marry, they throw off the restraints of chastity, and encourage secret lovers; and while each of the men live openly with one woman only, or with none, yet they indulge in promiscuous criminal intercourse to an incredible extent. Now, which social system is the more honorable and manly, the more virtuous and pure, the one more in accordance with Nature and the laws of Nature's God, – a pretended and a corrupt monogamy, or an open and honest polygamy? Which manifests the more base and selfish passion, – the man who espouses the partners of his love, and takes them to his home and his heart, and provides for them and their children, or the man who steals away from his house in the dark, and indulges his dishonorable and degrading passion in secret places, and then abandons the partners of his guilty pleasure to a life of wretchedness and shame and want?

> "Domestic happiness, thou only bliss
> Of Paradise that has survived the fall!
> Though few now taste thee unimpaired and pure,
> Forsaking thee, what shipwreck have we made
> Of honor, dignity, and fair renown!
> Till prostitution elbows us aside
> In all our crowded streets; and senates seem
> Convened for purposes of empire less
> Than to release the adulteress from her bond."

THE TASK

CHAPTER VIII:

THE NECESSARY RELATION OF MONOGAMY TO IMMORALITY AND CRIME

MARRIAGE PREVENTS CRIME

It is an acknowledged fact that crime is much more prevalent among unmarried persons than among the married; for the married man's family becomes a pledge to society for his good behavior nor can the married woman disgrace herself without disgracing also her husband and her children. That system, therefore, which provides marriage for the greater number must be the more favorable to the promotion of public virtue and morality. It has already been demonstrated that polygamy provides for the marriage of the greater number of the women than monogamy can; and it will not be difficult to prove that it also conduces to the marriage of the greater number of the men: for there are always a great many men who will not marry, so long as they can obtain the gratification of their propensities without marriage, which they can do as long as there are so many unmarried women as there must be where ever monogamy prevails. The more rich and luxurious monogamous society becomes, the more abandoned women there will be, and the fewer marriages and the more crime. But let the system of polygamy be adopted, and then all the women will be wanted for wives; and, as they can then obtain husbands and homes of their own, but few will prefer to follow a loose and vicious course of life. And then the men, being deprived of the opportunity of illicit indulgence, will be compelled to marry; and their marriage will refine and humanize them, and preserve them from many of those vices and immoralities to which they are now addicted. There are many crimes against which the moral sentiment of humanity revolts, but which are constantly forced upon mankind by the tyranny of monogamy, and which nothing but a return to the purer system of polygamy can restrain and prevent. Among many of these crimes and moral evils caused or aggravated by monogamy, and which would be greatly diminished by polygamy, I can mention only a few.

ADULTERY

The violation of the marriage-vow constitutes the crime of adultery, – a crime which has always been regarded with the greatest detestation among mankind, and which, in ancient times, was punished with death. The definition of adultery, like that of marriage, depends upon the social system which we adopt. According to the system of monogamy, if any married person has sexual intercourse with anyone, except his own wife, or her own husband, then he or she is guilty of adultery; but if the other party to the same act be unmarried, then that unmarried person is not guilty of adultery, but of fornication only. That is, if a married man has intercourse with another man's wife, then both are guilty of adultery; but if an unmarried man has intercourse with a married woman, then she is guilty of adultery, but he is not. According to the system of polygamy, if any man has intercourse with another man's wife, they are both guilty of adultery; but if any man has intercourse with an unmarried woman, then both are guilty of fornication. That is, it is the married or unmarried state of the woman, and not of the man, that determines the nature of the crime; and both parties to the same act are always by this system held guilty of the same offence. A careful examination of the laws of God and of Nature will enable us to determine which of these definitions is correct, and will also assist us in the determination of the more important question, Which social system is right?

1. If a married woman admit any other man to her bed except her husband, her offspring becomes spurious, or at least uncertain, and her husband may have another man's child imposed upon him instead of his own, to be supported, and to inherit his estate; but no such uncertainty occurs from the intercourse of one man with several women.

2. If a wife admit the embrace of another lover, it always implies an alienation of her affections from her husband: but it does not imply

an alienation of her husband's affections to take another woman, for his first wife is not always capable of fulfilling his conjugal desires; and it is sometimes as much out of regard to her health and comfort as to his own gratification, that he is impelled to take another.

3. If a woman is having intercourse with several men at the same time, she is living in uncleanness, and in constant liability of inducing within herself, and communicating to all her lovers, the most loathsome and incurable diseases; her mind and heart become hopelessly depraved, and she incurs the utter loss of all self-respect and all public estimation: but no such diseases of body or degradation of character attach to the man who is living with several women.

These natural laws are fully ratified and confirmed by the divine law: "The man that committed adultery with another man's wife, the adulterer and the adulteress shall surely be put to death." "But if a man entice a maid that is not betrothed, and lie with her, he shall surely endow her to be his wife." "Because he hath humbled her, he may not put her away all his life." "And Nathan said to David, Thou art the man. Thus saith the Lord, I delivered thee out of the hand of Saul, and I gave thee thy master's house and thy master's wives into thy bosom; and gave thee the house of Israel and of Judah, and if that had been too little, I would moreover have given thee such and such things. Wherefore hast thou despised the commandment of the Lord to do evil in his sight, and hast taken the wife of Uriah the Hittite to be thy wife? Now, therefore, the sword shall never depart from thy house, because thou hast despised me, and hast taken the wife of Uriah the Hittite to be thy wife."[246] It seems unnecessary to cite further proofs. The entire Bible confirms the definition of adultery as given by the system of polygamy.

The civil laws of those States practicing monogamy, in defining adultery, are full of contradictions and obscurities. Their theory requires that all married persons, both men and women, who have intercourse with any others except their own husbands or their own wives, should be called adulterers, and considered

---

246   Ex. xxii. 16; Lev. xx. 10; Deut. xxii. 22-29; 2 Sam. xii. 7-10

equally criminal; but with an open Bible before them, and living Nature all around them, they approach, sometimes, very near to the distinctions set forth in polygamy. The following is Dr. Noah Webster's definition: "*Adultery.* Violation of the marriage-bed; a crime or civil injury which introduces, or may introduce, into a family, a spurious offspring. In common usage, adultery means the unfaithfulness of any married person to the marriage-bed. *By the laws of Connecticut*, the sexual intercourse of any man with a married woman is the crime of adultery in both; such intercourse of a married man with an unmarried woman is fornication in both, and adultery of the man, within the meaning of the law respecting divorce; but not a felonious adultery in either, or the crime of adultery at common law, or by the statute. This latter offence is, in England, proceeded with only in the ecclesiastical courts."

This definition, according to the laws of Connecticut, is the very one which polygamy requires, with the exception of that part of it relating to divorce; and doubtless the God-fearing legislators of the "Land of Steady Habits" who framed this statute were more familiar with the Bible than with Roman codes, and, besides, had very little respect for the authority of popes or councils. In Massachusetts, also, the statute requires that "when the crime is committed between a married woman and a man who is unmarried, the man shall be deemed guilty of adultery." *Rev. Stat, of Mass.*, 1860. In most of the States of the American Union, however, the laws define adultery, according to common usage, as the theory of monogamy requires. And the consequence is, that it is regarded as a very trifling crime by the statutes of those States; the common penalty being only one hundred dollars' fine, or six months' imprisonment, even this light penalty being rarely inflicted; for the public conscience is so depraved by the false definitions of monogamous jurisprudence in respect to this crime, that few men will prosecute and few juries will convict either an adulterer or an adulteress.

"The frequency of crimes has washed them white."

Yet, with a curious inconsistency, whenever an injured husband appeals to the higher law of God, and assumes the awful responsibility to inflict with his own hand the penalty of death to the adulterer, the multitude applaud, or, at least, excuse the vindictive act; and men of undoubted respectability are thus impelled to private revenge, not only in the heat of resentment, when the guilty parties are first detected, but even in cool blood, and as an afterthought for vindicating personal and family honor. And, when he is arraigned for trial, the jury, sympathizing with him as the injured husband, are almost sure to acquit him with applause. Instances of such homicides are, unhappily, too common to require authentication. Since this is the state of our public morals, who are the barbarians if we are not? What is barbarism but private revenge? In what does civilization consist, if not in maintaining the sacred supremacy of law, and in furnishing adequate protection and vindication of life and honor? But the monogamous law of adultery is so contradictory to the divine law, and so absurdly at variance with common sense and common justice, that injured marital honor now has no redress but a barbarous one. A revision of the law concerning adultery, defining the crime, as polygamy does, in accordance with the laws of God, and enforcing it by an adequate penalty, is all that is necessary to disarm the assassin, and to invest the law itself with that majesty and sanctity which a true Christian civilization demands.

MURDER

It is a notorious fact, that, where the system of monogamy prevails, the most common cause of murder is unhappy marriages. Husbands murder their wives, and wives murder their husbands, or incite others to do it, almost every week. When love turns to hatred, it is the bitterest kind of hatred; and when people hate each other, their hatred becomes the more intense, the more closely they are bound together. The bonds of matrimony are softer than silk, and sweeter than wreaths of flowers, so long as mutual love and mutual confidence subsist; but when these are banished from the domestic altar, and their places usurped by distrust and jealousy, then those bonds become heavier than iron shackles, and more corroding than fetters of brass. Under such circumstances, a separation of some kind is eagerly desired. This desire is spontaneous and instinctive; but the marriage-vow has been so solemnly uttered and recorded, that there can be no honorable separation but death. Then the dreadful crime of murder is conceived and cherished and pondered in the mind, until it takes complete possession of it. The idea of murder is begotten between the desire of dissolving the marriage and the desire of maintaining one's public honor. And both desires cannot be gratified in any other way. Divorce is dishonorable. It occasions endless talk and scandal, and divulges family secrets. It makes one inevitably notorious. It often involves immense expense. Persons, therefore, whose desires are naturally impetuous, and who are determined to obtain a speedy separation from their hated husbands or wives, are peculiarly liable to this crime. They study out a plan that promises complete success. They are quite sure that they can manage to murder their companions without being found out. At all events, they often do murder them, and run the risk of being found out, as well as the additional risk of divine punishment in the world to come. Many cases of murder for this cause never are found out but enough are discovered to prove that the dreadful crime is one of frequent occurrence. It has been brought to light that some men have murdered a number of wives, and some women a number of husbands in succession. The nursery story of Bluebeard may be a horrible fiction; but it is a fiction founded on fact: there must be some verisimilitude about it, or it could never have interested so many generations as it has. Many well-authenticated instances of wife-murder have occurred for which no excuse of jealousy or domestic infelicity can be urged, and which can only be accounted for on the ground of men's capricious desires and love of change. The history of Henry VIII., king of England, and his six wives, most of whom were successively murdered to make room for their successors, is an obvious and an authentic instance.

Now, polygamy furnishes the only sufficient preventive of this horrible crime; for almost any man would sooner support an extra wife, if the usages of society would allow it, than to take the life of his present wife, at the imminent risk of his own. And many men will do it, and are now doing it, even against the usages of society, and in spite of the regulations of monogamy. Thus King Henry II., less sanguinary, or more independent of public opinion, than his brilliant descendant above mentioned, still permitted his queen Eleanor to live, and to wear the crown, though he often preferred the society of the fair Rosamond to hers, and often repaired to her sylvan bowers at Woodstock to enjoy it. And most of the sovereigns of Europe have followed his example; but, like Charles II. and the four Georges, they keep their mistresses nearer court than at Woodstock.

DIVORCE

The marriage-relation is designed to be a permanent and an inseparable one. The parties take each other by the hand, and mutually plight their troth, for better or for worse, to love and to cherish, in prosperity and in adversity, in health and in sickness, till death shall part them. Such a union is most honorable: it is most admirable. But, under the system of monogamy, it is often impracticable. Although the laws of Christ allow of but one cause for divorce, – the unfaithfulness of the wife to the marriage-vow, – and although every State that practises monogamy claims to be a Christian State, yet civil laws allow of divorce for the most trifling causes. The excuse is made, that, when married persons are unhappy in their marriage-relation, divorce alone can prevent neglect and abuse; and it may prevent murder. So they allow them to commit one great crime to prevent their committing another and a greater. This is, of course, fallacious reasoning. But, if it were most exact reasoning, the remedy is dangerous, unnecessary, and directly at variance with the laws of God. Polygamy is a safer and a surer remedy or rather preventive of both divorce and murder than any violation of divine law can be. The laws of God and of Nature always harmonize with each other; and the only manner in which we can perfect our civil laws is to bring them into perfect accordance with the former.

Most men who desire a divorce would prefer polygamy, if it were practicable and lawful. A man does not often undertake to repudiate his loved, present wife, until he begins to desire another. And that other one is already selected and already loved; but the love cannot be consummated. And nothing but the desire of consummating this love carries him through with the divorce. For, if the law of the land favors the divorce, there still remains the law of God to oppose it; and hence divorces are usually difficult, expensive, annoying, and slow. It took Henry VIII. five years, with all his wealth and power, to divorce himself from his first wife, Catharine of Aragon, in favor of Anne Boleyn, with whom he was desperately in love all the while. If she had yielded to his solicitations, and granted him illicit gratification, it is not at all probable that he would ever have prosecuted the divorce to its termination. And thus is every divorce more or less tedious, and it ought to be. Christianity forbids it, the wife resists it, children plead, and friends expostulate against it, the world wonders and stares; and yet, in spite of all opposition, the vehement passions of men often drive them through it. Yet the greatest suffering of all is that of the man's own conscience, who persists in it. To do such violence to the most solemn laws of God and the most honorable sentiments of mankind is no light crime, whatever the laws of the State may term it. Polygamy furnishes the only preventive of this great social evil. If a man loves another woman, and is resolved to have her, let him take her, and keep her, and keep his first one also. Napoleon Bonaparte never would have divorced Josephine, had polygamy been deemed lawful and proper. Yet no man ever had a fairer pretext for divorce upon any mere prudential considerations than he had. Her virtue was unquestionable. It was not only above reproach; it was above suspicion. But all hopes of her having offspring had failed. His desire for an heir was most intense, most natural, and most commendable. It seemed to be all that was wanting to secure the stability of his throne, the good of his people, and the peace of the world. Yet, according to the system of monogamy, the only manner in which these very desirable ends could be attained was by the divorce of Josephine, by whose alliance he had been brought to more public notice, and been greatly assisted in his successful career, and who was one of the loveliest and noblest women that ever wore a crown. The divorce was consummated, the reasons for it were publicly announced; but the moral sense of the world was; shocked, and Napoleon was at once pronounced a tyrant and a monster. And this act is still held by many to be the turning-point both in his personal character and in his public career. Before this, all his history is bright; after it, all is dark. One cannot, even now, after so long a time, contemplate the tears of Josephine and the subsequent disasters of Napoleon, without cursing the narrow bigotry of monogamy, and wishing that the golden age of polygamy had returned before his day.

At the court of David, King of Israel, even the rape and the incest of Tamar were not so unpardonable as her abandonment. Although shocked and indignant at the brutal violence of her half-brother Amnon, yet her tenderness could not deny some pity to the intensity of his passion. "Nay, my brother, do not force me," she said. "Speak to the king; for he will not withhold me from thee." But when his lust had been sated, and he commanded her to be gone, she refused to go; saying, "This evil in sending me away is greater than the other."[247] Then he caused her to be put out forcibly, and the door to be bolted. It was this insulting divorce added to her forcible humiliation that broke her heart. The latter she might forgive, the former she could not; and she rent her purple robes, and went out crying with her hand upon her head. It was this cruel repudiation that whetted the dagger of Absalom to avenge her wrongs, and it was this that fills up the measure of Amnon's guilt in the judgment of every honest heart. God did not require David to put away Bathsheba after he had once ravished her, and would not have permitted him to do so, had he desired it, although he had obtained her by blood and fraud. His punishment must come in some other manner. Their marriage, once consummated by cohabitation, was complete and indissoluble. How differently would a similar case be now decided by the ecclesiastical courts of modern Europe! Can men's judgment be more just than God's?

PROCURING ABORTION

The murder of the child *in embryo* is a crime prohibited by law, and most repugnant to humanity. Yet it is one which the system of monogamy is obliged to wink at and tolerate. This horrid crime is becoming more and more common every year, till it is now somewhat fashionable, especially as it is more commonly practised by fashionable people. Not many years ago, the person who dispensed drugs for such vile purposes was a hag; branded as a villain, or looked upon as a hateful Locusta, whose fit dwelling-place was some dark cave among volcanic mountains, and whose fit companions were venomous serpents and wild foxes: but it is now currently reported that one of the popular compounders of these death dealing drugs is deemed worthy of the honor of knighthood,[248] and is appointed physician extraordinary to the queen. Almost every newspaper now contains a well-displayed advertisement, addressed "to the ladies," setting forth the powerful properties of some specific for "removing obstructions," and "bringing on the

---

247   2 Sam. xiii.

248   Sir (?) James Clarke

monthly periods," with entire certainty; and although these drugs will be "sure to cause miscarriage," yet they are at the same time so "mild and safe as not to be injurious to the most delicate constitution." Such are some of the most impudent claims of the modern abortionist. But I cannot go on.

For full details I beg to refer my readers to the public journals of the day.

But the manufacturers and the consumers of drugs for these abominable practices are not the only ones responsible for the crime. Monogamy is responsible for it. The entire social system is corrupt. The most respectable merchants and apothecaries deal in these drugs, the most respectable journals advertise them, everybody reads about them; yet no protesting voice is raised, either against the use of them or the traffic in them. The ministers of religion, the proper censors of the public morals, are silent: the subject is too indelicate for them to allude to. The police-magistrates and other officers of the law make no effort to bring the guilty parties to justice, except in the most shocking and notorious instances, where the life of the mother is taken, as well as that of the child.

Intelligent and respectable physicians, who have the best opportunities of knowing, state that this vice is now practised more commonly by married women than by the unmarried; and it is not difficult to account for it. Under the system of monogamy, the wife attempts too much, and physical impossibilities are expected and required of her. She alone undertakes to supply all her husband's conjugal wants, and to gratify all his amorous desires; and she is quite conscious that even in the bloom of her youth, in perfect health, and in the height of her charms, she is scarcely capable of doing it: and she dreads to have anything happen to her to make her less capable. Especially if she has already borne one child, and has passed through the long period of lactation, she remembers its effect upon herself and upon her husband with alarm. She fancies herself in danger of losing her hold upon his affections, which she wishes to retain, of course, as long as possible. She therefore takes drugs to prevent fruitfulness, and to preserve her form and beauty, in order to prevent her husband's affections being lavished upon others.

And if the system of monogamy be right, then this motive is commendable, and the reasoning based upon it is entirely valid. No wife can be blamed for wishing to prevent her husband from forming illicit attachments, and thus bringing dishonor upon himself and all his house; and the only means at her command for preventing it is to concentrate all his affections upon herself.

But polygamy is capable of suppressing this vice, or, at least, of greatly diminishing it, by removing its most powerful motives. Under the system of polygamy, the burdens as well as the privileges of the women are more equally distributed. No woman is required or expected to be always prepared for her husband's embraces, nor does she claim any more than she is able to receive, or than he is voluntarily inclined to bestow. If she is full of life, and in vigorous health, and is capable of fulfilling her conjugal duties alone, it is well: her husband is a happy man. But, if she is not able, it is still well. Her husband need not be unhappy; for he can espouse another, without reproach to her or dishonor to himself.

FECUNDITY OUGHT TO BE PROMOTED, NOT DESTROYED

The laws of God and of Nature concur in bearing unqualified testimony to the desirableness of offspring. It is the proper fruit of marriage, of which love is the blossom. The blossom yields a delicious but an evanescent pleasure but the fruit, after diligent culture and careful preservation, is a source of perpetual delight and honor. "Be fruitful, and multiply, and replenish the earth and subdue it," constitutes the most important part of the divine blessing pronounced upon the first married couple, – a benediction repeated, in substance, upon the occasion of every subsequent marriage the particulars of which are recorded in the Holy Bible. When the parents of Rebecca sent her away to become the wife of Isaac, they blessed her, and said, "Be thou the mother of thousands of millions;" and when Boaz espoused Ruth the Moabitess, the people that were in the gate, and the elders, said, "The Lord make the woman that is come into thy house, like Rachel and Leah, which two did build the house of Israel." "Lo, children are a heritage of the Lord, and the fruit of the womb is his reward. As arrows are in the hand of a mighty man, so are the children of the youth. Happy is the man that hath his quiver full of them." "Thy wife shall be as a fruitful vine by the sides of thy house, thy children like olive-plants round about thy table. Behold that thus shall the man be blessed that feareth the Lord."[249]

---

249   Ps. cxxvii., czzviii

As fruitfulness, on the one hand, is always declared to be a blessing, in the Bible, so barrenness, on the other hand, is declared to be a curse. The most affecting and the most memorable prayers of females recorded therein are those which beg for offspring; and the most grateful thanksgivings are those for children borne by them. But the unnatural and unholy system of monogamy which now prevails has so strangely perverted our desires, that it seems to change the divine blessing into a curse, and the curse into a blessing. If women would now dare to pray for what they wish, they would pray for barrenness, instead of fruitfulness. Now, there must be something radically wrong in a social system which thus presumes to reverse the course of Nature, and to contradict the divine assurances of blessing and of cursing; and which has so fatally and deeply poisoned the mysterious springs of life, and polluted the most inviolable sanctuaries of female purity and maternal love.

"Our Maker bids increase: who bids abstain,
But our destroyer, foe to God and man?"

I doubt whether there can be any form of licentiousness more abhorrent to the laws of God and of Nature than this "Murder of the Innocents." Even fornication cannot be so great a sin. The unmarried woman who has a child in the natural way, and who bestows upon it a mother's love and a mother's care, cannot thereby become so guilty as the married woman who wilfully destroys her offspring, or who prevents her fruitfulness. There is great danger lest the general smattering of medical knowledge among us may do more harm than good. There is, alas! a positive certainty that presumptuous quacks, who know only enough of Nature to have lost their reverence for her laws, are leading many of our honorable women astray, and are poisoning the best blood in our land. These women, like our common mother Eve, from unholy and intensely selfish motives, prompted and countenanced by our system of monogamy, are plucking the fruit of the tree of knowledge of good and evil, and intermeddling with those functions of Nature which ought to be let alone. No honorable physician, who is master of his profession, will degrade that profession so much as to descend to such vile practice. His business is not to destroy life, but to save it. He, at least, has learned the most profound respect for the laws of our being

"A little learning is a dangerous thing;
Drink deep, or taste not the Pierian Spring.
There shallow draughts intoxicate the brain;
But drinking largely sobers us again."

We had better know nothing of the laws of gestation than to know only enough to evade or violate them; for they cannot be violated with impunity. The time will come when the young wife who now destroys her unborn offspring, or who otherwise wilfully and wickedly tampers with her reproductive powers, will surely mourn their loss, and will mourn as one that cannot be comforted. Like Rachel, she will beg and pray for fruitfulness, and say, "Oh! give me children, or else I die;" but, not like Rachel, she will beg and pray in vain. Those delicate organs once weakened by violent or unnatural means rarely regain their normal condition, and one voluntary abortion may be followed by many involuntary miscarriages. She loses all, and she is guilty of all; and some day she will surely feel both her loss and her guilt, till it becomes, like the punishment of the first murderer, a burden too heavy to be borne. Never can she know by blissful experience the sweetness of a mother's love; that pure and fond and tender and changeless affection, which so inspires and ennobles the female character. Never can she become quite free from the jealous suspicions of her husband, who, against his will and all his better judgment, is a perpetual prey to the green-eyed demon. Never can the spacious halls and gloomy apartments of their solitary home resound with the innocent glee of their children's voices; no baby in the cradle; no "daughter singing in the village choir" or the Sunday-school concert; no son to graduate from school or college, or to inherit and transmit to future generations the family name and wealth and honors.

This is no fancy sketch nor far-fetched representation, but is a faithful portraiture of many of our New-England families. The curse of God is already upon us, and our native population is even now giving way to the more prolific races of English, Celts, and Germans. God gives the land to those who obey his marriage-laws to "be fruitful, and multiply and replenish the earth, and subdue it." As the Israelites drove out the ancient Canaanites who made their children pass through to Moloch, and as they took possession of their fruitful fields and vineyards, already planted, and of their towns and cities, already built; so these poorer, more natural and less artificial immigrants are dispossessing us. I quote once more from the Massachusetts Registration Report for 1866, page 18.

BIRTH-RATE IN MASSACHUSETTS

"In England, during the twenty-six years 1838-1863, with a population of about eighteen million, the average birth-rate was 3.33 percent. In Massachusetts, it has never been so high. In the seven years 1852-1858, it was 2.90. In the five years immediately preceding the war, 1856-1860, it was 2.85. During the four years of war, 1862-1865, the birth-rate was 2.46. We find it now rising, not to the old standard of 2.85 or 2.90, but to 2.69."

Page 28 reads as follows, —

"The foreign-born population of Massachusetts, by the census of 1865, was 265,486, the American population 999,976, and the population of unknown nativity 1,569. The last it is not easy to divide; it seems nearer the probable truth to divide them equally. We have, then, 1,000,761 Americans, and 266,270 foreigners. And they produced in 1866, —the Americans 16,555 children, the foreigners 17,530 children; that is to say, a child was born to every 60 45/100 Americans, and to every 15 19/100 foreigners; the latter class being four times as productive as the former."

The birth-rate, therefore, of the Americans of Massachusetts for the year 1866 was only 1.65 percent; while that of the foreign population was 6.59 percent. At this rate, not many generations will be required for them to dispossess us.

But it is unnecessary to the satisfactory analysis and comparison of the two marriage-systems to go on, to any greater length, with this painful dissection of vice, or to array any further statistical proofs in confirmation of the inherent licentiousness of monogamy. It would be easy to show that the galling bondage of restricted marriage has had, and is now having, a similar effect upon the great social evils of insanity, suicide, and self-pollution, which it has upon those other forms of vice which have been analyzed above, and to prove that polygamy would tend to mitigate them also. If these hints of mine are seized upon and properly developed by some more capable writer, and so clearly and happily set forth as to lead to a practical reform, it will be honor enough for me to have indicated its necessity and demonstrated its possibility.

CHAPTER IX:

OBJECTIONS TO POLYGAMY ANSWERED

A few pages will now be devoted to a consideration of the objections which have been urged against the system of polygamy. And it may be proper to say, that if there should be any objections to it which are not here answered to everyone's satisfaction, yet the superiority of this system is still maintained and proven, as long as the previous demonstrations remain valid; the objections to the contrary notwithstanding. It is often the case that a proposition may be true, and at the same time it may not be possible to answer all the objections to it. There are unanswerable objections to a democratic or popular form of government; and yet for some nations, such a form of government may, on the whole, be the best one.

DOES POLYGAMY CAUSE JEALOUSY?

It has been objected that polygamy cannot be reasonable or right, since it causes jealousy among the different women in the same family. But it cannot be proved that jealousy is confined to any particular social system: it is, unfortunately, too common to every system. It is inherent in human nature, and must be regarded as one of its inseparable infirmities. Yet, so far from being most violent under the system of polygamy, the opposite is the fact; for it is always most violent when secret intrigue is carried on, and when the dreaded rival does not sustain an open and an acknowledged relation to the husband, but when the tenderness between him and that rival, whether real or suspected, is only secretly indulged: so that monogamy really furnishes more occasion for the exercise of this cruel passion than polygamy. In the latter system, the claims of the different women are acknowledged and understood; the parties all stand in well-defined relations to each other, and violent jealousy, under such circumstances, must be comparatively rare.

IS POLYGAMY DEGRADING TO WOMEN?

It has also been objected, that polygamy cannot be reasonable and right, since it places men and women on terms of social inequality; it exalts man, and degrades woman; it makes her dependent on his will; it demands of her undivided love and fidelity towards him, while he is permitted to lavish his affections upon as many as he may please. But all this is not degrading to her. It is the only thing that saves her from degradation. The experience of every age and of every community has proved that many men cannot and will not content themselves with one woman. There must be polygamy, or else there must be prostitution; and prostitution is wickedness, and wickedness is degradation.

Nor is there anything degrading in woman's dependence upon man. This dependence is natural, and honorable to her. It is the very position which she herself voluntarily and instinctively assumes towards him. The entire code of polite, social intercourse between the two sexes is founded on this principle of her nature. Not only in times of real danger, but at all times, she loves to lean upon the strong, brave arm of man, and willingly confesses her own timidity and weakness. And these qualities are so far from degrading her, that they only render her the more attractive and lovely. The manly gallant is as ready to afford assistance as she is to accept it. In riding, in walking, in dancing, in sailing, in bathing, in the public assembly, in the social gathering, and everywhere where it is possible to receive attention and accept assistance and protection, it is equally pleasing and ennobling for her to receive, and for him to bestow them.

WOMAN'S RIGHTS

They are her rights, – her woman's rights. I believe in a woman's rights, and I believe that polygamy is the system that can best assure them to her; for, as it is a mathematical certainty that there are more women than men in the world, some men must assume the protection of more than one woman each, or some women must be deprived of their rights. The most sacred and the most precious of all her rights are her rights to a husband and a home; and it is no more a degradation to her to share that home and that husband with another woman than it is to share other benefits and other attentions from the same man, in common with other women. No woman considers herself degraded to walk abroad with her hand upon a man's arm while another woman has her hand upon the other arm; thus they often appear in public, at balls and concerts and lectures and churches. For the time being, they are both willingly dependent upon his protection and his bounty and he is also dependent upon each of them for the benefits of their companionship and the charms of their society. He could not so fully enjoy those entertainments without them. For example, there are two female friends residing together, and mutually dependent upon each other for many of their social enjoyments, and for much of their intellectual and moral culture. A worthy young man of their acquaintance calls upon them frequently, and admires them both and they enjoy his visits, for neither of them have any other male associate. At length he invites them both to a public entertainment. Neither of them would be willing to leave her friend, and go with him alone; nor could he well endure the thought of enjoying himself abroad with one, while the other would be deserted and neglected at home, – the other who would enjoy the entertainment so much, and whose enjoyment would so much enhance theirs. Now, if this triple companionship shall ripen into friendship, and the friendship into love, and the love shall result in a triple marriage, where is the degradation? Would it not be still more heartless to desert either of the friends now, when each heart is thrilling with the harmonious music of the triple love? Let the words of divine wisdom answer, —

"Two are better than one, . . . and a threefold cord is not quickly broken."

There is a want in the female nature which impels her to seek and to appreciate the society of a male friend, which no number of associates of her own sex can fully satisfy. I have stood by the gates of the cotton-mill, and seen the multitudes of female operatives stream out of an evening, and I marked their lonesome appearance as they're paired to their respective homes. Homes, did I say? Ah! anything but homes, – their boarding houses. There I have seen them sit down, by scores, to the dinner-table, and eat their dinners in the utmost silence, as if each one was entirely isolated from all social and agreeable companionship. Oh, what loneliness! how hard! how bitter! Yet many of them were radiant with the charms of womanhood, and each one capable of adorning and blessing a home, but which few of them will ever enjoy; for they are not only the unwilling victims of poverty and toil, but the willing votaries of fashion, and the unconscious slaves of monogamy.

MASCULINE POWER AND FEMININE COMPLAISANCE

Those qualities of mind and person which impel a woman to seek the protection of the stronger sex, arising from her natural weakness and timidity, are really those very qualities which inspire the deepest admiration; yet, should a man happen to display these feminine qualities, they only render him supremely contemptible. A man must be strong, self-reliant, and courageous. No woman can devotedly love a man, unless she sees, or thinks she sees, in him a power of mind or of body, or of both, which Nature has denied to her. It is this power which she intuitively admires and venerates and worships, even though its exercise over her may be arbitrary and tyrannical. The Sabine matrons loved their Roman lords none the less because they had seized them with the strong hand; and a woman is always and everywhere more ready to forgive the too great ardor and boldness of a lover than his unmanly timidity and shame. For a wife to look up to her husband for authority and guidance is as natural as to look to him for protection from danger; and this is as natural as breathing. It is therefore true, though it may seem hard to some to admit it, that it is his right and duty to exercise authority, and her right and privilege to practise complaisance and submission.

> "Whence true authority in man; though both
> Not equal, as their sex not equal seemed;
> For contemplation he, and valor formed;
> For softness she, and sweet attractive grace;
> He for God only, she for God in him.
> His fair large front and eye sublime declared
> Absolute rule; and hyacinthine locks
> Round from his parted forelock manly hung
> Clustering, but not beneath his shoulders broad;
> She, as a veil, down to the slender waist
> Her unadorned golden tresses wore,

Disheveled, but in wanton ringlets waved,
As the vine curls her tendrils, which implied
Subjection, but required with gentle sway," &c.

PARADISE LOST, Book iv.

Yet while God and Nature have constituted man the superior to woman in strength and courage and authority, these principles do not render her relation to man one of degradation or even of general inferiority; for there are many other and no less admirable qualities in which she surpasses him. Her moral and religious sentiments are more susceptible, and her intellectual perceptions are truer and keener in respect to those matters requiring delicacy of taste and refinement of mind. Her humane sympathies are also stronger; she is sooner moved by the sentiments of compassion, benevolence, and charity. Blessings on her gentle heart! What a dreary world would this be without woman! And it is only polygamy that appreciates and appropriates her. Monogamy neglects her, spurns her, corrupts her, and degrades her.

IF A MAN MAY HAVE A PLURALITY OF WIVES, WHY MAY NOT A WOMAN HAVE A PLURALITY OF HUSBANDS?

Because a woman's heart is so constituted, that it is impossible for her to cherish a sincere love for more than one husband at the same time. It is even difficult for her to believe that a man can cherish a sincere and honest love for more than one woman at the same time. It is difficult for her to believe it; for she cannot comprehend it. Her own instincts revolt against the thought of a plurality of husbands, and, judging his feeling by her own, she does not see how a man can want, or at least can truly love, a plurality of wives. But, as this point involves a constitutional difference of sex, it is one in which we must be aware that our feelings cannot guide us. A man can never know the infinite tenderness and the infinite patience of a mother's love, except imperfectly, by reason and observation. His experience does not teach him. His paternal love does not exactly resemble it. So a woman can never know the purity and sincerity of a man's conjugal love for a plurality of wives, except by similar observation and reason. Her conjugal love is

407

unlike it. Her love for one man exhausts and absorbs her whole conjugal nature: there is no room for more. And if she ever receives the truth that his nature is capable of a plural love, she must attain it by the use of her reason, or admit it upon the testimony of honest men.

THE SUN AND THE PLANETS; OR MARRIAGE LIKE GRAVITATION

It would be as impossible and as unnatural for a pure-minded, virtuous woman to have more than one husband, as for the earth to have more than one sun; but it is not unnatural nor impossible for a pure and noble-minded man to cherish the most devoted love for several wives at the same time: it is as natural for him as it is for the sun to have several planets at the same time, each one dependent on him, and each one harmonious in her own sphere. To each planet the sun yields all the light and heat which she is capable of receiving, or which she would be capable of receiving, were she the only planet in the sky. Each planet attracts the sun to the utmost of her weight, – the exhaustion of her power; and the sun returns her attraction to an exactly equal degree, and no more. Not one planet nor two, nor all combined, are able to exhaust his power, or move him from his sphere. One more illustration: if a strong man holds one end of a cord, and a little child the other, and they pull towards each other, the tension of the cord is measured by the strength of the child, and not by that of the man. The same degree of power is felt at each end of the cord. The strength of the child is exhausted, that of the man is not. He can draw several children to him, sooner than they could unitedly draw him to them. A similar relation exists, naturally, between the male and the female. He is the sun; they are the planets. He is strong, they are weak. Let us not find fault with the ordinances of God, nor attempt to resist his will.

MASCULINE RESPONSIBILITY AND CARE

The responsibilities of the man are in proportion to his strength and authority. He must assume the care and provide for the support of the family; and his female companions will submit to this authority, if they are wise and prudent, with all the grace and gentleness which distinguish their sex.

"Thy husband is thy lord, thy life, thy keeper,
Thy head, thy sovereign; one that cares for thee
And for thy maintenance; commits his body
To painful labor, both by sea and land;
To watch the night in storms, the day in cold,
While thou liest warm at home, secure and safe;
And craves no other tribute at thy hands,
But love, fair looks, and true obedience, —
Too little payment for so great a debt.
Such duty as the subject owes the prince.
Even such a woman oweth to her husband;
And when she's forward, peevish, sullen, sour,
And not obedient to his honest will,
What is she but a foul contending rebel,
And graceless traitor to her loving lord?
I am ashamed that women are so simple
To offer war where they should kneel for peace;
Or seek for rule, supremacy, and sway,
When they are bound to serve, love, and obey.
Why are our bodies soft and weak and smooth,
Unapt to toil and trouble in the world;
But that our soft conditions and our hearts
Should well agree with our external parts?"

TAMING THE SHREW act v. scene ii.

The capacity of a man to attract and support several women must depend upon the amount of his talent, his fortune, and his benevolence, as well as upon his physical strength and vitality. There are some men who are scarcely able to attract the love and provide for the support of one woman; others are well able, if they were willing, to maintain several wives, but they are too penurious and too selfish to attempt it: and such men do not deserve the love of one. But there are others who are both able and willing, and who can as well love and provide for several as for one, and even better; for, if a man of immense vitality and corresponding mentality have but one, she must necessarily suffer from the superabundance of his power, and perhaps, like Semele in the too ardent embraces of Jove, may prove an early victim to the powerful demonstrations of his love. But even should he use the utmost tenderness, and never forget to restrain his burning ardor, yet, so long as he lives under the system of monogamy, such a husband must often be the occasion of the keenest suffering to a delicate woman. It is a source of constant pain and grief to her that she cannot come up to her husband's capacity, nor satisfy his conjugal requirements. She often tortures herself with the thought that he cannot love her, for she feels herself so much his inferior, and so utterly unworthy of his love. She often says that she knows he wishes her to die, that he might marry another. She wishes herself dead. She is madly jealous of every other woman who comes within the circle of their acquaintance, even though her husband may have no fancy for her; but the poor wife fears he may have, and this constant fear is worse than the worst reality. But, on the other hand, if he were a polygamist, and this same woman were one of his wives, she would then be happy and content. For she would continue to receive from him all the demonstrations of love she is capable of enduring, while she would joyfully contribute her share towards completing the capacity of his. Then it would constitute her happiness to behold him happy, and to enjoy the consciousness of having done what she could to make him so. She now *rejoices* in his abundant vitality, and *is proud* of his superiority. And when his manliness, his dignity, and his power are radiated upon her beaming countenance, and reflected thence, it is then that her heart is filled with the utmost delight and satisfaction of which it is susceptible. Having become his wife, she is so entirely devoted to him, that she almost loses in him her own identity. She throws herself upon his ample breast and within his infolding arms, and yields both her person and her will to his control; and she only regrets, when she has given up all, that she has not more to give.

> "You see me, Lord Bassanio, where I stand,
> Such as I am; though for myself alone
> I would not be ambitious in my wish
> To wish myself much better; yet for you,
> I would be trebled twenty times myself;
> A thousand times more fair, ten thousand times

More rich:

That only to stand high on your account,

I might, in virtues, beauties, livings, friends,

Exceed account; but the full sum of me

Is an unlessoned girl, unschooled, unpractised;

Happy in this, she is not yet so old

But she may learn; and happier than this,

She is not bred so dull but she can learn;

Happiest of all, is, that her gentle spirit

Commits itself to yours to be directed,

As from her lord, her governor, her king.

Myself and what is mine, to you and yours

Is now converted: but now I was the lord

Of this fair mansion, master of my servants,

Queen o'er myself; and even now, but now,

This house, these servants, and this same myself,

Are yours, my lord; I give them with this ring."

MERCHANT OF VENICE, act iii. scene ii.

CRITIQUE: BY J. A. H., ESQ.

SPRINGFIELD, MASS., Sept. 25, 1869

To the Author of "The History and Philosophy of Marriage"

Dear Sir, — I have read carefully your little work, and will, as briefly as possible, notice a few conclusions, which seem faulty to my mind; and, to the best of my ability, will state wherein I should differ with you. First, as to your position that man is not capable of loving one woman, and her only, and that woman is pre-eminently devoted to one man; thus making man a promiscuous animal, while the opposite is true of woman. Laying aside the exceptions, I think it can be shown that this is false doctrine, and that your conclusions are unwarrantable from the premises. For we find, that, in nature, most animals in a wild state are mated: so, through the whole range of the feathered tribe in a state of nature, the same is true; and the reason why the same law is not observable among domesticated animals and birds is, I think, attributable to man's interference. From this I urge that *God* has made all his creatures monogamous in their instincts.

Second, your statistics to show that there are more women than men will work very well when the test is applied to such thickly populated and peculiarly situated States as these in New England, and some of the Middle States; but you will scarcely claim any great weight in the slight differences manifest to support your theory. You evidently rely somewhat upon your observation that females mature at a much earlier age than males, to support your statistics, and on both, to support your theory that the *Creator* has thus made provision for polygamy. It may be true, that, in low latitudes, females do mature younger; but I believe that this is not true of Northern climes, and that, on the average, males will be found to be fit for fathers as soon as the opposite sex are fit to become mothers.

Third, in reviewing the lives of the Caesars as an example of the condition of morals in the Roman empire too, you overlook some facts, in drawing conclusions, quite inexcusable. You attribute all of their vices and sin to the social system of monogamy, and point to the polygamous nations of the East for comparisons, to the credit of the later. While it is true, no doubt, that all of iniquity which human cunning could devise was chargeable to the Romans, yet *Sodom* the city of the plain, was the just subject of God's wrath as the penalty of this same vice which is imputed to the Caesars, and to the Romans as a people, —this, too, among a polygamous people: this would seem to indicate that *Sodomy* is not necessarily the child of monogamy. And, further, I believe that today, the only nation on the civilized globe that stands charged with *Sodomy* is *Turkey*, and the Turks are a polygamous people! If this does not prove that monogamy is not responsible for our sins, it tends to show, I think, that the remedy does not lie in a plurality of wives.

Fourth, when the countries of the East were sparsely inhabited, or, in fact, when the world was comparatively without inhabitants, the need for the application and working of your theory may have existed; but it does not exist now. Why *Jesus Christ* did not rebuke polygamy, I do not know. His silence on this point proves nothing; if it did, I could cite many specific sins of an equally disgusting character passed over by him without a command; but I suppose he thought that the practical working of Christianity would effectually break down polygamy; and so it has. Wherever Christians have planted the standard of Calvary, this bane to womanhood disappears. Christ, no doubt, saw these things *in futuro*, and refrained from uprooting their entire social system; leaving it to time.

I could extend my remarks *ad infinitum*; but I think I have said enough. I think the work is worthy the perusal of all men who are of a thinking turn of mind, and, so far as I can judge, it is excellently written. As designed for an extensive sale, I regret I cannot predict a success; for the great army of *martyrs* (women) to the theory will stifle it if possible. Again: there are matters treated in the work (possibly unavoidable) which delicacy would prevent many from reading, and fathers and husbands from taking into their families; and, finally, I own, that, until I read this work, I was not aware that so much could be said in favor of polygamy.

J. A. H.

THE AUTHOR'S REPLY

Boston, Oct. 28, 1869

J. A. H., Esq., Springfield, Mass.

Dear Sir, —Your critique of "The History and Philosophy of Marriage" has come to hand, in which you state my views, somewhat erroneously, to be, "that man is not capable of loving one woman, and her only; . . . thus making man a promiscuous animal, while the opposite is true of woman." These allegations I respectfully deny. They are scarcely fair; for I have strongly objected to all "promiscuous" intercourse, throughout my treatise and it is my main charge against enforced monogamy that it tends to promote it. I am sorry to be misunderstood. I say a pure and honest plural *marriage* should be permitted to some men of superior vitality and great reproductive power, on account of the unfortunate imbecility or barrenness of some women. I admit that monogamy is the normal type of marriage between perfectly healthful persons; but, as the women are less healthful and more numerous than the men, the two inequalities should correct each other. (Pp. 62, 170, 198, 248, &c.)

1. You assert that animals in a state of nature are not polygamous, and hence that our Creator has not designed that man should be. I admit that this may be true of carnivorous beasts of prey and of solitary habits, but is not true of herbivorous and omnivorous animals of social habits; for they are usually polygamous: but man is both omnivorous and social, and hence by this analogy he should be polygamous. The gallinaceous birds are also polygamous, while birds of prey are not; but the analogy in this case is too remote to be of much benefit to either side of the question: when we shall have acquired wings, we shall neither marry, nor be given in marriage.

2. You say, my "statistics to show that there are more women than men will work very well in New England," &c., but not generally. My proposition is this, "The number of *marriageable* women always exceeds the number of marriageable men . . . except in those States in which the population is largely made up by foreign immigration;" and I cite public documents to prove that this is true of "more than one hundred million of the population of Europe," and of many different States in America (p. 45); and I challenge you to produce any contrary statistics, except in cases affected by immigration as aforesaid. These public documents and other authentic statistics have established *five important facts*: (1) That about half the population of every State consists of children under age, (2) of whom the majority are males; (3) that, after marriageable age, the females are more numerous, (4) on account of the greater mortality of male children; and (5) that the whole number of females exceeds the whole number of males. It is a necessary conclusion, therefore, that the number of marriageable females must still more exceed the number of marriageable males. This last proposition is often true, even when, on account of immigration, the whole number of males exceeds the whole number of females. I invite your special attention to an examination of the statistics of Pennsylvania. (See Table, p. 47.)

In the year 1860, the whole number of males in that State was 1,454,419, and the number of females 1,451,796; hence there were 3,723 more males than females. Yet at the same time there were more *marriageable* women than men, for there were 11,902 more males than females under fifteen years of age; therefore there were 7,179 more females than males over fifteen, while there were 10,826 more females than males between the ages of fifteen and twenty, and 17,588 more females than males between the ages of twenty and thirty.

Your assertion, that the earlier maturity of women "is not true in Northern climes," &c., is unsupported by any reason or authority, while it has a color of truth; for there are some exceptions in extreme polar regions: but the rule as I give it is correct of nine-tenths of the race; and I cite every respectable work on physiology in proof of it.

3. You object to my "charging the vices of the Caesars to their monogamy," and triumphantly point to the Sodomy of polygamous Turkey, and of ancient Sodom itself, in support of this objection. My reason for relating the

family history of the Caesars was not so much to charge all their vices to their monogamy as to give a true picture of their social life and their marriage-system at a time distinguished by the concurrence of two great events, world; — the conquest of Northern Europe, which imposed the system of Roman monogamy upon the civilized and the introduction of Christianity, by an early perversion of which that system was invested with the sanctity of a religious institution, and many of its repulsive vices were perpetuated by the most religious people, and have thus come down to modern times. In the analysis and discussion of these vices, special reference was had to prostitution and divorce; and the least possible allusion was made to Sodomy, on account of its remote relation to marriage, and its comparative absence from our Western civilization; and all allusion to it would have been omitted if faithfulness to historical truth had allowed. Yet, although its discussion does not necessarily belong to the marriage-question, it is closely connected with its history, since it arises from one of the perversions of the amorous propensity. Other readers of "The History and Philosophy of Marriage" have therefore noticed the same omissions which you have: they, too, have pointed to Sodom and to Turkey; and because I have not attempted to prove that every Roman vice was derived from their monogamy, or was stimulated by it, they will not admit that I have proved any of them to have been. Hence I am obliged to meet the issue fully; to lay aside all fastidious scruples; and to state what I have gathered of the origin of Sodomy, and its relation to the early history of marriage.

The rise of this detestable vice in Europe is proved to be connected with that of enforced monogamy. This marriage-system first appeared in Greece during the second period of its history, and Sodomy immediately followed in its train. There are no traces of it, as Mr. Lecky remarks ("History of European Morals," vol. ii. p. 311), in Homer or in Hesiod; but the dramatic poets and the artists of the monogamous period of Grecian history abound in allusions to it; yet Mr. Lecky errs, I think, in attributing its rise to the Grecian games for there is little doubt that it was an importation from Phoenicia, whence it is well known the Greeks were accustomed to borrow very largely at that period, and where its history can be traced back, even to the time of the deluge.

In the ninth chapter of Genesis, it is stated that Ham, one of the sons of Noah, and a monogamist, *had seen his father's nakedness*; a very common Hebrew euphemism to imply something much worse: for it is further said, that when "Noah awoke from his wine, and knew what his younger son had *done unto him,*" he forthwith cursed his posterity to the latest generation, —an apparently absurd and unjust penalty for seeing an indecency; but really, if my interpretation be correct, it was only a very just and very proper denunciation of that unnatural vice, which has always been hereditary in that race. It was in Palestine and Phoenicia that the family of Canaan, the accursed son of Ham, settled (Gen. x. 15-19), where they were all addicted to this vice; from the corruption of which, and of kindred vices, named in Leviticus (chapters eighteen and twenty), the invading Israelites were warned to beware, and for which it is therein expressly declared, that the Canaanites were doomed to destruction.

In later years, the Carthaginians, a Phoenician colony, exerted a similar corrupting influence upon Rome (Lecky, "European Morals," i. 177, ii. 320); for it was six years after the first Punic War, in the year of the city 520, that the first divorce occurred at Rome (Lecky, ii. 317), which soon became notoriously common there, as well as the more odious vice of Sodomy. The Romans had already imbibed a taint of this vice, along with their monogamy, from the Greeks, at a very early period; but the wars with Carthage increased it greatly. The first Punic War lasted nearly a quarter of a century, and gave ample time for the adoption of such foreign practices as wars are always apt to introduce. Many Romans had been long detained as prisoners at Carthage, and had learned the language and the licentious manners of that city: at the close of the war, the two states were brought into intimate commercial relations, and an inundation of Punic vice was the inevitable consequence. Nor was that corrupt city suffered to endure. The voice of the aged Cato, who visited Carthage during the next war to arrange an exchange of prisoners, and who saw the corruptions of the city with the experienced eye of a censor, was as the voice of God, when, on his return to Rome, he closed his frequent speeches in the senate with the ominous and terrible sentence, *et preterea censeo Carthaginem esse delendam* ("I insist that Carthage must be destroyed"). Our remaining knowledge of the social systems of the Sidonians, the Tyrians, and the Carthaginians, is quite meagre, at best: but it is demonstrable that polygamy was rare in those states; that some approach to enforced monogamy was first attempted; and that some notions of that doctrine, since called the Malthusian doctrine, which discourages an increase of population on grounds of political economy, were first current there; for both Polybius, and Aristotle in his " Politica," assert that the Carthaginian polity most resembled that of Sparta, where it is well known the social and political systems were inseparably blended. The Spartans were monogamous; they discouraged a rapid increase of population; they suppressed the maternal instincts by taking the children from their mothers at a very early age, to be brought up at the public nurseries and schools, exposing the feeble infants to perish, and raising none but the strongest. At Carthage, it is also known, that the families of the nobles were small and few (Heeren's Ideen, vol. ii, part 1, p. 118), and extremely jealous of each other: hence their failure to support Hannibal in Italy; hence his recall, his disasters, and the rapid ruin of the state.

In respect of the Sodomy of modern Turkey, I deny that it was introduced by the polygamous Turks themselves, but assert that it has obviously been inherited and propagated there by the miserable degenerate sons of degenerate Greek and Roman and Phoenician sires. And this is only an illustration and confirmation of the theological opinion, that the utter extermination of the Canaanites by the invading Hebrews was a dire necessity, that they might not be contaminated by their vices, those very vices which are now destroying the victorious Turks, who, in their greater mercy, spared the unarmed and the vanquished.

4. You admit that polygamy was anciently allowed for the more rapid increase of population, when the world was new, but object, that such a need does not exist now. The objection is specious, but unsound. The world is no longer new; but it is still unpeopled. The first law of God — "Increase and multiply and replenish the earth, and subdue it" —has never been sufficiently obeyed. The earth is not replenished, and not subdued. It does not contain, today, one-twentieth part of the population which it might easily support, and support with even more ease than its present population. The Malthusian doctrine is now regarded by most moralists to be as unphilosophical as it is selfish, cruel, and unnatural. The greater portion of the earth is even now but a new farm, and the present inhabitants but the first pioneers of improvement, who are breaking up the prairies, felling the forests, extracting the stumps, and gathering out the stones; our children's children will only begin to live in comfort and abundance upon a cultivated earth.

The first want which the poet Milton ascribes to the primitive gardeners in Eden is still our greatest want, — the want of "more hands."

5. The silence of Jesus concerning polygamy I shall still claim as an argument in its favor, notwithstanding your observations. My arguments need not be repeated here.

6. The reluctance of the women to adopt a polygamous system has also been anticipated in my work. The conservative element in the female character, and the subserviency of the sex to fashion and to public opinion, are all well known, and all designed, I believe, by our Creator, for our common good. Yet because they cannot, at once, see the propriety and necessity of the system of plurality of wives, this fact should not deter us from its investigation; for, if it should prove to be a purer and better system, we shall be sure of their approval in the end; and, when it is once approved and practised, the fairer sex, so far from being its "martyrs," will be the principal gainers by it.

7. I am fully aware that I attempt the discussion of a very delicate subject, and that my book is open to objections on that score; but it is only, as the Bible is, necessarily so, in order to state such facts as ought to be known, and such as are essential to a philosophical examination of the history of marriage. (See Preface.)

For your final complimentary remarks, I return my grateful acknowledgments.

THE AUTHOR

www.ingramcontent.com/pod-product-compliance
Ingram Content Group UK Ltd.
Pitfield, Milton Keynes, MK11 3LW, UK
UKHW042000010225
454478UK00006B/25